400

M. H. Richmond.

D1506681

CAMBRIDGE GREEK TESTAMENT FOR SCHOOLS AND COLLEGES

GENERAL EDITOR: R. ST JOHN PARRY, D.D.,
FELLOW OF TRINITY COLLEGE

THE EPISTLE OF PAUL THE APOSTLE

TO THE

ROMANS

CAMBRIDGE UNIVERSITY PRESS

C. F. CLAY, Manager

LONDON : FETTER LANE, E.C.4

NEW YORK : THE MACMILLAN CO.
BOMBAY
CALCUTTA } MACMILLAN AND CO., LTD.
MADRAS
TORONTO : THE MACMILLAN CO.
OF CANADA, LTD.
TOKYO : MARUZEN-KABUSHIKI-KAISHA

THE EPISTLE OF PAUL THE APOSTLE

TO THE

ROMANS

Edited by

R. ST JOHN PARRY, D.D.

Fellow of Trinity College, Cambridge

WITH INTRODUCTION AND NOTES

First ed.
1912

Cambridge:
at the University Press
1921

First Edition 1912
Reprinted 1921

*Printed in Great Britain
by Turnbull & Spears, Edinburgh*

PREFACE

THE Commentary on the Epistle to the Romans in this series had been entrusted by the late General Editor to Dr Bebb of Lampeter. It was only when Dr Bebb's engagements made it impossible for him to complete the task, that the work was entrusted by the Syndics of the Press to the present editor. No one can be more conscious than the editor himself how much has been lost by the change and how inadequately the trust has been fulfilled. It would, in any case, have been impossible to include, within the limits necessarily imposed, an even relatively complete treatment of this Epistle: and the difficulty of approaching to such a treatment, as was possible, has been increased by the pressure of other occupations. The most that can be hoped is that this edition may serve as an introduction to the study of the Epistle. I have aimed at giving a clear statement of the conditions under which it was written and of the general argument as illustrating and illustrated by those conditions. In the Commentary I have desired to give a close exposition of the text and of the sequence of thought, leaving the larger treatment of theological subjects and the wider illustration of thoughts and language to be sought in the great commentaries.

My obligations to previous writers will be seen by the references throughout the book. But there are some which must be explicitly acknowledged. There are few pages which do not reveal debts to the classical English edition of Drs Sanday and Headlam, and to the Prolegomena to the Grammar of the New Testament of Professor J. H. Moulton, a work whose constant usefulness to the student makes him impatient for its completion. If I add to these the posthumously published lectures and commentaries of Dr Hort, I am acknowledging a debt which all Cambridge theological students will recognise as not admitting of exaggeration. Finally I wish to express my most grateful acknowledgments to Mr J. H. A. Hart, Fellow and Lecturer of S. John's College, for his generous assistance in looking over the proofs and many most useful criticisms and suggestions.

TRINITY COLLEGE, CAMBRIDGE.
Michaelmas, 1912.

NOTE

The Greek Text adopted in this Series is that of Dr Westcott and Dr Hort with the omission of the marginal readings. For permission to use this Text the thanks of the Syndics of the Cambridge University Press and of the General Editor are due to Messrs Macmillan & Co.

CONTENTS

INTRODUCTION

1. Genuineness.

THE genuineness of the Epistle to the Romans is common ground for the great majority of critics. The few attempts to impugn it are based upon arbitrary and subjective methods which have no foundation in the known history and ignore the ordinary canons of literary criticism. It may be taken as admitted that the whole Epistle is genuine, even if it is composite, with the possible exception of xvi. 25—27, which section is, on arguable grounds, referred by some critics to a Pauline author writing from the point of view of the Epistle to the Ephesians and the Pastoral Epistles, on the assumption that these Epistles also are Pauline but not S. Paul's.

The literary history of the Epistle begins early. It was undoubtedly known to and used by the author of 1 Peter[1], probably by Hebrews, James[2], and Jude (24, 25). It is quoted (not by name) by Clement R. and used by Ep. Barnabas, Ignatius, Polycarp, and perhaps Hermas[3]. Justin Martyr and Athenagoras were familiar with it. It appears in the Canon of Marcion[4], in the Muratorian Canon, and is cited by Irenaeus, Clement of Alexandria and Tertullian. No Epistle, except 1 Corinthians, has an earlier or more continuous record[5].

---

[1] See S. H. pp. lxxiv f., Hort, 1 *Peter*, pp. 4 f.

[2] Cf. Hort, *Epistle of S. James*, xxiv f. and pp. 66 f., but S. H. pp. lxxvii f. doubt, and Mayor, *S. James*, pp. lxxxviii f. takes James to be prior.

[3] *New Testament in the Apost. Fathers*, Oxford, 1905.

[4] S. H. p. lxxxiii.

[5] The question of the relation of the Epistle to the *Testaments of the XII Patriarchs* (S. H. p. lxxxii) has been reopened by Charles (*Testaments*, pp. lxxxvi f.) who regards the Testaments as prior to S. Paul, and used by him.

2. INTEGRITY.

The integrity of the Epistle has been impugned, on grounds
which can be regarded as serious, only in connexion with cc. xv.,
xvi. The questions raised about these chapters are discussed in
the commentary and additional notes. It is sufficient to say
here that the only point on which a strong case has been made
out against the integrity relates to c. xvi. 1—23, which is regarded
by many critics as a short letter, or fragment of a letter, of
S. Paul to the Church in Ephesus. The arguments for this
hypothesis and the reasons for rejecting it are given in the
commentary. If the hypothesis is accepted, it postulates a
very early combination of the two letters, antecedent to the
period which is covered by our documentary evidence. Such
a combination would be not likely to be made, except on
an occasion when a collection of S. Paul's letters was being
made. We have in all probability a combination of two letters
in the case of the second Epistle to the Corinthians, at a
date, again, antecedent to documentary evidence. As both
parts of the assumed combination in Romans were written
from Corinth, and the two fragments combined in 2 Corinthians
were written to Corinth, the hypothesis would increase the
probability that a collection of Pauline letters was made at a
very early date at Corinth. It would naturally include
1 Corinthians, and 1 and 2 Thessalonians, both written from
Corinth, and possibly Galatians on the same ground. The
hypothesis implies that copies of letters written from Corinth
were made and deposited with the Church there. But in all this
there is no more than an interesting hypothesis.

3. DATE AND PLACE.

The date of the Epistle can be obtained with unusual certainty from the evidence afforded by the Epistle itself. S. Paul
has not yet visited Rome (i. 10, xv. 22 f.), but he intends to visit
it as soon as he has carried out his immediate purpose of a
journey to Jerusalem (xv. 25). The special object of this
journey is to carry to the Church in Jerusalem, for the benefit
of the poor, a contribution from the Churches of Macedonia

and Achaea (xv. 26, Asia is not mentioned). He has already preached the Gospel as far as Illyricum and so rounded off his missionary labours in Asia and Greece (xv. 19, 23) and hopes to resume them in Spain (xv. 24) after he has visited Rome, preached there (i. 13) and received from the Church in Rome spiritual refreshment and a good send-off for his labours in Spain (xv. 24).

The situation thus indicated is closely similar to the situation described in the Acts as characterising his stay in Greece during the three winter months after his departure from Ephesus (Acts xix. 21, xx. 2—4, xxi. 15, xxiv. 17). It agrees further with the references in 1 Cor. xvi. 1 f. and 2 Cor. viii., ix. to the contribution for the poor saints in Jerusalem. All indications thus point clearly to the winter of 56—57 (55—56 ; see Chronological Table, p. xlviii).

The place of this Epistle in the order of S. Paul's writings is, therefore, clearly marked. It comes after 1 and 2 Corinthians, and before Philippians, etc. Its place in reference to Galatians depends upon the view taken of that Epistle and is discussed in the edition of Galatians in this Commentary.

As regards the place of writing, that too is fixed at Corinth by the above consideration, and this conclusion is perhaps confirmed by the reference to Gaius (xvi. 23, cf. 1 Cor. i. 14) and Erastus (*ib.*, cf. 2 Tim. iv. 20). It is possible however that the concluding chapter was written from Kenchreae ; as Phoebe was apparently the bearer of the letter (xvi. 1 f.), and S. Paul appears to have gone to Kenchreae with a view to sailing to Syria, when his plans were changed by the discovery of a conspiracy formed against him by 'the Jews' (Acts xx. 3). It is at least possible that the circumstances which led to this change of plans may have occasioned the insertion of the paragraph (xvi. 17—20) in the last chapter.

4. OCCASION AND CIRCUMSTANCES.

The immediate occasion of the letter is quite clearly and directly stated in the letter itself. S. Paul, it appears, does not regard the Church of Rome as in need of his teaching or assistance (i. 11, 12, xv. 14), nor has he received any appeal or invitation from them. His own keen interest in their welfare has long inspired him with an ardent desire to visit them : but his missionary labours and the need of supervision of the Churches of his own foundation have been the immediate and constant call (xv. 22). It is only now, when the field of missionary work in the Eastern Mediterranean has been covered, and the needs of the Churches met (xv. 23), that he is able to consider what field of labour is marked out for him next. His call throughout has been to break new ground for the Gospel (xv. 20, 21). He did indeed hope that even in Rome itself he might find scope for missionary work (i. 13), and that hope, by strange and unexpected ways, was, as we know, amply fulfilled (Phil. i. 12 ff.). But he has now decisively turned his mind towards Spain, as the next great opportunity (xv. 24, 28). But, in order to enter upon that great field under the most favourable conditions, he desires to secure for himself the natural and most effective base of operations. As he had evangelised South Galatia from Antioch, Macedonia from Philippi, Achaia from Corinth, Asia (the province) from Ephesus, so he decides that before attacking Spain he must secure in the highest degree the sympathy and support of the Church in Rome (xv. 24 *b*, cf. i. 11, 12). But he is confronted here by new circumstances. In all the other cases, he first founded the Church in the local capital and could then claim the assistance of his converts for further missionary efforts, almost as a right (cf. Phil. i. 4 f.). In Rome, the Church was not of his founding : it was already in existence and in a flourishing condition. He is consequently obliged to invite himself to Rome and to appeal for their support on the general grounds of Christian duty and charity. The delicacy of the situation, as it presented itself to S. Paul, is marked by the character of the section in which he makes the appeal (xv. 14—29), where the eagerness of the Apostle of the Gentiles, the confidence of the Christian appealing to Christians for help in their highest work, and the sensitive courtesy of one who will not offer himself to any but the most willing hosts, combine to form an exquisite picture of the mind of S. Paul.

It would appear that a step in preparation for this visit had already been taken. Aquila and Priscilla (or as they are here named Prisca and Aquila, xvi. 3) had been at Ephesus (Acts

xviii. 18); they had been left there by S. Paul on his first passing visit, no doubt to prepare the way for that longer stay which he then intended and afterwards carried out (Acts xviii. 19, 21, 26). No doubt S. Paul found them there on his return, and they shared his missionary labours in Ephesus and the province of Asia. But now, as he writes, they are at Rome. It is reasonable to conclude that when, at Ephesus, the plan of a visit to Rome was definitely formed (Acts xix. 21), it was also decided that these two faithful companions and fellow workers should return to that city, to which at any rate Prisca probably belonged, prepare the way for S. Paul's own visit, and send him information as to the state of the Church there. It is perhaps even allowable to conjecture that, if c. xvi. 3—16 belongs to the Epistle, the numerous greetings, involving so much detailed knowledge of the Christians at Rome, may have been occasioned by a letter or letters received from them.

The immediate occasion, then, of the letter is S. Paul's desire to enlist the sympathy and assistance of the Roman Church for his contemplated mission to Spain. And the form which the letter takes is primarily dictated by the same desire. He could not appeal to the Roman Christians, as he could to Churches of his own converts, to promote and aid his preaching of the Gospel in an untouched land, without putting before them expressly the character of the Gospel which he preached. No doubt some account of this, but hardly a full or clear account, had reached Rome. No doubt in these latter days they had learnt more of it from Aquila and Priscilla. But the Apostle needs full and intelligent and wholehearted support: and consequently he lays before the Romans the fullest statement, which we have, of the Gospel as he was wont to present it for the conversion of Gentiles. He is determined that they shall thoroughly understand his position before they pledge their support. There were, as we shall see, other circumstances and influences which led to this systematic exposition of his theme, or rather dictated the terms in which it should be made. But the simple and sufficient explanation of his choice of the Roman Church to be the recipients of such a statement is to be found in the reason he had for writing to that Church at all. It is eminently characteristic of S. Paul's method that the needs of a particular occasion should have given rise to this elaborate and profound exposition of some of the fundamental elements of Christian truth. And it is of the highest importance both for the understanding of the Epistle itself, alike of what it includes and of what it omits, and for estimating its relation to his other Epistles, that we should constantly bear in mind the particular occasion from which it sprang.

So far we have been considering the explicit indications, which this Epistle itself affords, of the immediate purpose with which it was written. We must now examine, rather more widely the circumstances in which S. Paul came to write it.

The winter sojourn at Corinth marks the close of an extraordinarily interesting epoch in S. Paul's work. For some eight years he had been engaged in the evangelisation of Asia Minor, Macedonia and Achaia: and he had now completed that vast work (xv. 19). He had planted the Gospel in the principal towns of each province of the Roman Empire, which lay in the path between Jerusalem and Rome: and from these towns he, either in person or by his assistants, had evangelised the surrounding countries. He had spent a considerable time in revisiting and confirming all the Churches of his foundation in Galatia, Macedonia and Achaia ; in the province of Asia, he had spent nearly three years in founding and building up Churches. Throughout these labours he had been careful to keep in touch with the Church in Jerusalem : after his first mission, as an apostle of the Church in Antioch (Acts xiii. 1—3), warned perhaps by the difficulties which arose in Antioch on his return from that mission, he had made a practice of visiting Jerusalem before each new effort. He has now in his company at Corinth representatives of many, perhaps of all these Churches (xvi. 16 and Acts xx. 4 with Rom. xvi. 16): and his immediate object in returning to Jerusalem again is to carry thither, in company with their representatives, the charitable contributions of the Gentile Churches for the poor Christians in that place. The high importance of this object, in his eyes, is emphasised by the two facts, that for it he delays his cherished project of going to Rome and Spain, and that he persists in his determination in spite of actual perils incurred, and dangers clearly foreseen. These facts bring out the supreme importance to him of the two sides of his missionary work, the first, the evangelisation of Gentiles, the second, the building up of one Church in which Jew and Gentile should be closely knit, by bonds of brotherhood, in the new Israel springing from the old stock. Anxious, as each and all of his Epistles show him to have been, to consolidate unity within each several community by insisting on all the qualities which marked the Christian brotherhood based on love, he was no less anxious, as is shown by his consistent policy, to consolidate into one spiritual whole all the brethren, of whatever stock or religion, throughout the world. His ideal of the Christian Church was embodied in the conception of the new Israel, sprung from the old stock, and fulfilling, with a wider and deeper interpretation than Jews had discovered, the prophetic hope of the inclusion of the Gentiles, all members of one body and owning allegiance to one Lord by one faith. The composition of the Epistle to the Romans finds him at the climax of this endeavour. It consequently involves an exposition of this idea with a view to enlist their sympathetic support.

The actual form, which the exposition, at least in great part, takes, was influenced by the experiences he had gone through in his apostolic work. From the very beginning of his ministry (Acts ix. 23, 29) he had been met by the uncompromising opposition of Jews, an opposition which greeted all efforts to preach Jesus as the Messiah. But with the development of work among the Gentiles, he had to face a growing and ultimately even more bitter antagonism within the Christian Church itself. The battle raged not about the admission of Gentiles. That formed one strain in the prophetic hope, and would appear to have been settled by S. Peter's action in regard to Cornelius. S. Paul's action raised the question of the conditions on which Gentiles were to be admitted, and of their status when admitted. The solution was no doubt already involved in S. Peter's action : but that left abundant room for differences of interpretation and reserves. Such differences and reserves S. Paul challenged directly by his assertion that faith in GOD as revealed in the one Lord Jesus Christ was the sole requisite for baptism, the sole condition of acceptance, and by his consequent denial that the Jewish law, the supreme instrument of salvation in the eyes of Jews, had now any further obligation, as of right, upon Christians. The position thus asserted exposed him to the unflinching attacks of a class of Judaizing Christians in every place in which he preached, growing in strength in proportion to the success of his preaching and the development of the Churches which he founded. The controversy takes shape for us in the Council at Jerusalem (Acts xv.) and the circumstances which led up to it. The Epistle to the Galatians shows it in its most explicit and critical stage. The battle raged throughout the period of what is called the third missionary journey. In the Second Epistle to the Corinthians we have clear indications that, as a controversy within the Church, it was approaching its conclusion. This is abundantly clear if we take the view that that Epistle is composite, and that cc. x.—xiii. are a fragment of an Epistle preceding cc. i.—ix. But even if the Epistle was written as it stands, it clearly marks the closing of the fight, though the apprehensions and passions which it had called forth are still in vigorous activity. The victory has been won by S. Paul, on the main principle involved and on the important deductions. There remained the last resort of the defeated and embittered party, the personal attack on the probity and character of the champion of their antagonists. But that, full of peril as it was to his person, was in effect an acknowledgment of defeat.

The influence of this experience upon the Epistle to the Romans is seen in the closely reasoned exposition of the relation of faith and law, and of grace and law (cc. i.—viii.): and more obviously, though not more truly, in the elaborate attempt to grapple with the difficulties which Israel's official rejection of the Gospel involved for a Christian who claimed the inheritance of Israel (cc. ix.—xi.). But it is of the utmost importance to notice the positive and essentially uncontroversial character of the treatment; and the calm confidence of tone throughout confirms the conclusion that in S. Paul's view the battle had been won, and it remained only to state the positive truths which had been involved and successfully defended. No doubt this temper was largely the result of the reception of his letter to the Galatian Churches and his own reception at Corinth.

In saying this, we do not ignore the signs which the Epistle itself contains of the seriousness and perils of the controversy. There is one, but only one, reference to danger threatening the unity of the Church (xvi. 17—20). There is one, but only one, indication of perils threatening his own person (xv. 30—32). Both these references are plain and urgent enough to show that the dangers were real. But they threaten, not as before, from the inside and even the very heart of the Church, but as from external foes who may at any time gain a lodgment within, but at present have none. The whole tone of the Epistle indicates that the writer was in comparatively calm waters. He can review the struggles and trials of the last few years, not as one who is in the thick of the fight, but as one who is gathering the fruits of long toil, of a victory hard fought and hard won, both on the arena of his own soul's experience and in the field of the propagation of the Gospel.

5. IMPERIALISM.

So far, then, we have seen that his intention of carrying out missionary work in Spain is the immediate occasion of his writing to the Romans an account of the Gospel which he carried to unconverted Gentiles; and the experiences of the work, which he had already carried through, dictate the character of presentation. And it might seem sufficient to stop here. But it has been argued with great force and persuasiveness by Sir William Ramsay, and the position has been illustrated by a very wide examination of contemporary conditions, that S. Paul was influenced, more deeply than had been realised, by his position as a Roman citizen, among the Jews of the Dispersion at Tarsus; that his realisation of the vast unity of the Roman Empire led him to conceive of the Christian Church as providing a religious bond for its component parts; and that his letter and visit to Rome gained a supreme importance in his eyes from these conceptions. Are we, then, to add this idea of imperial statesmanship to the influences which we have already seen to be operative at this stage of S. Paul's activity?

It is certainly an established fact that S. Paul's plan in his missionary work was to seize upon great centres of Roman administration in the provinces, and to make them the centres from which to propagate the Gospel. Thessalonica, Philippi, Corinth, Ephesus were the principal places which he took for his headquarters in the period of his independent activity. And Rome itself became a special object, when his work in these places was drawing towards completion. But the choice of such centres would be quite consistent with a wise consideration of the most effective means of evangelising the part of the world which lay readiest to his hand, and would not necessarily involve such a conception as is attributed to him. It is true, of course, that much tradition, both among Jew and Gentile, favoured a tribal or national embodiment of religious ideas. But among the Jews there is considerable evidence of a wider conception. And, among Gentiles, the Stoic disregard of all such distinctions was already influencing the thought and practice of the contemporary world. No doubt, the obvious indications of the attempt to establish an imperial religion, in the worship of Rome and the Emperor already fostered in the provinces, and in particular in the province of Asia, would readily suggest to an observant mind the possibility that Christianity might supply the place of an imperial cult. To us looking back upon the historical development, and reading the end achieved under Constantine into the beginnings laid down by S. Paul, it seems all but inevitable that S. Paul must have had some thought of the possibility of such a development. But the deduction is not, as a matter of fact, inevitable. While it is impossible to disprove it, it is still safe to affirm that the evidence for it is all secondary and consists of deductions from the circumstances of his time and position rather than from any clear hint to be found in his writings. If we look to the latter for evidence of the wider conceptions under which he acted we shall find these to be such as are not favourable to the presence of the imperial idea. We may take two illustrations. It is fundamental to S. Paul's conception of the Gospel that it overleaps all distinctions of place, class, nationality and religion. The natural unity of mankind in its most comprehensive sense is insisted upon as the anticipation and even basis of the spiritual re-union in Christ. It is significant in this connexion that while S. Paul does recognise the family, as forming what we may call a multi-personal unit in the inclusive organism of the Christian body, he uses no similar language about political organisations. Illustrations are indeed taken from city life, but they are definitely metaphorical.   He may consistently have regarded the evangelisation of the various parts of the Roman Empire as a stage in and a basis for the wider evangelisation of the world; but of the organisation of an imperial Church there is no hint. Indeed it would appear that any organisation was beyond S. Paul's view, except such simple arrangements as would provide for the internal administration of the locally separated groups of Christians and the intercommunion of the several groups.   And we may see the reason for this in a second fundamental conception, which also gives ground for hesitating to attribute to S. Paul the imperial conception. In all his teaching, as we have it, it seems clear that the near return of the Lord was a constant, almost a dominating, element. The belief gave energy and fire to all he said or did that could bear upon the training of character in the individual and in the community, in preparation for that day. But it almost necessarily put out of thought such measures as would prepare the Church for prolonged activity upon earth and equip it for a relation to the powers of earth.   Where S. Paul speaks of these relations, he treats them solely as matters for the individual Christian to regulate for himself : he hardly considers the problems that even in this direction would arise; and indeed does little more than develop, and that not far, the Lord's own saying about rendering unto Caesar the things that are Caesar's.

Consequently, we do not think that a case is made out for attributing to S. Paul far-sighted views of the relation of the Church to the Empire.   And we do not include any thought of this kind among the influences which led him to write this Epistle.

6. READERS.

The evidence which the Epistle affords of the character and conditions of the readers to whom it was addressed may be divided into two classes.   The first class is the evidence directly given by particular passages.   The second is that which may be deduced from the nature of the topics handled and the method of handling them.

(1) In the first class, which is the more direct, we cite the following passages :

c. i. 6, 13 ; the readers appear here to be definitely included among the Gentiles. They are among the Gentiles to whom S. Paul has received grace and commission; and he feels it necessary to explain that he has hitherto been prevented from preaching among them, as he has preached among the rest of the Gentiles. c. xv. 14—21 is the second passage which definitely implies that as they were Gentiles he had a prescriptive right to address them; even though, as they were a Church not founded by himself, that right was limited by his self-imposed restriction which prevented him working on ground which others had made their own. A third passage which fixes the readers as at least predominantly Gentiles is c. xi. 25—32. We may add to these passages, though in a different degree of certainty, c. vi. 12—23 : the suggestion there made as to the state of the readers previous to their conversion is more consistent with the language S. Paul habitually uses about Gentiles than with his descriptions of Jews. It might, on the other hand, be felt that c. vii. 1 f. and c. viii. 3 f. were in no less a degree peculiarly applicable to Christians who had been Jews. But in qualification of this impression, it is clear that S. Paul regarded the whole pre-Christian world as having been in a real sense under dispensation of law (cf. iii. 14 f.), the Gentiles under law communicated through the inner witness of conscience, the Jews having in addition to this the positive revelation of GOD'S will in the covenant law. Both these passages in reality apply to the previous experience of all Christians : they take their several colours from the dominant experience of each class. On iv. 1 see the notes *ad loc.*

The conclusion to be drawn from these passages is that the Christians in Rome were a composite body, in which Gentiles formed the great majority ; and it is to them that the letter is primarily addressed.

(2) How far does the second class of evidence bear out this conclusion ? We have already seen that the circumstances of the Epistle and its object were the primary influence in dictating

the topics. But those circumstances were independent, to a large extent, of the Church in Rome; it had its influence chiefly so far as S. Paul considered its members fit and suitable to receive this presentation of his Gospel. But that again was the result of their position at the centre of the Empire and the assistance they could afford him in his work in Spain. Consequently we cannot expect to learn much about that Church from the Epistle itself; the less so, because S. Paul's acquaintance with them as a body was entirely at second hand. Thus in cc. i.—xi. the topics seem to be exclusively chosen with a view to making clear the principles of this Gospel and the methods of his preaching. In cc. xii.—xv., on the other hand, where he deals with the application of the Gospel to conduct, we might expect to find more of specific bearing upon the conditions in Rome. But here too the main themes are such as might have been addressed to any progressive body of Christians. Two sections, perhaps, offer some special light. (1) In c. xiii. 1—9 S. Paul deals, at greater length than elsewhere, with the relation of Christians to the civil power; and this may have been due to special conditions which had arisen at Rome (see below); though there is little in the treatment, except its explicitness, to tell us what those conditions were. (2) Again, in cc. xiv.—xv. 13 we have a discussion of the duties of the strong and the weak, as regards certain external practices and observances. Both the tone and the topics of the discussion are inconsistent with the supposition that S. Paul was combating any definite Judaistic propaganda at Rome. They rather point to the common danger of laying too much stress on external observances; and, in the particular instance of food, to some general form of asceticism which appears to have been a widespread characteristic of the higher religious feeling of the times, among Gentiles, perhaps, even more than among Jews. The contrast with the Epistle to the Galatians, where S. Paul uses so much of the principles, which he expounds in this Epistle, to combat a decided and powerful Judaistic propaganda, endorses this conclusion.

It might, at first sight, appear that the large use of the Old Testament and the familiarity with those Scriptures, which he throughout assumes in his readers, afford strong ground for

thinking that the majority at least were Jews. But this conclusion is countered by the observation that all the evidence
points to the fact that, at least in S. Paul's work, the nucleus of
every Gentile Church was found in those Gentiles who had been
in the habit of attending the synagogue: and that we find, as
a consequence of this, that the Old Testament was familiar to,
and indeed was the Bible of the early Churches, even when
they were certainly composed in the main of Gentiles, as was
the case at Corinth. It is a significant confirmation of this
conclusion, that our New Testament Scriptures seem to have
begun to acquire a canonical character from their association
with the Old Testament Scriptures in the public readings in the
congregation.

We conclude then on this line of evidence, as on the former,
that the Church in Rome was at this time predominantly, though
by no means exclusively, Gentile.

7. HISTORY OF THE ROMAN CHURCH.

If we ask, further, what evidence we have as to the founding
and development of the Church in Rome at this early period,
we find little material for anything but reasonable conjecture.
Perhaps the most important evidence is to be drawn from
S. Paul's own attitude to this Church as expressed, in particular, in c. xv. 14—30. A careful reading of that passage
shows that the writer has a sensitive delicacy in approaching
the Roman Christians and as it were inviting himself to visit
them and to preach among them. He lays emphatic stress on
the help and advantage he hopes to gain from intercourse with
them, his long cherished desire to visit them, his confidence in
their progress and competence in all Christian feeling and
practice; he feels indeed that he has something to contribute
to them (v. 15); but he makes much more of the mutual advantage to be gained by the visit (cf. i. 11, 12), and on the
especial support he hopes to gain for his mission to Spain.
This manner of approaching a Church is peculiar to this Epistle,
though there is in some degree a parallel in the Epistle to the
Colossians, to whom again he had not himself preached, in the
care he takes to explain his deep interest in them (Col. i. 9,

ii. 1 f.). The key to this attitude is no doubt given by the principle which he refers to in *v.* 20. The foundation of the Church in Rome has been laid by others; and he will by all means avoid the appearance of trenching upon the sphere of others.

Who those others were, we have no direct evidence to show. The tradition of a visit of S. Peter at this early period has small historic foundation. And although the argument from silence is precarious, it is in the highest degree improbable, considering the whole tone of the passage we have just referred to, that S. Paul would have abstained from all allusion to S. Peter, if he had indeed been in any sense the founder of the Roman Church.

The only passages in the Acts that throw any light upon the subject are ii. 10 and xviii. 2. In the first passage, among the foreign Jews staying at Jerusalem at Pentecost are mentioned οἱ ἐπιδημοῦντες Ῥωμαῖοι, Ἰουδαῖοί τε καὶ προσήλυτοι. The note is of course natural; it would be natural, that is to say, that Jews from Rome should be present on this occasion. But the special mention of Jews from that particular city and the definite description of them as temporarily residing in Jerusalem and including 'Jews and proselytes' may be a hint, such as S. Luke sometimes gives, of special importance attached by him to their presence and to the presence of both classes. It is a reasonable conjecture that some of these 'Jews and proselytes' would carry back to Rome news of the events of Pentecost and the account of what led up to them, and would at least prepare the way for the reception of the Gospel, both among Jews and among those Gentiles who had more or less attached themselves to the synagogues in Rome.

In the second passage (Acts xviii. 2) we are told that S. Paul, on his arrival at Corinth, 'found a certain Jew by name Aquila, a native of Pontus by race, lately come from Italy, and Priscilla his wife, because Claudius had ordered that all the Jews should depart from Rome,' and that 'he at once joined them, and because he was of the same craft continued to live with them, and they plied their trade' of tent-making. The connexion with Aquila and Priscilla which S. Paul here formed is evidently of high importance in the writer's view. This appears both from the full description of these persons and the statement of their reason for being in Corinth. But with the reserve, which so often tantalises us in the Acts, he omits to tell us whether Aquila and Priscilla were already Christians. It seems however to be implied that they were. S. Paul lived with them throughout his stay in Corinth: for the change mentioned in *v.* 7 refers only to his place of preaching: from which it would appear that they were either already Christians or were converted by S. Paul. But we should expect to have been told if the latter were the case (cf. *v.* 8). There is moreover another slight indication, pointing in the same direction, in the precise words 'all the Jews' (πάντας τοὺς Ἰουδαίους). The 'all' is not required, if the object is merely to refer to Claudius' decree of expulsion against the Jews. It is in point, if S. Luke wishes to indicate that the decree included both Christian and non-Christian Jews. It would explain why Aquila and Priscilla were expelled though they were Christians.

This leads us to consider the one piece of relevant information, which we derive from Suetonius. Suetonius (*Claud.* c. 25) tells us, 'Judaeos impulsore Chresto assidue tumultuantes Roma expulit.' It is agreed that Suetonius and S. Luke are referring to the same incident, to be dated A.D. 49 or 50. Suetonius gives us the reason for the decree. There had been constant disturbances among the Jews at the instigation of one Chrestus. It is probable that Chrestus is a vulgar rendering of Christus: and that the cause of the disturbances was either some general excitement in connexion with Messianic expectation, or, as a consideration of all the circumstances makes more probable, dissensions which arose from the preaching of the Gospel, such as are recorded at Corinth (Acts xviii. 12 f.). If we may suppose that events followed something of the same course at Rome and Corinth; that in Rome also the Jews tried to suppress the growing movement by appeal to the civil authorities, and, on their refusal to interfere, took the law into their own hands, we get a natural explanation of the violent disturbances which prompted the decree. The civil authorities, 'caring for none of these things,' would visit their wrath indiscriminately upon both parties to the quarrel. In this case we may conjecture that Aquila and Priscilla were among the

Christian Jews expelled from Rome. And we should further conclude that by the date of the decree the number of Christians was already considerable enough to make these disturbances serious ; and, moreover, that the character of the Gospel preached was such as to arouse the bitter opposition of Jews who remained impervious to its call, that is to say, that it appealed to and made great way among Gentiles. This does not imply that it was specifically Pauline in character, but is consistent with the conclusion we have already arrived at that the Church was predominantly Gentile. It is not unreasonable to conclude that the Church at Rome took its beginnings first from the reports brought from Jerusalem after Pentecost and afterwards from the preaching of the Gospel by returned pilgrims on later occasions. It is even possible that Aquila may himself have been one of these. It is tempting to search c. xvi. for other hints. The remarkable description of Mary (*v.* 6 ἥτις πολλὰ ἐκοπίασεν εἰς ὑμᾶς) may point to a part taken by her in this early stage : and the still more remarkable description of Andronicus and Junias may possibly imply that they were among those who had brought the Gospel to Rome and so were distinguished among the Apostles (*v.* 7 ἐπίσημοι ἐν τοῖς ἀποστόλοις). If that was so, we should have to find among the original evangelists not only returning pilgrims, but Jews from the East travelling for purposes of business, or even for the definite purpose of propagating the Gospel.

Whatever was the origin of the Church, it had by the date of this Epistle clearly become numerous and important. Its development was of a sufficiently substantial character to make S. Paul feel that its support would be not only desirable but in a high degree advantageous to him in his contemplated work in Spain. Of its constitution we can learn little. It seems to have included a number of groups, probably distinguished by the different houses to which they gathered for worship, instruction and mutual society (xvi. 5, 14, 15), or as forming subsections of social groups in which they were already classified (*vv.* 10, 11). By what organisation these various groups were held together there is no evidence. The common address of the Epistle implies that there was such an organisation ; and the analogy of other churches and the natural requirements of the situation point to the same conclusion. But in the absence of definite statement, we cannot be more precise. As to the classes of persons who were included, we gather from c. xvi. that there were both Jews and Greeks, freemen, and, apparently in large proportion, slaves. It would be indeed natural that the Gospel should spread most freely among the foreigners from Greece and the East, who were resident in Rome in large numbers, whether for ordinary purposes of business or as attached to the household of wealthy residents. There is nothing to show that the upper class of Romans had yet come within its influence (contrast perhaps 2 Tim. iv. 21).

8. CHARACTER AND CONTENTS.

In character the Epistle to the Romans is a true letter. It has the definite personal and occasional elements which mark the letter. It may be almost described as a letter of introduction. The writer introduces himself to the Romans, with a full description of his authority, office and employment. He takes pains to conciliate their sympathies for an object in which he desires to enlist their help. With a characteristic combination of refined delicacy and intense earnestness he claims their attention and interest. He emphasises his own interest in them, by the repeated account of his desire to visit them, and by his explanations of his delay; and he takes the opportunity of the presence in Rome of some first-hand acquaintances to convey a long list of personal greetings. He carefully explains the immediate occasion of his writing, as well as its ultimate purpose, and gives an account of his present circumstances and plans.

This character of the Epistle has been to some extent obscured owing to the fact that it contains the most systematic account, that S. Paul has left us, of some aspects of his preaching: and readers have been led to consider that it is primarily a treatise, for instance, on justification by faith, and that the epistolary character is secondary and even adventitious. The effect of this mis-reading of the work has been twofold. It has led some to regard it as a treatise intended to be circulated among several churches; and to look upon the form in which it has been preserved to us as merely that one in which it was adapted for the Romans. Others have concluded that the main part of the epistolary setting is secondary and not in fact original; that, for instance, the sixteenth chapter has been wrongly added to the body of the treatise, being borrowed from a letter to the Church in Ephesus, not otherwise preserved. As regards the second of these views, it is perhaps enough to say that the epistolary character, as described above, is determined even more by the first and fifteenth chapters, than by the sixteenth; and that these chapters, at least, cannot be detached from the main body of the Epistle except by a process of mutilation. And, as regards the first view, the direct evidence in support of it is of the slightest, and may at the most point to a circulation of the Epistle in an abbreviated form by the Church in Rome itself, some time after it had been received. (See pp. 235 ff.)

But we have still to account for the systematic character of the main body of the letter. For it is this character which differentiates it from all the other Pauline epistles, except the Epistle to the Ephesians. It must then be shown that this character is consistent with that which the letter itself declares to be its direct object. We have already seen that the primary and direct object of the letter was to interest the Romans and to gain their support for a contemplated mission to Spain. With this in view S. Paul wishes to prepare the way for a visit; and Aquila and Priscilla have already preceded him to Rome, probably with the same object. But something more was needed than the establishment of personal relations. A connexion between S. Paul and the Christians in Rome had not hitherto been established. What they knew of each other had hitherto been matter only of hearsay and report. He has probably now received full information from his friends, Aquila and Priscilla, of the state of things in Rome: and he wishes the Roman Church, in its turn, to be as fully informed as possible of his own position and intentions. Consequently, in appealing for their support, he has to explain to them what it is he asks them to support. He wishes to expound to them his conception of the Gospel, as he preaches it to Gentiles, his missionary message. And he does so in a systematic exposition which covers the whole of the Epistle from i. 14—xv. 13.

It is important to lay stress on this missionary character of the aspect of his Gospel which he thus presents. It accounts both for what he includes and what he omits. In the first place, he is not primarily defending his personal action as an apostle of the Gentiles; though that is vindicated by the way. He has done that in the second Epistle to the Corinthians, which may be described as the Apologia *pro apostolatu suo*. Nor is he expounding his thought of the Church and the developed Christian life: of this subject again many elements are necessarily included, but in subordinate proportions and rather by hints and implications than by express statements. The full exposition of this aspect of his Gospel he gives in the Epistle to the Ephesians. The Epistle to the Romans contains, in contrast with them, the Apologia *pro evangelio suo*, an explanation of the Gospel committed to him and preached by him for the conversion of the Gentiles. And the explanation is given, not by way of controversy as against opponents, as it is in the Epistle to the Galatians, nor by way of justification of his action in the past as though he was submitting his case to judges, but simply as a full explanation offered to men whose support he hopes to enlist for his future work.

A brief summary of the argument of the systematic portion of the Epistle will illustrate this position.

It is significant that S. Paul begins, as he does in no other epistle, with a quite definite statement of the theme he intends to put before his readers. 'The Gospel is GOD's active power for saving men; its one condition in all cases is faith in GOD: and this is so, because GOD's righteousness, required to be assimilated by man if he is to be saved, is shown in the Gospel, as resulting from man's faith and leading to faith' (i. 16, 17, see notes). The theme then is that the Gospel is an act of GOD's power, to enable all mankind to be righteous as GOD is righteous; that the sole condition demanded of man is faith in GOD; that this condition, being a common human quality not limited by class or nation, marks the universality of the Gospel.

This theme is then worked out in four main divisions. First, it is shown that the actual state of man, whether Jew or Gentile, is so remote from exhibiting GOD's righteousness in human life, that the need for the exercise of GOD's power is manifest: this is supported by a broad view of contemporary conditions, as we may say historically, in cc. i.—v.: and by a penetrating analysis of the experience of the single soul, or psychologically, in cc. vi., vii. Concurrently, it is declared that the need is met by the act of GOD in the person and work of Jesus Christ, to be accepted and made his own by man, through faith (iv. 21—26, vi. 11, vii. 25). Secondly, it is shown that GOD's power acts, in response to faith, by the presence and working of the Holy Spirit, uniting men to each other and to GOD through union with Christ, and producing in them the development of that character which in men corresponds to the righteousness of GOD. The Holy Spirit is GOD's power in man (c. viii.). Thirdly, we have, what is in reality a digression, but a digression naturally occasioned by the course of the argument. In cc. ix., x., xi. S. Paul attempts to solve, what to him and to others was the most harrowing problem occasioned by the offer of the Gospel to the Gentiles, namely, the position of the great mass of Israel who rejected the very Gospel for which their own history had been the most direct preparation. Fourthly (cc. xii.—xv. 13), it is shown what character the power of the Gospel produces in its operation upon the daily life of men, in the transformation of personal character, in their relations to each other as members of the society of faith, and in their external relations to the societies of the world.

S. Paul, therefore, in this exposition sets before the Romans his view of the Gospel as a moral and spiritual power for the regeneration of human life; he explains and defends the condition postulated for its operation, the range of its action, and its effects in life. The last subject suggests a fuller treatment of the Christian life in the Church: but this is not given here; it is reserved, as a fact, for the Epistle to the Ephesians. It is not given here, because S. Paul's object, in writing the Epistle, limits his treatment to the purpose of explaining his missionary message.

It may be well here to point out, that the properly occasional character of the Epistle is seen not only in the introductory and concluding portions, where the need of Roman support gives the occasion: but in the treatment of the main subject, in which the occasion of the details is often given by the actual circumstances of S. Paul's experience and the time or stage at which he was writing. For instance, c. iv. on Abraham's righteousness is inspired by his desire to show that the Gospel righteousness was essentially of the same nature as the Old Testament righteousness when properly conceived. Again, in cc. ix.—xi. the consideration of the case of Israel bears directly upon the assumption made throughout that the Christian Church is the true Israel, preserved indeed in a remnant but, all the more for that, prophetically designated as the heir of the promises. This sums up and clinches the long sustained controversy with the Judaisers. Again, in c. vi. the insistence upon the power of the Gospel to inspire and maintain the highest standard of morality is the final answer to the charge which S. Paul had been forced to meet, in his controversy with Jews and Judaisers, that in abolishing law he was destroying the one known influence in favour of a sound morality, and guilty of propagating moral indifference or ἀνομία. And, in the last section, in c. xiv., he deals fully, though in general terms, with a practical difficulty which had confronted him at Corinth and no doubt elsewhere, and which he may have been informed of as existing at Rome, the treatment of scrupulous brethren. All these questions were, in different degrees, of immediate interest and importance. Some of them appear to have ceased to be so, not long after the Epistle was written, and they mark, emphatically, its intimate relation to the actual situation in which S. Paul found himself in those three winter months at Corinth.

The following analysis of the contents does not profess to give more than one presentation of the argument of the Epistle. It is constructed on the general supposition involved in the above account of its character.

A. Introduction, i. 1—17.

    i. 1—7. Address: (i) The writer's name, office and commission: the commission is defined by the trust received, the Person from whom, and the Person about and through whom it was received;

       (ii) the class and name of the persons addressed;

       (iii) the greeting.

i. 8.   Thanksgiving, for the widespread report of the faith of the Romans.

i. 9—15.   Assertion of the intimate interest the writer has in the readers, his desire to see them, his hope of mutual help, his debt to them in common with others.

i. 16, 17.   Statement of his theme:

The Gospel which he preaches is GOD'S power to effect salvation for everyone who believes;

for in it is revealed the nature of GOD'S righteousness, both as an attribute of GOD and as His demand from man, and the fact that it follows upon faith, and leads to faith, without distinction of race or privilege; as already indicated in the O. T. Scriptures.

B.   First vindication of the theme, drawn from the actual state of mankind: main antithesis πίστις and νόμος.

i. 18—iv. 25.   The need of righteousness is universal (i. 18—iii. 20) and it is adequately met (iii. 21—31) on lines already laid down in O.T. (iv.).

(i)   i. 18—ii. 16.   It is needed by Gentiles: they are sunk in sin, due to the neglect of knowledge consequent upon want of faith in GOD :

(ii)   ii. 17—iii. 20.   And by Jews; they have admittedly failed in spite of their privileged position, because (iii. 1 —20) they also have ignored the one condition of attainment.

(iii)   iii. 21—31.   The general failure is met by the revelation of GOD'S righteousness in Christ, through His Death, a propitiative and redemptive act ; and by the condition demanded of man, namely, faith in GOD through Christ ; one condition for all men corresponding to the fact that there is but one GOD over all.

(iv)   iv. 1—25.   This condition of righteousness is already laid down in the O.T. in the typical case of Abraham.

C.   Second vindication of the theme, drawn from a consideration of its ethical bearing and effect: main antithesis χάρις and νόμος.

v.—vii. 25.   The Gospel reveals a power which can do what it purports to do.

(i) v. 1—11. The power is a new life, given by God in love, through the death of Christ, open to faith, dependent upon the life of Christ, and guaranteed by the love of God.

(ii) v. 12—21. This power depends upon a living relation of mankind to Christ, analogous to the natural relation of mankind to Adam, and as universal as that is.

(iii) vi. 1—vii. 6. It involves the loftiest moral standard because it is

    (1) a new life in the risen Christ (vi. 1—14);

    (2) a service of God, not under law, but in Christ (15—23);

    (3) a union with Christ, which must bring forth its proper fruits (vii. 1—6).

(iv) vii. 7—25. It is therefore effective to overcome sin and achieve righteousness in the individual life, as personal experience shows that law could never do.

D. The nature and working of the power thus revealed. viii.

viii. 1—11. The power is, in fact, the indwelling Spirit, derived from God through Christ, communicating to the believer the life of the risen Christ, and so overcoming in him the death wrought by sin, as God overcame in Christ by raising Him from the dead.

viii. 12—39. The consequent character and obligations of the Christian life:

(*a*) It is the life of a son and heir of God, involving suffering as the path to glory (as in the case of Jesus) (12—25).

(*b*) It is inspired by the presence of the Holy Spirit and His active cooperation in working out all God's purpose in us and for us (26—30).

(*c*) It is due to God's exceeding love, an active force manifested in the sacrifice of His Son, in the Son's own love in His offering, triumph and intercession, as a power of victory from which no imaginable thing can separate those who are His (31—39; note the refrain, v. 11, 21, vi. 23, viii. 11, 39).

E. Israel's rejection of the Gospel (a typical case of man's rejection of God's grace, and in itself a harrowing problem). ix. 1—xi. 36.

ix. 1—4. Israel's rejection of the Gospel is a great grief and incessant pain to S. Paul, and a hard problem in the economy of redemption. But

(1) 6—13. God's faithfulness is not impugned by it:
for the condition of the promise was not carnal descent but spiritual, and not man's work but God's selection.

(2) ix. 14—x. 21. God's righteousness is not impugned
(*a*) because His selection must be righteous because
(i) 14—18, it is dependent on His Will which is righteous;
(ii) 19—21, it is directed towards the execution of His righteous purposes;
(iii) 22—33, it acts in accordance with qualities exhibited.
(*b*) because His selection is not inconsistent with moral responsibility for
x. 1—4, Israel's failure was due to neglect of attainable knowledge;
5—15, as is shown by the warnings of Scripture properly interpreted;
16—21, which Israel can be shown to have received. Consequently Israel is himself to blame.

(3) xi. 1—36. Israel is still not rejected by God for
(i) xi. 1—7. A remnant is saved, as in the time of Elijah, κατ᾽ ἐκλογὴν χάριτος.
xi. 8—12. The rest are hardened, as Scripture warns, but not with a view to their own ruin, but with a view to the call of the Gentiles and the rousing of Israel.
(ii) xi. 13—36. The present condition of Israel and Gentiles.
xi. 13—16. The privilege the Gentiles have received is derived from and belongs to Israel.
xi. 17—24. The Gentiles may fall away as Israel did, if they fail in the same way.

(ii) 20—22. He has delayed to visit them because (*a*) he will not build on another's foundation, (*b*) he has been engrossed by his proper work.

(iii) 23—29. This work now takes him to Spain, and he will visit them on the way, hoping for their support.

(iv) 30—33. He entreats their prayers on behalf of his visit to Jerusalem, for full success in that mission of brotherhood, and hopes to come to them in joy and to gain refreshment.

(2) xvi. 1—16. Commendations and greetings.

(3) xvi. 17—20. A final warning against possible dangers to their Christian peace.

(4) xvi. 21—23. Greetings from his companions.

(5) xvi. 25—27. A final solemn ascription of glory to GOD for the revelation of the Gospel.

9. JUSTIFICATION BY FAITH.

The group of words δικαιοῦν, δικαίωμα, δικαίωσις is so prominent in this Epistle as to mark one of its most definite characters. δικαίωσις is found only here in N.T. (iv. 25, v. 18): δικαίωμα occurs five times to an equal number in the rest of the N.T. (Lk., Heb., Rev.); δικαιοῦν occurs fourteen times, and eight times in Galatians, to sixteen times in the rest of the N.T. Two of the latter occurrences are in Acts (xiii. 39) in a speech attributed to S. Paul. The only document, outside the Gospels, Acts and Pauline Epistles, in which the word occurs is James (ii. 21, 24, 25).

The meaning of δικαιοῦν is to 'pronounce righteous.' This is the universal use, to which the only known exception in LXX. and N.T. is Isa. lii. 14 ff., where the context makes it necessary to interpret it to mean 'to make righteous.' The form of the verb (-οω) allows the latter meaning: but use, always a safer guide than etymology, is decisive as to its actual meaning. In this use, this verb is on the same level with other verbs formed from other adjectives implying moral qualities (ἀξιόω, ὁσιόω): and the explanation usually given of the peculiar use in these cases is, that moral change cannot be effected from without; only a declaration of the state can be made. This reasoning, however, cannot be pressed, when the agency of GOD is in question, and the effect of His action on human character. Consequently, the meaning of the word in S. Paul must be got directly from evidence of his use of it.

There is no question that in the Gospels the meaning 'to declare righteous' is alone found. The same meaning must be given to 1 Tim. iii. 16. In James ii. 21—25 the use is closely parallel to that of the Romans: and 1 Cor. iv. 4, vi. 11, Tit. iii. 7 are clearly connected with the use in the Romans, although the expression is not quite so explicit. In Acts xiii. 39 we have a distinct anticipation of the argument of this Epistle, if the words were actually spoken by S. Paul: if they are put into his mouth by S. Luke, then we have an echo. Consequently, to arrive at the meaning in S. Paul we must examine the use in Romans and Galatians: remembering that the universal use which he had before him gave the meaning 'to declare righteous.'

1. The sense 'to declare righteous' is clearly contained in the following passages where the context involves the thought of judgment:

> ii. 13. οἱ ποιηταὶ νόμου δικαιωθήσονται following *v.* 12 διὰ νόμου κριθήσονται and leading to *v.* 16 κρίνει (κρινεῖ) ὁ θεός.
>
> iii. 4. δικαιωθῇς ‖ νικήσεις ἐν τῷ κρίνεσθαί σε (qu.).
>
> iii. 20. οὐ δικαιωθήσεται πᾶσα σὰρξ after ὑπόδικος γένηται.
>
> viii. 33. θεὸς ὁ δικαιῶν· τίς ὁ κατακρινῶν; this carries with it ἐδικαίωσεν, *v.* 30.

2. δικαιοῦν, δικαιοῦσθαι are paraphrased by λογίζεσθαι εἰς δικαιοσύνην, and the like, in iv. 2, 3, 5, 8, 9, 11. Cf. ii. 26, ix. 8.

3. In other passages, where there is no such explicit interpretation in the context, the sense is settled partly by the precedent of the above-cited passages, partly by the elements in the several contexts; e.g.

> iii. 24. δικαιούμενοι δωρεάν must be interpreted in the same way as δικαιωθήσεται in *v.* 20; as also δικαιοῦντα in *v.* 26 and δικαιοῦσθαι *al.*, *vv.* 27, 30.
>
> v. 1. δικαιωθέντες obviously sums up the argument of the preceding chapter, and the word must have the same sense.

v. 9. The stages ἁμαρτωλῶν...δικαιωθέντες νῦν...σωθησόμεθα
are interpreted by the parallel ἐχθροὶ...κατηλλάγημεν...
σωθησόμεθα: the aorists κατηλλάγημεν, δικαιώθεντες both
point to the act of GOD which is the starting-point of the
process described in σωθησόμεθα. That act as expressed
by δικαιοῦν is His declaration of righteousness.

vi. 7. ὁ γὰρ ἀποθανὼν δεδικαίωται ἀπὸ τῆς ἁμαρτίας. The
same meaning is quite clearly necessary.

viii. 30. ἐκάλεσεν...ἐδικαίωσεν...ἐδόξασεν. Here the word
cannot have a different sense from what it has in *v.* 33:
= He declared righteous: the actual imparting of the
character is expressed in ἐδόξασεν. See notes *ad loc.*

It is clear that the only sense we can attribute to this word
in the Romans is 'to declare righteous.' It is significant that
the word occurs only in the first six chapters, in which S. Paul
is analysing the elements of the Christian state, and in viii. 30,
33 where he sums up the results of his analysis. In cc. xii. ff.,
where he is dealing directly with the development of the
Christian character, it does not occur.

It is unnecessary to give a detailed examination of the use
in Galatians, as it stands on all fours with that of the Romans.
The difference between the Epistles is that the fundamental
fact of justification by faith is rather asserted than elaborately
argued in the Galatians. The full argument is reserved for the
Romans. The use of the word in Galatians agrees with the
use in Romans.

It is further to be observed that when the verb is used in
the passive, the preposition which marks the agency of GOD
is παρὰ, not ὑπό (Rom. ii. 13; Gal. iii. 11), indicating rather the
judge than the effective agent; the only other form used is ἐνώπιον αὐτοῦ (Rom. iii. 20). Once we have τῇ αὐτοῦ χάριτι (Rom. iii.
24); it is an act of grace. Cf. κατὰ χάριν, iv. 4.

4. We pass now to the description of the state of man which
requires this declaration of righteousness, and the conditions on
which it is made. The state is the universal state of sin, shown
to characterise both Gentiles and Jews: it is shown that the
knowledge of GOD'S will, whether elementary in Gentiles or
even consummate in Jews, had not been sufficient to enable
man to do the Will: that as a matter of fact man had failed
in his efforts to do the Will, and by this road had not reached a

state on which he could claim a verdict of righteousness. It is assumed that this account of man's efforts is exhaustive, and shows that this way of man's 'works' is a blind alley. The emergency requires divine intervention. This way is found in Jesus Christ, the Son of GOD, who by His Death, as interpreted by His Resurrection, at once vindicated the righteousness of GOD (iii. 24 f. ; see comm.) and offered Himself as man, an acceptable sacrifice to GOD. In Him as man once for all GOD declares man (human nature) righteous. The question then arises how are men, as several persons, to be brought under this verdict of righteousness. And the answer is, only by their being united with Christ, by being actually, not merely potentially, included in His humanity as offered to and accepted by GOD. This inclusion is the purport of baptism (vi. 1—11), involving an inner, living union with Christ, and thus a passing from the old life to the new life in Him. In this new life, the man is a new creature ; as such he is reconciled to GOD ; he is under the influence of all the spiritual powers of Christ, who is his life; he is undergoing the process of salvation ; he is the subject of the working of GOD's glory. So far all is the act of GOD, proceeding from His grace, or free giving, the crucial instance of His love.

What is the contribution which man has to make, on his part ? If the life is to be his life, it must in some degree from the first involve such a contribution. There must be personal action on his part, unless it is to be a mere matter of absorption into the divine life and action. Yet it was just by the emphasis on the personal action of the man, that Gentile and Jew alike had gone astray. They had hoped to make peace with GOD result from an active pursuit of righteousness, the attempt to do what was right in detail: and they had failed. The stress had been laid inevitably upon acts rather than character, upon external laws rather than upon inner principles ; upon the fulfilment of a task rather than upon a personal relation. The right point of view must be sought in some conception, which would at once preserve the personal activity of the man and yet leave the effective action to GOD. And this S. Paul finds in the conception of faith.

The meaning of πίστις in the N.T. is always belief or faith, as a quality of man's spiritual activity, until in the latest books (Jude 3 f., 20, and perhaps, but very doubtfully, in the Pastoral

Epistles) it gets the meaning of the contents of faith or the Christian creed. But 'belief or faith' itself is used with different degrees of intensity. It may mean simply a belief of a fact: or belief of GOD's promises: from this latter use, it passes easily to its fuller meaning of belief or trust in GOD as true to His promises; and thus to the full sense, which we find in S. Paul and S. John, of trust in GOD as revealed in Jesus Christ, a trust involving not merely the acceptance of the revelation as true, but the whole-hearted surrender of the person to GOD as so revealed and in all the consequences of the revelation. The kernel of the thought is the active surrender of the whole person, in all its activities, of intellectual assent, of the positive offering of will and action, of unreserved love. It is none of these things separately, but all of them together: it being in fact a concrete and complex act of the personality itself, throwing itself whole, as it were, upon GOD Himself, in the recognition of the worthlessness of all human life apart from GOD and of the will and power of GOD to give human life its true worth. This act of faith involves, that is to say, the element of belief, the element of will and the element of love. And the object of the activity of each of these elements of the person is GOD, believed, loved, and willed.

It follows from this complex character of faith, that it will be found in different degrees of development, and even in varying forms of manifestation. Sometimes the element of belief will be dominant: sometimes belief will be reduced to a minimum, and the deeper elements of will and love, either together or in different degrees of prominence, will form the staple of the act. In the case of Abraham, which S. Paul takes as typical of righteousness before the Gospel, the belief is mainly belief in the trustworthiness and power of GOD: the element of will, unquestioning obedience to and service of GOD, comes to the fore: the element of love, not explicitly mentioned in Romans, is represented in O.T. by the name 'the friend of GOD.' And such differences in the proportion in which the elements of faith are found in particular cases, are a matter of common experience. In 'the woman that was a sinner' it was for her great love that her sins were forgiven: yet by her acts it is clear that the other elements of faith were present at

the back of her action. In the Gospel cases, where faith is the
condition and even the measure of the working of Christ's
power in miracle, the element of belief is again prominent,
but it is a belief not only in the power but in the character
of Jesus, which itself is an indication that the other elements
were in a degree present, though in varying degrees, in those
who threw themselves upon His mercy. Even where the faith
seems to be reduced to the mere element of belief, the personal
element in the ground for the belief itself implies in the believer
the working of the other elements in their characteristically
personal action.

Now S. Paul, while he uses πίστις and πιστεύω freely in
their various senses, still when he is using it in correlation with
χάρις and in contrast to νόμος and ἔργα, uses the words in this
full sense, of the personal act of surrender in all the elements
of personality. It involves acceptance of the revelation of GOD
in the Person of Jesus Christ: and consequently the object of
the act is described both as faith in GOD (iv. 5, 24; cf. 1 Thes.
i. 8; 2 Tim. i. 12; Tit. iii. 8) and faith in or of Jesus Christ (iii.
22, 26; Gal. ii. 16, 20, iii. 22; Phil. iii. 9, i. 29 *al.*). It includes
belief of the revelation but emphasises the movement of will
and love. It consequently determines, as far as the man himself
can determine it, the position of man in relation to GOD: and is,
for that reason, the occasion or ground of GOD's declaration of
the man's righteousness. That declaration implies that the
man, in the act of faith, is in the right relation to GOD, and
already qualified to be the subject of all those spiritual influences
which are involved in his living union with GOD in Christ.

If we ask why S. Paul so rigorously isolates this single
moment in the man's experience, and connects with it the bare
statement of the declaration of his righteousness, I think the
answer is clear. He presses his analysis to this ultimate point,
because he wishes to bring out the fundamental contrast of faith
and law, as qualifying man for GOD's approval, His declaration
of righteousness. It is only when the conception is thus reduced
to its simplest elements, that man's true part in righteousness
and his true method of attaining it can be made clear. The
fact is that righteousness as a state is wholly GOD's work in man;
man's part begins, at any rate in analysis, before that work begins,
when by his act of faith he accepts his true relation to GOD, and

puts himself into righteousness as a relation. Even in this act of faith, he is not acting *in vacuo*, he is moved by GOD : yet it is his own act, a complete act of his whole personality ; and as such it is the beginning of a course of action, which, although it is GOD's working in him, is yet his own personal action (Gal. ii. 20). But it is only by isolating, in analysis, this original act that the whole consequent process can be seen to be GOD's action in him, springing from his faith, not consequent upon his works.

If it be said (as by Moberly, Mozley, *al.*), that GOD's declaration of righteousness cannot be ineffective, must involve an imparting of righteousness, that is undoubtedly true in fact. But that truth is not conveyed by the word δικαιοῦν, and the word would seem to be intentionally chosen by S. Paul so as not to convey it ; just because S. Paul desires to analyse the relation, which he is asserting, into its elements in order to make its nature clear. Just as the man is considered as expressing himself in faith, before that faith expresses itself in life ; so GOD is considered as accepting the faith, as declaring the man righteous, before that declaration takes effect by His Spirit in the man's life. And yet it is misleading to speak as if it were a case of temporal succession, as if the moment of faith and justification were a stage in experience to be succeeded by another stage. It is only by a process of abstraction that that moment can be conceived at all : as it exists, it is already absorbed in the mutual interaction of the persons whose relation to each other is so analysed. Neither does man's faith stop at all or exist at all in its bare expression ; nor does GOD's declaration exist as a bare declaration. Yet in order to characterise the state into which this relation brings the man, it is necessary to analyse it into its elements, excluding, in thought, the immediate and necessary results of the combination of those elements.

What is that state ? It is the living union of the man in Christ with GOD. There is no moment in the history of that union, in which the power of GOD does not act upon the spirit of the man, however far we go back. But in the ultimate analysis of the state we reach the two elements, man's faith and GOD's acceptance : these determine the method in which the union acts : and as long as we realise that this analysis, this separation of the elements, is only a separation in thought, the result of a logical process, we avoid the danger of importing the sense of a 'fictitious' arrangement. We may perhaps say that there is a fiction present; but it is a logical fiction, made for the purpose of clear thinking; not an unreal hypothesis made by GOD.

It follows from this that throughout the long process of GOD's dealing with man in Christ, man's contribution to the result is solely his faith, in its full sense. The power which originates, supports and develops the new life is throughout the power of GOD, the Spirit working upon and in the man. Consequently not in the most advanced life of the saint, any more than in the first faltering steps of the novice, is there any thought of meritorious works. It is the apprehension, trust and love with which the man embraces what GOD gives in Christ, that is his contribution, his whole contribution to the divine working. But it is just this attitude and act of apprehension, trust and love which calls forth and gives play to and indeed is the full realisation of his own personality; because it is the realisation of the true and most complex and most satisfying relation in which his personality can be developed, his relation to GOD.

For the discussion of this question see S. H., pp. 28 ff.; Moberly, *Atonement and Personality*, p. 335; J. K. Mozley, *Expositor*, Dec. 1910; Hort on 1 *Peter*, p. 81 f. and *James* ii. 22 (p. 63); Hastings, *DB.* art. Romans (Robertson); Du Bose, *The Gospel according to S. Paul*, pp. 69 ff.

10. TEXT.

It is unnecessary to enumerate the MSS. and Versions in which this Epistle is found. The reader may be referred to the articles in the *Encyclopaedia Biblica* (F. C. Burkitt), Hastings' *Dictionary of the Bible* (Nestle, Murray, *al.*), Sanday and Headlam (*Romans*, § 7) and Prof. Lake (*The Text of the New Testament*). The notation followed in the critical notes is the same as that adopted by Sanday and Headlam.

A selection of passages in which noteworthy variations of text occur is subjoined.

11. Critical Notes.

i. 1. Ἰησοῦ Χριστοῦ WH. txt. Χρ. Ἰ. WH. mg. Tisch. with B
Vulg. codd. Arm. Aug. (once) Ambr. Ambrst. and Latin Fathers.
The form Χρ. Ἰ. is confined to the Pauline letters (excl. Hebr.),
except Acts xxiv. 24, and increases in relative frequency with
time. It is more frequent than Ἰ. Χρ. in Eph., Phil., Col., and
is the dominant form in 1 and 2 Tim. Taking all the epistles it
occurs slightly more frequently than Ἰ. Χρ. (83—77), but this is
due mainly to its frequency in 1 and 2 Tim. In the Epistles up
to and including Rom. it is decidedly the rarer form (30—56)
and probably therefore more likely to be changed by scribes into
the other form, than the converse. The difference in significance
is slight: in Χρ. Ἰ. the Χρ. is perhaps rather more definitely a
proper name than in Ἰ. Χρ.; cf. S.H.

7. ἐν Ῥώμῃ om. Gg schol. 47 : for this omission cf. Add. Note,
pp. 235 f.

16. πρῶτον om. Bbg Tert. marc. 5, 13 [WH.].

32. ποιοῦσιν—συνευδοκοῦσιν. WH. Tisch. -οῦντες in each case
B and perhaps Clem. Rom. 35. DE Vulg. Orig. lat. and other
Latin Fathers had this Greek Text, but showed their doubts of
it by adding *non intellexerunt* (οὐκ ἐνόησαν D). WH. mark the
clause as corrupt, as involving an anti-climax. But see note.

ii. 2. δὲ WH. txt. γὰρ WH. mg. Tisch. The evidence is
fairly balanced. The sense is clear for δὲ : and the substitution
of γὰρ was probably due to the γὰρ of the preceding clause, i.e.
mechanical.

16. ἐν ᾗ ἡμέρᾳ WH. txt. with B alone. ἐν ἡμέρᾳ ᾗ WH. mg. A.
73. 93. tol. al. ἡ. ὅτε WH. mg. אDEGKL al. d.e.g. Vg. al.

iii. 9. προεχόμεθα : προκατέχομεν περισσόν D*G 31 : Antiochene
Fathers, Orig. lat. Ambrst. The variant is a gloss and involves
taking τί as the object of προκ. So syr^sch ap. Tisch. also omits
οὐ πάντως.

28. γὰρ. אAD*EFG al. plur. Latt. Boh. Arm. Orig. lat.
Ambrst. Aug. Tisch. WH. RV. mg. οὖν BCDᶜKLP al. plu. Syrr.
Chrys. Theodot. RV. WH. mg. The combination for γὰρ of אA
Boh. with the Western evidence is strong : and internal evidence
is in its favour.

iv. 1. εὑρηκέναι is found in most MSS. either before Ἀβραὰμ
or after ἡμῶν. B 47* alone omit it, and perhaps Chrysostom.

The sense in the context almost demands the omission: and the variation in position of εὑρ. suggests a gloss.

19. οὐ ins. before κατενόησεν DEFGKLP. om. Vulg. MSS. Syr. Lat. Orig. lat. Epiph. Ambrst.: a clearly Western reading; the sense is not materially affected.

v. 1. ἔχωμεν has an overwhelming support of MSS. It also makes the best sense (see note *ad loc.*).

3. καυχώμεθα: καυχώμενοι BC Orig. bis al. 'a good group' S.H. The influence of the context is ambiguous, as (v. 2 καυχώμεθα, v. 11 καυχώμενοι): the part. is slightly the more difficult, and perhaps the more characteristic reading.

6. εἰ γε B only WH. txt† : other readings are ἔτι γὰρ (with ἔτι below) Tisch. with most MSS. εἰς τί γὰρ, εἰ γὰρ, ἔτι are other variants. Text makes far the best sense. To account for the variants, H. suggests that εἴπερ was the orig. reading ; cf. 2 Cor. v. 3, v. l.; Rom. iii. 30; 2 Thes. i. 6.

14. μὴ om. 67 mg. and three other cursives. Latin Fathers: Orig. lat. freq. grk once, d. It is not easy to explain καί if the negative is omitted. It looks like a hasty attempt to correct a difficult expression.

viii. 2. σε al. με: om. Arm. perh. Orig. Neither pronoun is quite apt: and WH. app. argue for total omission.

11. διὰ τοῦ ἐνοικ. gen. ℵACP² al., Boh. Sah. Harcl. Arm. Aeth.: Clem. Alex. Cyr. Hier. Chrys. ad 1 Cor. xv. 45, Cyr. Alex.: accus. BDEFGKLP et Vulg. Pesh. Iren. lat. Orig. Did. lat. Chrys. ad loc. Tert. Hil. al. plur. The gen. is thus in the main Alexandrian; the accus. Western. S.H. place the preponderance of textual evidence slightly on the side of gen. The transcriptional evidence would appear to be on the side of the accus. as decidedly the harder reading: especially in view of the Alexandrian tendency to revision.

24. txt B 47 mg. only. RV. WH. τις, τί καὶ ἐλπίζει. T. R. Tisch. WH. mg. τί καὶ ὑπομένει ℵ*A 47 mg. WH. mg. RV. mg.

35. χριστοῦ. θεοῦ WH. mg.

ix. 5. WH. mg. σάρκα· ὁ ὢν ἐπὶ πάντων θεὸς ; see note *ad loc.*

x. 9. τὸ ῥῆμα B 71 Clem. Alex. and Cyril (?) om. rel. ὅτι Κύριος Ἰησοῦς B Boh. Clem. Alex. and Cyril (2ᶜᵉ). Κ—ον 'I—ουν rel.

xii. 11. τῷ κυρίῳ ℵABELP al. Vulg. Syrr. Boh. Gr. Fathers. καιρῷ DFG Latin Fathers. See comm. *ad loc.*

13. ταῖς χρείαις: μνείαις Western (Gr. Lat.). 'Some copies known to Theod. Mops.' WH. who suggest that it is a mere clerical error. The commemoration of martyrs arose as early as the middle of the second century. Cf. *Mart. Polyc.* xviii. S. H.

xiii. 3. τῷ ἀγαθῷ ἔργῳ. Cj. ἀγαθοέργῳ P. Young, Hort (probable). If this is read, then τῷ κακῷ is masc. = τῷ κακοέργῳ, the compound itself being avoided for euphony's sake. Cf. for a parallel in compound verbs, Moulton, p. 115. This reading certainly gives the best sense.

xiv. 13. om. πρόσκομμα and ἤ, B. Arm. Pesh. Cf. *v.* 20 and 1 Cor. viii. 9.

19. διώκωμεν CDE Latt. διώκομεν ℵABFGLPℶ.

xv. 8. γεγενῆσθαι ℵAELPℶ. γενέσθαι BCDFG.

19. πνεύματος B. add. θεοῦ ℵLP etc. Orig. lat. Chrys. etc. ἁγίου ACDFG Boh. Vulg. Arm. Aeth. etc.

31. δωροφορία (for διακονία). ἐν (for εἰς) BDFG.

32. ἐλθὼν—συναναπαύσωμαι, ℵAL Boh. Arm. Orig. lat. ἔλθω ...καὶ συν. Western and later MSS. B has ἔλθω and omits συναναπ.

διὰ θελήματος θεοῦ: Κυρίου Ἰησοῦ B, perh. clerical error for Χρ. Ἰησοῦ Western. Ἰησ. Χρ. ℵ* Ambst. txt ACLP Vulg. Syrr. Boh. Arm. Orig. lat. Chrys. Thdt. Lightfoot (*Fresh Revn* pp. 106 f.) suggests that the orginal had θελήματος alone. But there is no parallel to this use of the anarthrous θέλημα with a prep., and it seems difficult.

xvi. 20. For the place of the benedictions see Add. Note.

12. BOOKS.

The following list includes the principal books used and referred to in the Introduction and Commentary.

1. *Commentaries on the Epistle.*

> Field, Notes on Translation of the New Testament. Camb. Univ. Press, 1899.
>
> Gifford, Speaker's Commentary, reprinted, 1886. Giff.
>
> Hort, Prolegomena to Romans and Ephesians. Macmillan & Co. 1895.
>
> Liddon, Explanatory Analysis, 1896. Lid.

Lietzmann, Handbuch zum N.T. ed. H. Lietzmann. Tübingen, 1906.

Lipsius, Hand-Commentar zum N.T. Leipzig, 1893.

Rutherford, Romans translated. Macmillan & Co., 1900.

Sanday and Headlam (International Critical Commentary, 1895). S. H.

Weiss, B., Meyer's Kommentar : neu bearb. Göttingen, 1891.

Zahn, Commentar zum N.T. Leipzig, 1910.

2. *Commentaries on other Epistles* are cited sufficiently in the notes.

3. *Grammars and Dictionaries.*

Blass, Grammar of N.T. Greek, tr. by H. St J. Thackeray. Macmillan, 1898.

Burton, N.T. Moods and Tenses. Chicago, 1897.

Encyclopaedia Biblica, Cheyne and Black. London, 1899.

Hastings, Dictionary of the Bible. Edinburgh, 1898.

Herwerden, Lexicon Graecum suppletorium et dialecticum 1902--1904.

Kuhring, de praepos. Graec. in Chartis Aegyptiis usu. Bonn, 1906.

Mayser, Grammatik der Griechischen Papyri u.s.w. Teubner, 1906.

Moulton, J. H. Grammar of N.T. Greek. Vol. 1. Prolegomena. Edinburgh, 1906.

Thayer, Greek-English Lexicon of the N.T. (Grimm). Edinburgh, 1890.

Thackeray, Grammar of the O.T. in Greek. Vol. 1. Camb. Univ. Press, 1909.

Winer-Moulton, Grammar of N.T. Greek. Edinburgh, 1882.

4. *Linguistic.*

Dittenberger, Sylloge Inscriptionun Graecarum. Leipzig, 1883.

Milligan, Selections from the Greek Papyri. Camb. Univ. Press, 1910.

Nägeli, Der Wortschätz des Apostels Paulus. Goettingen, 1905.

Witkowski, Epistulae Privatae Graecae. Teubner, 1907.

5. *Other books of reference.*

Clemen, Religionsgeschichtliche Erklärung des N.T. (Giessen, 1909).

Dalman, The Words of Jesus. E.T. Edinburgh, 1902.

Davidson, Theology of O.T. Edinburgh, 1904.

Deissmann, Bibel Studien and Neue B. S. Marburg, 1895, 1897.

v. Dobschütz, Die Urchristlichen Gemeinden. Leipzig, 1902; and Probleme des Ap. Zeitalters. *Ib.*, 1907.

Dubose, The Gospel according to S. Paul. Longmans, Green & Co., 1907.

Ewald, De vocis Συνειδήσεως...vi ac potestate. Leipzig, 1883.

Hart, Ecclesiasticus. Camb. Univ. Press, 1909.

Hort, The Christian Ecclesia. Macmillan & Co., 1897. Judaistic Christianity. Macmillan & Co., 1894. Prolegomena to Romans and Ephesians. *Ib.*, 1895.

Journal of Theological Studies. Oxford University Press.

Knowling, Witness of the Epistles. Longmans, Green & Co., 1892.

Lake, The Earlier Epistles of S. Paul. Rivingtons, 1911.

Lightfoot, On a fresh Revision of the English N.T. Macmillan & Co., 1891. Biblical Essays. Macmillan & Co., 1893. Essays on Supernatural Religion. Macmillan & Co., 1889. Apostolic Fathers. Macmillan & Co., 1885-1890.

Mommsen, The Provinces of the Roman Empire. E. T. Bently, 1886.

Ramsay, The Church and the Roman Empire. Hodder & Stoughton, 1894. Paul the Roman Citizen and Traveller. *Ib.*, 1898. Pauline and other Studies. *Ib.*, 1906. Historical Commentary on the Epistle to the Galatians. *Ib.*, 1899.

Stanton, The Jewish and Christian Messiah. T. & T. Clark, 1886.

Texts and Studies. Camb. Univ. Press.

Weiss, Joh. Theol. Studien D. B. Weiss dargeb. Göttingen, 1897.

Zahn, Einleitung zum N.T. 2nd ed. Leipzig, 1900.

CHRONOLOGICAL TABLE.

Dates — Ramsay, *Pauline Studies*, 1906	Turner, *Hastings' D.B.*		Acts	Writings	Roman Emperors
B.C. 1	B.C. 7–6	The Nativity			A.D. 14 Aug. 19, Augustus d.
		Birth of Saul			
	A.D. 26	The Baptism			
	29	The Crucifixion and Resurrection	i.		
		Pentecost	ii.		
		The death of Stephen ...	vii. 54		
		Philip—Samaria—Caesarea ...	viii. 4–40		
A.D. 32 Jan. 25	35–36	Conversion of Saul... ...	ix.		
34	38	Saul's first visit to Jerusalem	ix. 26		37 Mar. 16, Tiberius d.
		Saul's retirement to Tarsus			41 Jan. 24, Caligula d.
		S. Peter — Lydda — Joppa — Caesarea (Cornelius) ...ix. 32–xi. 18			
		Missionary activity in Phoenicia, Cyprus, Antioch ...	xi. 19–26		
		Barnabas at Antioch—Saul			
44	44	Death of Herod Agrippa I. ...	xii. 20		
45	46–47	Famine in Judaea—second visit to Jerusalem	xi. 27–xii. 25		
46 Mar. (or 47)	47 Apr.	First Missionary Journey	xiii.		
48 Aug. (or 49)	48 Nov.	Return to Antioch	xiv. 26		
50 early	49 Pentecost	Third visit to Jerusalem : the Apostolic Council	xv.		
	49 or 50	Expulsion of Jews from Rome	xviii. 2		
50 summer	49 Sept.	Second Missionary Journey ...	xv. 36		

50-51	50 late	Work in Macedonia	xvi. 12 f.	1-2 Thess.	
51 Sept.	49 or 50	Arrival at Corinth	xviii. 1		
52 summer	52 April	Gallio comes to Corinth	xviii. 12		
53 Feb.	52 Pente-cost	Departure from Corinth	xviii. 18		
53 Mar. Passover	52 June	Fourth visit to Jerusalem	xviii. 22		54 Jan. 13, Claudius d.
53 April	52 Aug.	Antioch		Gal. (Ramsay)	
53 summer		Galatian Churches visited	xix. 1		
53 Dec.		Arrival at Ephesus	xix. 2		
	52	Felix becomes procurator of Judea			
56 Mar.	55 April	Departure from Ephesus	xx. 1	1 Cor.	
		Macedonia		2 Cor.	
56 Dec.-57	55-56	Corinth	xx. 3	Gal., Romans	
57 Mar.	56	Passover at Philippi	xx. 6		
57 May	56	Pentecost at Jerusalem			
57-59 June	56-58	S. Paul's arrest and imprisonment at Caesarea	xxi. 34		
59 June	58	Festus succeeds Felix	xxiv. 27		
59 Aug.	58	S. Paul sails for Rome	xxvii. 1		
60 Feb.	59	Arrival at Rome	xxviii. 16		
60-62 Feb.	59-61	Imprisonment at Rome	xxviii. 30	Philip., Ephes., Coloss., Philem.	
62-66	61-64	Later Journeys		1 Tim., Titus	
67	64	S. Paul arrested at Nicopolis (?) or Troas			64 Aug., Nero's perse-cution begins
67	64-65	Imprisonment and execution at Rome		2 Tim.	
70	70	Capture of Jerusalem			68 Jan. 9, Nero d.

SOME ABBREVIATIONS

LXX. = the Septuagint Version of the Old Testament ; *ad loc.* = *ad locum* ; *al.* = *alibi* ; *cf.* = *confer* ; *cft.* = *confert* ; ct. = contrast ; *ib.* = *ibidem* ; *l.c.* = *locus citatus* ; mg. = margin ; *op. cit.* = *opus citatum* ; *s.v.* = *sub voce* ; vb. = verb ; || = parallel to ;)(= opposed to.

Abbreviated names of authors and books will be plain if the list of books (pp. xlv. ff.) is consulted.

ΠΡΟΣ ΡΩΜΑΙΟΥΣ

1 ¹Παῦλος δοῦλος Ἰησοῦ Χριστοῦ, κλητὸς ἀπόστολος, ἀφωρισμένος εἰς εὐαγγέλιον θεοῦ ²ὃ προεπηγγείλατο διὰ τῶν προφητῶν αὐτοῦ ἐν γραφαῖς ἁγίαις
³περὶ τοῦ υἱοῦ αὐτοῦ, τοῦ γενομένου ἐκ σπέρματος
Δαυεὶδ κατὰ σάρκα, ⁴τοῦ ὁρισθέντος υἱοῦ θεοῦ ἐν δυνάμει κατὰ πνεῦμα ἁγιωσύνης ἐξ ἀναστάσεως νεκρῶν,
Ἰησοῦ Χριστοῦ τοῦ κυρίου ἡμῶν, ⁵δι’ οὗ ἐλάβομεν χάριν
καὶ ἀποστολὴν εἰς ὑπακοὴν πίστεως ἐν πᾶσιν τοῖς
ἔθνεσιν ὑπὲρ τοῦ ὀνόματος αὐτοῦ, ⁶ἐν οἷς ἐστὲ καὶ
ὑμεῖς κλητοὶ Ἰησοῦ Χριστοῦ, ⁷πᾶσιν τοῖς οὖσιν ἐν
Ῥώμῃ ἀγαπητοῖς θεοῦ, κλητοῖς ἁγίοις· χάρις ὑμῖν
καὶ εἰρήνη ἀπὸ θεοῦ πατρὸς ἡμῶν καὶ κυρίου Ἰησοῦ
Χριστοῦ.

⁸Πρῶτον μὲν εὐχαριστῶ τῷ θεῷ μου διὰ Ἰησοῦ
Χριστοῦ περὶ πάντων ὑμῶν, ὅτι ἡ πίστις ὑμῶν καταγ-
γέλλεται ἐν ὅλῳ τῷ κόσμῳ. ⁹μάρτυς γάρ μού ἐστιν ὁ
θεός, ᾧ λατρεύω ἐν τῷ πνεύματί μου ἐν τῷ εὐαγγελίῳ
τοῦ υἱοῦ αὐτοῦ, ὡς ἀδιαλείπτως μνείαν ὑμῶν ποιοῦμαι
¹⁰πάντοτε ἐπὶ τῶν προσευχῶν μου, δεόμενος εἴ πως ἤδη
ποτὲ εὐοδωθήσομαι ἐν τῷ θελήματι τοῦ θεοῦ ἐλθεῖν
πρὸς ὑμᾶς. ¹¹ἐπιποθῶ γὰρ ἰδεῖν ὑμᾶς, ἵνα τι μεταδῶ
χάρισμα ὑμῖν πνευματικὸν εἰς τὸ στηριχθῆναι ὑμᾶς,

¹²τοῦτο δέ ἐστιν συνπαρακληθῆναι ἐν ὑμῖν διὰ τῆς ἐν
ἀλλήλοις πίστεως ὑμῶν τε καὶ ἐμοῦ. ¹³οὐ θέλω δὲ
ὑμᾶς ἀγνοεῖν, ἀδελφοί, ὅτι πολλάκις προεθέμην ἐλθεῖν
πρὸς ὑμᾶς, καὶ ἐκωλύθην ἄχρι τοῦ δεῦρο, ἵνα τινὰ
καρπὸν σχῶ καὶ ἐν ὑμῖν καθὼς καὶ ἐν τοῖς λοιποῖς
ἔθνεσιν.   ¹⁴Ἕλλησίν τε καὶ βαρβάροις,
σοφοῖς τε καὶ ἀνοήτοις ὀφειλέτης εἰμί· ¹⁵οὕτω τὸ κατ'
ἐμὲ πρόθυμον καὶ ὑμῖν τοῖς ἐν Ῥώμη εὐαγγελίσασθαι.
¹⁶οὐ γὰρ ἐπαισχύνομαι τὸ εὐαγγέλιον, δύναμις γὰρ
θεοῦ ἐστιν εἰς σωτηρίαν παντὶ τῷ πιστεύοντι, Ἰουδαίῳ
τε [πρῶτον] καὶ Ἕλληνι· ¹⁷δικαιοσύνη γὰρ θεοῦ ἐν
αὐτῷ ἀποκαλύπτεται ἐκ πίστεως εἰς πίστιν, καθὼς
γέγραπται Ὁ δὲ δίκαιος ἐκ πίστεως ζήσεται.

¹⁸Ἀποκαλύπτεται γὰρ ὀργὴ θεοῦ ἀπ' οὐρανοῦ ἐπὶ
πᾶσαν ἀσέβειαν καὶ ἀδικίαν ἀνθρώπων τῶν τὴν ἀλήθειαν ἐν ἀδικίᾳ κατεχόντων, ¹⁹διότι τὸ γνωστὸν τοῦ
θεοῦ φανερόν ἐστιν ἐν αὐτοῖς, ὁ θεὸς γὰρ αὐτοῖς ἐφανέρωσεν. ²⁰τὰ γὰρ ἀόρατα αὐτοῦ ἀπὸ κτίσεως κόσμου
τοῖς ποιήμασιν νοούμενα καθορᾶται, ἥ τε ἀΐδιος αὐτοῦ
δύναμις καὶ θειότης, εἰς τὸ εἶναι αὐτοὺς ἀναπολογήτους,
²¹διότι γνόντες τὸν θεὸν οὐχ ὡς θεὸν ἐδόξασαν ἢ
ηὐχαρίστησαν, ἀλλὰ ἐματαιώθησαν ἐν τοῖς διαλογισ-
μοῖς αὐτῶν καὶ ἐσκοτίσθη ἡ ἀσύνετος αὐτῶν καρδία·
²²φάσκοντες εἶναι σοφοὶ ἐμωράνθησαν, ²³καὶ ἬΛΛΑΞΑΝ
ΤῊΝ ΔΌΞΑΝ τοῦ ἀφθάρτου θεοῦ ἐν ὁμοιώματι εἰκόνος
φθαρτοῦ ἀνθρώπου καὶ πετεινῶν καὶ τετραπόδων καὶ
ἑρπετῶν.   ²⁴Διὸ παρέδωκεν αὐτοὺς ὁ θεὸς ἐν
ταῖς ἐπιθυμίαις τῶν καρδιῶν αὐτῶν εἰς ἀκαθαρσίαν
τοῦ ἀτιμάζεσθαι τὰ σώματα αὐτῶν ἐν αὐτοῖς, ²⁵οἵτινες
μετήλλαξαν τὴν ἀλήθειαν τοῦ θεοῦ ἐν τῷ ψεύδει, καὶ
ἐσεβάσθησαν καὶ ἐλάτρευσαν τῇ κτίσει παρὰ τὸν

κτίσαντα, ὅς ἐστιν εὐλογητὸς εἰς τοὺς αἰῶνας· ἀμήν.
²⁶ Διὰ τοῦτο παρέδωκεν αὐτοὺς ὁ θεὸς εἰς πάθη ἀτιμίας·
αἵ τε γὰρ θήλειαι αὐτῶν μετήλλαξαν τὴν φυσικὴν
χρῆσιν εἰς τὴν παρὰ φύσιν, ²⁷ ὁμοίως τε καὶ οἱ ἄρσενες
ἀφέντες τὴν φυσικὴν χρῆσιν τῆς θηλείας ἐξεκαύθησαν
ἐν τῇ ὀρέξει αὐτῶν εἰς ἀλλήλους ἄρσενες ἐν ἄρσεσιν,
τὴν ἀσχημοσύνην κατεργαζόμενοι καὶ τὴν ἀντιμισθίαν
ἣν ἔδει τῆς πλάνης αὐτῶν ἐν αὐτοῖς ἀπολαμβάνοντες.
²⁸ Καὶ καθὼς οὐκ ἐδοκίμασαν τὸν θεὸν ἔχειν ἐν ἐπιγνώσει, παρέδωκεν αὐτοὺς ὁ θεὸς εἰς ἀδόκιμον νοῦν, ποιεῖν
τὰ μὴ καθήκοντα, ²⁹ πεπληρωμένους πάσῃ ἀδικίᾳ πονη-
ρίᾳ πλεονεξίᾳ κακίᾳ, μεστοὺς φθόνου φόνου ἔριδος
δόλου κακοηθίας, ψιθυριστάς, ³⁰ καταλάλους, θεοστυ-
γεῖς, ὑβριστάς, ὑπερηφάνους, ἀλαζόνας, ἐφευρετὰς κακῶν,
γονεῦσιν ἀπειθεῖς, ³¹ ἀσυνέτους, ἀσυνθέτους, ἀστόργους,
ἀνελεήμονας· ³² οἵτινες τὸ δικαίωμα τοῦ θεοῦ ἐπιγνόντες,
ὅτι οἱ τὰ τοιαῦτα πράσσοντες ἄξιοι θανάτου εἰσίν,
οὐ μόνον αὐτὰ ποιοῦσιν ἀλλὰ καὶ συνευδοκοῦσιν τοῖς
πράσσουσιν.

2 ¹ Διὸ ἀναπολόγητος εἶ, ὦ ἄνθρωπε πᾶς ὁ κρίνων·
ἐν ᾧ γὰρ κρίνεις τὸν ἕτερον, σεαυτὸν κατακρίνεις, τὰ
γὰρ αὐτὰ πράσσεις ὁ κρίνων· ² οἴδαμεν δὲ ὅτι τὸ κρίμα
τοῦ θεοῦ ἐστιν κατὰ ἀλήθειαν ἐπὶ τοὺς τὰ τοιαῦτα
πράσσοντας. ³ λογίζῃ δὲ τοῦτο, ὦ ἄνθρωπε ὁ κρίνων
τοὺς τὰ τοιαῦτα πράσσοντας καὶ ποιῶν αὐτά, ὅτι σὺ
ἐκφεύξῃ τὸ κρίμα τοῦ θεοῦ; ⁴ ἢ τοῦ πλούτου τῆς χρηστότητος αὐτοῦ καὶ τῆς ἀνοχῆς καὶ τῆς μακροθυμίας
καταφρονεῖς, ἀγνοῶν ὅτι τὸ χρηστὸν τοῦ θεοῦ εἰς μετά-
νοιάν σε ἄγει; ⁵ κατὰ δὲ τὴν σκληρότητά σου καὶ
ἀμετανόητον καρδίαν θησαυρίζεις σεαυτῷ ὀργὴν ἐν
ἡμέρᾳ ὀργῆς καὶ ἀποκαλύψεως δικαιοκρισίας τοῦ θεοῦ,

[6]ὃς ἀποδώσει ἑκάστῳ κατὰ τὰ ἔργα αὐτοῦ· [7]τοῖς μὲν καθ' ὑπομονὴν ἔργου ἀγαθοῦ δόξαν καὶ τιμὴν καὶ ἀφθαρσίαν ζητοῦσιν ζωὴν αἰώνιον· [8]τοῖς δὲ ἐξ ἐριθίας καὶ ἀπειθοῦσι τῇ ἀληθείᾳ πειθομένοις δὲ τῇ ἀδικίᾳ ὀργὴ καὶ θυμός, [9]θλίψις καὶ στενοχωρία, ἐπὶ πᾶσαν ψυχὴν ἀνθρώπου τοῦ κατεργαζομένου τὸ κακόν, Ἰουδαίου τε πρῶτον καὶ Ἕλληνος· [10]δόξα δὲ καὶ τιμὴ καὶ εἰρήνη παντὶ τῷ ἐργαζομένῳ τὸ ἀγαθόν, Ἰουδαίῳ τε πρῶτον καὶ Ἕλληνι· [11]οὐ γάρ ἐστιν προσωπολημψία παρὰ τῷ θεῷ. [12]Ὅσοι γὰρ ἀνόμως ἥμαρτον, ἀνόμως καὶ ἀπολοῦνται· καὶ ὅσοι ἐν νόμῳ ἥμαρτον, διὰ νόμου κριθήσονται· [13]οὐ γὰρ οἱ ἀκροαταὶ νόμου δίκαιοι παρὰ [τῷ] θεῷ, ἀλλ' οἱ ποιηταὶ νόμου δικαιωθήσονται. [14]ὅταν γὰρ ἔθνη τὰ μὴ νόμον ἔχοντα φύσει τὰ τοῦ νόμου ποιῶσιν, οὗτοι νόμον μὴ ἔχοντες ἑαυτοῖς εἰσὶν νόμος· [15]οἵτινες ἐνδείκνυνται τὸ ἔργον τοῦ νόμου γραπτὸν ἐν ταῖς καρδίαις αὐτῶν, συνμαρτυρούσης αὐτῶν τῆς συνειδήσεως καὶ μεταξὺ ἀλλήλων τῶν λογισμῶν κατηγορούντων ἢ καὶ ἀπολογουμένων, [16]ἐν ᾗ ἡμέρᾳ κρίνει ὁ. θεὸς τὰ κρυπτὰ τῶν ἀνθρώπων κατὰ τὸ εὐαγγέλιόν μου διὰ Χριστοῦ Ἰησοῦ.

[17]Εἰ δὲ σὺ Ἰουδαῖος ἐπονομάζῃ καὶ ἐπαναπαύῃ νόμῳ καὶ καυχᾶσαι ἐν θεῷ [18]καὶ γινώσκεις τὸ θέλημα καὶ δοκιμάζεις τὰ διαφέροντα κατηχούμενος ἐκ τοῦ νόμου, [19]πέποιθάς τε σεαυτὸν ὁδηγὸν εἶναι τυφλῶν, φῶς τῶν ἐν σκότει, [20]παιδευτὴν ἀφρόνων, διδάσκαλον νηπίων, ἔχοντα τὴν μόρφωσιν τῆς γνώσεως καὶ τῆς ἀληθείας ἐν τῷ νόμῳ,—[21]ὁ οὖν διδάσκων ἕτερον σεαυτὸν οὐ διδάσκεις; ὁ κηρύσσων μὴ κλέπτειν κλέπτεις; [22]ὁ λέγων μὴ μοιχεύειν μοιχεύεις; ὁ βδελυσσόμενος τὰ εἴδωλα ἱεροσυλεῖς; [23]ὃς ἐν νόμῳ καυχᾶσαι, διὰ τῆς παραβάσεως

τοῦ νόμου τὸν θεὸν ἀτιμάζεις; ²⁴τὸ γὰρ ὄνομα τοῦ
θεοῦ δι᾿ ὑμᾶς βλαϲφημεῖται ἐν τοῖϲ ἔθνεϲιν, καθὼς
γέγραπται. ²⁵περιτομὴ μὲν γὰρ ὠφελεῖ ἐὰν νόμον
πράσσῃς· ἐὰν δὲ παραβάτης νόμου ᾖς, ἡ περιτομή σου
ἀκροβυστία γέγονεν. ²⁶ἐὰν οὖν ἡ ἀκροβυστία τὰ δι-
καιώματά τοῦ νόμου φυλάσσῃ, οὐχ ἡ ἀκροβυστία αὐτοῦ
εἰς περιτομὴν λογισθήσεται; ²⁷καὶ κρινεῖ ἡ ἐκ φύσεως
ἀκροβυστία τὸν νόμον τελοῦσα σὲ τὸν διὰ γράμματος
καὶ περιτομῆς παραβάτην νόμου. ²⁸οὐ γὰρ ὁ ἐν τῷ
φανερῷ Ἰουδαῖός ἐστιν, οὐδὲ ἡ ἐν τῷ φανερῷ ἐν σαρκὶ
περιτομή· ²⁹ἀλλ᾿ ὁ ἐν τῷ κρυπτῷ Ἰουδαῖος, καὶ περιτομὴ
καρδίας ἐν πνεύματι οὐ γράμματι, οὗ ὁ ἔπαινος οὐκ ἐξ
ἀνθρώπων ἀλλ᾿ ἐκ τοῦ θεοῦ.   3 ¹Τί οὖν τὸ
περισσὸν τοῦ Ἰουδαίου, ἢ τίς ἡ ὠφελία τῆς περιτομῆς;
²πολὺ κατὰ πάντα τρόπον. πρῶτον μὲν [γὰρ] ὅτι
ἐπιστεύθησαν τὰ λόγια τοῦ θεοῦ. ³τί γάρ; εἰ ἠπίστη-
σάν τινες, μὴ ἡ ἀπιστία αὐτῶν τὴν πίστιν τοῦ θεοῦ
καταργήσει; ⁴μὴ γένοιτο· γινέσθω δὲ ὁ θεὸς ἀληθής,
πᾶς δὲ ἄνθρωπος ψεύϲτηϲ, καθάπερ γέγραπται
          Ὅπωϲ ἄν δικαιωθῇϲ ἐν τοῖϲ λόγοιϲ ϲου
          καὶ νικήϲειϲ ἐν τῷ κρίνεϲθαί ϲε.
⁵εἰ δὲ ἡ ἀδικία ἡμῶν θεοῦ δικαιοσύνην συνίστησιν, τί
ἐροῦμεν; μὴ ἄδικος ὁ θεὸς ὁ ἐπιφέρων τὴν ὀργήν; κατὰ
ἄνθρωπον λέγω. ⁶μὴ γένοιτο· ἐπεὶ πῶς κρινεῖ ὁ θεὸς
τὸν κόσμον; ⁷εἰ δὲ ἡ ἀλήθεια τοῦ θεοῦ ἐν τῷ ἐμῷ
ψεύσματι ἐπερίσσευσεν εἰς τὴν δόξαν αὐτοῦ, τί ἔτι
κἀγὼ ὡς ἁμαρτωλὸς κρίνομαι, ⁸καὶ μὴ καθὼς βλασφημούμεθα [καὶ] καθώς φασίν τινες ἡμᾶς λέγειν ὅτι
Ποιήσωμεν τὰ κακὰ ἵνα ἔλθῃ τὰ ἀγαθά; ὧν τὸ κρίμα
ἔνδικόν ἐστιν.

          ⁹Τί οὖν; προεχόμεθα; οὐ πάντως, προῃτιασάμεθα

γὰρ Ἰουδαίους τε καὶ Ἕλληνας πάντας ὑφ᾽ ἁμαρτίαν
εἶναι, ¹⁰καθὼς γέγραπται ὅτι

Ογκ ἔϲτιν δίκαιοϲ ογδὲ εἷϲ,
  ¹¹ογκ ἔϲτιν ϲγνίων, ογκ ἔϲτιν ἐκzητῶν τὸν θεόν·
  ¹²πάντεϲ ἐξέκλιναν, ἅμα ἠχρεώθηϲαν·
  ογκ ἔϲτιν ποιῶν χρηϲτότητα, ογκ ἔϲτιν ἕωϲ ἑνόϲ.
  ¹³τάφοϲ ἀνεῳΓμένοϲ ὁ λάργΓΞ αγτῶν,
    ταῖϲ Γλώϲϲαιϲ αγτῶν ἐδολιογϲαν,
  ἰὸϲ ἀϲπίδων ὑπὸ τὰ χείλη αγτῶν,
    ¹⁴ὧν τὸ ϲτόμα ἀρᾶϲ καὶ πικρίαϲ Γέμει·
  ¹⁵ὀξεῖϲ οἱ πόδεϲ αγτῶν ἐκχέαι αἶμα,
  ¹⁶ϲγντριμμα καὶ ταλαιπωρία ἐν ταῖϲ ὁδοῖϲ αγτῶν,
    ¹⁷καὶ ὁδὸν εἰρήνηϲ ογκ ἔΓνωϲαν.
      ¹⁸ογκ ἔϲτιν φόβοϲ θεογ ἀπέναντι τῶν
        ὀφθαλμῶν αγτῶν.

¹⁹Οἴδαμεν δὲ ὅτι ὅσα ὁ νόμος λέγει τοῖς ἐν τῷ νόμῳ
λαλεῖ, ἵνα πᾶν στόμα φραγῇ καὶ ὑπόδικος γένηται πᾶς
ὁ κόσμος τῷ θεῷ· ²⁰διότι ἐξ ἔργων νόμου οὐ δικαιωθήσεται πᾶσα σὰρξ ἐνώπιον αὐτοῦ, διὰ γὰρ νόμου ἐπίγνωσις
ἁμαρτίας. ²¹νυνὶ δὲ χωρὶς νόμου δικαιοσύνη θεοῦ πεφανέρωται, μαρτυρουμένη ὑπὸ τοῦ νόμου καὶ τῶν προφητῶν, ²²δικαιοσύνη δὲ θεοῦ διὰ πίστεως [Ἰησοῦ] Χριστοῦ,
εἰς πάντας τοὺς πιστεύοντας, οὐ γάρ ἐστιν διαστολή.
²³πάντες γὰρ ἥμαρτον καὶ ὑστεροῦνται τῆς δόξης τοῦ
θεοῦ, ²⁴δικαιούμενοι δωρεὰν τῇ αὐτοῦ χάριτι διὰ τῆς
ἀπολυτρώσεως τῆς ἐν Χριστῷ Ἰησοῦ· ²⁵ὃν προέθετο
ὁ θεὸς ἱλαστήριον διὰ πίστεως ἐν τῷ αὐτοῦ αἵματι εἰς
ἔνδειξιν τῆς δικαιοσύνης αὐτοῦ διὰ τὴν πάρεσιν τῶν
προγεγονότων ἁμαρτημάτων ²⁶ἐν τῇ ἀνοχῇ τοῦ θεοῦ,
πρὸς τὴν ἔνδειξιν τῆς δικαιοσύνης αὐτοῦ ἐν τῷ νῦν
καιρῷ, εἰς τὸ εἶναι αὐτὸν δίκαιον καὶ δικαιοῦντα τὸν

ἐκ πίστεως Ἰησοῦ.   ²⁷Ποῦ οὖν ἡ καύχησις;
ἐξεκλείσθη. διὰ ποίου νόμου; τῶν ἔργων; οὐχί, ἀλλὰ
διὰ νόμου πίστεως. ²⁸λογιζόμεθα γὰρ δικαιοῦσθαι
πίστει ἄνθρωπον χωρὶς ἔργων νόμου. ²⁹ἢ Ἰουδαίων ὁ
θεὸς μόνον; οὐχὶ καὶ ἐθνῶν; ναὶ καὶ ἐθνῶν, ³⁰εἴπερ εἷς
ὁ θεός, ὃς δικαιώσει περιτομὴν ἐκ πίστεως καὶ ἀκροβυστίαν διὰ τῆς πίστεως. ³¹νόμον οὖν καταργοῦμεν
διὰ τῆς πίστεως; μὴ γένοιτο, ἀλλὰ νόμον ἱστάνομεν.

4 ¹Τί οὖν ἐροῦμεν Ἀβραὰμ τὸν προπάτορα ἡμῶν
κατὰ σάρκα; ²εἰ γὰρ Ἀβραὰμ ἐξ ἔργων ἐδικαιώθη, ἔχει
καύχημα· ἀλλ' οὐ πρὸς θεόν, ³τί γὰρ ἡ γραφὴ λέγει;
Ἐπίϲτεγϲεν δὲ Ἀβραὰμ τῷ θεῷ, καὶ ἐλογίϲθη αὐτῷ εἰϲ
Δικαιοϲγνην. ⁴τῷ δὲ ἐργαζομένῳ ὁ μισθὸς οὐ λογίζεται
κατὰ χάριν ἀλλὰ κατὰ ὀφείλημα· ⁵τῷ δὲ μὴ ἐργαζομένῳ, πιστεύοντι δὲ ἐπὶ τὸν δικαιοῦντα τὸν ἀσεβῆ,
λογίζεται ἡ πίστις αὐτοῦ εἰς δικαιοσύνην, ⁶καθάπερ
καὶ Δαυεὶδ λέγει τὸν μακαρισμὸν τοῦ ἀνθρώπου ᾧ ὁ
θεὸς λογίζεται δικαιοσύνην χωρὶς ἔργων

⁷Μακάριοι ὧν ἀφέθηϲαν αἱ ἀνομίαι καὶ ὧν ἐπεκα-
λύφθηϲαν αἱ ἁμαρτίαι,

⁸μακάριοϲ ἀνὴρ οὗ οὐ μὴ λογίϲηται Κύριοϲ ἁμαρτίαν.
⁹ὁ μακαρισμὸς οὖν οὗτος ἐπὶ τὴν περιτομὴν ἢ καὶ ἐπὶ
τὴν ἀκροβυστίαν; λέγομεν γάρ Ἐλογίϲθη τῷ Ἀβραὰμ
ἡ πίϲτιϲ εἰϲ Δικαιοϲγνην. ¹⁰πῶς οὖν ἐλογίσθη; ἐν περιτομῇ ὄντι ἢ ἐν ἀκροβυστίᾳ; οὐκ ἐν περιτομῇ ἀλλ' ἐν
ἀκροβυστίᾳ· ¹¹καὶ ϲημεῖον ἔλαβεν περιτομῆϲ, σφραγῖδα
τῆς δικαιοσύνης τῆς πίστεως τῆς ἐν τῇ ἀκροβγϲτίᾳ, εἰς
τὸ εἶναι αὐτὸν πατέρα πάντων τῶν πιστευόντων δι'
ἀκροβυστίας, εἰς τὸ λογισθῆναι αὐτοῖς [τὴν] δικαιοσύνην, ¹²καὶ πατέρα περιτομῆς τοῖς οὐκ ἐκ περιτομῆς
μόνον ἀλλὰ καὶ τοῖς στοιχοῦσιν τοῖς ἴχνεσιν τῆς ἐν

ἀκροβυστίᾳ πίστεως τοῦ πατρὸς ἡμῶν Ἀβραάμ. ¹³Οὐ γὰρ διὰ νόμου ἡ ἐπαγγελία τῷ Ἀβραὰμ ἢ τῷ σπέρματι αὐτοῦ, τὸ κληρονόμον αὐτὸν εἶναι κόσμου, ἀλλὰ διὰ δικαιοσύνης πίστεως· ¹⁴εἰ γὰρ οἱ ἐκ νόμου κληρονόμοι, κεκένωται ἡ πίστις καὶ κατήργηται ἡ ἐπαγγελία. ¹⁵ὁ γὰρ νόμος ὀργὴν κατεργάζεται, οὗ δὲ οὐκ ἔστιν νόμος, οὐδὲ παράβασις. ¹⁶Διὰ τοῦτο ἐκ πίστεως, ἵνα κατὰ χάριν, εἰς τὸ εἶναι βεβαίαν τὴν ἐπαγγελίαν παντὶ τῷ σπέρματι, οὐ τῷ ἐκ τοῦ νόμου μόνον ἀλλὰ καὶ τῷ ἐκ πίστεως Ἀβραάμ, (ὅς ἐστιν πατὴρ πάντων ἡμῶν, ¹⁷καθὼς γέγραπται ὅτι Πατέρα πολλῶν ἐθνῶν τέθεικά σε,) κατέναντι οὗ ἐπίστευσεν θεοῦ τοῦ ζωοποιοῦντος τοὺς νεκροὺς καὶ καλοῦντος τὰ μὴ ὄντα ὡς ὄντα· ¹⁸ὃς παρ' ἐλπίδα ἐπ' ἐλπίδι ἐπίστευσεν εἰς τὸ γενέσθαι αὐτὸν πατέρα πολλῶν ἐθνῶν κατὰ τὸ εἰρημένον Οὕτως ἔσται τὸ σπέρμα σου· ¹⁹καὶ μὴ ἀσθενήσας τῇ πίστει κατενόησεν τὸ ἑαυτοῦ σῶμα [ἤδη] νενεκρωμένον, ἑκατονταετής που ὑπάρχων, καὶ τὴν νέκρωσιν τῆς μήτρας Σάρρας, ²⁰εἰς δὲ τὴν ἐπαγγελίαν τοῦ θεοῦ οὐ διεκρίθη τῇ ἀπιστίᾳ ἀλλὰ ἐνεδυναμώθη τῇ πίστει, δοὺς δόξαν τῷ θεῷ ²¹καὶ πληροφορηθεὶς ὅτι ὃ ἐπήγγελται δυνατός ἐστιν καὶ ποιῆσαι. ²²διὸ [καὶ] ἐλογίσθη αὐτῷ εἰς δικαιοσύνην. ²³Οὐκ ἐγράφη δὲ δι' αὐτὸν μόνον ὅτι ἐλογίσθη αὐτῷ, ²⁴ἀλλὰ καὶ δι' ἡμᾶς οἷς μέλλει λογίζεσθαι, τοῖς πιστεύουσιν ἐπὶ τὸν ἐγείραντα Ἰησοῦν τὸν κύριον ἡμῶν ἐκ νεκρῶν, ²⁵ὃς παρεδόθη διὰ τὰ παραπτώματα ἡμῶν καὶ ἠγέρθη διὰ τὴν δικαίωσιν ἡμῶν.

5 ¹Δικαιωθέντες οὖν ἐκ πίστεως εἰρήνην ἔχωμεν πρὸς τὸν θεὸν διὰ τοῦ κυρίου ἡμῶν Ἰησοῦ Χριστοῦ, ²δι' οὗ καὶ τὴν προσαγωγὴν ἐσχήκαμεν [τῇ πίστει] εἰς τὴν

χάριν ταύτην ἐν ᾗ ἑστήκαμεν, καὶ καυχώμεθα ἐπ᾽ ἐλπίδι
τῆς δόξης τοῦ θεοῦ· ³οὐ μόνον δέ, ἀλλὰ καὶ καυχώμεθα
ἐν ταῖς θλίψεσιν, εἰδότες ὅτι ἡ θλῖψις ὑπομονὴν κατεργάζεται, ⁴ἡ δὲ ὑπομονὴ δοκιμήν, ἡ δὲ δοκιμὴ ἐλπίδα,
⁵ἡ δὲ ἐλπὶς οὐ κΑΤΑΙϹΧΫ́ΝΕΙ. ὅτι ἡ ἀγάπη τοῦ θεοῦ
ἐκκέχυται ἐν ταῖς καρδίαις ἡμῶν διὰ πνεύματος ἁγίου
τοῦ δοθέντος ἡμῖν· ⁶εἴ γε Χριστὸς ὄντων ἡμῶν ἀσθενῶν
ἔτι κατὰ καιρὸν ὑπὲρ ἀσεβῶν ἀπέθανεν. ⁷μόλις γὰρ
ὑπὲρ δικαίου τις ἀποθανεῖται· ὑπὲρ γὰρ τοῦ ἀγαθοῦ
τάχα τις καὶ τολμᾷ ἀποθανεῖν· ⁸συνίστησιν δὲ τὴν
ἑαυτοῦ ἀγάπην εἰς ἡμᾶς ὁ θεὸς ὅτι ἔτι ἁμαρτωλῶν ὄντων
ἡμῶν Χριστὸς ὑπὲρ ἡμῶν ἀπέθανεν. ⁹πολλῷ οὖν
μᾶλλον δικαιωθέντες νῦν ἐν τῷ αἵματι αὐτοῦ σωθησόμεθα δι᾽ αὐτοῦ ἀπὸ τῆς ὀργῆς. ¹⁰εἰ γὰρ ἐχθροὶ ὄντες
κατηλλάγημεν τῷ θεῷ διὰ τοῦ θανάτου τοῦ υἱοῦ αὐτοῦ,
πολλῷ μᾶλλον καταλλαγέντες σωθησόμεθα ἐν τῇ ζωῇ
αὐτοῦ· ¹¹οὐ μόνον δέ, ἀλλὰ καὶ καυχώμενοι ἐν τῷ θεῷ
διὰ τοῦ κυρίου ἡμῶν Ἰησοῦ [Χριστοῦ], δι᾽ οὗ νῦν τὴν
καταλλαγὴν ἐλάβομεν.

¹²Διὰ τοῦτο ὥσπερ δι᾽ ἑνὸς ἀνθρώπου ἡ ἁμαρτία εἰς
τὸν κόσμον εἰσῆλθεν καὶ διὰ τῆς ἁμαρτίας ὁ θάνατος,
καὶ οὕτως εἰς πάντας ἀνθρώπους ὁ θάνατος διῆλθεν ἐφ᾽
ᾧ πάντες ἥμαρτον–. ¹³ἄχρι γὰρ νόμου ἁμαρτία ἦν ἐν
κόσμῳ, ἁμαρτία δὲ οὐκ ἐλλογᾶται μὴ ὄντος νόμου,
¹⁴ἀλλὰ ἐβασίλευσεν ὁ θάνατος ἀπὸ Ἀδὰμ μέχρι
Μωυσέως καὶ ἐπὶ τοὺς μὴ ἁμαρτήσαντας ἐπὶ τῷ ὁμοιώματι τῆς παραβάσεως Ἀδάμ, ὅς ἐστιν τύπος τοῦ
μέλλοντος. ¹⁵ἀλλ᾽ οὐχ ὡς τὸ παράπτωμα, οὕτως [καὶ]
τὸ χάρισμα· εἰ γὰρ τῷ τοῦ ἑνὸς παραπτώματι οἱ πολλοὶ
ἀπέθανον, πολλῷ μᾶλλον ἡ χάρις τοῦ θεοῦ καὶ ἡ δωρεὰ
ἐν χάριτι τῇ τοῦ ἑνὸς ἀνθρώπου Ἰησοῦ Χριστοῦ εἰς

τοὺς πολλοὺς ἐπερίσσευσεν. ¹⁶καὶ οὐχ ὡς δι᾽ ἑνὸς
ἁμαρτήσαντος τὸ δώρημα· τὸ μὲν γὰρ κρίμα ἐξ ἑνὸς εἰς
κατάκριμα, τὸ δὲ χάρισμα ἐκ πολλῶν παραπτωμάτων
εἰς δικαίωμα. ¹⁷εἰ γὰρ τῷ τοῦ ἑνὸς παραπτώματι ὁ
θάνατος ἐβασίλευσεν διὰ τοῦ ἑνός, πολλῷ μᾶλλον οἱ
τὴν περισσείαν τῆς χάριτος καὶ [τῆς δωρεᾶς] τῆς δικαιοσύνης λαμβάνοντες ἐν ζωῇ βασιλεύσουσιν διὰ τοῦ
ἑνὸς Ἰησοῦ Χριστοῦ. ¹⁸Ἄρα οὖν ὡς δι᾽ ἑνὸς
παραπτώματος εἰς πάντας ἀνθρώπους εἰς κατάκριμα,
οὕτως καὶ δι᾽ ἑνὸς δικαιώματος εἰς πάντας ἀνθρώπους
εἰς δικαίωσιν ζωῆς· ¹⁹ὥσπερ γὰρ διὰ τῆς παρακοῆς τοῦ
ἑνὸς ἀνθρώπου ἁμαρτωλοὶ κατεστάθησαν οἱ πολλοί,
οὕτως καὶ διὰ τῆς ὑπακοῆς τοῦ ἑνὸς δίκαιοι κατασ-
θήσονται οἱ πολλοί. ²⁰νόμος δὲ παρεισῆλθεν ἵνα πλεονάσῃ τὸ παράπτωμα· οὗ δὲ ἐπλεόνασεν ἡ ἁμαρτία,
ὑπερεπερίσσευσεν ἡ χάρις, ²¹ἵνα ὥσπερ ἐβασίλευσεν ἡ
ἁμαρτία ἐν τῷ θανάτῳ, οὕτως καὶ ἡ χάρις βασιλεύσῃ
διὰ δικαιοσύνης εἰς ζωὴν αἰώνιον διὰ Ἰησοῦ Χριστοῦ
τοῦ κυρίου ἡμῶν.

6 ¹Τί οὖν ἐροῦμεν; ἐπιμένωμεν τῇ ἁμαρτίᾳ, ἵνα
ἡ χάρις πλεονάσῃ; ²μὴ γένοιτο· οἵτινες ἀπεθάνομεν
τῇ ἁμαρτίᾳ, πῶς ἔτι ζήσομεν ἐν αὐτῇ; ³ἢ ἀγνοεῖτε ὅτι
ὅσοι ἐβαπτίσθημεν εἰς Χριστὸν [Ἰησοῦν] εἰς τὸν θάνατον αὐτοῦ ἐβαπτίσθημεν; ⁴συνετάφημεν οὖν αὐτῷ διὰ
τοῦ βαπτίσματος εἰς τὸν θάνατον, ἵνα ὥσπερ ἠγέρθη
Χριστὸς ἐκ νεκρῶν διὰ τῆς δόξης τοῦ πατρός, οὕτως καὶ
ἡμεῖς ἐν καινότητι ζωῆς περιπατήσωμεν. ⁵εἰ γὰρ σύμφυτοι γεγόναμεν τῷ ὁμοιώματι τοῦ θανάτου αὐτοῦ, ἀλλὰ
καὶ τῆς ἀναστάσεως ἐσόμεθα· ⁶τοῦτο γινώσκοντες ὅτι
ὁ παλαιὸς ἡμῶν ἄνθρωπος συνεσταυρώθη, ἵνα καταρ-
γηθῇ τὸ σῶμα τῆς ἁμαρτίας, τοῦ μηκέτι δουλεύειν ἡμᾶς

τῇ ἁμαρτίᾳ, [7]ὁ γὰρ ἀποθανὼν δεδικαίωται ἀπὸ τῆς
ἁμαρτίας. [8]εἰ δὲ ἀπεθάνομεν σὺν Χριστῷ, πιστεύομεν
ὅτι καὶ συνζήσομεν αὐτῷ· [9]εἰδότες ὅτι Χριστὸς ἐγερθεὶς
ἐκ νεκρῶν οὐκέτι ἀποθνήσκει, θάνατος αὐτοῦ οὐκέτι
κυριεύει· [10]ὃ γὰρ ἀπέθανεν, τῇ ἁμαρτίᾳ ἀπέθανεν ἐφ-
άπαξ· ὃ δὲ ζῇ, ζῇ τῷ θεῷ. [11]οὕτως καὶ ὑμεῖς λογίζεσθε
ἑαυτοὺς εἶναι νεκροὺς μὲν τῇ ἁμαρτίᾳ ζῶντας δὲ τῷ θεῷ
ἐν Χριστῷ Ἰησοῦ.   [12]Μὴ οὖν βασιλευέτω ἡ
ἁμαρτία ἐν τῷ θνητῷ ὑμῶν σώματι εἰς τὸ ὑπακούειν
ταῖς ἐπιθυμίαις αὐτοῦ, [13]μηδὲ παριστάνετε τὰ μέλη
ὑμῶν ὅπλα ἀδικίας τῇ ἁμαρτίᾳ, ἀλλὰ παραστήσατε
ἑαυτοὺς τῷ θεῷ ὡσεὶ ἐκ νεκρῶν ζῶντας καὶ τὰ μέλη
ὑμῶν ὅπλα δικαιοσύνης τῷ θεῷ· [14]ἁμαρτία γὰρ ὑμῶν
οὐ κυριεύσει, οὐ γάρ ἐστε ὑπὸ νόμον ἀλλὰ ὑπὸ
χάριν.   [15]Τί οὖν; ἁμαρτήσωμεν ὅτι οὐκ ἐσμὲν
ὑπὸ νόμον ἀλλὰ ὑπὸ χάριν; μὴ γένοιτο· [16]οὐκ οἴδατε
ὅτι ᾧ παριστάνετε ἑαυτοὺς δούλους εἰς ὑπακοήν, δοῦλοί
ἐστε ᾧ ὑπακούετε, ἤτοι ἁμαρτίας εἰς θάνατον ἢ ὑπακοῆς
εἰς δικαιοσύνην; [17]χάρις δὲ τῷ θεῷ ὅτι ἦτε δοῦλοι τῆς
ἁμαρτίας ὑπηκούσατε δὲ ἐκ καρδίας εἰς ὃν παρεδόθητε
τύπον διδαχῆς, [18]ἐλευθερωθέντες δὲ ἀπὸ τῆς ἁμαρτίας
ἐδουλώθητε τῇ δικαιοσύνῃ· [19]ἀνθρώπινον λέγω διὰ τὴν
ἀσθένειαν τῆς σαρκὸς ὑμῶν· ὥσπερ γὰρ παρεστήσατε
τὰ μέλη ὑμῶν δοῦλα τῇ ἀκαθαρσίᾳ καὶ τῇ ἀνομίᾳ [εἰς
τὴν ἀνομίαν], οὕτω νῦν παραστήσατε τὰ μέλη ὑμῶν
δοῦλα τῇ δικαιοσύνῃ εἰς ἁγιασμόν· [20]ὅτε γὰρ δοῦλοι
ἦτε τῆς ἁμαρτίας, ἐλεύθεροι ἦτε τῇ δικαιοσύνῃ. [21]τίνα
οὖν καρπὸν εἴχετε τότε ἐφ᾽ οἷς νῦν ἐπαισχύνεσθε; τὸ
γὰρ τέλος ἐκείνων θάνατος· [22]νυνὶ δέ, ἐλευθερωθέντες
ἀπὸ τῆς ἁμαρτίας δουλωθέντες δὲ τῷ θεῷ, ἔχετε τὸν
καρπὸν ὑμῶν εἰς ἁγιασμόν, τὸ δὲ τέλος ζωὴν αἰώνιον.

²³τὰ γὰρ ὀψώνια τῆς ἁμαρτίας θάνατος, τὸ δὲ χάρισμα
τοῦ θεοῦ ζωὴ αἰώνιος ἐν Χριστῷ Ἰησοῦ τῷ κυρίῳ
ἡμῶν.

7 ¹ᴬΗ ἀγνοεῖτε, ἀδελφοί, γινώσκουσιν γὰρ νόμον
λαλῶ, ὅτι ὁ νόμος κυριεύει τοῦ ἀνθρώπου ἐφ' ὅσον
χρόνον ζῇ; ²ἡ γὰρ ὕπανδρος γυνὴ τῷ ζῶντι ἀνδρὶ δέδε-
ται νόμῳ· ἐὰν δὲ ἀποθάνῃ ὁ ἀνήρ, κατήργηται ἀπὸ τοῦ
νόμου τοῦ ἀνδρός. ³ἄρα οὖν ζῶντος τοῦ ἀνδρὸς μοιχαλὶς
χρηματίσει ἐὰν γένηται ἀνδρὶ ἑτέρῳ· ἐὰν δὲ ἀποθάνῃ
ὁ ἀνήρ, ἐλευθέρα ἐστὶν ἀπὸ τοῦ νόμου, τοῦ μὴ εἶναι
αὐτὴν μοιχαλίδα γενομένην ἀνδρὶ ἑτέρῳ. ⁴ὥστε, ἀδελφοί μου, καὶ ὑμεῖς ἐθανατώθητε τῷ νόμῳ διὰ τοῦ
σώματος τοῦ χριστοῦ, εἰς τὸ γενέσθαι ὑμᾶς ἑτέρῳ, τῷ
ἐκ νεκρῶν ἐγερθέντι ἵνα καρποφορήσωμεν τῷ θεῷ. ⁵ὅτε
γὰρ ἦμεν ἐν τῇ σαρκί, τὰ παθήματα τῶν ἁμαρτιῶν τὰ
διὰ τοῦ νόμου ἐνηργεῖτο ἐν τοῖς μέλεσιν ἡμῶν εἰς τὸ
καρποφορῆσαι τῷ θανάτῳ· ⁶νυνὶ δὲ κατηργήθημεν ἀπὸ
τοῦ νόμου, ἀποθανόντες ἐν ᾧ κατειχόμεθα, ὥστε δουλεύειν [ἡμᾶς] ἐν καινότητι πνεύματος καὶ οὐ παλαιότητι
γράμματος. ⁷Τί οὖν ἐροῦμεν; ὁ νόμος ἁμαρτία;
μὴ γένοιτο· ἀλλὰ τὴν ἁμαρτίαν οὐκ ἔγνων εἰ μὴ διὰ
νόμου, τήν τε γὰρ ἐπιθυμίαν οὐκ ᾔδειν εἰ μὴ ὁ νόμος
ἔλεγεν Οὐκ ἐπιθυμήσεις· ⁸ἀφορμὴν δὲ λαβοῦσα ἡ ἁμαρτία διὰ τῆς ἐντολῆς κατειργάσατο ἐν ἐμοὶ πᾶσαν ἐπιθυμίαν, χωρὶς γὰρ νόμου ἁμαρτία νεκρά. ⁹ἐγὼ δὲ ἔζων
χωρὶς νόμου ποτέ· ἐλθούσης δὲ τῆς ἐντολῆς ἡ ἁμαρτία
ἀνέζησεν, ¹⁰ἐγὼ δὲ ἀπέθανον, καὶ εὑρέθη μοι ἡ ἐντολὴ
ἡ εἰς ζωὴν αὕτη εἰς θάνατον· ¹¹ἡ γὰρ ἁμαρτία ἀφορμὴν
λαβοῦσα διὰ τῆς ἐντολῆς ἐξηπάτησέν με καὶ δι' αὐτῆς
ἀπέκτεινεν. ¹²ὥστε ὁ μὲν νόμος ἅγιος, καὶ ἡ ἐντολὴ
ἁγία καὶ δικαία καὶ ἀγαθή.   ¹³Τὸ οὖν ἀγαθὸν

ἐμοὶ ἐγένετο θάνατος; μὴ γένοιτο· ἀλλὰ ἡ ἁμαρτία, ἵνα
φανῇ ἁμαρτία διὰ τοῦ ἀγαθοῦ μοι κατεργαζομένη
θάνατον· ἵνα γένηται καθ᾽ ὑπερβολὴν ἁμαρτωλὸς ἡ
ἁμαρτία διὰ τῆς ἐντολῆς. ¹⁴οἴδαμεν γὰρ ὅτι ὁ νόμος
πνευματικός ἐστιν· ἐγὼ δὲ σάρκινός εἰμι, πεπραμένος
ὑπὸ τὴν ἁμαρτίαν. ¹⁵ὃ γὰρ κατεργάζομαι οὐ γινώσκω·
οὐ γὰρ ὃ θέλω τοῦτο πράσσω, ἀλλ᾽ ὃ μισῶ τοῦτο ποιῶ.
¹⁶εἰ δὲ ὃ οὐ θέλω τοῦτο ποιῶ, σύνφημι τῷ νόμῳ ὅτι
καλός. ¹⁷Νυνὶ δὲ οὐκέτι ἐγὼ κατεργάζομαι αὐτὸ ἀλλὰ
ἡ ἐνοικοῦσα ἐν ἐμοὶ ἁμαρτία. ¹⁸οἶδα γὰρ ὅτι οὐκ οἰκεῖ
ἐν ἐμοί, τοῦτ᾽ ἔστιν ἐν τῇ σαρκί μου, ἀγαθόν· τὸ γὰρ
θέλειν παράκειταί μοι, τὸ δὲ κατεργάζεσθαι τὸ καλὸν
οὔ· ¹⁹οὐ γὰρ ὃ θέλω ποιῶ ἀγαθόν, ἀλλὰ ὃ οὐ θέλω
κακὸν τοῦτο πράσσω. ²⁰εἰ δὲ ὃ οὐ θέλω τοῦτο ποιῶ,
οὐκέτι ἐγὼ κατεργάζομαι αὐτὸ ἀλλὰ ἡ οἰκοῦσα ἐν ἐμοὶ
ἁμαρτία. ²¹Εὑρίσκω ἄρα τὸν νόμον τῷ θέλοντι ἐμοὶ
ποιεῖν τὸ καλὸν ὅτι ἐμοὶ τὸ κακὸν παράκειται· ²²συνή-
δομαι γὰρ τῷ νόμῳ τοῦ θεοῦ κατὰ τὸν ἔσω ἄνθρωπον,
²³βλέπω δὲ ἕτερον νόμον ἐν τοῖς μέλεσίν μου ἀντιστρατευόμενον τῷ νόμῳ τοῦ νοός μου καὶ αἰχμαλωτίζοντά
με [ἐν] τῷ νόμῳ τῆς ἁμαρτίας τῷ ὄντι ἐν τοῖς μέλεσίν
μου. ²⁴ταλαίπωρος ἐγὼ ἄνθρωπος· τίς με ῥύσεται ἐκ
τοῦ σώματος τοῦ θανάτου τούτου; ²⁵χάρις [δὲ] τῷ θεῷ
διὰ Ἰησοῦ Χριστοῦ τοῦ κυρίου ἡμῶν. ἄρα οὖν αὐτὸς
ἐγὼ τῷ μὲν νοῒ δουλεύω νόμῳ θεοῦ, τῇ δὲ σαρκὶ νόμῳ
ἁμαρτίας. **8** ¹Οὐδὲν ἄρα νῦν κατάκριμα τοῖς
ἐν Χριστῷ Ἰησοῦ· ²ὁ γὰρ νόμος τοῦ πνεύματος τῆς ζωῆς
ἐν Χριστῷ Ἰησοῦ ἠλευθέρωσέν σε ἀπὸ τοῦ νόμου τῆς
ἁμαρτίας καὶ τοῦ θανάτου. ³τὸ γὰρ ἀδύνατον τοῦ
νόμου, ἐν ᾧ ἠσθένει διὰ τῆς σαρκός, ὁ θεὸς τὸν ἑαυτοῦ
υἱὸν πέμψας ἐν ὁμοιώματι σαρκὸς ἁμαρτίας καὶ περὶ

ἁμαρτίας κατέκρινε τὴν ἁμαρτίαν ἐν τῇ σαρκί, [4]ἵνα τὸ
δικαίωμα τοῦ νόμου πληρωθῇ ἐν ἡμῖν τοῖς μὴ κατὰ
σάρκα περιπατοῦσιν ἀλλὰ κατὰ πνεῦμα· [5]οἱ γὰρ κατὰ
σάρκα ὄντες τὰ τῆς σαρκὸς φρονοῦσιν, οἱ δὲ κατὰ
πνεῦμα τὰ τοῦ πνεύματος. [6]τὸ γὰρ φρόνημα τῆς
σαρκὸς θάνατος, τὸ δὲ φρόνημα τοῦ πνεύματος ζωὴ καὶ
εἰρήνη· [7]διότι τὸ φρόνημα τῆς σαρκὸς ἔχθρα εἰς θεόν,
τῷ γὰρ νόμῳ 'τοῦ θεοῦ οὐχ ὑποτάσσεται, οὐδὲ γὰρ
δύναται· [8]οἱ δὲ ἐν σαρκὶ ὄντες θεῷ ἀρέσαι οὐ δύνανται.
[9]Ὑμεῖς δὲ οὐκ ἐστὲ ἐν σαρκὶ ἀλλὰ ἐν πνεύματι, εἴπερ
πνεῦμα θεοῦ οἰκεῖ ἐν ὑμῖν. εἰ δέ τις πνεῦμα Χριστοῦ
οὐκ ἔχει, οὗτος οὐκ ἔστιν αὐτοῦ. [10]εἰ δὲ Χριστὸς ἐν
ὑμῖν, τὸ μὲν σῶμα νεκρὸν διὰ ἁμαρτίαν, τὸ δὲ πνεῦμα
ζωὴ διὰ δικαιοσύνην. [11]εἰ δὲ τὸ πνεῦμα τοῦ ἐγείραντος
τὸν Ἰησοῦν ἐκ νεκρῶν οἰκεῖ ἐν ὑμῖν, ὁ ἐγείρας ἐκ νεκρῶν
Χριστὸν Ἰησοῦν ζωοποιήσει [καὶ] τὰ θνητὰ σώματα
ὑμῶν διὰ τοῦ ἐνοικοῦντος αὐτοῦ πνεύματος ἐν ὑμῖν.

[12]Ἄρα οὖν, ἀδελφοί, ὀφειλέται ἐσμέν, οὐ τῇ σαρκὶ
τοῦ κατὰ σάρκα ζῆν, [13]εἰ γὰρ κατὰ σάρκα ζῆτε μέλλετε
ἀποθνήσκειν, εἰ δὲ πνεύματι τὰς πράξεις τοῦ σώματος
θανατοῦτε ζήσεσθε. [14]ὅσοι γὰρ πνεύματι θεοῦ ἄγονται,
οὗτοι υἱοὶ θεοῦ εἰσίν. [15]οὐ γὰρ ἐλάβετε πνεῦμα δουλείας
πάλιν εἰς φόβον, ἀλλὰ ἐλάβετε πνεῦμα υἱοθεσίας, ἐν ᾧ
κράζομεν Ἀββά ὁ πατήρ· [16]αὐτὸ τὸ πνεῦμα συμμαρ-
τυρεῖ τῷ πνεύματι ἡμῶν ὅτι ἐσμὲν τέκνα θεοῦ. [17]εἰ δὲ
τέκνα, καὶ κληρονόμοι· κληρονόμοι μὲν θεοῦ, συνκλη-
ρονόμοι δὲ Χριστοῦ, εἴπερ συνπάσχομεν ἵνα καὶ συν-
δοξασθῶμεν. [18]Λογίζομαι γὰρ ὅτι οὐκ ἄξια τὰ
παθήματα τοῦ νῦν καιροῦ πρὸς τὴν μέλλουσαν δόξαν
ἀποκαλυφθῆναι εἰς ἡμᾶς. [19]ἡ γὰρ ἀποκαραδοκία τῆς
κτίσεως τὴν ἀποκάλυψιν τῶν υἱῶν τοῦ θεοῦ ἀπεκδέχεται·

²⁰τῇ γὰρ ματαιότητι ἡ κτίσις ὑπετάγη, οὐχ ἑκοῦσα ἀλλὰ διὰ τὸν ὑποτάξαντα, ἐφ' ἑλπίδι ²¹ὅτι καὶ αὐτὴ ἡ κτίσις ἐλευθερωθήσεται ἀπὸ τῆς δουλείας τῆς φθορᾶς εἰς τὴν ἐλευθερίαν τῆς δόξης τῶν τέκνων τοῦ θεοῦ. ²²οἴδαμεν γὰρ ὅτι πᾶσα ἡ κτίσις συνστενάζει καὶ συνωδίνει ἄχρι τοῦ νῦν· ²³οὐ μόνον δέ, ἀλλὰ καὶ αὐτοὶ τὴν ἀπαρχὴν τοῦ πνεύματος ἔχοντες [ἡμεῖς] καὶ αὐτοὶ ἐν ἑαυτοῖς στενάζομεν, υἱοθεσίαν ἀπεκδεχόμενοι τὴν ἀπολύτρωσιν τοῦ σώματος ἡμῶν. ²⁴τῇ γὰρ ἑλπίδι ἐσώθημεν· ἐλπὶς δὲ βλεπομένη οὐκ ἔστιν ἐλπίς, ὃ γὰρ βλέπει τίς ἐλπίζει; ²⁵εἰ δὲ ὃ οὐ βλέπομεν ἐλπίζομεν, δι' ὑπομονῆς ἀπεκδεχόμεθα. ²⁶Ὡσαύτως δὲ καὶ τὸ πνεῦμα συναντιλαμβάνεται τῇ ἀσθενείᾳ ἡμῶν· τὸ γὰρ τί προσευξώμεθα καθὸ δεῖ οὐκ οἴδαμεν, ἀλλὰ αὐτὸ τὸ πνεῦμα ὑπερεντυγχάνει στεναγμοῖς ἀλαλήτοις, ²⁷ὁ δὲ ἐραυνῶν τὰς καρδίας οἶδεν τί τὸ φρόνημα τοῦ πνεύματος, ὅτι κατὰ θεὸν ἐντυγχάνει ὑπὲρ ἁγίων. ²⁸οἴδαμεν δὲ ὅτι τοῖς ἀγαπῶσι τὸν θεὸν πάντα συνεργεῖ [ὁ θεὸς] εἰς ἀγαθόν, τοῖς κατὰ πρόθεσιν κλητοῖς οὖσιν. ²⁹ὅτι οὓς προέγνω, καὶ προώρισεν συμμόρφους τῆς εἰκόνος τοῦ υἱοῦ αὐτοῦ, εἰς τὸ εἶναι αὐτὸν πρωτότοκον ἐν πολλοῖς ἀδελφοῖς· ³⁰οὓς δὲ προώρισεν, τούτους καὶ ἐκάλεσεν· καὶ οὓς ἐκάλεσεν, τούτους καὶ ἐδικαίωσεν· οὓς δὲ ἐδικαίωσεν, τούτους καὶ ἐδόξασεν. ³¹Τί οὖν ἐροῦμεν πρὸς ταῦτα; εἰ ὁ θεὸς ὑπὲρ ἡμῶν, τίς καθ' ἡμῶν; ³²ὅς γε τοῦ ἰδίου υἱοῦ οὐκ ἐφείσατο, ἀλλὰ ὑπὲρ ἡμῶν πάντων παρέδωκεν αὐτόν, πῶς οὐχὶ καὶ σὺν αὐτῷ τὰ πάντα ἡμῖν χαρίσεται; ³³τίς ἐγκαλέσει κατὰ ἐκλεκτῶν θεοῦ; θεὸς ὁ ΔΙΚΑΙῶΝ· ³⁴τίς ὁ ΚΑΤΑΚΡΙΝῶΝ; Χριστὸς ['Ιησοῦς] ὁ ἀποθανών, μᾶλλον δὲ ἐγερθεὶς [ἐκ νεκρῶν], ὅς ἐστιν ἐν δεξιᾷ τοῦ θεοῦ, ὃς καὶ ἐντυγχάνει ὑπὲρ ἡμῶν· ³⁵τίς

ἡμᾶς χωρίσει ἀπὸ τῆς ἀγάπης τοῦ χριστοῦ; θλῖψις ἢ
στενοχωρία ἢ διωγμὸς ἢ λιμὸς ἢ γυμνότης ἢ κίνδυνος ἢ
μάχαιρα; [36]καθὼς γέγραπται ὅτι

Ἕνεκεν coῦ θανατούμεθα ὅλην τὴν ἡμέραν,
ἐλογίσθημεν ὡς πρόβατα cφαγῆc.
[37]ἀλλ᾽ ἐν τούτοις πᾶσιν ὑπερνικῶμεν διὰ τοῦ ἀγαπή-
σαντος ἡμᾶς. [38]πέπεισμαι γὰρ ὅτι οὔτε θάνατος οὔτε
ζωὴ οὔτε ἄγγελοι οὔτε ἀρχαὶ οὔτε ἐνεστῶτα οὔτε
μέλλοντα οὔτε δυνάμεις [39]οὔτε ὕψωμα οὔτε βάθος οὔτε
τις κτίσις ἑτέρα δυνήσεται ἡμᾶς χωρίσαι ἀπὸ τῆς
ἀγάπης τοῦ θεοῦ τῆς ἐν Χριστῷ Ἰησοῦ τῷ κυρίῳ ἡμῶν.

9 [1]Ἀλήθειαν λέγω ἐν Χριστῷ, οὐ ψεύδομαι, συνμαρτυρούσης μοι τῆς συνειδήσεώς μου ἐν πνεύματι
ἁγίῳ, [2]ὅτι λύπη μοί ἐστιν μεγάλη καὶ ἀδιάλειπτος
ὀδύνη τῇ καρδίᾳ μου· [3]ηὐχόμην γὰρ ἀνάθεμα εἶναι
αὐτὸς ἐγὼ ἀπὸ τοῦ χριστοῦ ὑπὲρ τῶν ἀδελφῶν μου τῶν
συγγενῶν μου κατὰ σάρκα, [4]οἵτινές εἰσιν Ἰσραηλεῖται,
ὧν ἡ υἱοθεσία καὶ ἡ δόξα καὶ αἱ διαθῆκαι καὶ ἡ νομοθεσία καὶ ἡ λατρεία καὶ αἱ ἐπαγγελίαι, [5]ὧν οἱ πατέρες,
καὶ ἐξ ὧν ὁ χριστὸς τὸ κατὰ σάρκα, ὁ ὢν ἐπὶ πάντων,
θεὸς εὐλογητὸς εἰς τοὺς αἰῶνας· ἀμήν. [6]Οὐχ οἷον δὲ
ὅτι ἐκπέπτωκεν ὁ λόγος τοῦ θεοῦ. οὐ γὰρ πάντες οἱ ἐξ
Ἰσραήλ, οὗτοι Ἰσραήλ· [7]οὐδ᾽ ὅτι εἰσὶν σπέρμα Ἀβραάμ,
πάντες τέκνα, ἀλλ᾽ Ἐν Ἰσαὰκ κληθήσεταί σοι cπέρμα.
[8]τοῦτ᾽ ἔστιν, οὐ τὰ τέκνα τῆς σαρκὸς ταῦτα τέκνα τοῦ
θεοῦ, ἀλλὰ τὰ τέκνα τῆς ἐπαγγελίας λογίζεται εἰς
σπέρμα· [9]ἐπαγγελίας γὰρ ὁ λόγος οὗτος Κατὰ τὸν καιρὸν
τοῦτον ἐλεύcομαι καὶ ἔσται τῇ Σάρρᾳ υἱός. [10]οὐ μόνον δέ,
ἀλλὰ καὶ Ῥεβέκκα ἐξ ἑνὸς κοίτην ἔχουσα, Ἰσαὰκ τοῦ
πατρὸς ἡμῶν· [11]μήπω γὰρ γεννηθέντων μηδὲ πραξάντων

τι ἀγαθὸν ἢ φαῦλον, ἵνα ἡ κατ᾽ ἐκλογὴν πρόθεσις τοῦ
θεοῦ μένῃ, οὐκ ἐξ ἔργων ἀλλ᾽ ἐκ τοῦ καλοῦντος, ¹²ἐρρέθη
αὐτῇ ὅτι Ὁ μείζων δογλεγσει τῷ ἐλάσσονι· ¹³καθάπερ
γέγραπται Τὸν Ἰακὼβ Ηγάπησα, τὸν δὲ Ἡσαγ ἐμίσησα.

¹⁴Τί οὖν ἐροῦμεν ; μὴ ἀδικία παρὰ τῷ θεῷ ; μὴ
γένοιτο· ¹⁵τῷ Μωυσεῖ γὰρ λέγει Ἐλεήσω ον ἂν ἐλεῶ,
καὶ οἰκτειρήσω ὃν ἂν οἰκτείρω. ¹⁶ἄρα οὖν οὐ τοῦ θέλοντος
οὐδὲ τοῦ τρέχοντος, ἀλλὰ τοῦ ἐλεῶντος θεοῦ. ¹⁷λέγει
γὰρ ἡ γραφὴ τῷ Φαραὼ ὅτι Εἰς αγτὸ τογτο ἐξήγειρά σε
ὅπως ἐνδείξωμαι ἐν σοὶ τὴν δγναμίν μου, καὶ ὅπως διαγ-
γελῇ τὸ ὄνομά μου ἐν πάσῃ τῇ γῇ. ¹⁸ἄρα οὖν ὃν θέλει
ἐλεεῖ, ὃν δὲ θέλει σκληρύνει.   ¹⁹Ἐρεῖς μοι οὖν
Τί ἔτι μέμφεται ; τῷ γὰρ βουλήματι αὐτοῦ τίς ἀνθέστηκεν ; ²⁰ὦ ἄνθρωπε, μενοῦνγε σὺ τίς εἶ ὁ ἀνταποκρινόμενος τῷ θεῷ ; μὴ ἐρεῖ τὸ πλάσμα τῷ πλάσαντι Τί με
ἐποίησας οὕτως ; ²¹ἢ οὐκ ἔχει ἐξουσίαν ὁ κεραμεγς τοῦ
πηλοῦ ἐκ τοῦ αὐτοῦ φυράματος ποιῆσαι ὃ μὲν εἰς τιμὴν
σκεῦος, ὃ δὲ εἰς ἀτιμίαν ; ²²εἰ δὲ θέλων ὁ θεὸς ἐνδείξασθαι
τὴν ὀργὴν καὶ γνωρίσαι τὸ δυνατὸν αὐτοῦ ηνεγκεν ἐν
πολλῇ μακροθυμίᾳ σκεγη ὀργῆς κατηρτισμένα εἰς ἀπώλειαν, ²³ἵνα γνωρίσῃ τὸν πλοῦτον τῆς δόξης αὐτοῦ ἐπὶ
σκεύη ἐλέους, ἃ προητοίμασεν εἰς δόξαν, ²⁴οὓς καὶ ἐκάλε
σεν ἡμᾶς οὐ μόνον ἐξ Ἰουδαίων ἀλλὰ καὶ ἐξ ἐθνῶν—;
²⁵ὡς καὶ ἐν τῷ Ὡσηὲ λέγει

Καλέσω τὸν ογ λαόν μογ λαόν μογ
    καὶ τὴν ογκ ηγαπημένην ηγαπημένην·
²⁶καὶ ἔσται ἐν τῷ τόπῳ ογ ἐρρέθη [αγτοῖς] Ογ λαός
                    μογ γμεῖς,
    ἐκεῖ κληθήσονται γίοὶ θεοῦ ζῶντος.
²⁷Ἡσαΐας δὲ κράζει ὑπὲρ τοῦ Ἰσραήλ Ἐὰν ἦ ὁ ἀριθμὸς
τῶν γίων Ἰσραηλ ὡς ἡ ἄμμος τῆς θαλάσσης, τὸ γπόλιμμα

cωθήϲεται· ²⁸λόγον γὰρ ϲυντελῶν καὶ ϲυντέμνων ποιήϲει
Κύριοϲ ἐπὶ τῆϲ γῆϲ. ²⁹καὶ καθὼϲ προείρηκεν Ἡϲαίαϲ
  Εἰ μὴ Κύριοϲ Σαβαὼθ ἐγκατέλιπεν ἡμῖν ϲπέρμα,
  ὡϲ Σόδομα ἂν ἐγενήθημεν καὶ ὡϲ Γόμορρα ἂν
                                          ὡμοιώθημεν.

³⁰Τί οὖν ἐροῦμεν; ὅτι ἔθνη τὰ μὴ διώκοντα δικαιοσύνην
κατέλαβεν δικαιοσύνην, δικαιοσύνην δὲ τὴν ἐκ πίστεως·
³¹Ἰσραὴλ δὲ διώκων νόμον δικαιοσύνης εἰς νόμον οὐκ
ἔφθασεν. ³²διὰ τί; ὅτι οὐκ ἐκ πίστεως ἀλλ᾿ ὡς ἐξ
ἔργων· προσέκοψαν τῷ λίθῳ τοῦ προσκόμματος, ³³καθὼς
γέγραπται
  Ἰδοὺ τίθημι ἐν Σιὼν λίθον προσκόμματος καὶ πέτραν
                                          σκανδάλου,
  καὶ ὁ πιστεύων ἐπ᾿ αὐτῷ οὐ καταισχυνθήσεται.

10 ¹Ἀδελφοί, ἡ μὲν εὐδοκία τῆς ἐμῆς καρδίας καὶ
ἡ δέησις πρὸς τὸν θεὸν ὑπὲρ αὐτῶν εἰς σωτηρίαν. ²μαρ-
τυρῶ γὰρ αὐτοῖς ὅτι ζῆλον θεοῦ ἔχουσιν· ἀλλ᾿ οὐ κατ᾿
ἐπίγνωσιν, ³ἀγνοοῦντες γὰρ τὴν τοῦ θεοῦ δικαιοσύνην, καὶ
τὴν ἰδίαν ζητοῦντες στῆσαι, τῇ δικαιοσύνῃ τοῦ θεοῦ οὐχ
ὑπετάγησαν· ⁴τέλος γὰρ νόμου Χριστὸς εἰς δικαιοσύνην
παντὶ τῷ πιστεύοντι. ⁵Μωυσῆς γὰρ γράφει ὅτι τὴν
δικαιοσύνην τὴν ἐκ νόμου ὁ ποιήϲαϲ ἄνθρωποϲ ζήϲεται ἐν
αὐτῇ. ⁶ἡ δὲ ἐκ πίστεως δικαιοσύνη οὕτως λέγει Μὴ
εἴπῃϲ ἐν τῇ καρδίᾳ ϲου Τίϲ ἀναβήϲεται εἰϲ τὸν οὐρανόν;
τοῦτ᾿ ἔστιν Χριστὸν καταγαγεῖν· ⁷ἤ Τίϲ καταβήϲεται εἰϲ
τὴν ἄβυϲϲον; τοῦτ᾿ ἔστιν Χριστὸν ἐκ νεκρῶν ἀναγαγεῖν.
⁸ἀλλὰ τί λέγει; Ἐγγύϲ ϲου τὸ ῥῆμά ἐϲτιν, ἐν τῷ ϲτόματί
ϲου καὶ ἐν τῇ καρδίᾳ ϲου· τοῦτ᾿ ἔστιν τὸ ῥῆμα τῆς πίστεως
ὃ κηρύσσομεν. ⁹ὅτι ἐὰν ὁμολογήσῃς τὸ ῥῆμα ἐν τῷ
ϲτόματί ϲου ὅτι ΚΎΡΙΟΣ ΙΗΣΟΎΣ, καὶ πιστεύσῃς ἐν
τῇ καρδίᾳ ϲου ὅτι ὁ θεὸς αὐτὸν ἤγειρεν ἐκ νεκρῶν,

σωθήσῃ· ¹⁰καρδίᾳ γὰρ πιστεύεται εἰς δικαιοσύνην,
στόματι δὲ ὁμολογεῖται εἰς σωτηρίαν· ¹¹λέγει γὰρ ἡ
γραφή Πᾶς ὁ πιστεύων ἐπ᾽ αὐτῷ οὐ καταισχυνθήσεται.
¹²οὐ γάρ ἐστιν διαστολὴ Ἰουδαίου τε καὶ Ἕλληνος, ὁ
γὰρ αὐτὸς κύριος πάντων, πλουτῶν εἰς πάντας τοὺς
ἐπικαλουμένους αὐτόν· ¹³Πᾶς γὰρ ὃς ἂν ἐπικαλέσηται τὸ
ὄνομα Κυρίου σωθήσεται. ¹⁴Πῶς οὖν ἐπικαλέσωνται εἰς
ὃν οὐκ ἐπίστευσαν; πῶς δὲ πιστεύσωσιν οὗ οὐκ ἤκουσαν; πῶς δὲ ἀκούσωσιν χωρὶς κηρύσσοντος; ¹⁵πῶς δὲ
κηρύξωσιν ἐὰν μὴ ἀποσταλῶσιν; καθάπερ γέγραπται
Ὡς ὡραῖοι οἱ πόδες τῶν εὐαγγελιζομένων ἀγαθά. ¹⁶Ἀλλ᾽
οὐ πάντες ὑπήκουσαν τῷ εὐαγγελίῳ· Ἡσαίας γὰρ λέγει
Κύριε, τίς ἐπίστευσεν τῇ ἀκοῇ ἡμῶν; ¹⁷ἄρα ἡ πίστις ἐξ
ἀκοῆς, ἡ δὲ ἀκοὴ διὰ ῥήματος Χριστοῦ. ¹⁸ἀλλὰ λέγω,
μὴ οὐκ ἤκουσαν; μενοῦνγε

　Εἰς πᾶσαν τὴν γῆν ἐξῆλθεν ὁ φθόγγος αὐτῶν,
　καὶ εἰς τὰ πέρατα τῆς οἰκουμένης τὰ ῥήματα αὐτῶν.
¹⁹ἀλλὰ λέγω, μὴ Ἰσραὴλ οὐκ ἔγνω; πρῶτος Μωυσῆς
λέγει

　Ἐγὼ παραζηλώσω ὑμᾶς ἐπ᾽ οὐκ ἔθνει,
　ἐπ᾽ ἔθνει ἀσυνέτῳ παροργιῶ ὑμᾶς.
²⁰Ἡσαίας δὲ ἀποτολμᾷ καὶ λέγει

　Εὑρέθην τοῖς ἐμὲ μὴ ζητοῦσιν,
　ἐμφανὴς ἐγενόμην τοῖς ἐμὲ μὴ ἐπερωτῶσιν.
²¹πρὸς δὲ τὸν Ἰσραὴλ λέγει Ὅλην τὴν ἡμέραν ἐξεπέ-
τασα τὰς χεῖράς μου πρὸς λαὸν ἀπειθοῦντα καὶ ἀντι-
λέγοντα.　**11**　¹Λέγω οὖν, μὴ ἀπώσατο ὁ θεὸς
τὸν λαὸν αὐτοῦ; μὴ γένοιτο· καὶ γὰρ ἐγὼ Ἰσραηλείτης
εἰμί, ἐκ σπέρματος Ἀβραάμ, φυλῆς Βενιαμείν. ²οὐκ
ἀπώσατο ὁ θεὸς τὸν λαὸν αὐτοῦ ὃν προέγνω. ἢ οὐκ
οἴδατε ἐν Ἡλείᾳ τί λέγει ἡ γραφή, ὡς ἐντυγχάνει τῷ

θεῷ κατὰ τοῦ Ἰσραήλ; ³Κύριε, τοὺς προφήτας coy ἀπέκτειναν, τὰ θυσιαστήριά coy κατέσκαψαν, κἀγὼ ὑπελείφθην μόνος, καὶ ζητοῦσιν τὴν ψυχήν μου. ⁴ἀλλὰ τί λέγει αὐτῷ ὁ χρηματισμός; Κατέλιπον ἐμαυτῷ ἑπτακισχιλίους ἄνδρας, οἵτινες οὐκ ἔκαμψαν γόνυ τῇ Βάαλ. ⁵οὕτως οὖν καὶ ἐν τῷ νῦν καιρῷ λίμμα κατ' ἐκλογὴν χάριτος γέγονεν· ⁶εἰ δὲ χάριτι, οὐκέτι ἐξ ἔργων, ἐπεὶ ἡ χάρις οὐκέτι γίνεται χάρις. ⁷τί οὖν; ὃ ἐπιζητεῖ Ἰσραήλ, τοῦτο οὐκ ἐπέτυχεν, ἡ δὲ ἐκλογὴ ἐπέτυχεν· οἱ δὲ λοιποὶ ἐπωρώθησαν, ⁸καθάπερ γέγραπται Ἔδωκεν αὐτοῖς ὁ θεὸς πνεῦμα κατανύξεως, ὀφθαλμοὺς τοῦ μὴ βλέπειν καὶ ὦτα τοῦ μὴ ἀκούειν, ἕως τῆς σήμερον ἡμέρας. ⁹καὶ Δαυεὶδ λέγει

Γενηθήτω ἡ τράπεζα αὐτῶν εἰς παγίδα καὶ εἰς θήραν καὶ εἰς σκάνδαλον καὶ εἰς ἀνταπόδομα αὐτοῖς,
¹⁰σκοτισθήτωσαν οἱ ὀφθαλμοὶ αὐτῶν τοῦ μὴ βλέπειν, καὶ τὸν νῶτον αὐτῶν διὰ παντὸς σύνκαμψον.

¹¹Λέγω οὖν, μὴ ἔπταισαν ἵνα πέσωσιν; μὴ γένοιτο· ἀλλὰ τῷ αὐτῶν παραπτώματι ἡ σωτηρία τοῖς ἔθνεσιν, εἰς τὸ παραζηλῶσαι αὐτούς. ¹²εἰ δὲ τὸ παράπτωμα αὐτῶν πλοῦτος κόσμου καὶ τὸ ἥττημα αὐτῶν πλοῦτος ἐθνῶν, πόσῳ μᾶλλον τὸ πλήρωμα αὐτῶν.

¹³Ὑμῖν δὲ λέγω τοῖς ἔθνεσιν. ἐφ' ὅσον μὲν οὖν εἰμὶ ἐγὼ ἐθνῶν ἀπόστολος, τὴν διακονίαν μου δοξάζω, ¹⁴εἴ πως παραζηλώσω μου τὴν σάρκα καὶ σώσω τινὰς ἐξ αὐτῶν. ¹⁵εἰ γὰρ ἡ ἀποβολὴ αὐτῶν καταλλαγὴ κόσμου, τίς ἡ πρόσλημψις εἰ μὴ ζωὴ ἐκ νεκρῶν; ¹⁶εἰ δὲ ἡ ἀπαρχὴ ἁγία, καὶ τὸ φύραμα· καὶ εἰ ἡ ῥίζα ἁγία, καὶ οἱ κλάδοι. ¹⁷Εἰ δέ τινες τῶν κλάδων ἐξεκλάσθησαν, σὺ δὲ ἀγριέλαιος ὢν ἐνεκεντρίσθης ἐν αὐτοῖς καὶ συνκοινωνὸς τῆς ῥίζης τῆς πιότητος τῆς ἐλαίας ἐγένου,

¹⁸μὴ κατακαυχῶ τῶν κλάδων· εἰ δὲ κατακαυχᾶσαι, οὐ σὺ τὴν ῥίζαν βαστάζεις ἀλλὰ ἡ ῥίζα σέ. ¹⁹ἐρεῖς οὖν Ἐξεκλάσθησαν κλάδοι ἵνα ἐγὼ ἐνκεντρισθῶ. ²⁰καλῶς· τῇ ἀπιστίᾳ ἐξεκλάσθησαν, σὺ δὲ τῇ πίστει ἕστηκας. μὴ ὑψηλὰ φρόνει, ἀλλὰ φοβοῦ· ²¹εἰ γὰρ ὁ θεὸς τῶν κατὰ φύσιν κλάδων οὐκ ἐφείσατο, οὐδὲ σοῦ φείσεται. ²²ἴδε οὖν χρηστότητα καὶ ἀποτομίαν θεοῦ· ἐπὶ μὲν τοὺς πεσόντας ἀποτομία, ἐπὶ δὲ σὲ χρηστότης θεοῦ, ἐὰν ἐπιμένῃς τῇ χρηστότητι, ἐπεὶ καὶ σὺ ἐκκοπήσῃ. ²³κἀκεῖνοι δέ, ἐὰν μὴ ἐπιμένωσι τῇ ἀπιστίᾳ, ἐνκεντρισθήσονται· δυνατὸς γάρ ἐστιν ὁ θεὸς πάλιν ἐνκεντρίσαι αὐτούς. ²⁴εἰ γὰρ σὺ ἐκ τῆς κατὰ φύσιν ἐξεκόπης ἀγριελαίου καὶ παρὰ φύσιν ἐνεκεντρίσθης εἰς καλλιέλαιον, πόσῳ μᾶλλον οὗτοι οἱ κατὰ φύσιν ἐνκεντρισθήσονται τῇ ἰδίᾳ ἐλαίᾳ.   ²⁵Οὐ γὰρ θέλω ὑμᾶς ἀγνοεῖν, ἀδελφοί, τὸ μυστήριον τοῦτο, ἵνα μὴ ἦτε ἐν ἑαυτοῖς φρόνιμοι, ὅτι πώρωσις ἀπὸ μέρους τῷ Ἰσραὴλ γέγονεν ἄχρι οὗ τὸ πλήρωμα τῶν ἐθνῶν εἰσέλθῃ, ²⁶καὶ οὕτως πᾶς Ἰσραὴλ σωθήσεται· καθὼς γέγραπται

Ἥξει ἐκ Σιὼν ὁ ῥυόμενος,
    ἀποστρέψει ἀσεβείας ἀπὸ Ἰακώβ.
²⁷καὶ αὕτη αὐτοῖς ἡ παρ' ἐμοῦ διαθήκη,
    ὅταν ἀφέλωμαι τὰς ἁμαρτίας αὐτῶν.

²⁸κατὰ μὲν τὸ εὐαγγέλιον ἐχθροὶ δι' ὑμᾶς, κατὰ δὲ τὴν ἐκλογὴν ἀγαπητοὶ διὰ τοὺς πατέρας· ²⁹ἀμεταμέλητα γὰρ τὰ χαρίσματα καὶ ἡ κλῆσις τοῦ θεοῦ. ³⁰ὥσπερ γὰρ ὑμεῖς ποτε ἠπειθήσατε τῷ θεῷ, νῦν δὲ ἠλεήθητε τῇ τούτων ἀπειθίᾳ, ³¹οὕτως καὶ οὗτοι νῦν ἠπείθησαν τῷ ὑμετέρῳ ἐλέει ἵνα καὶ αὐτοὶ νῦν ἐλεηθῶσιν· ³²συνέκλεισεν γὰρ ὁ θεὸς τοὺς πάντας εἰς ἀπειθίαν ἵνα τοὺς πάντας ἐλεήσῃ.   ³³Ὦ βάθος πλούτου καὶ σοφίας καὶ

γνώσεως θεοῦ· ὡς ἀνεξεραύνητα τὰ κρίματα αὐτοῦ καὶ
ἀνεξιχνίαστοι αἱ ὁδοὶ αὐτοῦ.
    [34]Τίς γὰρ ἔγνω νοῦν Κυρίου; ἢ τίς ϲύμβουλος αὐτοῦ
                                            ἐγένετο;
    [35]ἢ τίς προέδωκεν αὐτῷ, καὶ ἀνταποδοθήσεται αὐτῷ;
[36]ὅτι ἐξ αὐτοῦ καὶ δι' αὐτοῦ καὶ εἰς αὐτὸν τὰ πάντα·
αὐτῷ ἡ δόξα εἰς τοὺς αἰῶνας· ἀμήν.

    12 [1]Παρακαλῶ οὖν ὑμᾶς, ἀδελφοί, διὰ τῶν οἰκτιρ-
μῶν τοῦ θεοῦ παραστῆσαι τὰ σώματα ὑμῶν θυσίαν
ζῶσαν ἁγίαν τῷ θεῷ εὐάρεστον, τὴν λογικὴν λατρείαν
ὑμῶν· [2]καὶ μὴ συνσχηματίζεσθε τῷ αἰῶνι τούτῳ, ἀλλὰ
μεταμορφοῦσθε τῇ ἀνακαινώσει τοῦ νοός, εἰς τὸ δοκι-
μάζειν ὑμᾶς τί τὸ θέλημα τοῦ θεοῦ, τὸ ἀγαθὸν καὶ
εὐάρεστον καὶ τέλειον.
    [3]Λέγω γὰρ διὰ τῆς χάριτος τῆς δοθείσης μοι παντὶ
τῷ ὄντι ἐν ὑμῖν μὴ ὑπερφρονεῖν παρ' ὃ δεῖ φρονεῖν, ἀλλὰ
φρονεῖν εἰς τὸ σωφρονεῖν, ἑκάστῳ ὡς ὁ θεὸς ἐμέρισεν
μέτρον πίστεως. [4]καθάπερ γὰρ ἐν ἑνὶ σώματι πολλὰ
μέλη ἔχομεν, τὰ δὲ μέλη πάντα οὐ τὴν αὐτὴν ἔχει
πρᾶξιν, [5]οὕτως οἱ πολλοὶ ἓν σῶμά ἐσμεν ἐν Χριστῷ, τὸ
δὲ καθ' εἷς ἀλλήλων μέλη. [6]Ἔχοντες δὲ χαρίσματα
κατὰ τὴν χάριν τὴν δοθεῖσαν ἡμῖν διάφορα, εἴτε προφητείαν κατὰ τὴν ἀναλογίαν τῆς πίστεως, [7]εἴτε διακονίαν
ἐν τῇ διακονίᾳ, εἴτε ὁ διδάσκων ἐν τῇ διδασκαλίᾳ, [8]εἴτε
ὁ παρακαλῶν ἐν τῇ παρακλήσει, ὁ μεταδιδοὺς ἐν ἁπλότητι, ὁ προϊστάμενος ἐν σπουδῇ, ὁ ἐλεῶν ἐν ἱλαρότητι.
[9]ἡ ἀγάπη ἀνυπόκριτος. ἀποστυγοῦντες τὸ πονηρόν,
κολλώμενοι τῷ ἀγαθῷ· [10]τῇ φιλαδελφίᾳ εἰς ἀλλήλους
φιλόστοργοι, τῇ τιμῇ ἀλλήλους προηγούμενοι, [11]τῇ
σπουδῇ μὴ ὀκνηροί, τῷ πνεύματι ζέοντες; τῷ κυρίῳ

δουλεύοντες, ¹²τῇ ἐλπίδι χαίροντες, τῇ θλίψει ὑπομένοντες, τῇ προσευχῇ προσκαρτεροῦντες, ¹³ταῖς χρείαις
τῶν ἁγίων κοινωνοῦντες, τὴν φιλοξενίαν διώκοντες.
¹⁴εὐλογεῖτε τοὺς διώκοντας, εὐλογεῖτε καὶ μὴ καταρᾶσθε.
¹⁵χαίρειν μετὰ χαιρόντων, κλαίειν μετὰ κλαιόντων.
¹⁶τὸ αὐτὸ εἰς ἀλλήλους φρονοῦντες, μὴ τὰ ὑψηλὰ φρονοῦντες ἀλλὰ τοῖς ταπεινοῖς συναπαγόμενοι. μὴ γίνεσθε
φρόνιμοι παρ' ἑαυτοῖς.   ¹⁷μηδενὶ κακὸν ἀντὶ κακοῦ ἀπο-
διδόντες· προνοούμενοι καλὰ ἐνώπιον πάντων ἀνθρώπων·
¹⁸εἰ δυνατόν, τὸ ἐξ ὑμῶν μετὰ πάντων ἀνθρώπων εἰρη-
νεύοντες·   ¹⁹μὴ ἑαυτοὺς ἐκδικοῦντες, ἀγαπητοί, ἀλλὰ
δότε τόπον τῇ ὀργῇ, γέγραπται γάρ Ἐμοὶ ἐκδίκησις,
ἐγὼ ἀνταποδώσω, λέγει Κύριος.   ²⁰ἀλλὰ ἐὰν πεινᾷ ὁ
ἐχθρός σου, ψώμιζε αὐτόν· ἐὰν διψᾷ, πότιζε αὐτόν· τοῦτο
γὰρ ποιῶν ἄνθρακας πυρὸς σωρεύσεις ἐπὶ τὴν κεφαλὴν
αὐτοῦ.   ²¹μὴ νικῶ ὑπὸ τοῦ κακοῦ, ἀλλὰ νίκα ἐν τῷ
ἀγαθῷ τὸ κακόν.   13 ¹Πᾶσα ψυχὴ ἐξουσίαις
ὑπερεχούσαις ὑποτασσέσθω, οὐ γὰρ ἔστιν ἐξουσία εἰ
μὴ ὑπὸ θεοῦ, αἱ δὲ οὖσαι ὑπὸ θεοῦ τεταγμέναι εἰσίν·
²ὥστε ὁ ἀντιτασσόμενος τῇ ἐξουσίᾳ τῇ τοῦ θεοῦ δια-
ταγῇ ἀνθέστηκεν, οἱ δὲ ἀνθεστηκότες ἑαυτοῖς κρίμα
λήμψονται.   ³οἱ γὰρ ἄρχοντες οὐκ εἰσὶν φόβος τῷ
ἀγαθῷ ἔργῳ ἀλλὰ τῷ κακῷ. θέλεις δὲ μὴ φοβεῖσθαι
τὴν ἐξουσίαν; τὸ ἀγαθὸν ποίει, καὶ ἕξεις ἔπαινον ἐξ
αὐτῆς·   ⁴θεοῦ γὰρ διάκονός ἐστιν σοὶ εἰς τὸ ἀγαθόν.
ἐὰν δὲ τὸ κακὸν ποιῇς, φοβοῦ· οὐ γὰρ εἰκῇ τὴν μάχαι-
ραν φορεῖ· θεοῦ γὰρ διάκονός ἐστιν, ἔκδικος εἰς ὀργὴν
τῷ τὸ κακὸν πράσσοντι.   ⁵διὸ ἀνάγκη ὑποτάσσεσθαι,
οὐ μόνον διὰ τὴν ὀργὴν ἀλλὰ καὶ διὰ τὴν συνείδησιν,
⁶διὰ τοῦτο γὰρ καὶ φόρους τελεῖτε, λειτουργοὶ γὰρ θεοῦ
εἰσὶν εἰς αὐτὸ τοῦτο προσκαρτεροῦντες.   ⁷ἀπόδοτε πᾶσι

τὰς ὀφειλάς, τῷ τὸν φόρον τὸν φόρον, τῷ τὸ τέλος τὸ
τέλος, τῷ τὸν φόβον τὸν φόβον, τῷ τὴν τιμὴν τὴν τιμήν.
⁸Μηδενὶ μηδὲν ὀφείλετε, εἰ μὴ τὸ ἀλλήλους ἀγαπᾶν·
ὁ γὰρ ἀγαπῶν τὸν ἕτερον νόμον πεπλήρωκεν. ⁹τὸ γὰρ
Οὐ μοιχεύσεις, Οὐ φονεύσεις, Οὐ κλέψεις, Οὐκ ἐπιθυμή-
σεις, καὶ εἴ τις ἑτέρα ἐντολή, ἐν τῷ λόγῳ τούτῳ ἀνακεφαλαιοῦται, [ἐν τῷ] Ἀγαπήσεις τὸν πλησίον σου ὡς
σεαυτόν. ¹⁰ἡ ἀγάπη τῷ πλησίον κακὸν οὐκ ἐργάζεται·
πλήρωμα οὖν νόμου ἡ ἀγάπη.   ¹¹Καὶ τοῦτο
εἰδότες τὸν καιρόν, ὅτι ὥρα ἤδη ὑμᾶς ἐξ ὕπνου ἐγερθῆναι,
νῦν γὰρ ἐγγύτερον ἡμῶν ἡ σωτηρία ἢ ὅτε ἐπιστεύσαμεν.
¹²ἡ νὺξ προέκοψεν, ἡ δὲ ἡμέρα ἤγγικεν. ἀποθώμεθα
οὖν τὰ ἔργα τοῦ σκότους, ἐνδυσώμεθα [δὲ] τὰ ὅπλα τοῦ
φωτός. ¹³ὡς ἐν ἡμέρᾳ εὐσχημόνως περιπατήσωμεν, μὴ
κώμοις καὶ μέθαις, μὴ κοίταις καὶ ἀσελγείαις, μὴ
ἔριδι καὶ ζήλῳ. ¹⁴ἀλλὰ ἐνδύσασθε τὸν κύριον Ἰησοῦν
Χριστόν, καὶ τῆς σαρκὸς πρόνοιαν μὴ ποιεῖσθε εἰς
ἐπιθυμίας.

14 ¹Τὸν δὲ ἀσθενοῦντα τῇ πίστει προσλαμβάνεσθε, μὴ εἰς διακρίσεις διαλογισμῶν. ²ὃς μὲν πιστεύει
φαγεῖν πάντα, ὁ δὲ ἀσθενῶν λάχανα ἐσθίει. ³ὁ ἐσθίων
τὸν μὴ ἐσθίοντα μὴ ἐξουθενείτω, ὁ δὲ μὴ ἐσθίων τὸν
ἐσθίοντα μὴ κρινέτω, ὁ θεὸς γὰρ αὐτὸν προσελάβετο.
⁴σὺ τίς εἶ ὁ κρίνων ἀλλότριον οἰκέτην; τῷ ἰδίῳ κυρίῳ
στήκει ἢ πίπτει· σταθήσεται δέ, δυνατεῖ γὰρ ὁ κύριος
στῆσαι αὐτόν. ⁵ὃς μὲν [γὰρ] κρίνει ἡμέραν παρ᾽ ἡμέραν,
ὃς δὲ κρίνει πᾶσαν ἡμέραν· ἕκαστος ἐν τῷ ἰδίῳ νοΐ
πληροφορείσθω· ⁶ὁ φρονῶν τὴν ἡμέραν κυρίῳ φρονεῖ.
καὶ ὁ ἐσθίων κυρίῳ ἐσθίει, εὐχαριστεῖ γὰρ τῷ θεῷ·
καὶ ὁ μὴ ἐσθίων κυρίῳ οὐκ ἐσθίει, καὶ εὐχαριστεῖ τῷ
θεῷ. ⁷Οὐδεὶς γὰρ ἡμῶν ἑαυτῷ ζῇ, καὶ οὐδεὶς ἑαυτῷ

ἀποθνήσκει· ⁸ἐάν τε γὰρ ζῶμεν, τῷ κυρίῳ ζῶμεν, ἐάν
τε ἀποθνήσκωμεν, τῷ κυρίῳ ἀποθνήσκομεν. ἐάν τε οὖν
ζῶμεν ἐάν τε ἀποθνήσκωμεν, τοῦ κυρίου ἐσμέν. ⁹εἰς
τοῦτο γὰρ Χριστὸς ἀπέθανεν καὶ ἔζησεν ἵνα καὶ νεκρῶν
καὶ ζώντων κυριεύσῃ. ¹⁰Σὺ δὲ τί κρίνεις τὸν ἀδελφόν
σου; ἢ καὶ σὺ τί ἐξουθενεῖς τὸν ἀδελφόν σου; πάντες
γὰρ παραστησόμεθα τῷ βήματι τοῦ θεοῦ· ¹¹γέγραπται
γάρ

Ζῶ ἐγώ, λέγει Κύριος, ὅτι ἐμοὶ κάμψει πᾶν γόνυ,
καὶ πᾶσα γλῶσσα ἐξομολογήσεται τῷ θεῷ.

¹²ἄρα [οὖν] ἕκαστος ἡμῶν περὶ ἑαυτοῦ λόγον δώσει
[τῷ θεῷ]. ¹³Μηκέτι οὖν ἀλλήλους κρίνωμεν·
ἀλλὰ τοῦτο κρίνατε μᾶλλον, τὸ μὴ τιθέναι πρόσκομμα
τῷ ἀδελφῷ ἢ σκάνδαλον. ¹⁴οἶδα καὶ πέπεισμαι ἐν
κυρίῳ Ἰησοῦ ὅτι οὐδὲν κοινὸν δι' ἑαυτοῦ· εἰ μὴ τῷ
λογιζομένῳ τι κοινὸν εἶναι, ἐκείνῳ κοινόν. ¹⁵εἰ γὰρ διὰ
βρῶμα ὁ ἀδελφός σου λυπεῖται, οὐκέτι κατὰ ἀγάπην
περιπατεῖς. μὴ τῷ βρώματί σου ἐκεῖνον ἀπόλλυε ὑπὲρ
οὗ Χριστὸς ἀπέθανεν. ¹⁶μὴ βλασφημείσθω οὖν ὑμῶν
τὸ ἀγαθόν. ¹⁷οὐ γάρ ἐστιν ἡ βασιλεία τοῦ θεοῦ βρῶσις
καὶ πόσις, ἀλλὰ δικαιοσύνη καὶ εἰρήνη καὶ χαρὰ ἐν
πνεύματι ἁγίῳ· ¹⁸ὁ γὰρ ἐν τούτῳ δουλεύων τῷ χριστῷ
εὐάρεστος τῷ θεῷ καὶ δόκιμος τοῖς ἀνθρώποις. ¹⁹ἄρα
οὖν τὰ τῆς εἰρήνης διώκωμεν καὶ τὰ τῆς οἰκοδομῆς τῆς
εἰς ἀλλήλους· ²⁰μὴ ἕνεκεν βρώματος κατάλυε τὸ ἔργον
τοῦ θεοῦ. πάντα μὲν καθαρά, ἀλλὰ κακὸν τῷ ἀνθρώπῳ
τῷ διὰ προσκόμματος ἐσθίοντι. ²¹καλὸν τὸ μὴ φαγεῖν
κρέα μηδὲ πεῖν οἶνον μηδὲ ἐν ᾧ ὁ ἀδελφός σου προσ-
κόπτει· ²²σὺ πίστιν ἣν ἔχεις κατὰ σεαυτὸν ἔχε ἐνώπιον
τοῦ θεοῦ. μακάριος ὁ μὴ κρίνων ἑαυτὸν ἐν ᾧ δοκι-
μάζει· ²³ὁ δὲ διακρινόμενος ἐὰν φάγῃ κατακέκριται, ὅτι

οὐκ ἐκ πίστεως· πᾶν δὲ ὃ οὐκ ἐκ πίστεως ἁμαρτία
ἐστίν.   15 ¹'Οφείλομεν δὲ ἡμεῖς οἱ δυνατοὶ τὰ
ἀσθενήματα τῶν ἀδυνάτων βαστάζειν, καὶ μὴ ἑαυτοῖς
ἀρέσκειν. ²ἕκαστος ἡμῶν τῷ πλησίον ἀρεσκέτω εἰς τὸ
ἀγαθὸν πρὸς οἰκοδομήν· ³καὶ γὰρ ὁ χριστὸς οὐχ ἑαυτῷ
ἤρεσεν· ἀλλὰ καθὼς γέγραπται Οἱ ὀνειδισμοὶ τῶν
ὀνειδιζόντων σε ἐπέπεϲαν ἐπ' ἐμέ. ⁴ὅσα γὰρ προεγράφη,
[πάντα] εἰς τὴν ἡμετέραν διδασκαλίαν ἐγράφη, ἵνα διὰ
τῆς ὑπομονῆς καὶ διὰ τῆς παρακλήσεως τῶν γραφῶν
τὴν ἐλπίδα ἔχωμεν. ⁵ὁ δὲ θεὸς τῆς ὑπομονῆς καὶ τῆς
παρακλήσεως δῴη ὑμῖν τὸ αὐτὸ φρονεῖν ἐν ἀλλήλοις
κατὰ Χριστὸν Ἰησοῦν, ⁶ἵνα ὁμοθυμαδὸν ἐν ἑνὶ στόματι
δοξάζητε τὸν θεὸν καὶ πατέρα τοῦ κυρίου ἡμῶν Ἰησοῦ
Χριστοῦ.

⁷Διὸ προσλαμβάνεσθε ἀλλήλους, καθὼς καὶ ὁ
χριστὸς προσελάβετο ἡμᾶς, εἰς δόξαν τοῦ θεοῦ. ⁸λέγω
γὰρ Χριστὸν διάκονον γεγενῆσθαι περιτομῆς ὑπὲρ ἀληθείας θεοῦ, εἰς τὸ βεβαιῶσαι τὰς ἐπαγγελίας τῶν
πατέρων, ⁹τὰ δὲ ἔθνη ὑπὲρ ἐλέους δοξάσαι τὸν θεόν·
καθὼς γέγραπται Διὰ τοῦτο ἐξομολογήϲομαί ϲοι ἐν
ἔθνεϲι, καὶ τῷ ὀνόματί ϲου ψαλῶ. ¹⁰καὶ πάλιν λέγει
Εὐφράνθητε, ἔθνη, μετὰ τοῦ λαοῦ αὐτοῦ. ¹¹καὶ πάλιν

Αἰνεῖτε, πάντα τὰ ἔθνη, τὸν κύριον,
καὶ ἐπαινεϲάτωϲαν αὐτὸν πάντεϲ οἱ λαοί.

¹²καὶ πάλιν Ἡσαίας λέγει
Ἔϲται ἡ ῥίζα τοῦ Ἰεϲϲαί,
καὶ ὁ ἀνιϲτάμενοϲ ἄρχειν ἐθνῶν·
ἐπ' αὐτῷ ἔθνη ἐλπιοῦϲιν.

¹³ὁ δὲ θεὸς τῆς ἐλπίδος πληρῶσαι ὑμᾶς πάσης χαρᾶς
καὶ εἰρήνης ἐν τῷ πιστεύειν, εἰς τὸ περισσεύειν ὑμᾶς ἐν
τῇ ἐλπίδι ἐν δυνάμει πνεύματος ἁγίου.

¹⁴Πέπεισμαι δέ, ἀδελφοί μου, καὶ αὐτὸς ἐγὼ περὶ
ὑμῶν, ὅτι καὶ αὐτοὶ μεστοί ἐστε ἀγαθωσύνης, πεπλη-
ρωμένοι πάσης τῆς γνώσεως, δυνάμενοι καὶ ἀλλήλους
νουθετεῖν. ¹⁵τολμηροτέρως δὲ ἔγραψα ὑμῖν ἀπὸ μέρους,
ὡς ἐπαναμιμνήσκων ὑμᾶς, διὰ τὴν χάριν τὴν δοθεῖσάν
μοι ἀπὸ τοῦ θεοῦ ¹⁶εἰς τὸ εἶναί με λειτουργὸν Χριστοῦ
Ἰησοῦ εἰς τὰ ἔθνη, ἱερουργοῦντα τὸ εὐαγγέλιον τοῦ θεοῦ,
ἵνα γένηται ἡ προσφορὰ τῶν ἐθνῶν εὐπρόσδεκτος,
ἡγιασμένη ἐν πνεύματι ἁγίῳ. ¹⁷ἔχω οὖν [τὴν] καύχησιν ἐν Χριστῷ Ἰησοῦ τὰ πρὸς τὸν θεόν· ¹⁸οὐ γὰρ
τολμήσω τι λαλεῖν ὧν οὐ κατειργάσατο Χριστὸς δι᾽
ἐμοῦ εἰς ὑπακοὴν ἐθνῶν, λόγῳ καὶ ἔργῳ, ¹⁹ἐν δυνάμει
σημείων καὶ τεράτων, ἐν δυνάμει πνεύματος [ἁγίου]·
ὥστε με ἀπὸ Ἰερουσαλὴμ καὶ κύκλῳ μέχρι τοῦ Ἰλλυρικοῦ πεπληρωκέναι τὸ εὐαγγέλιον τοῦ χριστοῦ, ²⁰οὕτως
δὲ φιλοτιμούμενον εὐαγγελίζεσθαι οὐχ ὅπου ὠνομάσθη
Χριστός, ἵνα μὴ ἐπ᾽ ἀλλότριον θεμέλιον οἰκοδομῶ,
²¹ἀλλὰ καθὼς γέγραπται

Ὄψονται οἷς οὐκ ἀνηγγέλη περὶ αὐτοῦ,
καὶ οἳ οὐκ ἀκηκόασιν συνήσουσιν.

²²Διὸ καὶ ἐνεκοπτόμην τὰ πολλὰ τοῦ ἐλθεῖν πρὸς
ὑμᾶς· ²³νυνὶ δὲ μηκέτι τόπον ἔχων ἐν τοῖς κλίμασι
τούτοις, ἐπιπόθειαν δὲ ἔχων τοῦ ἐλθεῖν πρὸς ὑμᾶς ἀπὸ
ἱκανῶν ἐτῶν, ²⁴ὡς ἂν πορεύωμαι εἰς τὴν Σπανίαν,
ἐλπίζω γὰρ διαπορευόμενος θεάσασθαι ὑμᾶς καὶ ὑφ᾽
ὑμῶν προπεμφθῆναι ἐκεῖ ἐὰν ὑμῶν πρῶτον ἀπὸ μέρους
ἐμπλησθῶ,—²⁵νυνὶ δὲ πορεύομαι εἰς Ἰερουσαλὴμ διακονῶν τοῖς ἁγίοις. ²⁶ηὐδόκησαν γὰρ Μακεδονία καὶ
Ἀχαία κοινωνίαν τινὰ ποιήσασθαι εἰς τοὺς πτωχοὺς
τῶν ἁγίων τῶν ἐν Ἰερουσαλήμ. ²⁷ηὐδόκησαν γάρ, καὶ
ὀφειλέται εἰσὶν αὐτῶν· εἰ γὰρ τοῖς πνευματικοῖς αὐτῶν

ἐκοινώνησαν τὰ ἔθνη, ὀφείλουσιν καὶ ἐν τοῖς σαρκικοῖς
λειτουργῆσαι αὐτοῖς. ²⁸τοῦτο οὖν ἐπιτελέσας, καὶ σφραγισάμενος αὐτοῖς τὸν καρπὸν τοῦτον, ἀπελεύσομαι δι'
ὑμῶν εἰς Σπανίαν· ²⁹οἶδα δὲ ὅτι ἐρχόμενος πρὸς ὑμᾶς ἐν
πληρώματι εὐλογίας Χριστοῦ ἐλεύσομαι.   ³⁰Παρα-
καλῶ δὲ ὑμᾶς [, ἀδελφοί,] διὰ τοῦ κυρίου ἡμῶν Ἰησοῦ
Χριστοῦ καὶ διὰ τῆς ἀγάπης τοῦ πνεύματος συνα-
γωνίσασθαί μοι ἐν ταῖς προσευχαῖς ὑπὲρ ἐμοῦ πρὸς
τὸν θεόν, ³¹ἵνα ῥυσθῶ ἀπὸ τῶν ἀπειθούντων ἐν τῇ
Ἰουδαίᾳ καὶ ἡ διακονία μου ἡ εἰς Ἰερουσαλὴμ εὐπρόσδεκτος τοῖς ἁγίοις γένηται, ³²ἵνα ἐν χαρᾷ ἐλθὼν πρὸς
ὑμᾶς διὰ θελήματος θεοῦ συναναπαύσωμαι ὑμῖν. ³³ὁ δὲ
θεὸς τῆς εἰρήνης μετὰ πάντων ὑμῶν. ἀμήν.

16 ¹Συνίστημι δὲ ὑμῖν Φοίβην τὴν ἀδελφὴν ἡμῶν,
οὖσαν [καὶ] διάκονον τῆς ἐκκλησίας τῆς ἐν Κενχρεαῖς,
²ἵνα προσδέξησθε αὐτὴν ἐν κυρίῳ ἀξίως τῶν ἁγίων,
καὶ παραστῆτε αὐτῇ ἐν ᾧ ἂν ὑμῶν χρῄζῃ πράγματι,
καὶ γὰρ αὐτὴ προστάτις πολλῶν ἐγενήθη καὶ ἐμοῦ
αὐτοῦ.

³Ἀσπάσασθε Πρίσκαν καὶ Ἀκύλαν τοὺς συνεργούς
μου ἐν Χριστῷ Ἰησοῦ, ⁴οἵτινες ὑπὲρ τῆς ψυχῆς μου
τὸν ἑαυτῶν τράχηλον ὑπέθηκαν, οἷς οὐκ ἐγὼ μόνος
εὐχαριστῶ ἀλλὰ καὶ πᾶσαι αἱ ἐκκλησίαι τῶν ἐθνῶν,
⁵καὶ τὴν κατ' οἶκον αὐτῶν ἐκκλησίαν. ἀσπάσασθε
Ἐπαίνετον τὸν ἀγαπητόν μου, ὅς ἐστιν ἀπαρχὴ τῆς
Ἀσίας εἰς Χριστόν. ⁶ἀσπάσασθε Μαρίαν, ἥτις πολλὰ
ἐκοπίασεν εἰς ὑμᾶς. ⁷ἀσπάσασθε Ἀνδρόνικον καὶ
Ἰουνίαν τοὺς συγγενεῖς μου καὶ συναιχμαλώτους μου,
οἵτινές εἰσιν ἐπίσημοι ἐν τοῖς ἀποστόλοις, οἳ καὶ πρὸ
ἐμοῦ γέγοναν ἐν Χριστῷ. ⁸ἀσπάσασθε Ἀμπλιᾶτον
τὸν ἀγαπητόν μου ἐν κυρίῳ. ⁹ἀσπάσασθε Οὐρβανὸν

τὸν συνεργὸν ἡμῶν ἐν Χριστῷ καὶ Στάχυν τὸν ἀγαπητόν
μου. ¹⁰ἀσπάσασθε Ἀπελλῆν τὸν δόκιμον ἐν Χριστῷ.
ἀσπάσασθε τοὺς ἐκ τῶν Ἀριστοβούλου. ¹¹ἀσπάσασθε
Ἡρῳδίωνα τὸν συγγενῆ μου. ἀσπάσασθε τοὺς ἐκ τῶν
Ναρκίσσου τοὺς ὄντας ἐν κυρίῳ. ¹²ἀσπάσασθε Τρύφαιναν καὶ Τρυφῶσαν τὰς κοπιώσας ἐν κυρίῳ. ἀσπάσασθε Περσίδα τὴν ἀγαπητήν, ἥτις πολλὰ ἐκοπίασεν
ἐν κυρίῳ. ¹³ἀσπάσασθε Ῥοῦφον τὸν ἐκλεκτὸν ἐν κυρίῳ
καὶ τὴν μητέρα αὐτοῦ καὶ ἐμοῦ. ¹⁴ἀσπάσασθε Ἀσύνκριτον, Φλέγοντα, Ἑρμῆν, Πατρόβαν, Ἑρμᾶν, καὶ τοὺς
σὺν αὐτοῖς ἀδελφούς. ¹⁵ἀσπάσασθε Φιλόλογον καὶ
Ἰουλίαν, Νηρέα καὶ τὴν ἀδελφὴν αὐτοῦ, καὶ Ὀλυμπᾶν,
καὶ τοὺς σὺν αὐτοῖς πάντας ἁγίους. ¹⁶Ἀσπάσασθε
ἀλλήλους ἐν φιλήματι ἁγίῳ. Ἀσπάζονται ὑμᾶς αἱ
ἐκκλησίαι πᾶσαι τοῦ χριστοῦ.

¹⁷Παρακαλῶ δὲ ὑμᾶς, ἀδελφοί, σκοπεῖν τοὺς τὰς
διχοστασίας καὶ τὰ σκάνδαλα παρὰ τὴν διδαχὴν ἣν
ὑμεῖς ἐμάθετε ποιοῦντας, καὶ ἐκκλίνετε ἀπ᾽ αὐτῶν·
¹⁸οἱ γὰρ τοιοῦτοι τῷ κυρίῳ ἡμῶν Χριστῷ οὐ δου-
λεύουσιν ἀλλὰ τῇ ἑαυτῶν κοιλίᾳ, καὶ διὰ τῆς χρηστο-
λογίας καὶ εὐλογίας ἐξαπατῶσι τὰς καρδίας τῶν
ἀκάκων. ¹⁹ἡ γὰρ ὑμῶν ὑπακοὴ εἰς πάντας ἀφίκετο·
ἐφ᾽ ὑμῖν οὖν χαίρω, θέλω δὲ ὑμᾶς σοφοὺς [μὲν] εἶναι
εἰς τὸ ἀγαθόν, ἀκεραίους δὲ εἰς τὸ κακόν. ²⁰ὁ δὲ θεὸς
τῆς εἰρήνης συντρίψει τὸν Σατανᾶν ὑπὸ τοὺς πόδας
ὑμῶν ἐν τάχει.

Ἡ χάρις τοῦ κυρίου ἡμῶν Ἰησοῦ μεθ᾽ ὑμῶν.

²¹Ἀσπάζεται ὑμᾶς Τιμόθεος ὁ συνεργός [μου], καὶ
Λούκιος καὶ Ἰάσων καὶ Σωσίπατρος οἱ συγγενεῖς
μου. ²²ἀσπάζομαι ὑμᾶς ἐγὼ Τέρτιος ὁ γράψας τὴν
ἐπιστολὴν ἐν κυρίῳ. ²³ἀσπάζεται ὑμᾶς Γάϊος ὁ ξένος

μου καὶ ὅλης τῆς ἐκκλησίας.   ἀσπάζεται ὑμᾶς Ἔραστος
ὁ οἰκονόμος τῆς πόλεως καὶ Κούαρτος ὁ ἀδελφός.

²⁵Τῷ δὲ δυναμένῳ ὑμᾶς στηρίξαι κατὰ τὸ εὐαγγέλιόν μου καὶ τὸ κήρυγμα Ἰησοῦ Χριστοῦ, κατὰ
ἀποκάλυψιν μυστηρίου χρόνοις αἰωνίοις σεσιγημένου
²⁶φανερωθέντος δὲ νῦν διά τε γραφῶν προφητικῶν κατ᾽
ἐπιταγὴν τοῦ αἰωνίου θεοῦ εἰς ὑπακοὴν πίστεως εἰς
πάντα τὰ ἔθνη γνωρισθέντος, ²⁷μόνῳ σοφῷ θεῷ διὰ
Ἰησοῦ Χριστοῦ [ᾧ] ἡ δόξα εἰς τοὺς αἰῶνας· ἀμήν.

NOTES

CHAPTER I.

A. i. 1—17. INTRODUCTION. ADDRESS 1—7. OCCASION 8—15. SUBJECT 16—17.

1—7. Address. The writer's (*a*) name and state, (*b*) office, (*c*) commission defined by a statement of (i) the Person from whom it was received, (ii) the Person of whom it dealt and through whom it came, (iii) the persons to whom it was directed, and is now in particular addressed, (*d*) greeting.

1. Παῦλος. Here, Gal., Eph., 1 and 2 Tim., Tit., no colleague is mentioned.

δοῦλος in the address here and Phil. i. 1, Tit. i. 1, only; cf. James i. 1; 2 Pet. i. 1; Jud. 1; Rev. i. 1; cf. also Gal. i. 10; Col. iv. 12; 2 Tim. ii. 24. The most absolute term for service, countenanced by our Lord Himself, cf. Mt. xx. 27 and n. Joh. xv. 15; cf. Isa. xlix. 3 f.; Jer. vii. 25, *al.* Regular O. T. term for prophets. Here adopted by S. Paul for himself, and the name, 'I. Χρ., substituted for Jehovah; cf. S. H.

'Ιησοῦ Χριστοῦ. The personal relation is the foundation of the Christian state whether of the apostle or of his readers (*v.* 6). 'Ιησ., the personal name, emphasises, as always, the human mission of the Lord, its character and object. Χρ., the official name, emphasises the position in the history of GOD's dealings with men, and the divine commission. N. the fourfold repetition *vv.* 1, 4, 6, 7 and cf. 1 Cor. i. 1—9.

κλητὸς ἀπόστολος. *v.* 7, κλητοῖς ἁγίοις: cf. 1 Cor. i. 1, 2 only. This group καλεῖν, κλῆσις, κλητός is characteristic of Pauline writings; Rev. xvii. 14 only in John. Evv. only Mt. ix. 13 ‖. They describe the call to service, whether accepted or rejected. The emphasis is on the invitation given, Gal. i. 1; cf. Mt. xxii. 3 f. ‖. See further n. on viii. 28. The added word describes the nature of the service required.

ἀπόστολος in its widest sense—a commissioned agent—then further defined in the following phrases. The nexus throughout the passage is by development of the implicit meaning into explicit statements, words forming the base of expanding thoughts. The name in its Christian use is derived from the Lord Himself, Mk iii. 14=Lk. vi. 13. See Add. Note H.

ἀφωρισμένος. Cf. Gal. i. 15: repeats and enlarges the idea of κλητός = separation from all other human relations for this single purpose of absolute service to the commission when the call came. It is a characteristic O. T. expression for the relation of Israel to GOD (as the κλητός); cf. the word Pharisee, of which it appears to be an assonant rendering.

εἰς εὐαγγέλιον θεοῦ. As the call and separation are of GOD, so is the object, GOD's Gospel.

For the spread of the Gospel as the aim of Christian service cf. 1 Thes. iii. 2; Phil. i. 5, ii. 22, iv. 3; Gal. ii. 7; 1 Cor. ix. 12; 2 Cor. ii. 12, viii. 18, x. 14; 2 Tim. i. 8; below, xv. 16, 19 al. The O.T. connexion is with the use of εὐαγγελίζεσθαι in Isa. xl. f., esp. lxi.; cf. Lk. iv. 18. It is the Lord's own word for His message, Mk i. 15, viii. 35 and Lk. iv. 43 al.

The phrase is anarthrous only here (cf. Rev. xiv. 6), and so emphasises the character of the object—for propagating good tidings of and from GOD.

On the word see Thayer and S. H. and Dalman, p. 102.

2. ὃ κ.τ.λ. This message is continuous with GOD's earlier revelation and fulfils it, cf. Heb. i. 1, 2.

προεπηγγείλατο. 2 Cor. ix. 5 only; cf. xv. 4; Gal. iii. 8; 1 Pet. i. 10; for the converse cf. Eph. i. 12.

διὰ τῶν πρ. α. ἐν γρα. ἁ. The fulness of the expression suggests that Gentiles are specially addressed: not simply 'the prophets,' but the prophets whom He inspired, whose utterances are preserved in writings which reproduce in their degree the divine character of the inspiration (ἁγίαις). It is the same GOD who used the prophets and now uses Paul, and for the same object.

γραφαῖς ἁγίαις, the permanent record of revelation; cf. xvi. 26; 2 Tim. iii. 16; 2 Pet. i. 20. Anarthrous, expressing the nature of the means by which the utterances of GOD are revealed, stating that there are scriptures, not appealing to the scriptures as known. Perhaps the earliest extant instance of the use of the phrase. The argument from prophecy was from the first addressed to Gentiles: cf. Acts viii. 28, x. 43, xxiv. 14. So with the Apologists great stress is laid on prophecy.

3. περὶ τοῦ υἱοῦ αὐτοῦ κ.τ.λ. 'His Son' is the subject of GOD's Gospel promised beforehand—the words go with the whole preceding clause taken as one idea; their meaning is developed in the participial clauses following, which are strictly parallel and explain the twofold character or nature in which 'His Son' was revealed to men, on the human side (κατὰ σάρκα) as the son of David, on the divine side (κατὰ πν. ἁγ.) as Son of GOD. Both characters are a fulfilment of prophecy, and together form the fundamental content of the Gospel. The article marks the uniqueness of the relation, ct. Heb. i. 2. The aorists of the participles point to two definite historic acts, the interpretation of which is the key to the mystery which makes 'His Son' the subject of GOD's Gospel. The consequence of the implied argument is then summed up in the full title Ἰ. Χ. τ. κ. ἡ.

τοῦ γενομένου...κατὰ σάρκα. For γεν. cf. Phil. ii. 7; Gal. iv. 4; Joh. i. 14. The entry into a new kind of existence is implied in all these passages: the special kind is marked here and Joh. *l.c.* as κατὰ σάρκα, that is, existence as a man, ἐν ὁμοιώματι ἀνθρώπου (Phil.), ἐκ γυναικός (Gal.). σάρξ here stands for human nature as such, including all that belongs to it (cf. 1 Tim. iii. 16), and not 'flesh' as contrasted with 'spirit'; cf. Westcott on Joh. i. 14, Thayer, s. v. 3.

ἐκ σπέρματος Δαυείδ. The Davidic descent is referred to as marking the fulfilment of prophecy: a commonplace in the primitive argument; cf. Acts ii. 29 f., xiii. 34 f. ; 2 Tim. ii. 8; Rev. iii. 7 (v. Swete); Mk xii. 35.

4. τοῦ ὁρισθέντος, "who was distinguished, from His brethren κατὰ σάρκα, as GOD's Son by an act of power," closely ‖ Acts xvii. 31, ἐν ἀνδρὶ ᾧ ὥρισεν κ.τ.λ., "by a man whom He marked out or distinguished for that office, by the warrant of raising Him from death." The fundamental notion of ὁρίζειν is to distinguish or mark off one object from others by drawing a line between them: so of local boundaries, of definitions, of appointments to specific work or office, of discriminations. Here, as in Acts *l.c.*, the line is drawn by the act of GOD in raising Jesus from the dead; that marked Him off from other men and indicated consequently His true character as, not David's son only, but Son of GOD. N. then that the word does not imply that He then *became* Son of GOD, as γενόμενος implies that He *became* man, but that His unique Sonship then became clear to men. Cf. also Acts xi. 29 with Field's note. Chrys. δειχθέντος, ἀποφανθέντος comes near to the meaning but does not express so fully the action of GOD.

Contrast ἔθηκε, Heb. i. 2; γενόμενος, *v.* 3, Heb. vi. 20; Col. i. 18; ἐποίησεν, Acts ii. 36; ἐχαρίσατο, Phil. ii. 9. These verbs can be used when it is a question of office and relation to man, but not of nature and relation to God.

υἱοῦ θεοῦ, anarthrous, as marking the character, not the individual merely.

ἐν δυνάμει, 'by an act of power'; cf. Acts ii. 33, τῇ δεξιᾷ=by His mighty Hand; 1 Cor. vi. 14; 2 Cor. xiii. 4; Eph. i. 19, 20; Heb. vii. 16. The resurrection of Jesus was an exercise of God's power, unique but inevitable, Jesus being who He was, unique but the warrant of consequent exercise of the same power on men in Christ; cf. also Phil. iii. 10. The phrase goes closely with ὁρισθέντος; for ἐν cf. 1 Pet. i. 5 (v. Hort); Rom. xv. 13, 19; 1 Cor. ii. 5; 2 Cor. vi. 7.

κατὰ πν. ἁγιωσύνης. κατὰ indicates the correspondence of this act of God with the nature of Him on whom it was exercised. It was natural that, Jesus being what He was, God should raise Him from the dead; cf. Acts ii. 24. It follows that πν. ἁγ. refers to the divine nature of Jesus, in contrast with σάρξ which indicates His true human nature. This divine nature is properly indicated by the genitive of quality. ἅγιος is the specific word in the Greek Bible for that which is essentially divine. It is used secondarily of persons and things as related to or belonging to God, cf. Hort, 1 Pet. p. 70; Davidson, *O.T. Theology*, pp. 256 ff.; Heb. ix. 14 (with Westcott's note). The al sen e of the article shows that we are dealing with the nature of the Son Himself.

ἐξ ἀναστάσεως νεκρῶν. The raising of Christ is the testimony of God to His nature; cf. Acts i. 22, ii. 24 *et passim*; 1 Cor. xv. 14 *al.* With ὁρισθέντος—the distinction was the immediate result of resurrection; cf. closely Acts xxvi. 23. The phrase ἀν. ν. (without articles, limited to Acts (4), Rom. (here), 1 Cor. xv. (3), Heb. vi. 2) describes most generally the fact and its nature=resurrection from death. νεκρῶν is gen. of definition, distinguishing this ἀνάστασις from other kinds (cf. Lc. ii. 34; Heb. vii. 11, 15; Acts vii. 37 *al.*).

’Ι. Χρ. τ. κ. ἡ. The full title sums up the argument implicit in the preceding clauses: the Son of God is the Man Jesus, the promised Christ, our Sovereign Lord, the one subject of the Gospel; cf. esp. Acts ii. 36, Phil. ii. 11. It occurs about 68 times in S. Paul, about 19 in the rest of N. T.

5. δι’ οὗ. He who is the subject of the Gospel is also the agent through whom God dispenses those powers which enable men to minister the Gospel; cf. Joh. i. 17; Gal. i. 1.

ἐλάβομεν. The subject of *v.* 1 is recovered—the apostolic commission exercised under the Lord. The aorist refers to the act by

which the commission was given; cf. 1 Cor. ii. 12, xv. 8, 9; 1 Tim.
ii. 7; 2 Tim. i. 11. The plural=we Christian apostles (ct. τῶν
προφητῶν a.) as 1 Cor. i. 23, ii. 12. But S. Paul certainly uses the
plural with direct, though perhaps not exclusive, reference to himself,
e.g. 2 Cor. x. *passim*; Moulton, p. 86.

χάριν καὶ ἀποστολήν. The close connexion of the words, and the
immediate context, prove that χάρις is here used in the specially
Pauline sense of the favour of GOD as extended to all mankind, with
especial reference to S. Paul's commission to the Gentiles, cf. Gal.
i. 15 f., a decisive parallel; Gal. ii. 7 f. Cf. Robinson, *Eph.* pp. 224 ff.,
"the freeness and universality of the Gospel." S. Paul felt that his
commission was a signal instance of GOD's free favour. Cf. also xv. 15;
Phil. i. 7; 1 Cor. xv. 10. ἀποστολή=commission.

εἰς ὑπακοὴν πίστεως, to promote obedience (to GOD) springing from
or belonging to faith in Him (not from keeping of law). The phrase
corresponds to εἰς εὐαγγέλιον θεοῦ in *v.* 1 and indicates the attitude of
recipients of the Gospel; their faith accepts and brings them to obey
Him who reveals Himself in the Gospel as their GOD. The genitive
is then a genitive of 'derivation or foundation' as in iv. 13; cf. Hort,
1 Pet. p. 89 (see the whole note). With ὑπακοή the genitive seems
never to be objective in N. T. (not even 2 Cor. x. 5). Obedience will
be the sign of the coming in of the Gentiles as disobedience was the
cause of the rejection of Israel; cf. x. 21; Isa. lxv. 12, lxvi. 4.
It is the proper outcome of faith, the acceptance of GOD's offer;
cf. 1 Pet. i. 2.

ἐν πᾶσιν τοῖς ἔθνεσιν. Cf. xv. 12, xvi. 26 = Gentiles: the πᾶσιν added
to emphasise the universality of the commission, cf. 13.

ὑπὲρ τοῦ ὀνόματος αὐτοῦ, i.e. of the Lord Jesus Christ. The name,
both in O.T. and N.T., stands for the Person as revealed for man's
acknowledgment; cf. Acts ix. 15. 3 Joh. 7 (where see Westcott's
add. note) is an exact parallel; Acts v. 41, ix. 16, xxi. 13, of suffering
on behalf of the Name they proclaimed. The full force comes out Phil.
ii. 9—11. The idea, not the word, is present 2 Cor. v. 20; Eph. vi. 20.
ὑπὲρ then=to gain acknowledgment of Him as revealed.

6. ἐν οἷς κ.τ.λ. A hint of the reason of his writing to them.
Cf. *v.* 13.

καὶ ὑμεῖς. Throughout the Epistle S. Paul primarily considers
Gentile Christians.

κλητοὶ 'Ι. Χρ. Called to belong to Jesus Christ, ‖ κλητὸς ἀπόστολος, *v.* 1, and κλητοῖς ἁγίοις, *v.* 7. The genitive stands for an
adjective, e.g. Χριστιανοι.

7. πᾶσιν κ.τ.λ. The local designation comes first, then the

foundation of their state in GOD'S love, then the demand thus made
on them for response.

All Christians in Rome are addressed, whatever their previous
history.

ἀγαπητοῖς θεοῦ, 'GOD'S beloved': a unique phrase, but cf. 1 Thes. i.
4, 2 Thes. ii. 13, and with ἅγιοι Col. iii. 12. GOD'S love for them is the
beginning, the call follows, and it is a call to respond to that love by
a life consecrated to GOD; cf. Eph. v. 1.

κλητοῖς ἁγίοις, called to be holy, as GOD is holy; cf. 1 Pet. i. 15,
16 (see Hort). Constructed as κλητὸς ἀπόστολος above. See note
on ἀγιωσύνης, *v.* 4.

χάρις ὑ. κ.τ.λ. The words, while reminding of the common forms
of salutation, have their full Christian sense. GOD'S favour and the
peace which it brings between man and GOD, and between man and
man, is the prayer of S. Paul for his readers. The stress is thrown
on χάρις by the interposition of ὑμῖν.

ἀπὸ θ. π. ἡ. κ. κ. 'Ι. Χρ. S. Paul's regular form except Col. i. 2,
1 Thes. i. 1 (2 Thes. i. 2, ἡμῶν is absent), till the Pastoral Epistles. Note
that here the Lord Jesus Christ is coordinated with GOD our Father
as the source of blessing (in *v.* 5 He is the Agent of the Father's
blessing): this coordination is highly significant; it appears in its
clearest form already in Epp. Thes. (n. esp. 1 Thes. iii. 11, 2 Thes. i. 12,
ii. 16): it combines the Christian experience and conviction as to the
Person of the Lord with the Lord's own teaching as to the Father-
hood of GOD into the theological conception which (cf. 2 Cor. xiii. 13)
was ultimately expressed in the Catholic dogma of the Trinity. See
S. H. *ad loc.* For a Jew the position is already implied in the first
phrase δοῦλος 'Ι. Χρ.

These introductory verses thus lay the foundations of the Gospel
in the nature and act of GOD as revealed through His Son—a fitting
introduction to an Epistle which is in fact a reasoned exposition of
the Gospel as preached to Gentiles by S. Paul. The main theological
conceptions are here stated or implied in a fully developed form, but
as attained through religious experience, not deduced or even interpreted by any philosophical method. In full accordance with all
other evidence as to the primitive development of Christian thought,
these conceptions are seen to be reached by the reflection upon the
fact of the Resurrection and the light thrown back from that fact
on the teaching, acts, and character of the Lord Jesus Christ.

8—17. Thanksgiving 8—10 *a* introduces the Occasion 10 *b*—15
and the Subject 16—17 of the Epistle.

He gives thanks to GOD for the wide report of their faith as heartily as (9) his prayers for them have been unceasing and (10) have embodied his eagerness to see them, (11) to help them and be helped by them, by the faith which each finds in the other; his prayers resulted in definite plans, hindered so far, to go to Rome and win fruit there also, by way of paying his debt, due to them as to others, of preaching the Gospel. He has been always ready to do this, for he has 'no shame' for the Gospel: it is an effective act of GOD'S power promoting salvation for all men, on the one condition of faith; because it reveals the true nature of GOD'S righteousness in men as starting from faith and leading to faith, in accordance with a fundamental declaration of the old dispensation.

8. εὐχαριστῶ. S. Paul follows his greeting always with thanks-giving or blessing (εὐλογητός), except in Gal. (θαυμάζω) and 1 Tim., Tit. Peculiar to this place are μου (exc. Phil. i. 3) and διὰ 'I. Xρ. This fulness of phrase corresponds to the fulness of state-ment in 1—7.

περὶ πάντων ὑ. Cf. πᾶσιν in vv. 5, 7.

ἡ πίστις ὑ. καταγγ. Cf. 1 Thes. i. 8, iii. 6; Philem. 5. **καταγγ.**, a weighty word, otherwise used only of the Gospel itself or some element in it (only Acts and Paul, 1 Cor., Phil., Col.). **ἐν ὅλῳ τῷ κόσμῳ,** a not unnatural exaggeration: he is writing from Corinth, the great commercial junction of the Empire.

9. γάρ introduces the personal reasons for his writing. He establishes personal relations with his readers before communicating his message, as he bases his commission on personal relations with the Lord. Cf. Col. i. 3 ff. (the other unvisited church to which he wrote); 2 Tim. i. 3. Note also the force of xv. 14—30.

μάρτυς…ὁ θεὸς κ.τ.λ. This form of emphatic assertion is specially used by S. Paul (only), when asserting the state of his own mind, 2 Cor. i. 23; Phil. i. 8; 1 Thes. ii. 5, 10; cf. Wisdom i. 6; and is no doubt occasioned by the misrepresentations of his motives made by opponents.

ᾧ λατρεύω κ.τ.λ. adds emphasis by express assertion of his whole-hearted devotion to GOD's service.

λατρεύω. Cf. Westcott on Hebr. p. 232, "marks the service of perfect subjection to a sovereign power"; uniformly expresses reli-gious service, voluntarily offered.

ἐν τῷ πνεύματί μου. The service rendered is spiritual, not ritual (cf. Phil. iii. 3), and offered by means of the central function of man's personality. The connexion seems to be, the Gospel absorbs my activity in the service of GOD, and it is therefore easy to under-stand my interest in you.

ἐν τ. εὐ. τ. υ. α. The sphere of activity: GOD's Gospel (*v.* 1) is also the Gospel of His Son, whose name is its epitome (*v.* 5) and who Himself is the author and commissioner (*v.* 5).

ὡς, how. μνείαν ὑ. ποι., make mention of; cf. 1 Thes. i. 2, Eph. i. 16 *al.*; always of prayer.

10. ἐπὶ, at. δεόμενος εἴ πως. Cf. Acts viii. 22; cf. Blass, p. 216. ἤδη ποτὲ, at long last.

εὐοδωθήσομαι, "in passive always tropical; to prosper, be successful," Thayer; 1 Cor. xvi. 2; 3 Joh. 2; but cf. Sept., Judg. xviii. 5; Tob. v. 21, xi. 5; so S. H. adopt early English vv., "I have a spedi way."

11. ἵνα τι μεταδῶ κ.τ.λ. The complex order and the indefinite τι...χάρισμα give a half apologetic tone to this expression of his object, leading at once to the correction τοῦτο δέ ἐστιν—if he benefits them they will also help him. χάρισμα, a concrete instance of GOD's χάρις, a gift of GOD. Cf. perhaps 1 Thes. ii. 8; 2 Cor. i. 11, suggesting that the particular gift is a fuller realisation of the Gospel, in thought and life, at once appealing to and stimulating their spirit, and particularly in its universal character; cf. below xv. 15 and 29.

εἰς τὸ στ. This gift will be to their strengthening, **or rather to** the common encouragement of writer and readers.

12. συνπαρ., only here. ἐν (cf. ἐπί, 2 Cor. vii. 7), no ‖, =in my feelings about you.

διὰ τῆς ἐν ἀλλήλοις κ.τ.λ. πίστις has its regular meaning, faith in GOD through Christ, ἐν ἀλλ., which we each find in the other: he piles up phrases to emphasise the reciprocity of benefit (συν., ἐν ἀλλ., ὑ. κ. ἐ.).

13. προεθέμην. He had got beyond prayers; he had made definite plans, but had been hindered by the exigencies of his work.

τινὰ καρπόν, again the apologetic τις. σχῶ, 'get,' as always.

14. The thought of the service he wished to render and the fruit he hoped to gain leads on to the statement of the motive and the theme of the Epistle. He has already got 'fruit,' and so is in debt to men of all classes and culture, and would wish to preach in Rome that he may be debtor to them too. This connexion is indicated by the asyndeton.

Ἕλλησίν τε καὶ βαρβάροις. Cf. Gal. iii. 28; Col. iii. 11 (Lightfoot's note); this is the division of mankind current among the inhabitants of the Empire, primarily depending upon language. It excludes, in Paul's mind, the Jew. In speaking of his debt, he thinks only of Gentiles: presently in speaking of the range of the Gospel, he includes

Jews. The Romans would now be included among Ἕλληνες: cf. Lightfoot, *l.c.* p. 217 *b*.

σοφοῖς τε καὶ ἀνοήτοις, a classification by culture; cf. 1 Cor. i. 18 f. : n. he was writing from Corinth.

ὀφειλέτης. Cf. 1 Cor. ix. 16 f. (Giff.); a debtor, he wishes to pay the debt in Rome too. But in what sense a debtor? Ramsay (*Pauline Studies*, p. 55) suggests that this is a reference to what he had gained from his intercourse with Greeks and his position as a Roman citizen. This he felt should be repaid by bringing to them the Gospel. But this seems farfetched. Nor does Giff.'s reference to 1 Cor. ix. 16 seem quite satisfactory. It is best taken in close connexion with καρπὸν σχῶ; cf. Phil. iv. 17. He has already 'got fruit' from these classes: he pays the debt by sowing the seed more widely among such.

15. τὸ κατ᾽ ἐμέ, subject to πρόθυμον, sc. ἐστιν. So far as I have to do with the matter—ref. to ἐκωλύθην, *v.* 13; cf. τὰ κατ᾽ ἐμὲ, Phil. i. 12.

16. ἐπαισχύνομαι. Cf. Mk viii. 38; 2 Tim. i. 8. There is no lack of readiness, because there is no need of reserve; the Gospel is its own vindication. The tremendous opposition he had lately experienced, especially at Corinth, seems to be in his mind.

δύναμις γὰρ θεοῦ κ.τ.λ. Cf. 1 Cor. i. 18 f. The Gospel is not a mere message whose ineffectiveness might shame the preacher: it is GOD's power for producing salvation. It is in fact GOD's word sent out into the world with mighty effect; cf. Acts x. 36: it reveals and provides a power for man to enable him to live the life which GOD means for him. It was a critical matter for S. Paul to show that in sweeping away law, as the condition of salvation, he was not destroying the one source of moral growth, that he was not antinomian, but setting free a new and mightier form of spiritual and moral health than any legal system did or could provide. The whole of this Epistle is directed to show that the Gospel alone provides and is such a power. This thought is developed in 1 Cor. i. 18—31; cf. also 1 Cor. ii. 5, iv. 20; 1 Thes. i. 5; (Heb. vii. 16).

Tr. 'GOD's power for salvation' closely together = GOD's effective means for saving men. The insertion of the article in A.V. and R.V. only weakens the force of the expression. There are other manifestations of GOD's power; cf. *v.* 20.

σωτηρίαν includes deliverance from the slavery of sin and full spiritual and moral health. See S. H. for the development of meaning. "It covers the whole range of the Messianic deliverance, both in its negative aspect as a rescuing from the Wrath...and in its positive aspect as the imparting of eternal life" (Mk x. 30 ‖;

Joh. iii. 15, 16, etc.); cf. 1 Thes. v. 9, 10, 11; *ib.* p. 24. Cf. Ps. xcviii. 2. It is a pity that the two adequate English translations *health* and *wealth* are both spoiled by custom, and we have to fall back upon the Latin 'salvation.'

παντὶ τῷ πιστεύοντι. For the connexion cf. Joh. i. 12. The range of the power is universal, both as proceeding from GOD who is one and also as offered on the single condition of faith, a common human faculty. The condition is stated here in its most absolute form, but the context shows that it means trust in GOD who gives the power through His Son. Acts ii. 44, iv. 32 *et passim* show that from the first this trust was the recognised distinction of Christians; from belief of the message its meaning rapidly developed into trust in the Person, who was Himself the message, and in GOD as revealed in the Person. So the aorist of the verb = to become a Christian; cf. Acts xix. 2: οἱ πιστεύοντες and πεπιστευκότες name Christians. It is in fact the response of the heart to the love of GOD, the source of the power. The basis of the Gospel as active in life is thus the personal relation between GOD and man in Christ. See Introd. p. xxxviii f.

Ἰουδαίῳ τε πρῶτον καὶ Ἕλληνι. The πρῶτον marks the historical sequence of revelation, consistently recognised by S. Paul. Cf. iii. 1, ix. 1 f., xi. 16 f., xv. 8, 9; Acts xiii. 46; Joh. iv. 22; Mt. xv. 24; S. H. add Acts xxviii. 24 f. The summing up of all mankind under the two religious divisions is the natural expression for a Jewish writer.

17. γάρ. The Gospel is GOD's power, with this wide range and single condition, because in it GOD's righteousness (which man needs if he is to answer to his true destiny) is revealed for man's acceptance as beginning, as far as the human condition is concerned, from faith and promoting faith.

δικαιοσύνη θεοῦ, not 'a righteousness of GOD,' but 'GOD's righteousness,' i.e. righteousness as belonging to the character of GOD and consequently required by Him in the character of men: so distinguished from any righteousness which man sets up for himself and thinks to acquire by himself; cf. x. 3; Phil. iii. 9; 2 Cor. v. 21; Eph. iv. 24; 1 Joh. ii. 29; Mt. vi. 33; and below, vi. 13 f. Cf. S. H. "It is righteousness active and energizing; the righteousness of the Divine Will as it were projected and enclosing and gathering into itself human wills." Cf. Ps. xviii. 2 *ib.*

This 'righteousness' is in fact man's σωτηρία, true state of health; and the Gospel, revealing it as following upon faith, puts it in the power of every faithful man to reach. Hence the Gospel is GOD's power, etc.

As the σωτηρία is that state of man in which he has made his own

the righteousness of GOD and so worked out in himself that image of
GOD (cf. Joh. i. 12) in which he was created, so we shall presently see
the converse is true—the damnation, destruction, of man lies in his
forsaking that task and reproducing in himself the image of the
beasts.

ἐκ πίστεως εἰς πίστιν, resulting, as far as the individual is concerned, from faith and promoting faith.   It is of the nature of
personal trust in one who is worthy of trust to deepen and widen
itself.   Ps. lxxxiii. 7 (lxxxiv. 8) (S. H.) is a good ‖: but 2 Cor. ii. 16
(*ib.*) is different.   It is important to observe that man's faith is the
source of man's righteousness only in a secondary degree.   The
primary source is GOD'S grace.

ἀποκαλύπτεται.   The Gospel is not a new principle in GOD'S
dealings with man, but a fresh revelation of what has always
been there.   This is emphasised by the quotation from Habakkuk,
and the argument about Abraham in c. iv.

καθὼς γέγραπται, Habakkuk ii. 4.   N. that in Hab. the reference
is to dangers from external foes and loyalty to Israel's king. This
is a good instance of the way in which S. Paul applies what is
occasional and local to the spiritual experience of man.

ὁ δὲ δίκαιος ἐκ πίστεως ζήσεται.   The stress is on ἐκ πίστεως—
the life which the man seeks to live, modelling himself, in his degree,
on the righteousness of GOD, requires and results from trust in GOD.

N. S. Paul seldom reaches such a degree of abstraction in his
statements as he does in these verses.   It is due to his desire to
state in the most summary form the character of the Gospel as he
conceived it.   But recalling *vv.* 2—7, we see that we are not even
here dealing with merely abstract principles : the Gospel itself is
essentially concrete in the Person of the Son : the power of GOD is no
impersonal force, but Christ Himself quickening men (cf. Phil.
iii. 12) ; salvation and faith are no mere technical terms, but
personal activities and conditions ; GOD'S righteousness is not a
system of laws or ethics, but the character revealed in Jesus
Christ ; our righteousness is that same character realised in ourselves.

B. i. 18—iv. 25. THE FIRST VINDICATION OF THE THEME. THE
UNIVERSALITY AND NEED OF THE GOSPEL JUSTIFIED HISTORICALLY.

i. 18—ii. 16. The Gospel is needed by Gentiles, because they are
under sin (i. 18—32), and have incurred the just judgment of GOD
(ii. 1—16).

i. 18—32. (18) This power and condition revealed in the Gospel meets the need of man; for in the actual state of man we can see that his life lies under GOD's wrath. Man has by unrighteous action overlaid the truth imparted to him: (20) the knowledge of GOD, communicated through the visible creation as a means of conceiving the invisible character of GOD, His power in life and His divine character, has been rejected; (21) men have failed to respond with appreciation and thanksgiving; losing the sense of their own destiny and submitting their intelligence to the influence of blind reasonings and passions, (22) with a false assumption of cleverness, they have substituted for the image of GOD, in which they were created, the likeness of the mere animal nature. (24) As a consequence, left by GOD to their own devices, under the unclean rule of their own desires, they have taken the false instead of the true view of their due allegiance, substituted in their worship the creature for the Creator, and as a consequence perverted even the natural uses of the body to vile and unnatural indulgence; (28) their will refusing to act upon the knowledge of GOD, GOD has allowed them to surrender themselves to all spiritual and moral ills, personal and social; (32) for they knowingly and willingly faced the verdict of death, and both practise and promote the practice of such things as incur that verdict.

The revelation of the Gospel is the revelation of the righteousness of GOD in the Person of Jesus Christ, and of that righteousness as a power for reproducing itself in man, if man will trust it, or rather Him. This is paralleled by a statement of the consequences of man's refusing to trust his knowledge of GOD, as seen in the lives and characters of men as they actually are, a revelation of GOD's wrath; the state of man shows both the need of power for recovery, and the condition in man for its action, namely recovered faith.

As GOD's righteousness is revealed in life, the Life of Jesus Christ, so GOD's wrath is revealed in life, the life of men putting themselves into antagonism with GOD, choosing to be under His wrath.

In this section S. Paul summarises his observations of contemporary conditions and generalises from it and from his judgment on history, in order to estimate the actual needs of man and the cause of his condition, as vindicating the character of the Gospel and its universal necessity, if man is to be delivered.

18. γὰρ gives the reason for the revelation just described and for the condition of its effectiveness.

ἀποκ. ὀργὴ θεοῦ. The revelation here spoken of is the revelation through the actual facts of human life, just as the Gospel revelation is revelation through the actual facts of the divine life seen in the Man Christ Jesus, the Incarnate Son.

ἀποκαλύπτεται, as above, of a general fact or principle governing the relations between God and man.

ὀργὴ θεοῦ, fundamentally = the relation between God as righteous and man as sinner. It is seen under present conditions in the progress of sin and growing alienation. The final issue will be seen in the final judgment. As with σωτηρία, so with ὀργή, we have the double sense of present alterable condition, and future final determination. The eschatological reference is, therefore, always implied, but not exclusive; cf. 1 Thes. i. 10, ii. 16, Lightfoot; Joh. iii. 36, Westcott, n.; Eph. v. 6; *infra*, iii. 5, ix. 22. It is opposed to σωτηρία (1 Thes. v. 9), ζωή (Joh. iii. 36), φῶς (Eph. v. 9). The verb is never used with θεός in N.T., though frequently in O.T. (but cf. Mt. xviii. 34; Lk. xiv. 21).

ἀπ᾽ οὐρανοῦ, used originally literally and now metaphorically of the seat of God's Presence, and so the place of origin of His judgments and commissions now and hereafter, the home indeed of all spiritual matters; so here the judgment on man's defections is represented as revealed from thence, in contrast with all earthly opinions and judgments; cf. Mt. xvi. 19, xxi. 25; Lk. xv. 18. Cf. Dalman, p. 219 f., E.T.

ἀσέβεια, the violation of reverence; ἀδικία, the violation of righteousness: sin is regarded as a contempt of God's claims on man, or as a breach of His will however revealed.

τῶν...κατεχόντων. The participial clause describes the action of man which constitutes him ἀσεβῆ and ἄδικον.

τὴν ἀλήθειαν. The next clause shows this to be quite general = the truth or true condition of man in his relation to God; both the truth of man's nature and destiny, cf. Joh. viii. 32; James i. 18, v. 19, and of God, in His revealed character and dealings; cf. 2 Thes. ii. 10—13. Cf. Hort on 1 Peter, p. 87.

ἐν ἀδικίᾳ marks the condition created by man himself under which he holds the truth; it is the combination of the possession of the truth and this selfmade condition which constitutes the act and state of sin. All sin is due to will acting against knowledge.

κατεχόντων. κατέχειν means either (1) to possess, 1 Cor. vii. 30, xi. 2, or (2), less frequently, to restrain or keep under restraint, Lk. iv. 42; 2 Thes. ii. 6, 7. Here the sequence of thought is decisive in favour of the first meaning: it is essential to the argument that the primary condition which makes an act or state sinful, should be set down here; namely, that the sinner knows what he is doing. Cf. Origen, *Philocal.* 73 (ed. Robinson). The compound has the force of real or full possession; cf. Moulton, p. 111 f. Contrast Lk. viii. 15.

19. διότι gives the reason for the wrath. For (Blass, p. 274) they knew GOD (19—21 a, expanding τὴν ἀλ. κατ.), but did not act on this knowledge (21 b—23, expanding ἐν ἀδικίᾳ). There should be a full stop or colon after κατεχόντων: as v. 18 introduces the whole section.

τὸ γνωστὸν τ. θ. = that element in or aspect of GOD which can be known. GOD can be known by man only in part: but that partial knowledge is true and adequate to man's capacity and sufficient and indispensable for his life. He is revealed partially in nature, including human nature, with relative completeness in the Son. For the construction cf. Blass, p. 155, Winer-M., p. 295. This is not a case of the neuter adjective standing for an abstract substantive; the genitive is partitive.

φανερόν ἐ. ἐν αὐτοῖς = ' is clear in them.' They have a clear knowledge of GOD so far as He can be known to man. Cf. Wisdom xiii. 1 which S. Paul certainly has in mind; but he defines the situation with a much closer grip.

ὁ θεὸς γὰρ κ.τ.λ. explains the fact of the clearness of this knowledge: it was due to a self-revelation of GOD through creation.

20. τὰ γὰρ ἀόρατα…θειότης are best treated as parenthetic—explanatory of ἐφανέρωσεν—the revelation of GOD through nature and human nature is true as far as it goes, but it is confined to His power both in nature and in morals, and His character as Divine Ruler and Lawgiver. Cf. generally Lk. xviii. 18 f.

τὰ ἀόρατα αὐτοῦ ‖ τὸ γν. τ. θ.; cf. Acts xiv. 15 f., xvii. 22 f. The argument from the natural order was the first argument addressed to Gentiles, as the argument from the O.T. order was the first argument addressed to Jews. The invisible things of GOD, His spiritual and moral attributes, are brought within the range of man's mental vision through a conception gained by reflection upon the things He has made. There is a play on the double meaning of ὁρᾶν as applied to sensual and mental vision, the transition to the second being marked by νοούμενα; cf. Col. i. 15 f.; Heb. xi. 27.

ἀπὸ κτίσεως κόσμου, temporal: ever since there was a world to be the object of sense and thought, and minds to feel and think. Not, as Giff., = ἀπὸ τοῦ ἐκτισμένου κόσμου; this would require articles and be tautologous; cf. Mk x. 6, xiii. 19; 2 Pet. iii. 4.

τοῖς ποιήμασιν, dat. of means. καθορᾶται = are brought within the range of vision.

νοούμενα, being conceived or framed into conceptions, made objects of thought; cf. Isa. xliv. 18; qu. Joh. xii. 40: and n. Heb. xi. 3, esp. the connexion of πίστει and νοοῦμεν.

ἥ τε ἀΐδιος α. δύναμις καὶ θειότης explain τὰ ἀόρατα. The primary conceptions of the Maker, formed by reflection upon things, are power and divinity. The fundamental assumption implied is that there must be a Maker—things could not make themselves, and man obviously did not make them. This assumption might well be taken by S. Paul as universally agreed. From that he sees man's reflection passing to the conception of power, and lasting or spiritual power; the conception of divinity is a further step, logically if not chrono-logically, first involving hardly more than antithesis to man and nature, but growing more complex with continued reflection; it involves qualitative conceptions of the Maker, not merely quanti-tative conceptions of His Power. The very abstract term θειότης (only here in N.T.; cf. Acts xvii. 29 and Wisdom xviii. 9) is used because the conceptions of God's nature vary so widely with time and place. The term covers every conception of a Being, antecedent and superior to creation, which man has formed or can form.

ἀΐδιος. Only here and Jude 6 in N.T.; Sept. only Wisdom vii. 26; frequent in class. Gk for lasting, eternal; e.g. Plato, *Timaeus*, 40 B, ζῶα θεῖα ὄντα καὶ ἀΐδια.

δύναμις. Esp. used of God's power in creation, old and new. Cf. above, v. 4.

εἰς τὸ may either express 'purpose' (viii. 29) or simple result (xii. 3): here generally taken of 'purpose,' in which case it must be connected with ἐφανέρωσεν above. But there is force in Burton's argument for 'result' (*M. T.* § 411). Cf. Moulton, p. 219. N. A.V. and R.V. invert text and margin.

ἀναπολογήτους, ii. 1 only. They have no defence as against God.

21. διότι picks up and expands the theme of v. 19.

γνόντες, aor. = having received or gained knowledge of God. ‖ τὴν ἀλ. κατέχοντες.

ἐδόξασαν = did not ascribe the due honour to God for what they knew to be His acts; cf. Acts xi. 18; Mt. xv. 31, *al.*

ηὐχαρίστησαν. They lacked the temper which should have led them δοξάζειν.

ἐματαιώθησαν. Vb only here; cf. 1 Cor. i. 20 f., iii. 20, and esp. Eph. iv. 17. The adjective implies absence of purpose or object, futility: so = they became μάταιοι, turning from the true object of all thought they invented vain and meaningless objects for themselves.

διαλογισμοί in S. Paul always in a bad sense; cf. 1 Cor. iii. 20, which perhaps gives the source of the use. It seems to imply the working of the intellect without correction by facts; cf. xiv. 1. ἐν perhaps instrumental—they lost the true thread by their speculations.

καὶ ἐσκοτίσθη κ.τ.λ. Cf. Eph. iv. 17 f., missing the true aim, they lost the true light.

καρδία more nearly corresponds to ' mind ' than to ' heart.' So here ἀσύνετος, unintelligent ; cf. x. 6, 8. Associated with thought and will (*v*. 24 ; 1 Cor. iv. 5) more usually than with feeling (Rom. ix. 2), see S.H. There is the same tragic irony here as in 1 Cor. i. 20 f. ; cf. Wisdom xi. 15.

22. φάσκοντες. The asyndeton shows that this is an explanation of the preceding sentence. φ. of false allegations, Acts xxiv. 9, xxv. 19 and here only.

23. ἤλλαξαν. Cf. Ps. cvi. (cv.) 20 ; cf. *infra* 25. The consequence of their false conception is a false religion, substituting inferior objects of worship for the one true object. The construction is a survival of poetic usage. Cf. Soph. *Antigone* 495 (Lietzmann).

τὴν δόξαν. Here apparently = the manifestation of GOD as an object of worship ; cf. *v*. 21. ‖ τὸ γνωστὸν τ. θ. the manifestation of GOD as an object of knowledge.

24. The consequences seen in the moral condition, to which GOD handed man over. Man by ignoring the truth is led to neglect the worship of GOD for the worship of creatures, and thence (24) to failure in due respect to his own body and (26) consequent misuse of the body for unnatural ends, and (28) misapplication of the mind to devising conduct which ignores his own true end and all social claims.

παρέδωκεν ὁ θ. Cf. *vv*. 26, 28 ; cf. iv. 25, and for the converse Phil. ii. 12. This surrender of man to the consequences of his own choice is also the act of man himself, cf. Eph. iv. 19. But it is still an act of judgment on the part of GOD. See S. H., Giff., Moberly, *Atonement and Personality*, p. 15 f.

ἐν ταῖς ἐπιθυμίαις τ. κ. α. The desires, uncontrolled by the choice of man's true end, are the occasions of sin.

τοῦ ἀτιμάζεσθαι. The gen. expressing result, as generally in S. Paul, cf. Moulton, p. 217, = the use of the body for purposes not intended ; cf. πάθη ἀτιμίας below, and n. esp. Col. ii. 23 (note in C.G.T.). ἐν αὐτοῖς requires us to take ἀτιμάζεσθαι as pass.

25. οἵτινες. Quippe qui, "seeing that they," repeats *v*. 23 with amplification.

τὴν ἀλήθειαν τοῦ θεοῦ. Quite comprehensive = the truth about

God and themselves and their relation to Him; so τῷ ψεύδει the false theory or statement of man and God which they adopted; cf. 2 Thes. ii. 11, 1 Joh. ii. 27.

ἐσεβάσθησαν. Here only in N.T., and O.T. only Hos. x. 5 Aq. = they made their objects of worship.

ἐλάτρευσαν. Of full religious service. See Westcott, *Hebr.* ref. above, *v.* 9.

παρὰ τὸν κτ., to the neglect of. Winer-M., p. 504; n. the tragic irony of the antithesis.

ὅς ἐστιν εὐλ. κ.τ.λ. Cf. ix. 5, 2 Cor. xi. 31, in each case a mark of deep emotion.

26. διὰ τοῦτο. Wilful rejection of God's self-revelation undermines self-respect, purity, and the whole sphere of duty.

πάθη ἀτιμίας. The gen. is descriptive—shameful passion. The thought of misuse is included in ἀτιμία; cf. ix. 21; as φυσική and κατὰ φύσιν mark a right use.

27. ἀπολαμβάνοντες, 'receiving as due.'

28. ἐδοκίμασαν, 'they thought not fit' (cf. Field, *ad loc.*). The verb implies approval after testing: the infinitive is epexegetic. τὸν θεὸν closely with the verb; cf. in passive construction 1 Thes. ii. 4. They tested or proved God and decided not to keep Him, etc.

ἔχειν, pres. = to keep, maintain what they had received. ἐν ἐπιγνώσει = rather 'intimate' than 'full' knowledge, close application of mind rather than mastery, though the latter follows in due degree. Cf. Robinson, *Eph.* 248 f.; Moulton, p. 113; cf. iii. 20, x. 2; Phil. i. 9; cf. 2 Cor. xiii. 5 f.

ἀδόκιμον νοῦν—νοῦς the mind as originating purposed action, good or bad. ἀδόκιμος, unable to stand the test which is properly applied to it; cf. 2 Cor. *l.c.*; Heb. vi. 8.

29. This catalogue of sins emphasises the false relations of man to man as following upon the false relation of men to God and the false conception of the proper use of man's own nature. The classification is only partially systematic, 29 a the mental dispositions, 29 b—31 the dispositions seen in various kinds of action.

32. οἵτινες κ.τ.λ. define once more the root of the evil—rejection of known truth—here as to the fixed judgment of God on such acts and persons.

τὸ δικαίωμα = the just decision or claim, cf. ii. 26, viii. 4; Lk. i. 6, not so much of the judge as of the legislator. The word and its cognates used of a judge seem always to imply acquittal.

πράσσοντες. Practise—methodically and deliberately. ποιοῦσιν = commit the acts, without necessarily implying deliberation.

συνευδοκοῦσιν, join with deliberate and hearty purpose. There is a true climax. A conspiracy of evil is worse than isolated actions, because it indicates the set tendency of the heart. Cf. S.H.; cf. Lk. xi. 48; Acts viii. 1, xxii. 20. N. the *Test. of the Twelve Patriarchs*, Ash. vi. 2, καὶ πράσσουσι τὸ κακὸν καὶ συνευδοκοῦσι τοῖς πράσσουσιν. Charles regards this passage as the original of our verse here.

CHAPTER II.

1—16. GOD's wrath, thus revealed in human life through the consequences of man's rejection of GOD, is also seen in the judgment of GOD upon man's conduct—the only just judgment (1) because all men being implicated no man has the right to judge, and (4) a just judgment because GOD has offered man the opportunity of repentance and (5) judges wilful wrongdoing (6) by the main tendencies of a man's life, (9) without favour to any privileged race, (12) in accordance with opportunities given even to Gentiles and (14) the use made of knowledge admittedly possessed even by Gentiles. This section is closely connected with the preceding by the διὸ and by the verbal and sense echoes (ἀναπολόγητος, πράσσεις).

1. ἀναπολόγητος κ.τ.λ. The consequence of this state of man, being universal, is that there is no excuse for men judging their neighbours. The statement is quite general; but vv. 9—11 show that the Apostle is thinking in particular of the Jew's wholesale condemnation of Gentiles and justification of himself.

κρίνεις...κατακρίνεις, the mere attitude of judgment is a condemnation of thyself; cf. Mt. vii. 1 f.; Lk. vi. 37.

τὸν ἕτερον, thy neighbour or thy fellow-man; cf. xiii. 8; 1 Cor. vi. 1, x. 24, al.

τὰ γὰρ αὐτὰ πράσσεις, whether you realise it or not—developed, for the Jew, in vv. 21 f.

2. τὸ κρίμα τοῦ θεοῦ. The ὀργή is now conceived as an act of judgment.

κατὰ ἀλήθειαν, in accordance with truth—i.e. the true facts of GOD's nature and man's condition. Moral judgment ought to express the actual mind of the judge in relation to the case submitted to him. This is the case with GOD's judgment, not with man's as here considered. Man can judge only so far as he is making his own the mind of GOD; cf. 1 Cor. v. 3. GOD's judgment is just because it corresponds to facts.

3. The nexus seems to be this: do you calculate that this correct attitude towards sin in others will exempt your case from being considered by GOD, or are you merely indifferent to His merciful dealing with you? The case is put in the most general way and

applies to all theoretic judgment of others ; but the crucial instance
in mind is the Jew ; cf. *vv.* 17 ff.

ἐκφεύξῃ, shalt clean escape ; cf. Lk. xxi. 36; Heb. ii. 3.

4. χρηστότητος.   The word has special reference to GOD's
generous gifts to men ; cf. xi. 22 ; Eph. ii. 7 ; Tit. iii. 4.   Here=the
generosity which has conferred graces and benefits which the man,
who presumes to judge, mistakes for special excellences of his own,
and so makes light of the Giver ; e.g. cf. *vv.* 17 f.

τῆς ἀνοχῆς, 'forbearance,' iii. 26 ; cf. Acts xvii. 30.   μακρο-
θυμία=the long continuance of χρηστότης and ἀνοχή in spite of men's
ways : a favourite word with S. Paul.   Cf. Ps. vii. 11, the adjective
freq. of GOD in O. T.; cf. 1 Pet. iii. 20.

ἀγνοῶν.   Once more man misses the aim which GOD proposes.

τὸ χρηστὸν.   The neut. adj. for the abstract subst.=ἡ χρηστότης.
For the thought, 2 Pet. iii. 15.

ἄγει, 'is (always) leading thee,' a good instance of the linear
action of the present, describing tendency not fulfilled.

5. δὲ κ.τ.λ. =however you are deceiving yourself all the while, in
fact you are storing up wrath.

κατὰ τὴν σκλ.   Deut. ix. 27 ; cf. Mt. xix. 8; Acts vii. 51.   κατὰ,
the hardness and unrepentant heart is the measure of the wrath
stored up.

ἀμετανόητον.   Only here.

θησαυρίζεις.   Cf. James v. 3.   Contrast Mt. vi. 23.   It is the man's
own act.

ἐν ἡ. ὀ.   Rev. vi. 17 only in N.T.; cf. Zeph. i. 15, 18, ii. 3.

καὶ ἀποκαλύψεως.   When there will be no evading the true facts.

δικαιοκρισίας.   Hos. vi. 5 (Quinta Orig. *Hex. ad loc.*) only in
Greek Bible; =righteousness in judging, excluding favouritism.

6. ὃς ἀποδώσει.   Cf. Ps. lxii. 3 ; Prov. xxiv. 12.

τὰ ἔργα.   The judgment will correspond to the man's real character
as shown by the works he produces, not as merits that earn but as
evidence of character : the works are then described in *vv.* 8 f. as the
main effort and tendency of a man's life, the temper which governs
him, and the aims he affects.

7. τοῖς μὲν.   Explanatory, therefore the asyndeton.   The rhythmical movement and the balanced antitheses of these clauses decide
two ambiguities : (1) ζητοῦσιν governs the preceding accusatives ;
(2) there should be a colon at θυμός ; θλ. κ. στ. begin the second pair
of antitheses.   The whole structure is noticeable.   Cf. Joh. Weiss
Theol. Stud. D. B. Weiss *dargeb.*, Göttingen, 1897.

καθ' ὑπομονὴν ἔ. ἀ.   The temper by which the life is directed.

ὑπ. =perseverance against opposition. The gen. ∝ in good work; cf. 1 Thes. i. 3.

δόξαν καὶ τ. κ. ἀ. with ζητοῦσιν, describing the aims of the life; cf. i. 23, 24. The reflection of the known character of GOD in his own life is a man's proper aim: and the gift of GOD by which that aim is ultimately secured is ζωὴ αἰώνιος, which again is represented in the third clause as δ. κ. τ. καὶ εἰρήνη. The three words here, then, describe the perfected life of man, his true aim. For δόξα in this sense cf. ix. 23; 2 Cor. iii. 18; for τιμή cf. 1 Pet. i. 7 (see Hort, ref. Ps. viii. 6; Rom. ix. 21; 2 Tim. ii. 20); for ἀφθαρσία cf. 1 Cor. ix. 25, xv. 42; 1 Pet. i. 4; Eph. vi. 24 (see Robinson) =immortality.

ζωὴν αἰώνιον. Cf. vi. 23; Gal. vi. 8; cf. Dan. xii. 2; 2 Macc. vii. 9; 4 Macc. xv. 3 only *ap*. LXX. In Synoptics, of the life of the coming age, cf. Mk x. 17, 30. Eternal life, the peculiar condition of GOD, is His consummate gift to man, operative in present conditions but consummated only in the future, the sum and crown of all His other gifts; cf. also vi. 22; 1 Tim. i. 16, vi. 12; Tit. i. 2, iii. 7; cf. Westcott on Joh. iv. 14.

8. ἐξ ἐριθίας. From the literal sense of 'work for hire,' through the political sense of 'self-seeking or partisan factiousness' (cf. Gal. v. 20), the word gets the general ethical sense of 'self-seeking' (cf. Phil. ii. 3; James iii. 16) to the disregard of service, whether of GOD or man. So =μισθαρνία, ambitus, Wetst. *ad loc*. Here in sharp contrast to καθ' ὑπ. ἔ. ἀ. (See Hort on James iii. 14.)

ἀπειθοῦσι κ.τ.λ. sum up the description given i. 21—32. Disobedience to known truth is again the condition of judgment; cf. xi. 30—33.

τῇ ἀληθείᾳ includes as above, i. 18, truth of act and life as is emphasised by the parallelism with δ. κ. τιμ. κ. ἀφθ. ζητοῦσιν, and so)(τῇ ἀδικίᾳ.

ὀργὴ καὶ θυμός. N. the change of construction : "ὀργή the settled feeling, θυμός the outward manifestation," S. H.

9. θλίψις καὶ στενοχωρία. These words must be separated from ὁ. κ. θ.: they begin the second pair of antitheses; the adoption of the false and wrong aim worries and narrows the whole life; cf. viii. 35; 2 Cor. iv. 8, vi. 12. But the direct reference here again is to the final state, consequent on judgment.

ἐπὶ π. ψ. κ.τ.λ. pick up and enforce τοῖς ἐξ ἐρ. κ.τ.λ. and emphasise the universality of the judgment and the single condition τὰ ἔργα; the underlying thought then comes to the surface in Ἰουδαίου κ.τ.λ.; for this pair of antitheses the dominant thought is the universality of the judgment, as in the first pair its certainty and quality.

10. εἰρήνη replaces ἀφθαρσία, wider and more ethical : peace with GOD and man, characterising the true life ; in contrast also with ἐξ ἐριθείας.

11. οὐ γάρ ἐστιν προσωπολημψία. The fundamental quality of the righteous judge. Cf. Deut. x. 17 ; Mt. xxii. 16 ‖ Lk. xx. 21 ; Gal. ii. 6 ; Eph. vi. 9, *al.*

παρὰ τῷ θεῷ, 'with GOD,' that is, in Him and His acts, as judge ; for this use of παρά (for ἐν) due to reverence, cf. Hort on James i. 17 (p. 30), cft Mk x. 27.

12—16. These verses bring out, further, the principle of judgment in accordance with the opportunities a man has had and the use he has made of them. Privilege does not exempt from judgment but heightens responsibility ; nor does the absence of privilege exempt, provided there is some knowledge which demands corresponding action. The special object of these verses is to justify the in-clusion of Gentiles under the judgment of GOD. In *v.* 17 we pass to the case of the Jew.

12. ὅσοι. All without distinction.

ἀνόμως. The antithesis ἐν νόμῳ and διὰ νόμου and the parallel τὰ μὴ νόμον ἔχοντα, prove that ἀν.=without law (not 'against law,' as 1 Tim. i. 9 (?)) ; cf. 1 Cor. ix. 21. In fact it is arguable that ἄνομος should always be taken in this sense in N. T. See on 14.

ἥμαρτον, in accordance with the whole preceding argument, implies acting against knowledge, even though that knowledge has not been given in explicit law ; *v.* 4 f. explain how it was given. See Add. Note D, on ἁμαρτία, p. 213.

Aor. most simply taken as 'timeless' ; cf. Moulton, p. 134 ; Burton, § 54, who calls it 'collective.' The aorist expresses fundamentally 'action at a point' or action simply in itself without time reference. A special difficulty arises in the indicative because the augment gives a reference to past time : but as the present is properly durative, it is natural that the necessity for expressing simple action should lead to the use of the aorist in this sense, in spite of the effect of the augment : so I take it here and iii. 23 and tr. 'all that sin.' Other-wise, it should be translated by the future perfect, under the influence of the future in the apodosis.

13. οὐ γάρ justifies the latter clause of 12. If law is a ground of sinning, law must be done, if a verdict of acquittal is to be gained.

δικαιωθήσονται. A clear case of the forensic use of δικαιοῦν=shall be acquitted. See Introduction, p. xxxvi.

14. ὅταν γάρ. The principle of *v.* 13 applies to Gentiles, only we have to think not of explicit law, but of knowledge of right and wrong evidenced in their conscience and utterances.

Suspicion has been cast on these verses (14, 15) on the ground that they interrupt, both the rhythmical antitheses, and the argumentative structure of the passage (*v.* 16 returning to *v.* 13). Some take them as a later comment, though in strict accordance with the principles of the passage; some as a marginal note by S. Paul himself. But their genuineness is indicated by the fact that they are not only in accordance with but strictly necessary to the argument; for it is essential to make it clear here in what sense Gentiles are in relation to law : only if in such relation could they be amenable to judgment. Cf. J. Weiss, *op. cit.* p. 218 n.

ἔθνη. Gentiles as such.

τὰ μὴ νόμον ἔχοντα. The admitted condition of ἔθνη.

φύσει with ποιῶσιν = without the help of an external revelation in law; cf. Eph. ii. 3 (n. Robinson) ; Gal. ii. 15, iv. 8. φύσις, morally neutral, depends on man's use ; cf. i. 26, ii. 27.

τὸ τοῦ νόμου = the acts prescribed by such a revealed law.

ἑαυτοῖς εἰσὶν νόμος. Here S. Paul boldly applies the term νόμος to the condition which has just been described as ἄνομος. They have no law outside themselves ; but the knowledge of GOD, which they have, takes the place of revealed law and may even be called law for them. It is a good instance of the way in which S. Paul goes behind the ordinary use of language and cuts down to the vital nerve of thought. See further in ch. vii., viii. 1—4.

15. οἵτινες explains the preceding phrase.

ἐνδείκνυνται, 'give proof of'; cf. ix. 17; cf. 2 Cor. viii. 24; Eph. ii. 7 ; i.e. by their actions. The fact that moral goodness is found in Gentiles is assumed throughout this argument as much as the fact that all sin.

τὸ ἔργον τοῦ νόμου. Not the law itself, but that effect which is produced by the law in those who have it. Not = "the course of conduct prescribed by the law " (S. H.) ; that could hardly be described as 'written in the heart'; but "the knowledge of GOD's will, of right and wrong," which is found in all human consciousness, and in a heightened degree in those who have an external law; cf. vii. 7 f. ; ‖ therefore to i. 19, 21, and different from iii. 20, 28 ; cf. Gal. v. 19 ; perhaps James i. 4 ; 1 Thes. i. 3 ; 1 Cor. ix. 1 ; Mt. xi. 19. (Ewald, *de voce* συνειδήσεως p. 17, after Grotius, qu. S. H.)

γραπτὸν ἐν τ. κ. α. Cf. for the metaphor 2 Cor. iii. 2. On καρδία the seat of knowledge and will, see above, i. 24. Cf. Weiss, *Theol.* p. 250.

συνμαρτυρούσης κ.τ.λ., explain the nature of the ἔνδειξις; cf. i. 21.
The cpd vb only here and viii. 16, ix. 1. In the two latter places
the force of the συν- is clear from the context. Here apparently the
other witness is 'their actions'; cf. 2 Cor. i. 12. It is possible,
however, that the συν- is merely 'perfective.' Cf. Moulton, p. 113.

τῆς συνειδήσεως. The primary idea of the word is (1) 'consciousness' as due to reflection, on the model of the use of the verb
συνειδέναι ἑαυτῷ τι, 'to be conscious of an experience good or bad';
on this follows the meaning (2) 'experience' as the sum of reflective
consciousness or self-knowledge, subjective always; and (3) so the
'feeling' which admits or rejects as alien a new candidate for admission into a man's sum of experience; then (4), as a special
development of the last meaning, 'conscience' as suggesting moral
judgments. See Add. Note, p. 208. Here = (2) 'their conscious experience'; the effect of the law is recognisably part of their mental
equipment or consciousness, their stock of ideas; the next clause
then explains how their consciousness bears this witness.

μεταξὺ ἀλλήλων = as between each other, in mutual intercourse:
it is the mutual intercourse of men which arouses the moral
judgment, even when that moral judgment is exercised upon the
man's own experience, as here; cf. S.H. This is an instance of the
development of personality by social relations. Cf. Ward, *The Realm
of Ends* (1911), p. 366.

τῶν λογισμῶν. Their thoughts exhibit moral judgments, pre-
supposing that knowledge which is the effect of the law. For
λογισμοί cf. 2 Cor. x. 5 only, freq. in LXX. Here = reflexion
passing moral judgment on the contents of consciousness. (In
4 Macc. = reason as master of the passions and champion of piety.)
This interpretation seems to be necessitated not only by the regular
use of λογισμός but also by the context; n. esp. τὰ κρυπτὰ τῶν
ἀνθρώπων, 16.

ἢ καὶ ἀπολογουμένων. The approval of conscience rarer than the
condemnation, but not unknown.

16. ἐν ᾗ ἡμέρᾳ κ.τ.λ. = at the assize (by the judgment) of GOD who
judges not by privilege or appearance but by the secret contents of a
man's heart: to be taken with the whole of the preceding sentence,
as supporting the analysis of the Gentile state by appeal to the
method by which GOD judges. Gentiles clearly have this knowledge,
etc., if judged as GOD judges by the unseen state of their hearts.

For ἡμέρα in this sense cf. 1 Cor. iv. 3, perh. also above, *v.* 5.

If to avoid the obvious difficulties of this interpretation we look for
some other connexion for ἐν ᾗ ἡ., we must go back to *v.* 12 and regard

the two clauses introduced by γὰρ as parenthetic. The objections to such a conception of the passage may be modified, if we remember that it was in all probability dictated, and we can imagine that in the speaker's pause, while these two clauses were being written down, his mind recurred to the main subject of the paragraph, and he concludes with the thought of the final assize.

κρίνει. If we read the present, the stress is laid on the general principles of GOD's judgment; if the future (κρινεῖ, cf. iii. 6) on the certain judgment itself.

κατὰ τὸ εὐαγγέλιόν μου. The judgment was a primary element of the Gospel as presented to Gentiles (Acts xvii. 31, xxiv. 25), and as a judgment of character, rather than of acts : and this quality of the judgment was involved in its being administered through the agency of Christ Jesus, who is Himself the judge, as being Himself the standard, of human goodness.

17—iii. 20. The Gospel is needed by Jews, who have also failed through ignoring the one condition of righteousness.

17. Under the same principle comes the Jew, who has full and privileged opportunities (21) and yet makes ill use of them by open unrighteousness (25) from the consequences of which no privilege can deliver him in face of a judgment which considers character and not privilege. (iii. 1) His advantage was an exceptional trust given by GOD, which his failure does not impair, as on GOD's part, though it justifies his punishment, but not himself. (9) He is, therefore, as sinning against knowledge, a state foreseen in O. T., under the same condemnation as the Gentile, law having given to him the knowledge which makes wrongdoing into sin.

This section shows explicitly that the Jew belongs to the class τῶν τὴν ἀλήθειαν ἐν ἀδικίᾳ κατεχόντων. They possess the truth, vv. 17—20, ἐν ἀδικίᾳ, 21 ff. Here, as there is no dispute as to fact, the Jew obviously possessing the truth, the main argument is directed to his supposed plea, that his specially privileged position exempts him from condemnation (iii. 1—20).

It is important to realise that the whole stress is laid on acting upon knowledge, whether embodied in human consciousness or in an external law; it is this duty of obedience which is the characteristic demand of the pre-Christian dispensation; and its exposition leads to the conclusion that all have sinned and are amenable to judgment, as all have failed to obey law, in one form or another. Cf. S.H., p. 58, Lft, Gal. iv. 11, Hort, R. & E. p. 25.

17. εἰ δέ. Apodosis v. 21; on the construction cf. Winer-M., p. 711 (who keeps εἰ δέ), Blass, p. 284 (who prefers ἴδε ; so Field ad

loc.). If we read εἰ δέ it is a case of anacoluthon, of a quite intelligible kind. The nexus supports εἰ δέ. He is passing from the case of the Gentile to the case of the Jew with his special conditions; and the particle of contrast is required.

Ἰουδαῖος)(Ἕλλην marks nationality, but suggests too all that the distinctive nationality meant to the Jew; cf. Gal. ii. 4.

ἐπονομάζῃ. Only here in N. T. The ἐπί gives the force of a specific name, differentiating a part in a wider class. So here=not ἄνθρωπος only, but Ἰουδαῖος. Cf. Plato, *Protag.* 349 A, σοφιστὴν ἐπονομάζεις σεαυτόν.

ἐπαναπαύῃ κ.τ.λ. These clauses enumerate the details of the true prerogatives of the Jew, as called by GOD; so

καυχᾶσαι, in a good sense; all your boasting is in GOD and His dealings with you; cf. v. 11, 2 Cor. xi. 7.

18. τὸ θέλημα. Cf. Lft, *Revision*, p. 106, ed. 1; p. 118, ed. 2 (S. H.).

δοκιμάζεις. As above, i. 28, 'approvest, after testing.'

τὰ διαφέροντα=the things that are better, the better courses of conduct; cf. Phil. i. 10, and for the verb 1 Cor. xv. 41; Gal. iv. 1.

κατηχούμενος=being taught—all teaching at this time being oral; cf. Lk. i. 4; Gal. vi. 6.

19. πέποιθάς τε passes to the Jew's conviction of his true relation to other men.

ὁδηγὸν. Perh. an echo of Mt. xv. 14; cf. S. H.

20. ἔχοντα=as one who has.

τὴν μόρφωσιν=the true shaping. The Law was a true expression of the knowledge and truth of GOD; cf. vii. 12. On μορφή as the proper expression of the inner reality cf. Lft, *Phil.* 127 f.

τῆς γν. κ. τῆς ἀλ. Cf. τὸ θέλημα—all in the most general form.

ἐν τῷ νόμῳ. With ἔχοντα.

21—29. The nexus is marked by the particles—οὖν (21) sums up the privileges and introduces, in the form of questions, the contrast in the actual facts; γὰρ (24) implies the answer yes to the preceding questions and justifies it; γὰρ (25) explains how the event has come about, in spite of the privileges; οὖν (26) draws the conclusion, as to the relative position of Jew and Gentile; γὰρ (28) explains this conclusion as resting on the essential superiority of the moral and spiritual to the external and ritual.

21. οὖν. Well then, does practice correspond to prerogative? If not, prerogative does not exempt from judgment. The charge is put in the form of questions, by way of convicting the Jew in his own

conscience. He cannot plead not guilty. Much more forcible than bare statements.

22. ἱεροσυλεῖς. Cf. Acts xix. 37. S. H. refers to Jos. *Antiq.* iv. 8, 10; Lft, *Supern. Rel.* p. 299 f. ; Ramsay, *Ch. & R. E.* p. 144 n. ; Deut. vii. 26. The antithesis is less clear than in the former cases. The charge seems to be that, though they regard idols as 'abominable' things, they do not hesitate to make pecuniary advantage out of robbing temples.

23. ἀτιμάζεις; S. H. and Giff. support ἀτιμάζεις. and treat it as a direct statement summing up the points of the preceding questions. Yet the interrogative form is more forcible here too. The claim explicitly brings the Jews under the same imputation as the Gentiles, i. 21.

24. τὸ γὰρ ὄνομα κ.τ.λ. Isa. lii. 5; the words are adopted (practically in LXX. form), but in a new sense. Here of the contempt brought upon the Name of GOD by the lives of His professed worshippers; cf. xiv. 16; 1 Tim. vi. 1; Tit. ii. 5; 2 Pet. ii. 2.

25. περιτομὴ μὲν γὰρ κ.τ.λ. The explanation of the awful contrast between the formal condition of the Jew and his actual condition. περιτομή is the symbol of the whole covenant relation of the Jew with GOD. The symbol has no effect unless the condition imposed by the covenant is kept. It did not either excuse from or enable to obedience. Disobedience evacuates the formal position of all meaning. The 'weakness' of the covenant as a spiritual force is not however developed till ch. vii.

νόμον πράσσῃς, 'if you practise law,' in the tenour of your life: the absence of the article and the vb πράσσειν throw stress on the general character of the life, as distinct from particular acts; cf. vv. 1—3.

παραβάτης νόμου. So 'a law breaker'—in general.

26 f. It follows that the formal positions of Jew and Gentile may be reversed.

ἡ ἀκροβυστία. Abstract for concrete = the Gentiles ; to emphasise the absence of the formal condition.

τὰ δικαιώματα—the ordinances in detail as rules of life.

27. ἡ ἐκ φύσεως ἀκρ. This introduces the distinction between the external symbol and the spiritual condition.

τὸν νόμον τελοῦσα, 'if it keep...' or 'by keeping...': perhaps better = 'which keeps...,' τελοῦσα, adjectival, owing its position to the fact that there is a second adj., ἐκ φύσεως.

διὰ γράμματος καὶ περιτομῆς = under a condition of written law and circumcision : an advantageous condition as far as it goes. γρ.

is the external form of revelation, as περ. is the external form of the covenant. The emphasis is on the character of these forms; therefore anarthrous; and 'letter' is a better translation than 'scripture.' For this abstraction of the external form of scripture cf. vii. 6; 2 Cor. iii. 3. For διά *w.* *gen.*, expressing a condition or state, cf. iv. 11, viii. 25, xiv. 20; cf. Blass, p. 132 f.

28. The grammar is ambiguous, but the sense is clear. The outward state and sign, if they are to have spiritual value, demand a corresponding inward state; which itself has value, even if the outward is absent.

29. ἐν τῷ κρυπτῷ. Cf. *v.* 16; 1 Pet. iii. 4.

περιτομὴ καρδίας. Here the symbol becomes the reality; cf. Deut. x. 16; Jer. iv. 4, ix. 26; Ezek. xliv. 7; Acts vii. 51, S. H.

ὁ ἔπαινος. An allusion to Ἰουδαῖος, Judah = praise; cf. Gen. xxix. 35, xlix. 8, Giff.

CHAPTER III.

1—20. A brief statement of the true nature of the Jew's position, to be fully dealt with in chh. ix., x. (See p. 55.) The argument is thrown into the form of a dialogue.

1. τὸ περισσὸν = excess, good or bad. Mt. v. 37; cf. 1 Cor. viii. 8; 2 Cor. iii. 9. Here = advantage or relative gain.

2. πρῶτον μὲν γάρ.... The enumeration is not carried out, but cf. ix. 4, 5. γάρ simply introduces an explanation of the preceding statement. "γάρ saepe ponitur ubi propositionem excipit tractatio," Bengel on Lk. xii. 58, *ap.* Winer-M. p. 568 (*b*).

The drift of this very condensed argument is—the Jews received in charge the revelation of GOD's will and purpose in the scriptures; the failure of some to believe, when Christ offered them the consummation of that revelation, does not affect the validity of the revelation or diminish the privilege of the Jew as offered to him by GOD. The scriptures are still there ready to be used and a charge upon believers; the advantage of the Jew is still for him to take. The failure of some only emphasises by contrast the faithfulness of GOD.

ἐπιστεύθησαν. This pass. only in S. Paul; cf. 1 Cor. ix. 17; 1 Thes. ii. 4, *al.*

τὰ λόγια τοῦ θεοῦ. Heb. v. 12; 1 Pet. iv. 11; Acts vii. 38 only. The last passage is a close parallel in argument.

On the meaning cf. Westcott, *Hebr. l.c.*; Lft, *Supern. Rel.* p. 172 ff.; Sanday, *Gospels*, etc. p. 155. Orig. = brief sayings, oracles; but by use the word came to mean the scriptures. Cf. Clem. R. 1 *Cor.* liii. 1; and probably here it means the whole written record, but specifically as the utterance of GOD's Mind and Will.

3. τί γάρ; Phil. i. 18 only. Introduces an objection which must be met. The passage is closely condensed.

εἰ ἠπίστησαν. ἀπιστεῖν always = to disbelieve (from ἄπιστος = unbelieving), even prob. 2 Tim. ii. 13. The aor. refers to the definite act of the rejection of the Gospel, the climax of τὰ λόγια τοῦ θεοῦ; cf. xi. 20, and for the limitation in τινες cf. x. 16 and ix. 6, xi. 25.

τὴν πίστιν τοῦ θεοῦ, the faithfulness of GOD—apparently the only place in N.T. where the gen. in this or cognate phrases is subjective; but the sense is determined by ἀληθής *infra*; and the thought ‖ 1 Cor. i. 9; Heb. x. 23; 1 Thes. v. 24, *al.* S. H. qu. Lam. iii. 23; Ps. Sol. viii. 35 (only in LXX.). For πίστις in this sense cf. Mt. xxiii. 23; Gal. v. 22; 1 Tim. v. 12 (?); Tit. ii. 10. See Lft, *Gal.* p. 157; Hort, 1 *Pet.* p. 81.

καταργήσει. This seems to be a 'volitive' future, near akin to the 'deliberative' subjunctive: 'shall it really annul'='are we to allow it or suppose it to annul.' Cf. Moulton, pp. 150, 239; cf. ix. 20, appy the only ‖. For the thought cf. ix. 6, xi. 29. For καταργεῖν cf. iv. 14; Gal. iii. 17, *al.* Paul only exc. Lk. (1), Heb. (1); from the literal sense 'to make sterile or barren,' Lk. xiii. 7, the metaph. follows—'to deprive of effect, abrogate, annul.'

4. μὴ γένοιτο. Cf. S. H.; characteristic of S. Paul, and esp. of this group of epistles; expresses the vehement rejection of a possible but false inference.

γινέσθω δὲ κ.τ.λ. Let GOD prove or be proved.... **ἀληθής,** only here and Joh. iii. 33, viii. 26, of GOD=true to His word.

πᾶς ἄνθρ. ψ. Ps. cxv. 2 (cxvi. 10).

ὅπως ἂν κ.τ.λ. Ps. l. 6 (li.) (here νικήσεις for νικήσῃς). N. that LXX. mistranslate the Hebrew='when thou judgest.' S. Paul adopts the mistranslation, which puts it as though GOD Himself were on trial. Cf. S. H. **δικαιωθῇς**=be acquitted. For coord. of aor. subj. and fut. indic. see Blass, p. 212. Burton, §§ 198, 199.

5. εἰ δὲ introduces, in order to remove, a difficulty suggested by this argument: if the confession of man's sin has for its result the vindication of GOD's righteousness, is not that a justification of the sin? It is met by an appeal (1) to a fundamental postulate of GOD's judgment, (2) to a fundamental axiom of man's conduct (*v.* 8). It is not examined in its own elements till ch. xi.

ἡμῶν, of us men.

θ. δικ., righteousness in GOD; here of the character of GOD as a righteous judge.

συνίστησιν establishes by way of proof (cf. v. 8, Gal. ii. 18) from the literal sense 'construct a whole of various parts.'

τί ἐροῦμεν. Characteristic of this Ep.; cf. μὴ γένοιτο, above.

μή, can it really be that...? Puts a question with the implication of a decided negative. Is it a wrong thing to punish that conduct which brings into greater clearness the righteousness of GOD?

τὴν ὀργήν. The wrath which has been already described (i. 18 f.) in judgment.

κατὰ ἄνθρωπον. In S. Paul only; cf. esp. 1 Cor. ix. 8; Gal. iii. 15;

cf. the vocative in ix. 20 : = after a merely human manner, so here 'after an ordinary way of men's speaking, in their bold blaming of GOD.' Common in classical Greek (cf. Wetstein), but with a different reference : in class. Gk = the normal, truly human, what is right and proper for man; in S. Paul = the merely human, what men do and say when uninfluenced by the divine grace and not responding to their true destiny. So it strikes a note of apology.

6. ἐπεί, 'or else,' 'otherwise'; cf. Field on xi. 22; cf. xi. 6; 1 Cor. xiv. 16, xv. 29; Heb. ix. 17. A good classical use; cf. Wetstein. Only in S. Paul and Heb.

πῶς κρινεῖ κ.τ.λ. It is a fundamental postulate that GOD is the Judge.

7. εἰ δὲ. The difficulty is restated more fully and is shown to imply the principle that 'the end justifies the means'; and that is a *reductio ad absurdum* of the argument.

ἐν τῷ ἐ. ψ. = in the fact of, or by, my lie.

ψεῦσμα. Only here = acted lie, falseness to trust, etc.

ἐπερίσσευσεν. The aor. used for a single typical case.

ἔτι, after that result. κἀγὼ, just I, whose conduct has led to that result.

8. καὶ μή. In loose construction after τί; strictly τί μὴ ποιήσωμεν κ.τ.λ. is required; but the insertion of the statement that this was actually charged against S. Paul breaks the construction.

καθὼς βλασφημούμεθα. S. Paul's polemic against the obligation of the law brought upon him the charge of antinomianism; cf. vi. 1 f.

ὧν τὸ κρίμα. The clear statement of the position furnishes its own condemnation, and the subject is for the time dismissed.

9. τί οὖν; well then, this being so, what follows? Cf. Joh. i. 21; *infra*, vi. 15, xi. 7 only. Cf. above on μὴ γένοιτο, τί οὖν ἐροῦμεν;

προεχόμεθα; 'are we surpassed? are we at a disadvantage?' So R.V. (not mg., not A.V.); see Field, *ad loc*. He shows (1) that there is no example of the mid. = the active 'are we better than these?' (2) that προέχεσθαι = to excuse oneself, always requires an accus.; (3) that προέχεσθαι = pass. of προέχειν, to surpass, is supported by a ||, and natural; qu. Plut. *T.* II. p. 1038 c after Wetstein.

With the meaning settled, it remains to ask, who are *we*? and what is the connexion? The question must be taken, dramatically, as put into the mouth of Jews. It has been just shown that while they had an exceptional privilege, their use of this privilege brought

them under judgment. The privilege itself might then appear to be
a penalty, the greater call only an occasion of greater condemnation
(cf. closely vi. 15). The answer given does not go to the root of the
matter—that again is reserved for chh. ix. 30—x. 13—but deals with
it only for the purpose of the immediate argument; all have sinned,
and as sinners all are equally condemned; yet in a certain sense (n. οὐ
πάντως) Jews are in a worse state, because they have sinned against
clearer light; yet, again, not to such an extent as to put them at
a disadvantage in regard to the new dispensation of the Gospel.
The universality of grace covers the universality of sin, and is for
all adequate and complete (*vv.* 21 f.).

This horror-struck question of the Jews, then, rises immediately
out of the preceding verses, and the answer completes the statement
of their case in comparison with Gentiles. The vigorous dramatic
form of expression is due to the depth of feeling with which S. Paul
sympathises with his brethren after the flesh.

οὐ πάντως. 1 Cor. v. 10 only; not altogether that, either. See
above.

προητιασάμεθα only here in Greek appy. So προενάρχομαι, 2 Cor.
viii. 6; προελπίζω, Eph. i. 12 (first); προκυροῦν, Gal. iii. 17. The ref.
is esp. to i. 18, ii. 1, 9.

ὑφ᾽ ἁμαρτίαν. Cf. Moulton, p. 63, for the disuse of the dative
after ὑπό. Cf. vii. 14; Mt. viii. 9. = in subjection to sin and therefore needing deliverance. The whole object of these chapters is to
show the universal need of the Gospel.

πάντας includes on this side the παντί of i. 16.

10—18. This string of quotations is adduced to justify from
Scripture the assertion of *v.* 9. On the Rabbinic practice of stringing
quotations cf. S. H., who instance also ix. 25 f., 2 Cor. vii. 16, *al.*
The references are (W. H.) Ps. xiv. (xiii.) 1 ff., v. 9, cxl. (cxxxix.)
3, x. 7 (ix. 28); Isa. lix. 7 f.; Ps. xxxvi. (xxxv.) 1. The quotation is
free in 10, 14, 15—17. On the reaction of this passage on text of
Psalms cf. S. H.

11. συνίων, for form, as from συνίω, cf. Moulton, pp. 38, 55,
Hort, Introduction to App. i. 167, Thackeray, *Gr. of O.T. Gk*, pp. 244,
250.

12. ἠχρεώθησαν. Cf. Lk. xvii. 10 (ἄχρειος). Lost their use,
became good for nothing.

13. ἐδολιοῦσαν. Hebr. 'make smooth their tongue,' R.V. mg.,
Ps. v. 9 only, in Gk Bible. Prop.=deceived; form=imperf. with
aor. term. Cf. Thackeray, *op. cit.* p. 214.

19. οἴδαμεν δέ. What is the connexion? The disadvantage of

the Jew has been shown not to be complete—Scripture being adduced
to support the statement that all are under sin. So far Jew and
Gentile are equal. But the Jew is brought more signally and
definitely under God's judgment, just because of his possession of
the law : the utterance of the law is in a special degree addressed to
him ; and he is less able, consequently, even than the Gentile to
maintain any plea against God. These verses, then, explain the
qualification contained in οὐ πάντως. In a certain sense he is at a
disadvantage as compared with the Gentile. Greater privilege involves greater responsibility. (So with Gifford, practically, though
not in detail.) We may say then, also, that we have here the final
answer to τί τὸ περισσὸν τοῦ 'I. (iii. 1). It was a true advantage to
have fuller light, even though it brought greater condemnation (cf. ἐν
δὲ φάει καὶ ὄλεσσον).

οἴδαμεν δὲ. δέ carries us back to v. 9, οὐ πάντως.

οἴδαμεν. Almost=of course.

ὁ νόμος. Not=τὰ λόγια, v. 2, but in its common sense 'the Mosaic
law.' S. Paul presses the point that the injunctions of the law are
meant for those who receive them, and by them the Jew is condemned, as against the plea of the Jew that his privileged position
exempts him from judgment. Cf. Gifford, ad loc. and on ii. 3.

φραγῇ. 2 Cor. xi. 10, Hebr. xi. 33 only. ἐμφράττειν more common
w. στόμα ; cf. Wetst.

ὑπόδικος. Only here in N.T. ; =liable to an action. The dative
seems always to be used of the person injured, not of the judge.
The metaphor, then, suggests a trial as between God and His
people.

20. διότι explains how law produces this effect. This sentence,
while having particular reference to the Jew, is thrown into the most
general form, so as to bring the Jew into line with the Gentile, and
then to sum up in one conclusion i. 18—iii. 19.

ἐξ ἔργων ν., put in the most general form : if works done in
obedience to law are taken as the basis of judgment.

οὐ δικαιωθήσεται, forensic. Cf. Gal. ii. 16, as ὑπόδικος ; will not
be acquitted when judged. Qu. Ps. cxliii. (cxlii.) 2.

ἐπίγνωσις. See n. on i. 28. Realisation of sin as sin is the specific
effect of law. Law is therefore educational, cf. Gal. iii. 24, but not in
itself a moral or spiritual force, cf. i. 32. The sentence here is not
strictly wanted for the argument, but crops up as an element in
S. Paul's view of law. It anticipates and is developed in c. vii. It is
important to observe that in i. 19—iii. 20 S. Paul bases his assertion of
the universality of sin and the consequent universal need of man, not

upon theory but on observation—his experience of human life, both
in Jewish and Gentile circles, generalised by the help of history. It
is a historical justification of the need of the Gospel, confirmed by
the testimony of scripture and by general experience. In c. vii. he
reaches the same conclusion by the searching analysis of his own
inner experience, treated as typical—what may be called the psychological justification. Cf. Giff. on iii. 18 *ad fin.*

21—31. The failure of Jew and Gentile alike is met by the new
dispensation of the Gospel, with the condition it demands of man,
faith. The argument having explained 'the revelation of wrath,'
returns to the statement of i. 16, 17, and amplifies it in a series of
summary propositions, which are developed and explained in cc. v. ff.
(21) Under the present dispensation, in the absence of law, there
has been an open declaration of GOD'S righteousness, not in itself
new because it is the same righteousness as the law and the prophets
declare, but new in the clearness of the declared condition by which
it is to be attained by man, i.e. faith in Jesus Christ, and in its
extension to all who have that faith, without distinction of race or
person; (23) for as sin is found in all and all fall short of that
divine likeness which GOD propounds to man, (24) so all are now
declared righteous, without merit on their part, by GOD'S free act
of grace, by means of that redemption and deliverance which is in
Christ Jesus. (25) He is indeed GOD'S appointed agent of propitiation, on condition of faith, by the instrumentality of His Blood,
shed to exhibit GOD'S righteousness which His patient endurance of
men's sins through so long a time had obscured, as the characteristic
message of the present season, that in the knowledge of all He may
be righteous and declare righteous all who begin with faith in Jesus.
(27) So there is no resting on privilege, where faith is the one
condition of acceptance with GOD, (28) a condition open to all
mankind (29) corresponding to the fact that there is but one GOD
for all men, who from covenanted and uncovenanted alike demands
nothing but faith. (31) This view of GOD'S revelation, so far from
annulling law, alone establishes it.

21. νυνὶ = ἐν τῷ νῦν καιρῷ, *v.* 26, as things now are, under the
Gospel dispensation.

χωρὶς νόμου, apart from law. The idea is that man no longer
has to look to law as GOD'S revelation of Himself, but to the Person
and character of Jesus Christ, not against or inconsistent with law
but fulfilling it; cf. Hort, *Jud. Chr.* p. 19; 2 Cor. iii. 12—18.

δικαιοσύνη θεοῦ. GOD'S righteousness as characteristic of Him,
and therefore the norm for human character; cf. Mt. v. 48.

πεφανέρωται, has been made manifest, and stands there for all to see; cf. xvi. 26 ; 2 Tim. i. 10 ; Ti. i. 3 ; esp. 1 Pet. i. 20; cf. Joh. i. 11, 14 ; 1 Joh. i. 2.

μαρτυρουμένη κ.τ.λ., so xvi. 26 marks the continuity of GOD's self-revelation : pres. part., because the law and the prophets still speak in the scriptures. The phrase sums up the O.T. revelation, the positive law and the comments of the prophets; cf. Mt. v. 17, xi. 13; Joh. i. 45 ; Acts xxviii. 23.

22. δικαιοσύνη δὲ, the phrase repeated with a qualification (not of law but by faith), introducing the distinctive condition, and so bringing into emphasis the fact that GOD's righteousness is the true aim which man must set before himself for realisation in his own life, so far as he may.

διὰ πίστεως 'I. Χρ. Phil. iii. 9 ; Gal. ii. 16. Gen. obj. = faith in Jesus Christ as the manifestation of GOD's righteousness ; see n. on i. 17. Both this and the next phrase (εἰς π. τ. π.) qualify δικαιοσύνη θεοῦ.

εἰς π. τ. π., i. 16, shows that faith is not one condition but the only condition imposed on man.

οὐ γάρ ἐστιν διαστολή. x. 12.

23. πάντες γάρ...τ. θ. resumes i. 19—iii. 20. ἥμαρτον is the 'constructive' or summary aorist, "which regards the whole action simply as having occurred, without distinguishing any steps in its progress" (Moulton, p. 109 ; cf. Burton, *M. T.* § 54), and so should be translated by the perfect 'have sinned,' and is naturally co-ordinate with the durative present, describing the actual state; see on ii. 12.

ὑστεροῦνται. The middle of this verb seems to imply, not merely to fall short of a goal (act.), but to be lacking in something of which the need is felt or at least obvious. Cf. Mt. xix. 20 with 1 Cor. viii. 8 and 2 Cor. xi. 5 with Phil. iv. 12 ; Heb. xii. 15: ' comes short of ' A.V., 'fall short of' R.V. both therefore seem inadequate translations. Perhaps 'lack' will do. Their lives and characters obviously show the lack of ' the glory of GOD.'

τῆς δόξης τοῦ θεοῦ consequently = that exhibition of GOD in their own character, which is man's proper work : implying the idea of Gen. i. 26, 27 ; cf. 1 Cor. xi. 7 ; 2 Cor. iii. 18, and Irenaeus, " vivens homo gloria Dei," and probably *infra*, v. 2 and n. 1 Cor. vi. 20. See S. H. *ad loc.* GOD is not seen in them as He ought to be seen. The same thought is expressed by the verb in i. 21. See n. on ii. 7.

24. δικαιούμενοι δωρεὰν κ.τ.λ., 'being declared righteous (so far as they are so declared) by a free act of GOD.' The participle adds

a third element to the description of the universal state, and returns to the thought of *v.* 22, εἰς πάντας τ. π., introducing the further specification of the means of 'justification.' δωρεάν is the emphatic word and is therefore expanded by τῇ α. χάριτι, ‖ χωρὶς νόμου, *v.* 21.

τῇ αὐ. χ. The free grace of GOD is the source of justification; πίστις, the human condition; ἡ ἀπολ. the means: αὐτοῦ is emphatic —by *His* gift, not by *their* desert.

διὰ τῆς ἀπολυτρώσεως. Cf. Heb. ix. 15; Westcott, *ib.* p. 295. The scriptural idea of ἀπολύτρωσις is redemption from an alien yoke: orig. of Egypt, then of any yoke other than that of GOD; here the yoke of sin. The word implies the cost of redemption to him that brings it about; and does not involve (as used) a price paid to the alien master. The whole class of words is specially characteristic of S. Paul, in accordance with the essentially historical and experimental character of his religious position. The point here is, then, that man is delivered from that general state of sin by the free act of GOD working through Jesus Christ, and requiring only trust on the part of man for its realisation.

τῆς ἐν Χρ. 'Ι. ἐν Χρ. 'Ι. and ἐν Χρ. always relate to the glorified Christ, not to the historic Jesus, S. H.

25. ὃν προέθετο κ.τ.λ., explains in a very condensed way how GOD redeems man by Christ Jesus.

προέθετο, cf. πεφανέρωται, *v.* 21; cf. Heb. ix. 26. Vb occurs only i. 13, Eph. i. 9; means (1) to purpose, (2) to publish: here, only, the latter, 'set forth on His part'; cf. Polyb. ii. 19. 1; iii. 62. 1 (=proponere, ob oculos ponere, Schweigh.). The whole passage dwells on the new revelation given by GOD, for the purpose of doing what could not be done by the emphasised elements of the former revelation; so it is not so much yet the purpose of GOD as the revelation of that purpose which is in question. The 'publication' was given (aor.) in the Resurrection and Ascension as the act of GOD (cf. i. 4).

ἱλαστήριον. The thought of the redemption of man from his subjection to sin raises the question of GOD's dealing with sin: the fact of permitted sin affects both man's conception of the righteous-ness of GOD, and his actual relation towards GOD. Here, then, S. Paul cuts deeper; but still all is summary and here unexplained (see viii. 1). ἱλαστ. consequently expresses the character of the ascended Lord, as making acceptable to GOD those who were not. in and by themselves acceptable. He in His Person and Work is the agent of propitiation. And the way in which He has achieved propitiation vindicates the righteousness of GOD (ἐν τῷ αὐ. .αἱ.) and offers righteousness to men (διὰ πίστεως). The context, then, leads us to take ἱλ. as an adjective (accus. masc.), and this is justified by use current at the time, and by the true interpretation of LXX. (cf. Deismann, B. S. I. p. 128; S. H., ad loc.; cf. Westcott, Epp. Joh. pp. 39, 83 f.; Heb. ii. 17).

διὰ πίστεως, the means by which man makes the propitiation his own.

ἐν τῷ αὐ. αἵματι, the means by which He effects propitiation. Eph. ii. 13 (cf. Col. i. 20), Eph. i. 7 (cf. 1 Joh. i. 7; 1 Pet. i. 19), explain the idea : the Blood shed on the Cross and offered from the Throne is that which makes man acceptable to God, puts away his sin (ἄφεσις, not πάρεσις), brings him home from the far country, makes him at peace where he was at enmity. So that the Blood indicates not only the Death, but always also the Life offered to God and communicated to man; this is indicated here by ἐν Χρ. Ἰησ., v. 24, see above; cf. Westcott, Epp. Joh. pp. 34 f. ἐν τῷ θανάτῳ could not be substituted here; cf. Acts xx. 28. ἐν, instrumental=διὰ w. gen. The two phrases διὰ πίστεως, ἐν τῷ a. al. are ∥.

εἰς ἔνδειξιν κ.τ.λ. This phrase depends on προέθ. ἱλ. : while διὰ τὴν πάρεσιν...καιρῷ all go together, and explain the need of ἔν-δειξιν.

τῆς δικαιοσύνης αὐτοῦ. The character of God as righteous might seem to be impugned by His allowance of sin, and required to be vindicated. It was vindicated, because the Cross showed God's eternal hostility to sin; cf. S. H.

διὰ τὴν πάρεσιν κ.τ.λ. πάρεσις only here = letting go, passing by; cf. Acts xiv. 16, xvii. 30; cf. ii. 4; Mk ix. 19; Lk. xviii. 7; 2 Pet. iii. 15.

ἐν τῇ ἀνοχῇ explains τὴν πάρεσιν.

26. πρὸς τὴν ἔνδειξιν, the exhibition already referred to, i. 17.

τῆς δικαιοσύνης αὐτοῦ. Here in the wider sense of i. 17, etc., His righteousness in itself and as offered to man.

εἰς τὸ εἶναι κ.τ.λ. sums up both strains. καὶ δικαιοῦντα = even when He justifies.

τὸν ἐκ πίστεως. See v. 30.

πίστεως Ἰησοῦ. Cf. Rev. xiv. 12, the only other place where the exact phrase occurs. The simple name Ἰ. is relatively rare (after Evv. and Acts). In S. Paul, its use always emphasises 'the Humanity'—generally in reference to the Resurrection (e.g. viii. 11), but also in reference to the whole Life and Character exhibited on earth. So the Christian confession is Κύριος Ἰησοῦς and the denial of it ἀνάθεμα Ἰησοῦς (1 Cor. xii. 3; 2 Cor. xi. 4; Phil. ii. 10); the manner

of the Life on earth is a precedent for and vindication of the manner
of the Apostles' lives (2 Cor. iv. 5—11; cf. Gal. iv. 17); truth is there
seen as man can see it (Eph. iv. 21); parallel in thought, though not
in expression, are 1 Joh. iv. 3, 15; Rev. i. 9; Joh. xiv. 1. So here=
faith in Jesus as, in His human Life and Character, revealing as man
can see it the righteousness of GOD.

27. ποῦ οὖν ἡ καύχησις; Cf. ii. 17, 22. This whole practice and
temper of mind is here set aside, as inconsistent with the truth of
man's common relation to GOD. The class of words is almost confined to S. Paul.

διὰ ποίου νόμου; under what kind of law? So better than *by*...;
cf. iv. 3; n. on iii. 27. The law which required for its satisfaction
works might leave room for assertion of personal superiority; but
a law of which the only requirement is faith or trust can leave no
room for such; all that is done in that case is done by GOD. With
τῶν ἔργων τοῦ νόμου must be supplied, and the reference is to the claim
of the Jew. But in νόμου π. a wider sense of νόμος is introduced.

διὰ νόμου πίστεως. A unique phrase. S. Paul cuts to the nerve
of νόμος here, as = GOD's revealed will. That will is now revealed in
Christ Jesus; He is now GOD's law. Man does law only as Christ
is it and does it in him, and this requires faith in Christ; so it is a
law requiring not works but faith. The essence of faith as a basis of
morals is the acceptance of Another's works and a recognition that
all personal achievement is due to that Other. For a similar appeal,
as it were, to the deepest meaning of the word, cf. viii. 1, as startling
after the argument of c. vii., as it is here. Cf. for a similar paradox
James i. 25; Joh. vi. 29; 1 Joh. iii. 23.

28. γάρ. Context is decisive in favour of this reading: the clause
refers to the argument of i. 17, iii. 20, as supporting the statement
that boasting is excluded, and is not a fresh conclusion from *v.* 27.

29. ἢ Ἰουδαίων κ.τ.λ. presses the argument deeper; not only is
righteousness a matter of faith which all men can exercise, but GOD
is one—one and the same for all mankind; all men are in the same
relation to Him, and He will justify all on the same condition.

30. εἴπερ, if as is the fact; cf. viii. 9, 17; 2 Thes. i. 6;
2 Cor. v. 3 (v.l.); diff. 1 Cor. xv. 15=if as they maintain (with ἄρα).

εἷς ὁ θεός. Cf. 1 Cor. viii. 4; Gal. iii. 20; Eph. iv. 6; 1 Tim. ii. 5;
James ii. 19: always in S. Paul as giving the ground for the unity of
mankind and the universality of the Gospel.

ἐκ, διά. No essential difference: ἐκ=as the result of, in implied
contrast with ἐξ ἔργων νόμου; cf. ix. 31: διά=by means of the exercise
of faith, which is now open to them.

31. νόμον οὖν κ.τ.λ. An anticipatory caution, worked out in ch. vi. The Gospel does not abolish law by insisting on faith as man's sole contribution; it represents law as fulfilled in Christ, and in man if he has faith in Christ; see above on νόμου πίστεως. Practically a summary of the treatment of law in Mt. v. νόμος here is not limited to, though it includes, the Mosaic law.

ἱστάνομεν. A later form of ἵστημι; cf. Thackeray, p. 247; Moulton, p. 55. Only here simpl.; cf. Acts xvii. 15 (καθ.); 1 Cor. xiii. 2 (μεθ.). συνιστάνω, 2 Cor. iii. 1, iv. 2, v. 12, vi. 4, x. 12; Gal. ii. 18.

The difficulty of this passage lies in its condensation; the clue is found when we see in it a return to i. 17, and amplification of that passage, with a view to fuller exposition in chh. v. ff.; in fact it restates the subject of the Epistle. In interpreting, we must bear in mind, as we saw on i. 17, that Christ Jesus is throughout the concrete righteousness of GOD.

CHAPTER IV.

c. iv. This condition of faith is already seen in Abraham, typical of righteousness under the covenant of promise.

(1) Abraham was admittedly a righteous man: but how did he become so? (3) The scripture connects his righteousness with his faith. (6) So David makes forgiveness an act of GOD's grace. (9) Nor is this grace confined to the Covenant people; for in Abraham's case the covenant was not the precedent but the confirmation of his righteousness, (11*b*) so that he is father (according to the promise) of all that believe though uncovenanted and of the covenanted only so far as they share his faith. (13) For the promise was given not under law but under a state of righteousness due to faith. (14) If the law is a condition of inheritance of Abraham, then Abraham's faith has no effect, and the promise made to him is annulled—for the effect of the law is wrath; where law is not, neither is there transgression. (16) And the reason for this dependence upon faith is clear: it is that righteousness may be absolutely GOD's gift, and therefore free, in fulfilment of the promise, to all the true seed of Abraham, that is to those who derive from him not by the link of the law but by that of faith, by virtue of which he, as the promise said, is father of all of us who believe, both Jews and Gentiles, (17*b*) all standing before the same GOD in whom Abraham believed, the GOD who quickens the dead and ascribes being to that which is not: (18) the particular act of faith required absolute trust in Him who gave the promise in spite of supreme difficulties, trust both in the truth and in the power of GOD. (22) This trust was reckoned for righteousness. (23) The incident has reference to us: righteousness will be reckoned to us too for our trust in GOD: for us too He has shown His truth and power by raising Jesus our Lord from death, delivered up for our transgressions and raised for our justification.

The case of Abraham is taken to illustrate the preceding argument: the Jews would quote it as a clear case of justification under the old covenant, and therefore presumably under law; it would follow that the promise made to Abraham was limited to his descendants who

were under the covenant of law. S. Paul points out, to the contrary, that here all depended on faith, and on an act of faith parallel
to that which the Gospel demands. It follows that the principle of
δικαιοσύνη ἐκ πίστεως held under the old dispensation as under the
new; and that in this respect as in others the Gospel is not a breach
with the old, but a revival of its fundamental principles in a form
in which they reach their perfect exemplification; cf. iii. 21. The
case of Abraham was a current thesis of the Rabbinic schools; cf.
Lightfoot, *Gal.*, p. 158 ff.

1. τί οὖν ἐροῦμεν = what shall we say of Abraham?..., i.e. in
relation to the question of boasting and the source of righteousness.
Zahn (*Einl.* p. 95, A₂) punctuates ἐροῦμεν ; and takes [εὑρ.] Ἀβραὰμ
...θεόν as stating an opposed view: but this is too complicated.

τὸν προπάτορα ἡμῶν. Addressed to Gentiles (as well as Jews);
cf. 11, 12 and 1 Cor. x. 1. The spiritual lineage is an essential strain
in S. Paul's conception of religious history.

κατὰ σάρκα. If this goes with προπάτορα then the whole clause
must be taken as a difficulty raised by a supposed Jew disputant.
But it is better taken with ἐροῦμεν in relation to ἐξ ἔργων of v. 2 and
περιτομή, v. 9 ff. = as regards his human condition—his works and
the covenant of circumcision ; cf. Hort, *R. and E.*, p. 23.

2. εἰ γὰρ Ἀ. The question bears on our argument, for if
Abraham was justified from works, he has the right to boast, and
is an exception to our principle which would be a precedent for other
exceptions.

ἀλλ' οὐ πρὸς θεόν, sc. ἔχει καύχημα. Scripture shows that his
condition was due to a free act of GOD ; not therefore of works, not
therefore a subject for personal boasting.

3. τί γὰρ ἡ γρ. λ. Gen. xv. 6 ; Gal. iii. 6 ; James ii. 23.

ἐπίστευσεν. Here primarily of belief in GOD's word: but this
belief implied trust in the faithfulness and power of GOD, and was
therefore essentially faith in the full sense.

ἐλογίσθη, was reckoned for something more than it actually was
because it contained the seed, was the necessary precedent, of that
more. For the word in LXX. cf. Lev. vii. 8, xvii. 4, with the legal
sense of imputation familiar to the Jews; cf. S. H. ref., Weber, *Altsyn.
Theol.*, p. 233 ; cf. above ii. 26, ix. 8; 2 Cor. v. 19.

4. τῷ δὲ κ.τ.λ. S. Paul argues from the precise words of scripture: it was an act of faith that was met by the act of GOD. No
works are mentioned, therefore no works were included in the
consideration ; if there had been works, the language would have
expressed the act of GOD as conferring a due reward; but there is no

such suggestion in the words; they clearly imply a free favour on the part of God.

ἐργαζομένῳ has frequently the idea of working for hire, for a living, etc.; cf. 1 Thes. ii. 9, *al.*

5. ἐπὶ τὸν δικ. τὸν ἀσεβῆ. This goes beyond the strict relevance of the qu. in *v.* 3 and prepares the way for the enlargement of the idea by the qu., *vv.* 7, 8. πιστ. ἐπὶ brings into explicit statement the notion of trust, not expressed in *v.* 3. Cf. Moulton, p. 68, who suggests that the substitution of εἰς or ἐπὶ w. acc. for the simple dative after π. is peculiarly Christian, and coincides with the deepening of the sense of π. from belief to trust or faith. The change here is very significant, going, as it does, with the advance from the idea of God as simply faithful to His word (*v.* 3) to the idea of God as acting upon man.

τὸν δικαιοῦντα here, as above, =who declares righteous, *not* who makes righteous; iii. 24, 26, 30. See Introd. p. xxxvi.

τὸν ἀσεβῆ. Not of Abraham, but with the wider reference of the whole clause: of the sinner as ignoring or neglecting God; cf. i. 21. It here expresses the thought of the man about himself in the very act of trusting.

6. Δαυείδ. Ps. xxxii. 1, 2. The qu. emphasises the act of God in putting away man's sin, without naming conditions; and is used by S. Paul to bring out the wider reference of faith in God, not only as fulfilling promise but as removing and not imputing sin.

τὸν μακαρισμὸν = the blessing (art.)—the act of μακαρίζειν. *V.* 9 shows that here the blessing is not the congratulation of other men, but comes from God.

χωρὶς ἔργων. Conclusion drawn from the absence of any mention of works in qu.

9. ὁ μακ. οὖν. The blessing mentioned in the ps. is essentially the same as 'the reckoning' of *v.* 3; and the question is raised whether it extends to the circumcision only or to all. This is answered by insisting on Abraham's circumstances at the time.

10. ἐν περιτομῇ. The true place of περιτομή in the history of God's dealings with man: it was a sign (*v.* 4) of a state already existing and due to God's free gift.

11. περιτομῆς. The gen. of description—not practically different from περιτομήν.

σφραγῖδα. App. a common Jewish term for circumcision; cf. S. H., Wetst. *ad loc.*, "signum foederis, sigillum Abrahami." For the Jew circumcision marked the inclusion of the individual in the Covenant: here S. Paul treats it as a mark of the righteousness reckoned by God to Abraham as a result of his faith (a different interpretation), consequently not as excluding others, but as an outward sign and acknowledgment of Abraham's actual position; cf. Eph. i. 13.

εἰς τὸ εἶναι αὐ. π. The essential characteristic of A. was righteousness imputed to faith. Circumcision confirmed this, and consequently itself points to the lineage of A. being a lineage dependent on sharing his faith, not on sharing his circumcision.

δι' ἀκροβυστίας = while in a state of uncircumcision. = ἐν, v. 10; cf. ii. 27 n.

τὴν δικαιοσύνην = the same righteousness that was imputed to Abraham.

12. καὶ πατέρα περιτομῆς. περ. probably abstr. for concrete, =τῶν περιτεμνομένων.

τοῖς οὐκ ἐκ κ.τ.λ. Among the circumcised only those are sons of Abraham who follow in the steps of the faith which he had before he was circumcised. This is obviously the meaning, but requires the assumption of a primitive error in text. Hort suggests καὶ αὐτοῖς for καὶ τοῖς; W. H., appendix, *ad loc.*; cf. S. H. and Giff. The alternatives are to accept Hort's emendation or to omit τοῖς before στοιχοῦσιν.

13—16. The relation of law to promise is very briefly treated, just to meet the possible objection that the law is a condition of inheriting the promise, even though it was not an original condition of the promise itself.

13. οὐ γὰρ διὰ νόμου, γάρ = this is a full statement of the case, for law does not come in to qualify it.

διὰ νόμου, under conditions of law. Abraham was not under law when the promise was made; nor could the fact that his seed came under law affect the range or condition of the original promise; because promise and law have two quite different offices in God's hands: to make inheritance, really based on promise, depend on law is to evacuate the faith, which accepted the promise, of all meaning, and in fact to annul the promise; because while the promise is given to faith, the law has for its function to emphasise the nature of sin, and transgression can occur only when there is law.

ἢ τῷ σπέρματι αὐτοῦ, 'the seed' (Gen. xxii. 18) is introduced here as recipient of the promise, so as to enforce the above argument as applying to more than Abraham.

τὸ κλ. α. ε. κ. A free summary of the promises.

διὰ δικ. π., under conditions of a righteousness given in response to faith.

14. οἱ ἐκ νόμου, those who base a claim on law, and those only.

κεκένωται ἡ π. κ. κ. ἡ ἐ. The two principles are mutually exclusive. ἡ π.=the act of faith seen in Abraham.

κεκένωται=is made, by such a qualification, pointless; cf. 1 Cor. xv. 14, i. 17.

κατήργηται=is robbed of all meaning; cf. Gal. iii. 17.

15. ὁ γὰρ νόμος...κατεργάζεται. This verse indicates the true function of law, to show that it can have no effect upon the promise; it neither makes nor unmakes the kinship with Abraham, which is a kinship of character (faith) not of works. What the law does is to develop the moral sense of GOD's will; in doing so it inevitably creates the sense of guilt; it cannot in itself evoke faith.

οὐδὲ κ.τ.λ. This clause seems to be added almost automatically; at least its bearing on the context is very difficult to see. Is it possible that it is a primitive gloss? Otherwise=where law is not in question (as in the case of faith and promise), neither can transgression be in question (we have not to consider the acts and doings of Abraham and his true seed, as qualifying them for the promise, but only their attitude towards GOD, their faith). The subject is worked out in ch. vii.; cf. for similar anticipations iii. 20, 24.

16. διὰ τοῦτο κ.τ.λ. Here follows the positive side of the argument, of which the negative has been given—not ἐκ νόμου but κατὰ χάριν. Observe that νόμος as laying conditions upon men is contrasted with πίστις, as implying the action of GOD with χάρις. See below.

διὰ τοῦτο. Antecedent to ἵνα; for this cause, with this object; cf. Blass, p. 132, § 42, 1. Cf. 2 Cor. xiii. 10; 2 Thes. ii. 11; 1 Tim. i. 16; Phm. 15; Heb. ix. 15 (w. ὅπως).

ἐκ πίστεως, sc. ἡ δικαιοσύνη ἐστίν.

ἵνα κατὰ χάριν, sc. γένηται, that it might depend on and be measured by GOD's favour in contrast to man's earning; cf. iii. 24 and below, chh. v., vi.

εἰς τὸ εἶναι βεβαίαν. Only if righteousness is the free gift of GOD could the promise be guaranteed to all the seed : other conditions would have imported an element of insecurity.

παντὶ τῷ σπέρματι determines the meaning of τῷ σπέρματι in *v.* 13; contrast Gal. iii. 16.

τῷ ἐκ τοῦ νόμου. The promise is secure to these too, if besides starting from law they have Abraham's faith.

τῷ ἐκ π. It is implied that these have not τὸν νόμον; cf. iii. 30.

ὅς ἐστιν κ.τ.λ. expands and emphasises παντὶ τῷ σπέρματι. ἡμῶν, in the widest possible sense.

17. κατέναντι οὗ κ.τ.λ.   Cf. 2 Cor. ii. 17, xii. 19; and esp. Acts viii. 21: =κατέναντι τοῦ θεοῦ ᾧ ἐπίστ. ᾽Α.

The clause is to be taken with the main sentence, not with the relative clause : the promise to Abraham is secure for the faith of Abraham, wherever it is found, because the promise comes from and the faith rests on the one and the same GOD who, then as now, now as then, quickens, etc. (Giff., S. H. take it with the relative clause : W. H. and Lft, *ad loc.*, as above.)

τοῦ ζ. τ. ν.   As *v.* 19, the type is the birth of Isaac : the antitype is the quickening of man under the action of GOD's grace; cf. 1 Tim. vi. 13; cf. Joh. v. 21, 25 (n. connexion between καλεῖν and ζωο.).

καλοῦντος τὰ μὴ ὄντα ὡς ὄντα.   Cf. Hosea ii. 25; qu. ix. 25; *not*=calling into being things that are not (=εἰς τὸ εἶναι), but either 'naming things that are not as though they were' with reference to the imputed righteousness, or 'summoning to His service things that are not as though they were,' of the call of the descendants of Abraham in the lineage of faith. Then the making the unborn child the vehicle of the promise is typical of this. The context (ζωοπ.) points to the latter and fuller meaning, as also does S. Paul's use of καλεῖν; cf. S. H.

It was on the creative power of GOD that Abraham rested, as is further emphasised in *v.* 18.

18. παρ᾽ ἐλπίδα ἐπ᾽ ἐλπίδι, when hope was passed, he took his stand on hope and trusted, so that he became, etc.

19. καὶ μὴ ἀσθενήσας.   μὴ in N.T. and all later Greek is normally used with part.; cf. Moulton, pp. 170, 232.

κατενόησεν.   Really a μὲν clause—though he fully saw...yet (εἰς δὲ...).

20. εἰς=in regard to.

διεκρίθη.   Cf. Mt. xxi. 21; Mk xi. 23; James i. 6; =did not hesitate; cf. S. H. ; cf. Field, *ad loc.*   τῇ ἀπ., under the disbelief which was natural.

ἐνεδυναμώθη τῇ πίστει.   With S. H.=was empowered, by his faith, to beget a son; cf. Heb. xi. 11, 12, and Talmud qu. S. H.

ἐνδυναμοῦν.   Cf. 2 Tim. ii. 1; Eph. vi. 10. Formed from ἐνδύναμος; the preposition therefore does not govern a case following; cf. ἐνεργεῖν.

δοὺς δόξαν—because he acknowledged GOD's power to fulfil His promise; ct. i. 21.

21. πληροφορηθεὶς.   Cf. Heb. x. 22; see Lightfoot, *Col.* iv. 12; Kennedy, *Sources*, p. 119.   =persuaded, convinced. "Almost

exclusively Biblical and Ecclesiastical," Lft, *l.c.*   Eccles. viii. 11 only
in Sept.   "A word esp. common among the Stoics," S. H.—on
what authority?   One instance is quoted by Nägeli (p. 63) from the
Papyri (2nd cent. A.D.).

ὃ ἐπήγγελται, mid.

22. διὸ καί sums up and restates the argument, and so leads
to the statement of the parallel between Christians and Abraham,
justifying the conclusions of ch. iii.

23. οὐκ ἐγράφη δὲ κ.τ.λ.   Cf. xv. 4; 1 Cor. ix. 10, x. 11;
2 Tim. iii. 16.

24. τοῖς πιστεύουσιν = οἵτινες π.

ἐπὶ τὸν ἐγ. Ἰ.   (1) The trust is personal in a Personal Power, whose
Power and Character are revealed in the crucial act.   (2) The
raising of Jesus is a kind of antitype of the birth of Isaac.   Note
that the name Jesus is used alone to emphasise the historic fact—
τὸν κ. ἡ. = whom we acknowledge as Lord.

25. ὃς παρεδόθη διὰ τὰ π.   As iii. 25; cf. Isa. liii. 12 LXX.   Joh.
Weiss (*op. cit.*), p. 172, points out that the two clauses are an
instance of the Hebrew tendency to parallelism, and that consequently they must not be regarded as independent statements of
distinct elements in the process of redemption; the verbs might be
interchanged without affecting the sense; cf. viii. 32; Gal. ii. 20;
Eph. v. 2, 25.   Cf. below, v. 9, δικ. ἐν τῷ αἵματι α.

ἠγ. διὰ τὴν δικαίωσιν ἡ.   Another summary statement developed
later.   διά = with a view to.

δικαίωσιν.   v. 18 only; justification as an action = διὰ   τὸ
δικαιοῦν ἡ.

From one point of view, the resurrection of Christ as the act of
GOD is the testimony of GOD to the perfection of the Humanity of
Christ as well as to His Divinity, the declaration of the complete
righteousness of Jesus.   As it is through that perfect Humanity, and
by union with It, that the Christian is made one with the Christ, the
object of the Resurrection is the declaring righteous of those who, by
faith, accept the offered condition of righteousness.   This leads to
the actual making righteous: but that further thought is not included
in this statement; δικαίωσις is limited, as is δικαιοῦν, to the description of GOD's attitude to the sinner.   See Introd. p. xxxvi.

On the Resurrection, see S. H. add. note, pp. 116 ff., and on the
connexion of justification with the Resurrection cf. Gifford.

This concludes the first part of the Epistle, in which is set forth
what may be called an historical account of the relation of man, both
Jew and Gentile, to the revelation of GOD's Will and to the performance

of the same. It has been shown that the revelation of that Will in the Death and Resurrection of Christ answers to the necessities shown to exist both among Jews and Gentiles; the attitude of both to the Will of GOD and the character and issues of His dealings with them all point to the Gospel as the one adequate message of righteousness for man. The treatment then has been historical : the great ethical and spiritual principles involved have been used and stated, but not explained ; there follows now the description of these principles as seen by an analysis of the case of the individual sinner (v.—viii.) and of the sinning people (ix.—xi.); and then (xii. f.) the main characters of the Christian life are explained. The argument that follows, in fact, deals with the Gospel as a *power* of salvation.

C. cc. v.—vii. SECOND VINDICATION OF THE THEME. THE ETHICAL
NEED AND BEARING OF THE GOSPEL, AS A POWER WHICH EFFECTS
RIGHTEOUSNESS. The Power of the Gospel is explained, in
contrast with νόμος, as a gift (χάρις) of new life in Christ.

CHAPTER V.

v. 1—11. Introduction, describing the nature of the state in which
we are, under the power of the Gospel: (1) Since, then, we are
justified by GOD on the single condition of faith, let us maintain the
state of peace with GOD, by the help of Him, (2) by whom we have
been brought under this free favour of GOD, and ground our boasting
on hope of attaining the perfection of this state in the future full
manifestation of GOD in us ; (3) and no less in the present straitened
condition of our lives, (4) as an opportunity for endurance, proof of
character and hope, that hope which cannot disappoint us because
it is itself the effect of GOD's love in us ; (6) and that love, measured
by what was done for us in Christ's death for us while we were
enemies and sinners, will certainly complete our salvation by the
working of Christ's life in us. (11) So, finally, let us boast in
GOD by the help of our Lord Jesus Christ, through whom, as I have
said, we received that reconciliation which is now our state.

These verses describe the state of the Christian. It has been
shown to be due to GOD's free act of justification, requiring only
man's faith in Him ; it is, summarily, a state of peace with GOD ;
it was won by the Death of Christ, and is maintained by His Life ;
under present conditions it is a state of θλίψις, for the man must
be tested ; but the hope of maintaining and perfecting this state is
warranted by the fact that the love which gave it to us will surely
maintain us in it and perfect us for its complete realisation. The
thought comes out at once that the power of the Gospel is Christ
living in us: the section begins and ends with διὰ τοῦ Κυρίου ἡ. Ἰ.
Χρ.; cf. n. on i. 17; the subject is resumed and fully treated in c. viii.

1. δικαιωθέντες οὖν ἐκ πίστεως sums up the position gained.
Notice that in these chapters (v.—vii.) the word πίστις occurs only
in these first two verses : πιστεύω occurs once only (vi. 8), and then
in the simple sense of believe. The fact is that the first fundamental

act of trust, when it has once brought man under the justifying love
of GOD and the power of Christ's life, becomes a permanent though
progressive act of submission to and reliance upon that power, a
continued act of will realising that power in itself, which is, on
man's side, the determining characteristic of the Christian life and
is not by S. Paul described exclusively by any one name, but is
involved in all the exhortations, and summed up in the phrases τὸ
πνεῦμα τῆς ζωῆς ἐν Χρ. 'Ι. (viii. 1) and πνεῦμα υἱοθεσίας (viii. 15).

εἰρήνην. Cf. Acts x. 36; Joh. xvi. 33. With χάρις, it is the unfailing element in S. Paul's salutations, and gives him his characteristic
phrase 'ὁ θεὸς τῆς εἰρήνης (xv. 33, xvi. 20; 2 Cor. xiii. 11; Phil. iv. 9
(cf. 7); 1 Thes. v. 23; 2 Thes. iii. 16 (ὁ κύριος τ. ε.); cf. Col. iii. 15;
Heb. xiii. 20). The cardinal passage is Eph. ii. 14—17. Like χάρις,
it has special reference to the call of the Gentiles, but as involved
in the wider conception of the establishment of man as man in a state
of peace with GOD by the removal of sin. The first step is the
justification of man upon faith : then that state has to be maintained.

ἔχωμεν, *al.* ἔχομεν. A.V. 'we have,' R.V. 'let us have.' The mood
of exhortation is clearly required by the context (against Field, *ad
loc.*); S. Paul is passing from the description of the fundamental
initial act of GOD in bringing man into this state, to the character
and duties of the state so given. The verb ἔχειν is durative = to
maintain hold on, and here it has its strict sense—let us maintain
(better than the ambiguous 'have') peace; this requires further
activities in man, and the continual help of the Lord; cf. Moulton,
p. 110.

διὰ τ. κ. ἡ 'Ι. Χρ. The fuller name is given because each
element in it is an assurance that the help will be given and will be
effective, and ought to be claimed.

2. δι' οὖ καὶ, the Person, who has brought us into this state
by His Death and Resurrection, will help us to maintain it by His
Life.

τὴν προσαγωγήν. Eph. ii. 18, iii. 12 only. Vb 1 Pet. iii. 18;
cf. Joh. xiv. 6; Heb. iv. 14 f. The vb in LXX. freq. of bringing
persons and sacrifices before GOD for acceptance. Here of the initial
approach; in Eph. iii. 12 of continual right of access.

ἐσχήκαμεν, 'we obtained'—the 'constative' of ἔχω; Moulton, p.
145.

τῇ πίστει. Perh. = for our faith—the way has been opened for
faith to approach God.

εἰς τὴν χάριν ταύτην. The demonstrative clearly shows that the

reference is to God's free favour shown to man in justifying him.
The dominant meaning of χάρις in the Bible is God's favour shown
to man, the effect of His love. The word is a favourite with S. Paul,
and has special but not exclusive reference to the light thrown upon
God's favour, by the inclusion of the Gentiles. This thought is
implied here. They have been brought within the range of God's
favour, as described; cf. Hort, 1 *Pet.* p. 25 f., 49, 66 f.; Robinson,
Eph. p. 221 f.; cf. Gal. v. 4; 1 Pet. v. 12.

ἐστήκαμεν, 'we stand'; cf. Moulton, p. 147; Burton, § 75, etc.;
1 Pet. v. 12; cf. 1 Cor. xv. 1.

καυχώμεθα. Indic., to be taken with δι' οὗ. Here is the Christian
opportunity for boasting; cf. iii. 27.

ἐπ' ἐλπίδι τῆς δόξης τ. θ. The ground of Christian boasting is
not a privileged or exclusive state, but a hope that by the work of
the Lord Jesus Christ the glory of God will be revealed in man;
it rests, then, on God's favour and embraces mankind; cf. on iii. 23,
Col. i. 27.

3. οὐ μόνον δέ, ἀλλά. *v.* 11, viii. 23, ix. 10; 2 Cor. viii. 19; cf. 1 Tim.
v. 13. With the ellipse only in S. Paul; not only is the hope of the
future revelation a ground of boasting, but also the process of θλίψις,
by which, under conditions of the present life, it is being worked
out; cf. Joh. xvi. 33; Acts xiv. 22. The idea is fully worked out in
2 Cor. iv. 8—12.

ἡ θλίψις. xii. 12; 2 Thes. i. 4.

4. δοκιμή. (1) The process of testing, 2 Cor. viii. 2; (2) the result
—the temper given to the steel, Phil. ii. 22; 2 Cor. ii. 9, ix. 13,
xiii. 3 : here the latter; cf. 1 Pet. i. 6 ff.; James i. 2, 12. θλίψις produces
in the Christian endurance or resistance, and this Christian endurance tempers character; the tempered character, as evidence of
God's working so far, itself produces hope; and this hope, so
grounded and won, cannot disappoint him who has it.

5. καταισχύνει, in this connexion = brings the shame of disappointment; cf. Ps. xxi. 6; *infra* ix. 33; Phil. i. 20.

ὅτι ἡ ἀγάπη κ.τ.λ. *vv.* 5—10 enlarge upon the strength of the
reasons for hope, an *a fortiori* argument from the love of God, as
already shown in our call and justification in Christ, to the willing-
ness and ability of that love for the completion of His work. Cf.
viii. 35, 39.

ἡ ἀγάπη τοῦ θεοῦ = the love which is characteristic of God in His
eternal nature, and therefore in His relation to man, constituting
His true relation to man and making the Incarnation divinely
natural; further, this love is, as it were, by the agency of the Holy

Spirit, resident in man, and becomes to him the power of moral
and spiritual action by which the new character is originated and
gradually developed in the processes of life.   It is not the mere
sentiment of affection, but an influence of the divine activity which
creates its own image in its object and vitalises it into a life like
its own.   A faint reflection of this divine operation is seen in the
way in which a father's or a friend's love influences character.   The
fundamental passage is Joh. xvii. 26; cf. 1 Joh. iv. 12 *et passim*.   In
S. Paul note particularly 2 Thes. iii. 5 (Lft's note) and 2 Cor. v. 14;
Eph. iii. 19; *infra* viii. 35, 36.

ἐκκέχυται.   Cf. Acts ii. 17, 18, 33.

ἐν ταῖς κ., the love of GOD has flooded our hearts.

διὰ πν. ἁγ. τ. δ. ἡ.   Cf. viii. 9, 11, 15.   The gift of the Spirit
is almost always referred to as a definite act in the past (ἔδωκεν,
ἐλάβετε); cf. 1 Cor. ii. 12; 2 Cor. i. 22; Gal. iii. 2; Eph. i. 13, *al.*
but n. pres. 1 Thes. iv. 8 ref. Ezek. xxxvii. 14.   Pentecost was the
date of the giving of the Spirit to the Church; baptism with the
laying on of hands is the date for each individual.

πν. ἁγ.   The first mention of the Holy Spirit in this epistle: the
truth here indicated is developed in ch. viii.

6.   εἴ γε.   "Si quidem, 2 Cor. v. 3 (v. l.); Eph. iii. 2, iv. 21; Col.
i. 23 (classical)," Blass, p. 261.   = if, as you will not dispute.

The connexion seems to be this: Christ's death for us when we
were still outside the operation of the Spirit is such an overwhelming
proof of GOD's love, that it must surely justify all the confidence we
can put in it, now that by the indwelling of the Spirit it is a vital
power within us.   The connexion of these sentences is obscure: it
is perhaps best to take εἴ γε...ἀπέθανεν as protasis, μόλις γὰρ...
ἀπέθανεν (8) as parenthesis; πολλῷ οὖν (9) picks up the apodosis:
then *v.* 10 in a very characteristic way repeats the main thought in a
parallel pair of antithetic clauses.   The whole 6—10 incl. is an expansion of *v.* 5*b*.

ἀσθενῶν, having 'no power of ourselves to help ourselves.'   The
word is specially chosen to mark the contrast with the new power
which is in the Christian: not used quite in this way elsewhere.

ἔτι, with ὄντων, cf. *v.* 8, A.V., R.V.   But ἔτι almost invariably
precedes the word it qualifies, except with negatives (e.g. Rev. viii.
16) or rarely when it has special emphasis.   So better here with
κατὰ καιρὸν, 'while there was yet opportunity,' before the case was
hopeless.   The rhythm of the sentence points the same way.

ἀσεβῶν marks not the weakness, but the relation to GOD.

7, 8 emphasise the uniqueness of this act of love.   This parenthesis

makes an anacoluthon, a constant mark in S. Paul of deep
feeling.

7. δικαίου—ἀγαθοῦ. Both masc. The idea is that the appeal
of a righteous character hardly stirs the emotion; the good man with
more that touches the heart may inspire such an act. Those for
whom Christ died were neither.

τολμᾷ = 'has the spirit to die'; cf. Field, *ad loc.*, qu. Eur. *Alc.*
644.

8. συνίστησιν. Cf. iii. 5.

9. πολλῷ οὖν μᾶλλον. *A fortiori.* The hope of progress and
perfection (*v.* 2) which depends on the love of God is justified *a
fortiori* by our experience of that love in the act of justification.

σωθησόμεθα δι' αὐ. ἀπὸ τῆς ὀργῆς. The description, on the
negative side, of the σωτηρία which is the result of the power of the
Gospel (i. 16). The ὀργῆς (cf. i. 18 f.) consists now in a state of sin
and hereafter in the consequences] of that state being persevered in.
Note that justification does not remove the conflict with evil; it
reveals God's attitude of love to us and in us, and consequently
enables us to engage in that conflict with hope.

10 repeats the *a fortiori* argument with amplification (cf. Eph. ii.
11 f.). The two clauses are exactly ‖ *vv.* 6 and 9.

κατηλλάγημεν ref. to δικαιωθέντες; cf. the aorists below. Vb and
subst. pec. to Rom. and 2 Cor. (*al.* 1 Cor. vii. 11). ἀποκαταλλ.
Eph., Col. only. διαλλ. and συναλλ., implying mutual reconciliation
(cf. Mt. v. 24), are never used in this connexion. Always therefore of God reconciling (not, as being reconciled). It marks the
same stage as δικαιοῦν; the means employed is the Death of Christ;
man's state, which necessitates it, is that of ἐχθροί, ἀπηλλοτριωμένοι.
The fullest passage is 2 Cor. v. 18 f.

διὰ τοῦ θανάτου τ. υ. α. Cf. Col. i. 20; see vi. 2 ff.

σωθησόμεθα includes both the maintenance of the state of peace
and the final result; as does σωτηρία.

ἐν τῇ ζωῇ αὐτοῦ. This again is worked out in vi. 2 f. =the
resurrection life of the Lord as the sustaining environment and
inspiration of the new life of the Christian; cf. 2 Cor. iv. 10, 11;
Eph. iv. 18 ff.

11. οὐ μόνον δέ, ἀλλὰ returns to *v.* 3. This return, after so long
a break, is made easier by the parallelisms pointed out above. καυχώμενοι, part. for indic.; cf. Moulton, p. 224.

ἐν τῷ θεῷ. The essentially personal character of the whole relation is emphasised: our boast is not in a transaction or a state,
but in God Himself and by the help of our Lord Jesus Christ—so

summing up the whole argument. God loved, justified through
Christ, gave the Spirit, will finish what He has begun.

N. This passage then marks the transition from the antithesis
between πίστις and νόμος, as ground of justification, to the antithesis
of χάρις and νόμος, as ground of the saving of man's life; the faith
in God, which accepts His justification, must lead us on to trust His
good will and power to perfect the new life, which is the life of Christ
in us. This is the supreme instance of His χάρις, His free favour to
man. The range and manner in which this χάρις works are developed
in the following sections.

12—21. This state depends upon a living relation of mankind to
Christ, analogous to the natural relation to Adam, and as universal
as that is. So it comes to pass that there is a parallel between
the natural state of man and his new condition: by one who was
man the sin which has been shown to be universal entered into man's
world, and this sin was the cause of man's death, extending to all
men because all actually sinned; (13) for that sin was in the world
just in the degree that law was (sin not being reckoned without
law) (14) is proved by the fact that death held supreme sway from
Adam to Moses, even though the men of that time sinned not, as
Adam did, against a positive external command (but only by falling
away from the inner standard of well-doing which they had from
God). [So far Adam is connected with men merely as the first
sinner; their state was due to their own sins, and those not quite
like Adam's sin.] Now Adam is a type of Him that was to come.
(15) There is a parallel between the transgression of Adam, and the
gift of God in Christ; but only a qualified parallel: (a) it was the
fall of the single man that led to the death of all, a human
origin; the gift is the free favour of God in giving what He does
give to all in the single man, and that man Jesus Christ, the
Ascended Son. (16) Again (β) the effect of God's gift is out of all
proportion to the result which followed upon one man's having
sinned; for while the judgment of God followed upon one sin and
involved condemnation, the gift of God follows upon many sins and
involves acquittal of all. (17) For it is obvious that the sway of
death established by one man's sin, and through his action, is far
more than overthrown by the kingship realised in life by the help
of the one (man) Jesus Christ, which they will gain who accept
the superabundance of the favour of God and His generous
gift of righteousness (there is far more than a restoration of what
was lost). (18) With these qualifications then the parallel may be
stated: As one man's transgression so affected all men as to bring

them under God's condemnation, so also one man's enacted
righteousness affects all men so as to bring them into a state of
justification which involves life; for just as the disobedience of the
one man was the means whereby all were put into the condition of
sinners, so also the obedience of one man will bring all into the
condition of righteous men (if, as has been shown, they exercise
faith). (20) Now law, whether pre-Mosaic or Mosaic, was imported
into man's experience to multiply the fall; but where the acts and
state of sin were thus multiplied, the favour of God was shown in
still greater abundance in order that, in antithesis to the reign
gained by sin in the state of death, the favour of God might gain
sovereignty in a state of righteousness leading to life eternal by the
aid and working of Jesus Christ our Lord.

This is perhaps the most condensed passage in all S. Paul's
writings. It is consequently almost impossible to give an interpretation with confidence. The fundamental thought appears to be
to establish the universal range of the power of the Gospel, as
answering to the universal range of sin and man's need. The
universality is then based in each case on the relation of the whole
race to one man. As regards sin, its universality is related, in
a way which must be called obscure, to the connexion of the race
with Adam; their humanity is derived from him; and his fall has
its results in them; this seems rather to be concluded from the
observed fact that all came under the sentence of death pronounced
on him for his fall, than upon any theory that in some sense
they sinned in him; they died (15, 17) because of his sin, but also
they sinned themselves; it was the death rather than the sin
that they inherited, and individually they justified, so to speak,
the verdict of death by their own sin. What they inherited was a
nature liable to death; they made it, each for himself, a sinful
nature. Note that it is not said that men sinned in Adam or because
Adam sinned; but that man died because Adam sinned; death
established the mastery thus initiated because men also sinned. At
last the vicious series was broken: one Man broke the universal
practice of sin, enacted righteousness and by so doing brought within
the reach of all men justification, as God's free gift, and a power to
realise that justification in their own lives, a power which brings life
because it is His own life imparted to them. Thus is the sovereignty
of the favour of God established instead of the sovereignty of sin
and death. The relation to the one Man, in this case, is a relation
of imparted life, as in the former case it is a relation of entailed
death. In each case the entail is realised for each person by his

own act: in the first case, by an act of sin; in the second case, by an act of faith. The Second Adam broke the entail by the fact that He did not sin (*v.* 18); and that condition He imparts by communication of His own life. See Additional Note, p. 210.

The analysis of the structure is this: the anacoluthon in *v.* 12 is due to the interruption of the intended statement of the universality of χάρις and ζωή, by the expansion of the thought of the sway of death. The completion of the original idea is then undertaken in *vv.* 15, 16, 17, but only by noting certain qualifications of the parallel which is to be drawn; then, *v.* 18 f., the parallel is finally stated.

διὰ τοῦτο. The Christian state being as described in *vv.* 1—11, it follows that GOD's act in the Gospel has a universal range.

δι' ἑνὸς ἀνθρώπου ἡ ἁμαρτία κ.τ.λ. Adam's sin, by the mere fact, brought sin into the world of created humanity; sin was no longer a possibility but a fact.

καὶ διὰ τῆς ἁμ. ὁ θάνατος, the death we know: death as we know it came into man's experience by the act of Adam. The question is not raised, still less answered, whether without sin man's nature would have been liable to death; S. Paul is dealing with our experience of death and its natural associations, alike for Jew and Gentile, as the destruction of life and separation from GOD. It was sin which gave death this character, and this character, reinforced by the sins of men, led to the tyranny of death over the human spirit. It appears therefore that S. Paul is not distinguishing between physical and moral death, but regarding death as a fact in its full significance in relation to the whole nature of man. See p. 218.

καὶ οὕτως. καὶ is the simple conj. and the clause is part of the ὥσπερ sentence, not the apodosis; that would require οὕτως καὶ.

ὁ θάνατος διῆλθεν. The primary stress is on the universality of death, initiated by one sin, reinforced by sin in every man. The universality of sin has already been argued. The order throws stress on εἰς π. ἀ. The aorists are ' constative,' they " represent a whole action simply as having occurred without distinguishing any steps in its progress"; Moulton, p. 109.

ἐφ' ᾧ πάντες ἥμαρτον. These words must be taken strictly; the range of death included all men because all sinned. The death, which received its character from Adam's sin, retained its character because each and every man in turn sinned. All principles of interpretation require us to take sin here in the same sense as in ch. i. 18 f. There it is clear that sin involves conscious neglect of knowledge of GOD and His Will, in however elementary a degree.

It is an individual act against light. To suppose that ἐν Ἀδάμ is to be supplied, is to suppose that the most critical point of the argument is unexpressed. ἐφ ᾧ=' on the ground that '; cf. 2 Cor. v. 4; Blass, p. 137.

13. ἄχρι γὰρ νόμου=just so far as there was law there was sin. It has been shown (ii. 14, 15) that there was law, in a certain and true sense, before the law given to Moses; action against this law was sin, and the fact that it was so is here confirmed by the consideration that the penalty of sin, death, was obviously present in the world before the law of Moses was given. γὰρ then introduces a fresh piece of evidence of the universality of sin—for death, as understood by sinners, was there, therefore sin, sin in proportion to knowledge. So I take ἄχρι ν.=up to the degree of law, just to the extent to which law was present. So ἁμαρτία, anarthrous—men's acts had the character of sin. See Additional Note, p. 210.

ἁμαρτία δὲ, sc. but that law was present, and therefore men's acts were sins, is shown by the reign of death; the law in question is shown to be the law described in ii. 14 f., because the reign of death, the punishment of sin, extended over men who did not sin as Adam did against a positive external command. The two verses 13, 14 together justify the statement πάντες ἥμαρτον. See Add. Note, p. 213.

14. ἐβασίλευσεν, the 'constative aorist'; Moulton, p. 109.

ἀπὸ Ἀδὰμ μέχρι Μωυσέως, in the interval between Adam, who sinned against positive law, and Moses who delivered positive law. In the case of Adam and of those who lived under the Mosaic law there could be no doubt that πάντες ἥμαρτον.

ἐπὶ τοὺς μὴ ἁμ. It is noticeable that as sinners men are here distinguished from Adam: their sin was of a different kind; but still it was sin, action against light, though the light came in a different way, that is, through the inner experience of the knowledge of GOD; i. 18 f.

ἐπὶ τῷ ὁμ. τ. π. Ἀ. The dominant fact in the sin of Adam was that he acted in spite of a positive command: other men acted in spite of the inner light.

ὅς ἐστιν τύπος τοῦ μέλλοντος. τοῦ μέλλοντος=' of Him who was to come.' Adam is typical of Christ in his natural relation to men. The words introduce the parallel now to be stated: tr. ' and he is a type,' etc.; and so there is a parallel in the relations, but a parallel with qualifications. So ἀλλά, not γάρ, follows.

15. τὸ χάρισμα here is the gift of justification offered in Christ; in range this has as large an effect as the fall; but in quality

it is far greater, as it leads to life, the other to death. This conclusion is not fully stated till *v.* 17.

εἰ γὰρ τῷ τοῦ ἑνὸς κ.τ.λ., the fall of one man led to the death of all (note, not to the sin). οἱ πολλοὶ denominate πάντες in contrast to ὁ εἷς; cf. Lft, *ad loc.* There are two steps omitted here; Adam's fall lead to his death, death thus introduced spread because all sinned. So, ultimately, it was owing to one man's sin that the many died. Similarly, in the parallel clause, the individual condition of faith and the actual result (ζωή) are omitted.

ἡ χάρις τοῦ θεοῦ, the favour of God. ἡ δωρεά, His generous giving, emphasises χάρις; and then this χάρις is further described as the favour of the Ascended Lord, the one Man (cf. 2 Cor. xiii. 14 and viii. 9), to bring out the parallel. The words express the attitude of GOD to sinning man—His love in all its fulness; not the effect of that love.

ἐπερίσσευσεν, 'superabounded'—in its very nature as an act of infinite love, and, as will be shown presently, in its effects. But here the nature of the act alone is in question. If its effects were in question, the aorist would scarcely stand.

εἰς τοὺς πολλούς, with ἐπερίσσευσεν, abounded in fact, as shown in its effects; what those effects were is then expressed, generally in δώρημα, δικαίωμα, specifically (17 f.) by ἐν ζωῇ βασ., and both expressions united in (18) δικαίωσιν ζωῆς.

16. καὶ οὐχ—τὸ δώρημα. Still more condensed. δώρημα is the concrete effect or result of χάρις and δωρεά.

δι' ἑνὸς ἁμαρτήσαντος, through one man and his sin (death came into the world); the gift came after many sins.

The v.l. ἁμαρτήματος is a true gloss: the absence of the article makes the phrase = through one man's sin: the participial form of the phrase emphasises the responsibility of the act.

τὸ μὲν γὰρ κ.τ.λ. This is explained and must be interpreted by the second γὰρ clause, *v.* 17.

κρίμα. GOD's decision upon the act of sin led to the imposition of a penalty. ἐξ ἑνός. Neuter.

κατάκριμα. See Deissmann, *B. S.* II. p. 92. A very rare word. Papyri seem to show that it = a burden imposed upon an estate in consequence of a legal judgment: so a judicial penalty of any kind: 'poena condemnationem sequens.'

χάρισμα. The gift which GOD gives, after many sins, leads to acquittal.

δικαίωμα. Here = acquittal,)(κατάκριμα: justification is a sentence of acquittal, though on condition of faith.

17. τῷ παραπτώματι. παραπτ. is used throughout of the actual fall, whether of Adam, or as repeated in his descendants, v. 20.

ἐβασίλευσεν, ‘ingressive,’ gained its sovereignty : τῷ—παραπτ., the instrument ; διὰ τοῦ, the agent. The one was the agent, his fall the instrument by which death entered and established its sovereignty : repeats 12a.

πολλῷ μᾶλλον. The idea seems to be that the state of those who receive God’s gift is far more than a mere deliverance from death ; it is a new life and actual sovereignty.

οἱ...λαμβάνοντες. Here is expressed the condition for realising God’s gift, its reception by faith, parallel to the (unexpressed) condition of the extended sovereignty of death, the sin of each man.

τῆς δωρεᾶς τῆς δικαιοσύνης=righteousness as offered in Christ. Here again the excess of God’s love finds expression : it is not merely justification (δικαιοῦν, δικαίωσις), acquittal, which is given ; but positive righteousness under the operation of the new life of Christ in men.

ἐν ζωῇ. The antithesis of 1 Cor. xv. 22.

βασιλεύσουσιν. An exact antithesis would be ἡ ζωὴ βασιλεύσει ; but this abstract expression would not represent the vivid thought of the condition of those who receive, etc., as sharing not only the life but the sovereignty of the Lord ; cf. Eph. ii. 5, 6. The future is used because of the hypothesis implied in οἱ λαμβάνοντες ; it includes not only the future glorified state of the redeemed but their present share in the Lord’s already established sovereignty.

διὰ τοῦ ἑνὸς Ἰ. Χρ. It is not necessary again to emphasise the Human Nature by repeating ἀνθρώπου ; it is understood. N. that Ἰ. Χρ. means Jesus as Ascended Christ. He is the Agent through whom God’s gift comes to men.

18. ἄρα οὖν. The parallel is now summed up without the qualifications, in the simplest form.

ὡς δι’ ἑνὸς κ.τ.λ. The best way of translating seems to be to turn εἰς πάντας ἀνθρ. into a statement—all men were affected. The prepositional form seems almost to be chosen in order to avoid a definite statement as to the nature of the nexus between the one man and all men.

εἰς κατάκριμα, sc. θανάτου ‖ εἰς δικ. ζωῆς.

δι’ ἑνὸς δικαιώματος. Possibly as above, ‘through one man’s acquittal,’ as an accomplished fact ; but the antithesis to παράπτωμα, and the parallel with τῆς ὑπακοῆς (v. 19), suggest the rendering ‘righteous act’ or ‘enacted righteousness.’ We have to choose between an inexact antithesis here, or a difference in the meaning of δικαίωμα here and in v. 16.

εἰς δικαίωσιν ζωῆς, for an acquittal, carrying with it not the mere negative setting aside of sin, but the positive gift of life.

ζωῆς.   The gen. of definition—an acquittal involving life.

19. ὥσπερ γὰρ κ.τ.λ.   The antithesis is repeated in another form, for clearness of thought.

παρακοή.   This word is substituted for παράπτωμα as definitely involving the personal action.

κατεστάθησαν.   Cf. James iv. 4.   =were brought into the condition of sinners—i.e. under the doom of death; the condition then realised by their own sins.

δίκαιοι καταστ., shall be brought into the condition of righteous or justified men—again the condition to be realised by their own faith; marked by the future tense.

20. νόμος δὲ κ.τ.λ.   The effect of law, whether the inner law or the law of Moses, was to multiply the fall, i.e. to occasion in each the fall which had taken place in Adam (cf. ch. vii.), so that each became a sinner by his own act in rejecting knowledge; cf. 'every man is the Adam of his own soul.'

παρεισῆλθεν.   The force of the compound is that law came in as an additional element in man's experience, not as it were on the direct line of natural development but as an extra imported element, both the inner light and the outer law being especial gifts of GOD.

ἵνα πλεονάσῃ.   Cf. iii. 19, vii. 7 ff., esp. 13, 14.   We cannot avoid taking ἵνα as final.   The knowledge of GOD's will was necessary for man's moral development; it was necessary to make what was sin to be realised as sin (iii. 20).

οὗ δὲ κ.τ.λ.   The resources of GOD's favour were abundantly equal to this multiplied demand upon it.

ὑπερεπερίσσευσεν, 'became still more abundant.'

21. ἵνα ὥσπερ κ.τ.λ.   Here the reign of death is shown to be as a matter of fact the reign of sin in the atmosphere of death; a summary again of i. 18 f.

ἐν τῷ θανάτῳ.   The ‖ εἰς ζωὴν shows that ἐν here is not instrumental, but describes the sphere or atmosphere in which sin reigned.

ἡ χάρις κ.τ.λ., the grace or favour of GOD might gain its sovereignty under the condition of righteousness leading to eternal life by the action and agency of the Ascended Man Jesus Christ, now our Lord.   χάρις, as throughout, describes not the state of man but the attitude of GOD towards man.

διὰ δικαιοσύνης=in or under a condition or state of righteousness:

cf. 17 *b* and for διὰ ii. 27 n. The elaborate phrasing is due to the difficulty of getting an exact antithesis. The exact verbal antithesis would be ἡ δικαιοσύνη ( )(ἡ ἁμαρτία) β. ἐν ζωῇ ( )(ἐν τῷ θαν.); but the true power of sovereignty is not man's righteousness but GOD's grace; so ἡ χάρις is put as the subject; then δικαιοσύνη expresses the state of man under the sovereignty of χάρις, and is therefore introduced by διὰ; and for ἐν ζωῇ (cf. 17 *b*) the description of the new atmosphere in which man is or the new power by which man lives (already implied in ἡ χάρις) is substituted εἰς ζ. αἰ. as the end to which all tends; and the whole argument is summed up in the phrase διὰ 'Ι. Χρ. τ. Κ. ἡ., which comes almost as a refrain (cf. vii. 17, viii. 23).

It is essential throughout the passage to bear in mind the argument of i. 18—iii. 31, and in particular the position there made plain that the sinful state is made actual in each man by his own act, just as the state of righteousness to be made actual in each man requires the personal act of faith.

Then in ch. vi. S. Paul passes from this description of GOD's favour or grace in its range, effectiveness and purpose to consider man's duty as the object of this grace.

CHAPTER VI

(1) Are we to conclude that the state of sin is to continue, as a provocative, so to speak, of the graciousness of GOD; the more sin the greater grace? (2) It is a monstrous thought; the fundamental characteristic of our Christian position is that when we became Christians we died to sin and our sinful life, (3) it is elementary that in baptism into Christ we shared His death, (4) His burial, and His resurrection by the manifest act of the Father; now we are in a new life and our conduct must be correspondingly new. (5) For baptism involved union of our nature to Christ's both in His death and His resurrection; (6) His death implies the destruction of the old nature, the abolition of the rule of sin; His resurrection, shared by us—a freeing from death and sin, a living to GOD —implies that we are dead to sin and in Him living to GOD (so that sin is in the highest degree unnatural to this new creature). (12) Therefore both the use and the obedience of even your mortal body must be rendered no longer to sin for unrighteous work, but to GOD for righteousness; the authority of sin being broken because you are not under law but under grace. (15) Not under law, but not therefore free to sin, for that were a return to the old slavery; but under grace, you are under a new slavery (to use human language), willingly adopted; (19) your very members must be turned from the old slavery to the new. (20) For that was a state of slavery and freedom—freedom as against the claims of righteousness, slavery to the claims of sin and its result in death: (21) from that slavery you are freed and brought into a new slavery to GOD; with its proper result, sanctification, leading to its end, eternal life. (23) For all that is earned from sin is death: but GOD gives, of His free grace, eternal life by communion with Christ Jesus our Lord.

The section deals with the response natural in those who are under GOD's grace. It is, incidentally, a repudiation of the charge made against S. Paul that, by denying the obligation of law, he was destroying the support and the obligation of a holy life. It gives consequently the true basis for a Christian ethics : and the fundamental point is the new life in union with and dependence on Christ.

1. τί οὖν ἐροῦμεν; as always, introduces a question putting a case which might occur to the reader.

ἐπιμένωμεν. So far the emphasis has been chiefly upon the free grace of GOD as justifying; this might suggest that human effort is not required: and S. Paul meets this by pointing out that as GOD justifies in Christ alone, communion with Christ is necessary for the individual actualisation of justification, and this involves a characteristic life.

ἡ χάρις, that the generosity and marvel of GOD's free favour may be multiplied by increasing the demand upon it.

2. οἵτινες, the appeal is to the character of the Christian—'seeing we are men who…'.

ἀπεθάνομεν definitely refers to baptism as explained *vv.* 3 f. τῇ ἁμαρτίᾳ=our sin, the state of sin in which we were; cf. Gal. ii. 19.

3. ἢ ἀγνοεῖτε, vii. 1 only; cf. οὐ θέλω ὑ. ἀγνοεῖν i. 13, xi. 25; 1 Cor. x. 1, xii. 1 *al.*; as always, appealing to an admitted principle of Christian instruction.

It has been suggested that here and in 1 Cor. xv. 4 we have a reference to a primitive Baptismal Confession of the Death, Burial and Resurrection. See Clemen *Erklärung*, p. 172.

ἐβαπτίσθημεν, only Evv., Acts and Paul. With εἰς Χρ. only here and Gal. iii. 27:=were brought by baptism into union with Christ: this community of life is the fundamental thought of the passage, as determining the natural and necessary character of the Christian life.

εἰς Χρ. Ἰησ. The union is with the full life of the Son as seen both in His Humanity and in His ascended state.

εἰς τὸν θάνατον αὐ.: the first stage of the Christian life is death, a death, in its kind, of the same quality as the death of Jesus (cf. 2 Cor. iv. 10), i.e. a death to sin, cf. *v.* 10.

4. συνετάφημεν. Col. ii. 12 only; cf. 1 Cor. xv. 4; Acts xiii. 29. It is remarkable that S. Paul, alone in N.T. outside the Gospels, lays stress on the Burial: he alone was not an eyewitness of the circumstances of the Death, and therefore for him the burial was of high significance, in its evidential value.

εἰς τ. θ. Closely with τοῦ β.—through that baptism into His Death.

ἵνα. The purpose of this sharing the death and burial is negative as regards the old life of sin, but positive also, that we might enter into the atmosphere of the new life and walk in it.

διὰ τῆς δόξης τοῦ πατρός, here δόξα is used of the manifest action of the Father in the raising of Christ; διά, instrum.; cf. Joh. xi. 40, Col. i. 11. The resurrection of Christ is a revelation of the Father.

τοῦ πατρός. Cf. Joh. v. 21; Acts i. 4, 7, ii. 33 (only in A); Eph. ii. 18, iii. 14; Col. i. 12 (?); 1 Pet. i. 17; 1 Joh. i. 2, 3, ii. 1, 15 *al.* (7); 2 Joh. (3); Rev. (4).

The use of ὁ πατήρ absolutely is dominantly characteristic of S. John (but cf. also Mt. xi. 25 f. ‖ Lk.; xxiv. 36 ‖; xxviii. 19). It occurs in S. Paul and Acts only as above (but n. Gal. iv. 6). This is the only place where it is used alone in connexion with the resurrection; and consequently it calls marked attention to the character of the resurrection as an act not of power only but of the love of the Father to His Son, and through the Son to those that are His. This thought emphasises the obligations of the new life which has its ultimate source in that love.

οὕτως therefore covers the whole thought of the ὥσπερ clause: as in rising Christ left all that was dead behind, as that rising was due to the Father's love and power, as we share that rising, so we must leave our dead selves behind and walk etc.

ζωή is the principle of life, not the manner of life (cf. Gifford and see Lft, Igna. Rom. 7); the fresh vigour of a new principle of life (cf. viii. 2) is the motive power of Christian conduct (περιπατήσωμεν). This is the answer to *v.* 1.

5. γάρ expresses what was implied in καὶ ἡμεῖς, we are risen as Christ rose: this argument is continued to *v.* 11.

σύμφυτοι, here only N.T. Cf. ἔμφυτος, James i. 21. = if we have been born (γεγόναμεν) with a (new) nature characterised by or wearing the likeness of His death. The new nature is stamped with the likeness to Christ's death, as a death to sin; the idea is expanded in *v.* 6. συμφ. = 'of one growth or nature with.' γεγόναμεν, cf. xvi. 7, i. 3; James iii. 9. ὁμοίωμα, cf. viii. 3, Phil. ii. 7, implies true assimilation, but of things different. There is that in the Death of Christ which transcends the capacity of men, yet the life of the redeemed man is truly assimilated, in its degree, to that Death. R.V. supplies αὐτῷ and takes τῷ ὁμ. as instrumental; possible but not quite natural.

ἀλλὰ καὶ κ.τ.λ. = ἀλλὰ καὶ σύμφυτοι τῷ ὁμ. τῆς ἀν. ἐσόμεθα: explained by συνζήσομεν, *v.* 8 and ζῶντας, *v.* 11. The stamp of the risen Life of the Lord will also be shown in this new life—as a 'life to GOD,' and therefore not under sin. ἐσόμεθα is a logical future: it follows that our lives will show etc.

6. τ. γιν. ὅτι, almost = schooling ourselves to remember—the idea
is one which grows with experience of the new life—contrast εἰδότες
v. 9, cf. Moulton, p. 113. The point of the sentence lies in the ἵνα
clause—the object of our crucifixion with Christ was to deliver us etc.

ὁ παλ. ἡ. ἄνθρωπος : ἄνθρ. as often = human character, humanity :
two uses are to be distinguished, (a) ὁ ἔξω and ὁ ἔσω ἄνθρ. marking
the twofold character of human nature—mind and body; vii. 22;
2 Cor. iv. 16; Eph. iii. 16; cf. 1 Pet. iii. 4. This use goes back to
Plato. (b) ὁ παλαιὸς and ὁ καινὸς ἄνθρ. marking human nature as un-
regenerate or regenerate; so here; Eph. iv. 22 f.; Col. iii. 9. This use
seems to be peculiar to S. Paul, and is a notable link between Rom.,
Eph. and Col.; cf. S. H. For the idea cf. 2 Cor. v. 17; Gal. vi. 15.
It involves the thought of a new act of creation; and is perhaps
connected with the idea of 1 Cor. xv. 45 and so with c. v. above. A
further development of the thought is found in Eph. ii. 15.

συνεσταυρώθη, a more concrete expression of the idea of v. 5; cf.
Gal. ii. 20 (only, in this sense); also Gal. v. 24, vi. 14.

τὸ σῶμα τῆς ἁμαρτίας = the body as the instrument of sin ; the
body which sin had made its own—explained by the next clause and
v. 12. S. H. cf. vii. 24; Phil. iii. 21; Col. ii. 11. The body is the
organism of the human spirit ; the spirit is the source of all moral
action, both positive and negative; but the use of the body in sinful
ways has a cumulative effect upon the bodily activities, and by influencing impulses and habits makes it a ready instrument of the
sinning spirit, and of sin regarded metaphorically as an external
tyrannical force: all these acquired habits and impulses need to be
annihilated. Without metaphor = the body in which and by which
we sin. The result of this 'crucifixion' is to make the body an
instrument of righteousness, cf. xii. 1.

τοῦ μηκέτι δ. τοῦ *with infin.* is normally telic in N.T. = ' so as to...,'
' so that we are... '; cf. Phil. iii. 10 ; Moulton, p. 216 f. The purpose
is expressed by ἵνα, the result by τοῦ κ.τ.λ. So δουλεύειν pres.: so
that we are no longer in slavery to sin.

7. ὁ γὰρ ἀποθανών then enforces the completeness of this result :
= he that dies (cf. Moulton, p. 114) is acquitted of his sin for which
he is put to death—he has paid the penalty and is free from further
effects. This is not a merely general statement. As v. 8 shows, the
death here is a sharing of Christ's death : it is the voluntary self-
surrender of man to the penalty of his sin, and involves penitential
faith. Consequently it receives from GOD forgiveness, or acquittal from
his sin ; and sin has no more dominion over him. Cf. Moberly,
Atonement and Personality, pp. 39 f.

8.   εἰ δὲ ἀπεθάνομεν.   The death spoken of is not an absolute death, but relative only.   The force of these verses is to bring out the positive effects of this death: it is not only death to the old life but entry upon the new.   S. Paul thinks of death not as an end but as a transition from one life to another.

πιστεύομεν ὅτι is of the nature of a parenthesis=as we believe; it is even possible that there is a reference to a Christian common-place such as 2 Tim. ii. 12.

καὶ συνζήσομεν.   This is the real apodosis.   The future does not necessitate a reference to the future life, and in the context such a reference is very unnatural; it is rather the logical future marking the new life as fulfilling a promise or natural consequence.   So probably 2 Cor. xiii. 4; cf. *v.* 2.   Cf. ἐσόμεθα, *v.* 5.

9.   εἰδότες ὅτι, 'appeal to an elementary Christian belief,' Hort, 1 Pet. i. 18; cf. *v.* 3; 2 Cor. iv. 14, v. 6.   A stronger form is οὐκ οἴδατε ὅτι, *v.* 16, 1 Cor. iii. 16 *al.*

Χριστὸς κ.τ.λ.   The antithetic and rhythmical balance of these clauses suggests a well-known and well-used formula.   Cf. above *v.* 8.   It is possible that we have here, too, a fragment of a hymn or confession; cf. 2 Tim. ii. 8.   N. the rhythmical character stops at θεῷ.

οὐκέτι ἀποθνήσκει=never again dies: iterative, cf. Moulton, p. 114.

θάνατος α. κ.τ.λ.   His resurrection was a triumph over the sovereignty of death (cf. v. 14; 1 Cor. xv. 57) and has changed the meaning of death.

10.   ὃ γὰρ ἀπέθανεν, 'a kind of cognate accus. after the second ἀπέθανεν,' S. H.   His death that He died was a death once for all to sin.

τῇ ἁμαρτίᾳ.   Cf. *v.* 21, the sin that reigned by death: for the dative cf. *v.* 2.

ὃ δὲ ζῇ, 'the life that He lives is a life to GOD.'   It is clear that 'the Death' is not limited to the Death on the Cross.   The whole life of Jesus was a death to sin, culminating in the final act of the Cross.   So 'the life' here is not limited to the post-resurrection life: it is the life which He lived on earth, and still lives.   Cf. the very remarkable phrase, 2 Cor. iv. 10, τὴν νέκρωσιν τοῦ Ἰησοῦ followed by ἡ ζωὴ τοῦ Ἰησοῦ.   This meaning is well indicated by the strong 'perfectivised' ἀπέθανεν; cf. Moulton, p. 112.

11.   οὕτως κ.τ.λ. sums up the argument in answer to the question in *v.* 1.

ἐν Χρ. Ἰησοῦ, first time in this Ep. (iii. 24 is different).   The relation hitherto has been described by διὰ (v. 1, 11, 17, 21).   The idea then becomes explicit that the new life is life in Christ Jesus, as the ascended Lord, agent and source of the Christian life. As so often, it is the anticipatory mention of an idea which is developed later. See 23, vii. 4, viii. 2.

12 ff. The suggestion of *v.* 1 is reversed: the slave is free, the tyrant deposed, the service changed, the instruments of service refurbished, the power of service quickened.

μὴ βασιλευέτω, pres. of the continued reign, under these altered conditions.

ἡ ἁμαρτία, the sin which hitherto reigned.

ἐν τῷ θνητῷ ὑ. σ. Cf. 2 Cor. iv. 11 = even in your mortal body; the body, which yet must die, must not be allowed to minister to the deeper death.

ταῖς ἐπιθυμίαις α. Cf. i. 24. ἐπιθυμία (sing.) is used in a good sense only thrice in N.T. (Lk. xxii. 15; Phil. i. 23; 1 Thes. ii. 17); otherwise always in a bad sense, of the natural desire when not under the direction of νοῦς or πνεῦμα; cf. Gal. v. 16; Eph. iv. 22; 1 Pet. i. 14; 1 Joh. ii. 16.

13. μηδὲ παριστάνετε, do not continue to lend. παραστήσατε make a surrender once for all; cf. Moulton, p. 125. Cf. xii. 1.

τῷ θεῷ, for God's use.

ἐκ νεκρῶν ζ., as men that are alive after being dead.

τὰ μέλη, the component parts of the body. ὅπλα, instruments, tools (not merely for war); cf. xiii. 12; 2 Cor. vi. 7.

14. οὐ κυριεύσει, a promise, not a command.

οὐ γὰρ κ.τ.λ. Cf. 1 Cor. xv. 56: a verse which shows that this line of argument had been already developed by S. Paul in his oral teaching.

ὑπὸ νόμον...χάριν. The contrast is the keynote of this section: from the point of view of ethics, the Christian state is a state of grace, that is, a state in which man is the object of God's free favour and recipient of a new power of moral action, not a state of law, that is, a state in which man receives a revelation of God's will, but not the power to fulfil it. The statement of the contrast leads to the question of what freedom from law means, and that to a fuller account of what subjection to law means (c. vii.).

15—23. These verses, starting from the contrast just stated, describe the same conditions as in *vv.* 1—14 but from a slightly different point of view; there the two states of man have been described; here the two activities of the human will. What demand is made upon us as self-determining agents by this new condition of things? The answer is—a twofold demand; first to apprehend our true position, secondly to act upon it with the full purpose of will. The release from law is not a licence to sin but an obligation to free service.

τί οὖν; as τί οὖν ἐροῦμεν ; *v.* 1.

ἁμαρτήσωμεν, are we to commit sin, i.e. by definite acts? As sin may not be used to multiply grace, so it cannot be even used because grace has taken the place of positive law. The question is really raised whether the Christian has any law to which his life must conform, and, if he has, what kind of law?

16—23. These verses answer the question put in *v.* 15. The complexity of the passage is due to the fact that S. Paul wishes to explain that the Christian life is subject to law, but that the subjection differs from that of the Jew both in the character of the law and the nature of the subjection. (1) This new law is not a code of precepts but GOD's righteousness revealed in the life of Christ: the life of Christ is the model to which the Christian life must conform. And that, not merely because it is an external standard, but because the living Christ is the source, and naturally therefore determines the character, of the Christian life. This thought gets full and fearless expression in viii. 2, ὁ νόμος τοῦ πνεύματος τῆς ζωῆς ἐν Χρ. 'Ι. : but by that time the true place and character of preceptual law have been expounded, and there is no longer danger of confusion. (2) The nature of the subjection corresponds to the nature of the law: it is a whole-hearted self-surrender to GOD and to the life which embodies and reproduces, in those who so offer themselves, His righteousness. ὑπακοή here is very closely allied to πίστις, and might almost be described as 'faith in action'; cf. πίστις δι' ἀγάπης ἐνεργουμένη, Gal. v. 6.

It is this complexity of the subject which occasions the inaccurate antithesis in *v.* 16; the parenthetic explanation of *vv.* 19—21, and the multiplication of phrase (ὑπακοῆς, δικαιοσύνης...τύπον...θεῷ (22)).

16. οὐκ οἴδατε ὅτι, appeal to recognised principle.

ᾧ, neut.: the case is stated as generally as possible.

εἰς ὑπακοήν = with a view to obeying, for obedience—the proper attitude of the δοῦλος.

ἢ ὑπακοῆς εἰς δικαιοσύνην, the antithesis fails: we expect ἢ δικαιο-σύνης εἰς ζωήν. The reason for the change appears to be that the latter phrase could not yet be used without risk of misunderstanding: δοῦλοι δικαιοσύνης εἰς ζωήν could be fully accepted by a Jew as describing his state under law : consequently it is necessary to bring out the meaning both of ὑπακοή and of δικαιοσύνη; and this is done first by substituting these words, in spite of the inexact antithesis; and then by explaining their meaning in 17—18.

ὑπακοῆς. Consequently the gen. here is not objective after δοῦλοι but descriptive=slaves who obey.

εἰς δικαιοσύνην, with a view to righteousness—to secure and maintain righteousness. Righteousness here as generally=God's righteousness as revealed in Christ and made known in the gospel. Hence it can be used alternatively with τῷ θεῷ, vv. 18, 22.

17. χάρις δὲ τῷ θεῷ. The outburst of feeling is occasioned by the thought of the magnitude of the change which has been worked in them and in himself by God.

ἦτε δοῦλοι, really a μὲν clause, and to be translated 'while you were' or 'though you were.'

ὑπηκούσατε δὲ ἐκ καρδίας, the expansion of ὑπακοή, v. 16, as the effect of a deep heartwhole effort of self-surrender in response to the revelation of God: cf. exactly x. 9, 10, whence is seen the closeness of ὑπακοή as here used to πίστις. The aor. refers to the definite act of self-surrender made when they became Christians (contrast ἦτε).

εἰς ὃν παρεδόθητε τύπον διδαχῆς=τῷ τύπῳ τῆς διδαχῆς εἰς ὃν παρεδόθητε.

τύπον διδαχῆς, (1) not 'a type of doctrine' as some comm., e.g. the Pauline form of the Gospel as contrasted with the Judaistic: this is quite alien from S. Paul's manner of thought and expression (2 Tim. i. 13 has quite a different meaning from that usually given), and also to the whole drift of the context: but (2) the model of conduct which they have been taught in the Gospel: cf. Eph. iv. 20, οὐχ οὕτως ἐμάθετε τὸν χριστόν…. The gen. διδαχῆς= ὃν ἐδιδάχθητε. The 'model' in question is ὁ χριστός: the new righteousness being God's righteousness revealed in the character of the Christ: as Jesus ascended, He is here regarded not so much as the Master who claims, but as the personal Pattern who guides, the obedience of the surrendered life. This description of the object of obedience is therefore in line with the others (δικαιοσύνη, 18, 19, θεῷ, 22). For τύπος as a personal model for imitation cf. Phil. iii. 17; 1 Thes. i. 7; 2 Thes. iii. 9; 1 Tim. iv. 12; Tit. ii. 7; 1 Pet. v. 3.

παρεδόθητε. The correct interpretation of τύπος makes the use of this verb natural—they had been handed over, in their Baptism (aor.), to a new kind of life; || in thought to ἐβαπτίσθημεν εἰς Χριστόν, v. 3. Cf. 2 Cor. iv. 11.

18. ἐδουλώθητε τῇ δικαιοσύνῃ. The correct antithesis which was avoided in v. 16 is now given, because the sense in which ἡ δικ. is to be taken has been made clear in the preceding sentence; Art.=the righteousness of God revealed in Christ.

19. ἀνθρώπινον λέγω. An apology for the harsh word ἐδουλώθητε:

he calls it slavery, because the weakness of the flesh needs just such a masterful control as that word implies, and as it had lent itself to under its former master. The mastery of Christ is even more exacting and exclusive than the mastery of sin. Cf. Mt. v. 20. He developes this thought in *vv.* 19—21.

διὰ τὴν ἀσθ. gives the reason why he thinks the word δουλεία appropriate even to their new life.

ὥσπερ γὰρ κ.τ.λ. A summary of the state described in i. 18 f. Cf. ii. 14 f.

εἰς ἁγιασμόν = for hallowing, to be hallowed; the translation into character of the call expressed in the name ἅγιοι: submitting their lives to the influence of the revealed δικαιοσύνη: here, as generally, marks the process; cf. 1 Pet. i. 2; 2 Thes. ii. 13; 1 Thes. iv. 7. The hallowing is the work of the Spirit (cf. viii. 2) upon their surrendered lives.

20. γάρ. Make this effort, for your former freedom or slavery brought you such gain as now shames you.

21. εἴχετε, used you to enjoy. ἐφ᾽ οἷς = ἐκείνων ἐφ᾽ οἷς, from those things at which....

καρπόν here = the results of their slavery—so ὀψώνια—χάρισμα : in the one case earned and paid, in the other not earned but given.

22. δουλωθέντες δὲ τῷ θεῷ. The fullest expression of the service into which they have been brought.

ἔχετε. You bear your proper fruit; or perhaps imper.; cf. *v.* 19. N. the present of continued action.

23. τὸ χάρισμα. The concrete instance of God's χάρις.

ἐν Χρ. With ζ. αἱ. as *v.* 11: for the full name cf. n. on v. 21. N. refrain again.

CHAPTER VII.

(1) Your experience of human laws helps here: you are aware that law rules a man so long only as he lives—for instance marriage binds the wife during the life of her husband; but after his death she is free to marry another. (4) So you were under the law, but you died with the Christ, by the death of His Body, and that was a death to the law, so that you became united to Another, to Him who was raised from death just in order that (in Him) we might bear fruit to God. (5) For when the flesh was the condition in which we lived, the sinful states which we experienced under the influence of the law were so operative in our members that we bore fruit only for death, (6) but in our present condition we have been freed from all influence of the law, we are dead in respect of that character in which we were held under its influence, so that we are now rendering our due service under the influence of a fresh action of spirit and not by an antiquated action of literal precept.

A new illustration enforces the argument of the preceding section that freedom from law does not imply freedom to sin. There is a change of allegiance which has its analogue in human laws. The change chosen as an illustration is that of the law of marriage. This suggests not only allegiance but a union which is productive of offspring. The old union is of the self with the flesh or the 'old man'; under the influence of law that produced sin: the new union is of the self with Christ; it has been brought about by the self sharing the death of Christ, and consequently becoming united to His risen Life: this union involves as its product service to God under the inspiration of a fresh spirit. The progress in the main argument is in this emphasis on the new life as in Christ, developing vi. 11, 23.

If the illustration is to be pressed, the conception must be that there is a persistent self, first wedded to a nature of flesh and, under law, begetting sins; then that nature dies, the self is freed from it and its law, and is wedded to Christ. In this union it brings forth the new fruit. So in vi. 6 it is not the self, but the old character that was crucified with Christ, 'we,' 'ourselves,' were set free. There is a distinction between the self and the character which the self assumes whether ἐν σαρκί or ἐν πνεύματι. Cf. Gifford and S. H., *aliter* Lft.

1. νόμον. Quite general—not Roman or Jewish, but a general axiom of law.

ὁ νόμος= the law under which he lives, whatever it be.

2. κατήργηται ἀπό. Cf. Gal. v. 4: has been made, so to speak, non-existent as regards that law and so freed from it.

3. χρηματίσει, Acts xi. 26 only= will be called; cf. Wetst.

γένηται ἀνδρί. Cf. Lev. xxii. 12; Ruth i. 12 f.

τοῦ μὴ εἶναι. Cf. vi. 6 note.

4. ἐθανατώθητε, you were put to death, i.e. your former nature was slain but you yourselves survived to enter upon a new life, free from that law which bound the old nature, but with its own characteristic obligation. ἐθαν. corresponds to κατήργηται of v. 2. See vi. 8 n.

διὰ τοῦ σώματος τοῦ χριστοῦ. Cf. Heb. x. 10; Col. i. 22; 1 Pet. ii. 24, and perhaps 1 Cor. x. 16, apparently the only passages outside Evv. where the pre-resurrection Body is spoken of thus. Both Col. and 1 Pet. are parallel: and 1 Pet. so close that it must depend on this passage. *Infra* xii. 5= 1 Cor. xii. 27, we have the sense of the Body as the form of the Church, developed in Eph. i. 23 *et passim*. In Col. the words τῆς σαρκός are expressly added to mark the distinction.

διὰ τ. σ. Cf. vi. 3, 8. The thought is that as they were baptised into Christ, they shared the effects of His Death in the Body as well as those of His risen life. N. τοῦ χριστοῦ: the article marks the reference to the historic action.

εἰς τὸ γεν. So that you came to be wedded to another, i.e. than that old nature which was slain.

ἵνα. Closely with ἐγερθέντι.

καρποφορήσωμεν. Sc. under the influence of the new life imparted by the Risen Lord, constituting in each individual a 'new man' or character.

5. ἦμεν ἐν τῇ σαρκί= ὁ παλαιὸς ἄνθρωπος of vi. 6.

τὰ παθήματα τῶν ἁμ.: παθήματα only Paul, Heb. and 1 Pet. =(1) sufferings, cf. viii. 18, and commonly; (2)= experiences, here and Gal. v. 24= concrete instances of πάθος, the state in which the subject is regarded as not active but receptive of experiences. So here= the effects which our sins produced upon our nature. See vi. 6 n.

τὰ διὰ τοῦ νόμου. Developed and explained in *vv.* 7 ff. These experiences came through the influence of law upon the old nature.

ἐνηργεῖτο= were constantly being made operative, i.e. by the action

of ὁ πάλαιος ἄνθρωπος in reaction against law (τὰ διὰ τ. ν.) ; cf. Robinson, *Eph.* 247. ἐνεργεῖσθαι in S. Paul is always passive, implying an
agent, here the context shows that the agent is ὁ παλ. ἄνθρωπος.

6. κατηργήθημεν ἀπὸ νόμου=ἐθανατώθημεν τῷ νόμῳ ‖ v. 2.

ἀποθανόντες ἐν ᾧ κατειχόμεθα=being dead in or to that character
in which we were held in a state of subjection; ἀποθανόντες τῷ (or
ἐν τῷ) παλαίῳ ἀνθρώπῳ ἐν ᾧ κατ.; cf. Joh. v. 4 T. R., the only
other instance of the passive in N.T. Cf. Polyb. iv. 51. 1, θεωροῦντες
τὸν πατέρα...κατεχόμενον ἐν Ἀλεξανδρείᾳ. The old nature was the
prison in which we, our true selves, were detained.

ὥστε δουλεύειν=so that we are still servants (pres.) but in newness
of spirit etc. Cf. Burton, §§ 369 f.

ἐν καινότητι πνεύματος. ἐν circumstantial. Our service is rendered
in a new atmosphere marked by the presence in us of Spirit, i.e. the
Spirit of the life in Christ Jesus; cf. viii. 1.

παλαιότητι γράμματος=the worn-out system which was marked by
the dominance of written precepts. Cf. ii. 29; 2 Cor. iii. 6; S. H.
ii. 27. The antithesis occurs only in these passages; and contrasts
the external law with the internal quickening spirit.

vii. 7—25. The new life is effective to achieve righteousness in
each man, as the law could not do.

(7) Not that the law is itself sin, but it awakes the consciousness
of sin, as, for instance, covetousness is not felt as sin till it
is known to be a breach of law; sin gets its opportunity through
law. (9) In the personal experience, there is first a (non-moral)
existence unconscious of law; when a definite precept is brought
into this experience, sin springs to life, the man dies: for sin, like
some alien power, gets its opportunity by this precept, deceives the
man and slays him. (12) While therefore the law represents and
is even in detail the standard of holiness, righteousness and good,
(13) yet by this good, sin works death and proves itself so to be
downright sin, (14) because of the inevitable antithesis between the
spiritual character of the law, and the fleshly nature of the awakened
consciousness which makes it sin's slave. (15) It is in fact the
experienced antagonism of the conscious will and the fleshly practice;
the former witnesses to the goodness of the law; the latter to an
indwelling power, not the personal will, but sin; (18) in this fleshly
nature by itself there is nothing good; it even prevents the good will
actualising itself in practice; (20) but in that case, the practice
belongs not to the man but to the sin which possesses him. (21) So
we are driven by analysis of our experience to recognise, if not a

double personality, at least a person and a power, within consciousness; it is a principle of this twofold consciousness that the will sides
with the law of GOD while in the body there appears another, an-
tagonistic, law which enslaves a man: from this slavery I find in
myself no power to escape. (25) But thank GOD there is such a
power, not of me but within me, the help of Jesus Christ our Lord.
So that, to sum up all, in one and the same self there is a double
servitude: with my mind and heart I am a slave to GOD's law, with
my flesh I am a slave to sin's law.

This section then brings out the true character of the effect of law,
as the revelation in positive precepts of GOD's will for man. Its effect
is to give the knowledge of right and wrong, to awaken, that is, the
moral consciousness; this at once brings out the antagonism between
the nature of man as living in the flesh, and his will and intelligence,
which approve the law; the antagonism arises with the attempt to
act; the good will finds itself thwarted by something in the nature,
which, as not properly essential to the nature and yet finding its ready
instrument therein, is realised as a power lodged there and is called
sin. So definite and actual is this power felt to be in our experience
that S. Paul, interpreting that experience, describes it as a power
imposing, on all but equal terms with GOD, a law upon his nature,
a law which says 'thou shalt' in direct contradiction of GOD's law
'thou shalt not.' In this conflict he has found no help except in
the reinforcement of his will by the new spirit which has become
his, by the aid of Jesus Christ our Lord. This is developed in c. viii.
The law with all its goodness does not impart such a power. The
difficulty of the passage is due to the depth of the psychological
analysis to which S. Paul here subjects his own experience; he
analyses so thoroughly as to reach the common human element in
the individual experience. See Additional Note, p. 216.

7. τί οὖν ἐροῦμεν; Yet another suggestion stated, to be put aside.
If under law we are slaves to sin, under grace to righteousness, it
might be supposed that the law itself is sin: but as the law is a
revelation of GOD's will, such a supposition would be monstrous.

ἀλλά introduces the true statement of the case, which covers the
next few verses.

ἔγνων. Inceptive: I did not become conscious of sin but by the
law, making its claim on me for right action.

τήν τε γὰρ ἐπιθυμίαν. Cf. 2 Cor. x. 8 (ἐάν τε γὰρ). This isolated τε
introduces a particular example of the effect of law from the 10th
Commandment: almost=even, or in particular; cf. Shilleto, Dem.
F. L. § 176, crit. ann.

οὐκ ᾔδειν. I had remained without knowledge of the real meaning of covetousness, if the law had not kept saying.... Cf. Moulton, p. 200 f.

8. ἀφορμὴν...λαβοῦσα, 'having got a handle.' ἀφορμὴ=a starting point, base of operations, opportunity.

ἡ ἁμαρτία throughout the passage is treated as a concrete force or power. It is remarkable that S. Paul comes as near as possible to personifying the conception of sin, but does not actually use the idea of a personal author of evil: he here limits his account strictly to the analysis of actual experience; cf. S. H. p. 145. See Additional Note, p. 218.

διὰ τῆς ἐντολῆς. Closely with ἀφ. λ.: the positive command (ἐ.=a particular law) was the opportunity; cf. iii. 20, v. 20. The order of the phrases is due to the necessity of emphasising the manner of sin's entry into experience; διὰ τ. ἐ. is here unemphatic.

ἐν ἐμοί. S. Paul analyses his own experience as typical.

κατειργάσατο...π. ἐ. The idea seems to be that the impulses of man's nature are not recognised as being right or wrong, till the sense of right and wrong is awakened by a positive command: when this occurs, what were neutral impulses become 'lusts,' i.e. desires of what is forbidden; it is this perverse desire which is described as the work of 'sin,' impulses persisting when there is present the knowledge that they are wrong, and the will or true self is not yet strong enough to control them.

χωρὶς γὰρ κ.τ.λ. For apart from a knowledge of right and wrong sin has no power of action; there is no moral sense or moral judgment. Cf. 1 Cor. xv. 56, a passage which shows that the main idea had been represented already in S. Paul's teaching. For νόμος as imparting the sense of right and wrong cf. ii. 14 f.

9. ἐγὼ δὲ ἔζων κ.τ.λ. 'I was living unaffected by law once.' He goes back to a pre-moral state—not necessarily in actual memory of a completely non-moral experience, but comparatively: his life as a child was untouched by numberless demands of law, which accumulated with his moral development; at that period whole regions of his life were purely impulsive; one after another they came under the touch of law, and with each new pressure of law upon his consciousness the sphere, in which it was possible to sin, was enlarged. It was easy to carry this retrospect one step beyond memory and to see himself living a life of pure impulse before the very first voice of law reached him: and to regard such a stage as a typical stage in the general development of the moral sense in man.

ἀνέζησεν, 'sprang to life': only here and Lk. xv. 24 (=revived), not classical. We should perhaps recognise here an instance of the 'perfectivising' function of the preposition; cf. Moulton, p. 112. Both A. and R.V. 'revived': but the whole point is that at that moment sin for the first time came to life. For this use of ἀνά cf. ἀναβοᾶν, ἀναθυμιᾶσθαι, ἀνακύπτειν, ἀνατέλλειν.

10. ἐγὼ δὲ ἀπέθανον. Here of the death to the pre-moral life, a death by and in sin: *aor.* = became dead.

εὑρέθη = proved in my experience; more than ἐγένετο.

11. ἐξηπάτησεν κ.τ.λ. Here we get nearest to personification of ἡ ἁμ., with the echo of Gen. ii. 13; cf. 2 Cor. xi. 3; 1 Tim. ii. 14. The deceit lies in the representation of the satisfaction of the forbidden impulse as more desirable than obedience to the command.

12. ὁ μὲν κ.τ.λ. The antithesis is not expressed; an interruption is caused by the occurrence of one more false conclusion which has to be removed. Then the line of thought is resumed in *v.* 14.

δικαία = right.

13. τὸ ἀγαθὸν κ.τ.λ. Did that good thing, law, itself prove death to me?

ἡ ἁμαρτία. Sc. ἐγένετο ἐμοὶ θάνατος.

ἵνα φ. The effect of sin found to be death proves sin to be what it is.

διὰ τοῦ ἀγαθοῦ = διὰ τοῦ νόμου. **κατεργαζομένη**, by producing.

14. οἴδαμεν γὰρ ὅτι. Appeal to acknowledged principle.

πνευματικός introduces the final description of the internal conflict: it is a struggle of πνεῦμα against ἁμαρτία to win the mastery of σάρξ. In this struggle law is on the side of πνεῦμα, but only as a standard and revelation of right, not as a spiritual power strengthening man's will; that can only come from GOD, by an internal influence on man's πνεῦμα.

σάρκινος. Fleshy, made of flesh, marks the substance or component part of substance; σαρκικός marks character. A πνεῦμα may be σαρκικόν but cannot be σάρκινον. Cf. λίθινος, Joh. ii. 6; 2 Cor. iii. 3; ξύλινος, 2 Tim. ii. 20; see Westcott on Heb. vii. 16. Here the word is precise; his nature has in it a fleshy element; if this dominates the πνεῦμα, then the man is σαρκικός; if the πνεῦμα controls it, the man is πνευματικός. σάρξ describes the man in his natural state, including not merely his material body, but his mental and volitional operations so far as they are limited to or dominated by his earthly and temporal concerns. The evil belongs to σάρξ not in itself but in its wrong relation to spirit; so far as it is brought completely under the control of spirit, it too becomes πνευματική; hence explain 1 Cor. xv. 44 f. So πνεῦμα becomes σαρκικόν if it subordinates itself to σάρξ. Cf. 1 Cor. iii. 1 and 3 ff.

πεπραμένος, 'one that has sold himself under sin '='made a slave under sin,' not explanatory of σάρκινος but a further determination of the condition. Before law came, man was σάρκινος, but not πεπρ. ὑ. ἁμ.; now he is both. Metaph. only here in N.T.

15. γὰρ amplifies the idea of πεπραμένος ; he is no longer his own master but under a tyranny he hates.

ὃ κατεργάζομαι. The effects I produce are not the outcome of my own knowledge and purpose.

οὐ γινώσκω=I form no true conception of, I do not thoroughly realise—the durative present. Cf. ἐξηπάτησεν, *v.* 11.

πράσσω, put into practice. **ποιῶ,** commit in act.

17. νυνὶ δὲ. But, in this case, this being so.

οὐκέτι ἐγὼ. It is, when this point is reached, no longer my true self that is producing these effects, but the indwelling and alien tyrant.

18. οἶδα=I am fully conscious that....

τοῦτ' ἔστιν κ.τ.λ. A correction of the too wide **ἐν ἐμοί**; in his true self there is ἀγαθόν, the knowledge of and appreciation of law.

ἐν τῇ σαρκί. The evil is not the flesh, but alien from, though lodged in, the flesh.

παράκειται. Only here and 21.

19=15.

20=17.

21. ἄρα sums up the reiterated positions of *vv.* 15—20.

τὸν νόμον=this law of my condition : a new sense of the word involving some confusion of language. The law of his condition is that there are two laws at once in his complex nature, one a law of his mind, i.e. the law of GOD accepted by his mind, one a law intruded upon his 'members' by sin, embodying the law of sin. It is just possible however that τὸν νόμον=the law of GOD (cf. ἡ ὀργή) ; and tr. 'I find as regards the Law, that when I will to do the good ' (i.e. the bidding of this law) etc. This is strained, but diminishes the confusion. Cf. S. H.

τὸ καλὸν. The ideally true and right, as referred to a standard : **ἀγαθόν**=that which is good, as judged by effects.

22. τῷ νόμῳ τοῦ θεοῦ. The law of GOD, however revealed, but always in the form of positive command.

τὸν ἔσω ἄνθρωπον describes the inner core of personality, including mind and will. Cf. vi. 6 n.

23. ἐν τοῖς μέλεσιν describes the flesh as organised and active in various directions=the σῶμα in detail. Observe that S. Paul does not say 'of my members' but 'in my members.' He carefully avoids using language which implies that this law is proper to the flesh in its essential nature; it has its lodgment there, but the flesh is destined, and must be claimed, for other and higher allegiance.

τῷ νόμῳ τοῦ νοός μου=the law accepted by my mind, GOD's law made my own in apprehension and acceptance.

αἰχμαλωτίζοντα ‖ πεπραμένος, v. 14.

τῷ νόμῳ τῆς ἁμ. The law imposed by sin.

24, 25. A parenthetic exclamation, a cry for help, and the answer.

24. ἐκ τοῦ σ. τ. θ. τ. The man has become all but wholly involved in his body which sin has made captive to death. τ. θ. τ. this moral death.

Just as in *v.* 9 S. Paul's keen self-analysis carries him beyond actual memory into the imagination of a pre-moral state, so here he carries the analysis of the internal strife, perhaps beyond his actual experience, into the sympathetic realisation of the common human state and need, when man's spirit realises its extremity and does not yet see hope: though the very realisation is the first gleam of hope. Cf. S. H. See Additional Note, p. 218.

25. χάρις δὲ τῷ θεῷ. An exclamation—not in construction. For the phrase cf. 1 Cor. xv. 57.

διὰ 'Ι. κ.τ.λ. Sc. ῥυσθήσομαι or ἐρρύσθην. Law being the bare declaration of right had no power to move the living springs of action: that power comes from and through the Risen Lord imparting His own new life to man. This thought is developed in c. viii.

ἄρα οὖν sums up the whole statement of the condition of man in the face of law on the one hand, and of sin on the other.

αὐτὸς ἐγώ=I by myself and apart from any new or other power which may be available to change the balance of contending powers. It is important to remember that the whole section is an analysis of man's state under law, definitely excluding, for the moment, from consideration all action of GOD upon man's spirit except through the channel of communicated law. It has already been shown or as-sumed that there is such action, both in the case of Gentiles (ii. 14) and in Abraham's case (c. iv.) as typical of the pious Jew; here we are reminded that that action reaches its full and effective operation in the risen Lord. But it was necessary, by this analysis, to isolate, as it were, from these considerations, the case of man under law, in order to bring out the exact place of law in the moral and religious experience of man, and to show that more than law was needed by him and has been and is operative in him. See Additional Note on νόμος, p. 211.

τῷ μὲν νοΐ. The νοῦς is here used for the mind as capable of the

knowledge of GOD and His Will.   πνεῦμα seems to be avoided, because
it definitely suggests the direct connexion with and dependence upon
GOD as acting upon man's spirit; and that thought is for the moment
excluded.   The use of the word is almost confined to S. Paul.   Cf.
23, xii. 2; Eph. iv. 23; Col. ii. 18.   Here it includes apprehension
and inclination.

There is much to be said for Joh. Weiss' suggestion (*op. cit.*
p. 231 f.) that there has been here a primitive transposition of text,
so that originally ἄρα οὖν αὐτὸς...ἁμαρτίας preceded ταλαίπωρος...ἡμῶν.
The ταλαίπωρος clause would come most properly after the summary
of the all but desperate situation in ἄρα οὖν κ.τ.λ.   The last clause
(χάρις κ.τ.λ.) would come naturally at the end of the whole discussion; it contains the name which has so often already been used,
as a concluding refrain: and it marks the transition to viii. 1.

CHAPTER VIII.

D. VIII. THE NATURE OF THE POWER AND OF THE WORKING OF THE NEW LIFE EXPLAINED.

1—11. The power is the indwelling spirit.

(1) It follows from this examination of man's state under law, that in our present state, as effected by GOD, those who are made one with Christ Jesus are not under penalties. (2) For the new condition brought by the Spirit, which animates the new life we received on being united with Christ Jesus, liberated us once for all from the former tyranny. (3) GOD's law, barely declaring His will, could not do this because it was undermined by means of the flesh. But GOD Himself did the work of liberation, first, through His Son incarnate triumphing over sin even in the flesh, (4) and secondly and consequently through His Son in us, fulfilling the claim of law by conduct on the lines of spirit not of flesh. (5) It was in fact just this reinforcement of man's spirit which was needed, in the antagonism of spirit and flesh, to overcome the limitations of the latter and to bring it under the power of the spirit. (9) That work has now been done in Christians: GOD's Spirit dwells in them, because if they are Christ's they possess Christ's Spirit, which implies that their bodies are dead for all purposes of sin, their spirits a living power in the body for all purposes of righteousness, (11) for all purposes, because they are thus strengthened by the same Power which raised Christ Jesus from death, and will put life into their bodies, in themselves doomed to death, because it is GOD's Spirit dwelling in them.

This section then brings out the nature of the power of the Gospel in contrast with the description of the powerlessness of law. That power in fact is the power of the life of the Risen Lord in the Christian, bringing to bear upon the human spirit the whole moral and spiritual force of the Spirit of GOD Himself.

1. ἄρα. So, after this exposition, it becomes clear.

νῦν. As things now are, under the new dispensation.

κατάκριμα. In Christ there is no penal state following upon a verdict of condemnation, because in Christ men are acquitted (justi-fied); cf. v. 16 n.

τοῖς ἐν Χρ. ʼΙ. Those whose relation to GOD is determined by their union with Christ. Χρ. ʼΙ. always in this order after ἐν and εἰς (unless Gal. iii. 14).

2. ὁ γὰρ νόμος τ. πν. κ.τ.λ. The life in Christ Jesus is the new life of and in men, Christ's life in them, their life in Christ. This life has its instrument or vehicle, as it were, in the new spirit that is in men, new, because the result of their spirit being in union with and invigorated by Christ's Spirit (v. 9). This new or renewed spirit has its own law regulating its true condition, just as the old spirit had (vii. 21): and this law is embodied in the life and character of Christ; its first utterance is justification by faith which at once liberates a man from the tyranny of sin and death and dictates a corresponding manner of life; cf. n. on vi. 16—23. It is very re-markable that S. Paul should use this word νόμος to express any condition of the new life: it at least shows how far he is from having worked out a complete technical vocabulary. "He is using ν. here in the sense of Torah which is very much wider than ν. as ordinarily interpreted." J. H. A. Hart. In τ. πν. τ. ʒ. there is a reference to Gen. ii. 7: this is a new creation; cf. 2 Cor. v. 17.

ἐν Χρ. ʼΙ. Closely with ζωῆς; the whole phrase describes the 'new man.'

ἠλευθέρωσεν. Sc. as soon as it came into action. Cf. vi. 4, 8, 11.

ἀπὸ τοῦ νόμου τ. ἁ. κ. τ. θ. Either (1) the law imposed by sin, cf. vii. 23, 25, or (2) the law which gave sin its opportunity, cf. vii. 11. The first is more in accordance with usage in c. vii.; yet it obliges us to take νόμος in a different sense from v. 3.

3. γὰρ explains the method of liberation.

τὸ ἀδύνατον. For abstract ἀδυνασία: cf. τὸ γνήσιον, 2 Cor. viii. 8; τὸ δοκίμιον, James i. 3; 1 Pet. i. 7 (?); τὸ χρηστὸν, supra ii. 4; cf. Blass, p. 155=the incapacity, ineffectiveness, lack of power. The construction is pendent; cf. Blass, p. 283.

τοῦ νόμου. Here clearly of the law of GOD as apprehended by man.

ἐν ᾧ ἠσθένει=the quality by which it was in a state of weakness, brought to that weakness (by sin) by means of the flesh; cf. vii. 14 n. ἠσθένει=constantly proved weak.

ὁ θεὸς. The whole action described is the action of GOD.

τὸν ἑ. υἱὸν. "The emphatic ἑαυτοῦ brings out the community of nature between the Father and the Son, cf. v. 32, Col. i. 13," S. H. Add to 'nature' mind and purpose.

πέμψας. In this connexion only here and in Ev. Joh.

ἐν ὁμ. σ. ἁμ. Cf. Phil. ii. 7; Heb. ii. 17. ὁμ. does not mark
unreality but suggests a difference; cf. v. 14, vi. 5 n. The difference
here is indicated by the addition of ἁμ. The σάρξ which He assumed
never admitted the tyranny of sin, though it included the capacity
for temptation and sin. In these words S. Paul touches the very
nerve of the Passion, and indicates the supreme act of the divine
Love. See Moberly, *Atonement and Personality*, c. vi.

σ. ἁμαρτίας=human nature as it is under the dominion of sin.
This phrase comes most near to describing flesh as in itself sinful;
but that misunderstanding has already been fully guarded against.

περὶ ἁμαρτίας. περὶ = in the matter of, to deal with. ὑπέρ=on
behalf of. But the distinction between these prepositions is obscured
in the Greek of this time. ὑπὲρ is never used with the sing. (sin
as sin) but only with the plural (men's sins): περὶ with both. It
is probable that in περὶ ἁμαρτίας there is a direct allusion to the
sin-offering; cf. Lev. iv. *et passim*; Heb. x. 6 *al.* (cf. Heb. x. 26);
but the reference is also wider.

κατέκρινε τὴν ἁμ. Condemned it, gave a verdict against it in its
claim upon man : it was just this effective condemnation which law
had been unable to compass.

ἐν τῇ σαρκί. With κατέκρινε=in His flesh; cf. vi. 1—10, esp. 6, 7,
10. This parallel shows the reference to be primarily to the Crucifixion (cf. vii. 4); but the whole Incarnate Life showed the victorious
power over sin which culminated in the Death and Resurrection, and
constituted a verdict against sin's claim to man's nature. The whole
was one act of redemption of the flesh, i.e. of human nature: it is
that act in all its bearings which is in question here, in contrast with
τὸ ἀδύνατον τοῦ νόμου.

4. ἵνα. The object of the sending and the condemnation of sin.

τὸ δικαίωμα, the righteous claim of the law. The law as God's
revealed will has a claim over man : the same act which repudiated
the claim of sin provided for the fulfilment of the claim of the law.
Law and sin are here conceived as litigants for the ownership of man.

ἐν ἡμῖν. Not ὑφ' ἡμῶν : in us as renewed in Christ.

τοῖς μὴ κ.τ.λ. Not=if we walk, but in us in the character of men
whose principle of conduct is regulated not by flesh but by spirit. A
summary description of the true life of man, seen and made possible
in Christ.

κατὰ σάρκα...κατὰ πνεῦμα. This antithesis at last becomes explicit, and is developed in *vv.* 5—8. In vii. 25 the antithesis was
νοῦς and σάρξ ; here, when it is more a question of the roots of action,
it is πνεῦμα and σάρξ.

5. γάρ. Explains how walking after spirit leads to the fulfilment of the claim of law, by a series of contrasted clauses.

οἱ γὰρ κατὰ σάρκα ὄντες. Those who take flesh for their standard of reference and line of action.

τὰ τῆς σαρκὸς φρονοῦσιν. *φρονεῖν τά τινος* = to adopt a man's interests as your own, to side with him, be of his party: so here, not = have fleshly thoughts (*σαρκικὰ φρονοῦντες*), but side with the flesh, make its aims, characteristics and interests their own; cf. Mt. xvi. 23 ‖ Mk viii. 33 only. It is just this giving flesh its wrong place in the mutual relation of the elements of man's nature which makes it the instrument of sin.

6. τὸ φρόνημα. Almost = the policy, the leading idea, of the flesh when isolated and uncontrolled, i.e. of man as merely earthly. Only in this chapter.

7. τὸ φρ. τῆς σαρκὸς ἔχθρα εἰς θεόν. As before, it is the flesh as usurping and absorbing man's whole interest which is in question, not the flesh in general.

8. οἱ ἐν σαρκὶ ὄντες, those whose being is wholly involved in flesh, not = those who are living in this passing life.

9. ὑμεῖς δέ. Spirit, not flesh, is even now the atmosphere and inspiration of the Christian life.

ἐν πνεύματι. The human spirit (as shown by the contrast with *σάρξ*), which, in Christians, has become the channel or vehicle on and in which the divine Spirit works. *πν.* is that element in human nature by which man is capable of communion with GOD; and that communion reaches its culminating point when it is mediated by the life in and of Christ: then the Spirit of GOD not only speaks to or influences occasionally but dwells in the human spirit; and this is re-created, becomes new, as the spirit of the life in Christ Jesus; cf. Joh. iii. 34. Cf. S. H.

πνεῦμα θεοῦ ‖ πνεῦμα Χριστοῦ ‖ Χριστός. Cf. Acts ii. 33; *supra,* i. 4; v. 5; *infra,* 14. The Spirit is the Spirit of GOD because He is sent from GOD: He is the Spirit of Christ, because He comes as representative of Christ, and brings the living power, the life of the ascended Lord, into human lives : so as the result of His action Christ Himself dwells in man. See Moberly, *op. cit.* pp. 197 ff.

εἴπερ, if, as is admitted: an appeal to the acknowledged character of Baptism ; cf. vi. 1 ff. It is important to note that in all these sentences, no new teaching is being given, but appeal made to established truth.

εἰ δέ τις κ.τ.λ. To be a Christian is to have Christ's Spirit; not merely to have a spirit like Christ's. Cf. 1 Cor. ii. 14—16.

οὐκ. Cf. Moulton, p. 171; Blass, p. 254.

10. εἰ δὲ Χριστὸς ἐν ὑμῖν. The converse of ἐν Χριστῷ; the consequence of having Christ's Spirit.

διὰ ἁμαρτίαν = for the sake of, for the purposes of sin. Cf.
Mk ii. 27; 1 Cor. xi. 9; Blass, p. 132.

τὸ...πνεῦμα ζωή. The spirit is not merely alive, but a principle
of life in the man ; under its power the body too is alive.

διὰ δικαιοσύνην. For the purposes of righteousness ; cf. 4.

11. εἰ δὲ κ.τ.λ. Develops the thought implied in 10 that the
body, too, even now is quickened by the new life ; it has become
a ὅπλον δικαιοσύνης, vi. 13.

τὸ πν. τ. ἐγ. The resurrection of Jesus is a measure and warrant
both of the will and of the power of the Spirit of GOD, to bring life
into what is dead. Cf. iv. 24 and v. 6, 10, 11.

ζωοποιήσει. Cf. vi. 8. The reference is not to the final resurrection, but to the present spiritual quickening of the whole man, the
foretaste of that. The future is used, because a condition has to be
fulfilled by man, πίστις; cf. vi. 11 (with 8).

τὰ θνητὰ σώματα. Your bodies, dead though they be; cf. vii. 24
and vii. 4.

The whole context seems to be decisive in favour of this line of
interpretation. The section (viii. 1—11) balances the preceding
section (vii. 7—25). There the inability of the law by itself to
produce the higher spiritual life was shown; and the argument dealt
primarily and mainly with human life as it is now. Here the whole
object is to show that the Gospel provides just such a power as law
lacks, a power, that is, to revive and renew the human spirit so as to
enable it to mould and master the whole life. The life and death
spoken of are the spiritual life and death already described ; the
raising is the present liberation of the spirit which affects the body
also, making it too serve its true ends and live its true life. The
raising of Jesus is a proof both of the will and character and power
of that Spirit, which operated then and operates now through the
risen Life communicated now to man ; cf. vi. 2—11. The future
resurrection is not referred to; but it is of course implied as a consequence of the whole relation thus described between GOD and man.
Cf. closely 2 Cor. iv. 10, 11, iii. 18, v. 14—16. The thought of the
future resurrection life becomes explicit in v. 17. As v. 1—11 argued
that if GOD so loved us as to give His Son to die for us, He must love
us enough to complete His saving work in us through His Son; so
viii. 1—11 argues that if GOD had power and will to raise Jesus from
the dead, He must have power and will to raise us in and through
His Son from the death of sin.

12—39. The interpretation of the character and obligations of human life, under the power of the indwelling Spirit, in relation to creation and to GOD.

(12) If then all this is true, that our spirit in its warfare with the flesh is reinforced by GOD's Spirit, our life intimately dependent upon Christ living in us through that Spirit, then the duty of the Christian is clear; it is a duty not to the flesh but to the spirit, not to live as the flesh dictates, but to live as the spirit dictates, bringing through a fleshly death to a spiritual life all the doings and farings of the body; (14) *only so*, as always answering to the leading of the Spirit, do we act up to our character as sons of GOD—a character which has replaced that of slaves, which enjoins a free appeal to the Father's love and answers to the inner testimony of His Spirit acting upon ours—(17) *only so*, do we claim as children our share of the life of GOD in Christ, a share of present suffering as the means to a share in the future glory. (18) For we cannot disregard this character of fleshly death, of present sufferings : nor should we try to do so : they are the stamp placed upon creation to mark its vanity, its transitory character, its merely preliminary and preparatory quality : corruption in nature and in man is the evidence of a redemption now working through the breaking up of present conditions and one day to be manifested in the establishment of a glorious freedom : (23) our adoption to sonship is inchoate but incomplete, and a strain and trial now of mortal nature : hope is its inspiration : patience and endurance its condition : the joy and glory it points to are incomparably greater than the trials and troubles of the present.

(26) Corresponding to this present condition of our nature is the activity of the Spirit helping our infirmity, by supplementing our ignorant and feeble prayers with His indescribable intercessions known in their fullest meaning only to GOD, (28) to us known only as the incontestable labours of GOD Himself in carrying out His purpose for the creatures of His love, through the whole wonderful progress from the first idea He formed of them as to be sharers in the character of His Son, through His determination, call, justification, to that final consummation, in which He brings them to the full concrete realisation of His glory.

(31) And as our ultimate comfort and joy we reflect that all this unspeakable procedure rests upon the firm foundation of GOD's love —instanced by His not sparing His own Son : that act shows that He can grudge nothing to us in the fulfilment of His purpose—no voice can be raised against us, no judgment delivered, when His voice and judgment have been declared in Christ, dead or rather

risen from death, throned at God's right hand, interceding for us.
(35) Christ in His love has passed through all the possibilities of
human experience in bodily and spiritual pain: they cannot separate
us from Him.   He has faced and subjugated all the most tremendous
facts and forces and conditions and influences under which man is
placed: they cannot separate us from Him.   And to say that is to
say, that nothing can separate us from the love of God which is in
Christ Jesus our Lord.

Note the refrain v. 11, 21, vi. 23, vii. 25, viii. 11 (*al.*), 39.   This
section sums up the bearing of the whole preceding argument upon
the character and relations of human life: and ends in the sublime
assertion of the Love of God as the spring and root of all God's dealings with man, as revealed in the Gospel.   Then out of the very heart
of this overwhelming joy springs the tremendous problem of Israel's
rejection of the Love of God (cc. ix.—xi.).

12. ἄρα οὖν covers the whole argument from v. 12 and proceeds to
conclusions as to Christian conduct; but this purpose is interrupted
by the thought of the Spirit and the wide bearings of the relation of
sonship to God.   The subject of Christian conduct is resumed in
c. xii.   Here the main character of the Christian life is expounded.

ὀφειλέται.   Still debtors, but under a new allegiance. Cf. Gal.
v. 3; Mt. xviii. 21; Lc. vii. 41.

13. μέλλετε ἀποθνήσκειν.   The periphrastic future of the durative
present—you will continue in or be in a state of death ; ἀποθανεῖσθε =
you will die, of the single event; cf. Moulton, p. 114; Burton, § 72.
Consequently the reference is the same as in vii. 10, 11.

θανατοῦτε.   Sc. διὰ ἀμαρτίαν, v. 10; the durative present. Cf.
νέκρωσις, 2 Cor. iv. 10; νεκροῦν, Col. iii. 5, ct. aor. vii. 4. τὰς πράξεις
τοῦ σώματος, in a bad sense, because of the ‖ κατὰ σάρκα, and in
antithesis to πνεῦμα : the body's practices independent of spirit are
bad.

14. ὅσοι γὰρ.   You must do this, for only if so led by God's
Spirit, are you true sons.

15, 16.   Parenthetic, enforcing the description of Christians as sons.

15. ἐλάβετε.   Again an appeal to baptism.

πάλιν.   Though still δοῦλοι in a true sense (cf. vi. 18, 19, 22) the
spirit in which they serve is not a spirit of slavery but of sonship.

πν. υἱοθεσίας.   Cf. τὸ πνεῦμα τοῦ υἱοῦ αὐ., Gal. iv. 6.   It is a spirit
of sonship because it is the effect of the Spirit of His Son; cf. 9.

υἱοθεσίας = the status of sons by adoption, sonship by adoption;
cf. 23, ix. 4; Gal. iv. 5; Eph. i. 5 only.   It is the right of son and

heir, given out of the natural order, as in the case of Jacob. Cf.
Deissmann, *Bibelstudien* II. pp. 66, 67; the stress here is of course
on the sonship, not on the way it came; cf. Heb. xii. 7.

ἐν ᾧ κ.τ.λ. Corresponds to εἰς φόβον of the preceding clause—not
slaves to a master but sons to a Father: the reference seems to be
direct to the 'Lord's Prayer,' as the norm of Christian prayer, the
new basis of appeal to GOD.

'Αββά ὁ πατήρ. Cf. Mk xiv. 36; Gal. iv. 6. The repetition is
not merely for interpretation, but for emphasis; cf. S. H., Lft ad
Gal. *l.c.*, Chase, *Texts and Studies*, I. 3, p. 24.

ὁ πατήρ. Nom. for voc. (not merely a Hebraism; cf. Moulton,
pp. 70, 235).

16. αὐτὸ τὸ πνεῦμα κ.τ.λ. The absence of a conjunction suggests
that this is, in some sort, an explanation of the preceding phrases
(rather than an analysis of the consciousness, as S. H.). If this be
so, then the idea is that the Spirit, which makes man's spirit a spirit
of sonship, by inspiring this cry of man's spirit joins in testifying to
the true relation to GOD.

τέκνα θεοῦ. Cf. Phil. ii. 15; otherwise only in Joh.; cf. esp.
1 Joh. iii. 2. On the other hand Joh. never uses υἱοὶ θεοῦ of men (cf.
Mt. v. 9, 45; Lk. vi. 35, xx. 36; Apoc. xxi. 7; Heb. ii. 10, xii. 5 f.;
here 14, 19, ix. 26 (qu.); Gal. iii. 26, iv. 6, 7 only). υἱός rather describes
the dignity and privilege of the son, τέκνον the sharing in the life of
the father; cf. Westcott, *Epp. Joh.*, pp. 120, 121. So here τέκνα
is substituted, as the ground of κληρονομία, because the main thought
here is of the life possessed by Christians, not of the privilege.

17. Continues the thought of 15 and so the explanation of ζήσεσθε:
if children we share the life.

κληρονόμοι. The son has a part in the possessions of the father;
cf. Gal. iv. 1 f.

κληρονόμοι θεοῦ. Only here (n. Gal. iv. 7 διὰ θεοῦ): the idea of
hereditary succession is not applicable: the O.T. usage of κληρονομία
for 'sanctioned and settled possession' (cf. Hort, 1 *Peter*, p. 35)
suggests that the meaning here is 'possessors,' possessors of GOD
=possessors of the divine life (cf. 2 Pet. i. 4); and this agrees with
the use of τέκνα. Then

συνκλ. δὲ Χριστοῦ marks the condition of our possession; we are
so possessors only as sharing with Christ, by His life in us.

εἴπερ κ.τ.λ. S. H. suggest that there is a reference to a current
Christian saying; cf. 2 Tim. ii. 11. See above, vi. 9.

συνπάσχομεν...συνδοξασθῶμεν. These are the two essential characters of the divine life as revealed in Christ and, by union with Him,

in man; suffering under the present conditions, 'glory,' or un-
hampered revealing of the life, when present conditions are done
away in the future state. This truth is most fully worked out in
2 Cor. iii. 7—10, 18, iv. 7—v. 10. In that Ep. the sufferings themselves are declared to be the natural expression now of the life of
Christ in us, as they were in the case of Jesus, and in them the 'glory'
is even now present and seen ; so that the present life of suffering
presents a gradual growth in 'glory' (*ib.* iii. 18). The full and free
manifestation is reserved for the future state, but it is the object of
the present state, and already discernible in it; cf. also 1 Pet. iv. 13.
The συν. in each case marks the result of sharing the life of Christ.
συνδοξ. the aorist, and the next verse, show that the reference is to
the future revelation. N. that the fundamental idea of δόξα is manifestation in act or character, esp. of GOD manifested in Christ and
in the lives and character of Christians; cf. Phil. iii. 21; 2 Cor.
viii. 23.

18—26. In the preceding verses the thoughts worked out in
2 Cor. *l.c.* have been summarised. In these verses the Apostle includes a wider range of thought, characteristic of Eph. and Col.
Man's present state is shown to have its analogy in the whole
material creation, which is all undergoing a vital change, from the
transitory and perishable to the eternal and spiritual. The connexion
between man and creation lies in his physical nature; the full redemption of this nature, when it is brought under the complete control of
the spirit by the life of GOD communicated through Christ, will also be
the liberation of all the physical creation from the limitations under
which it now lies. The whole conception is difficult but sublime in
the extreme. It is based upon the idea that the living GOD must
in the end bring His whole creation to be, in its parts and degrees, a
perfect manifestation of His own character and life. Cf. Eph. iii. 9,
10; Col. i. 16 ff.

18. λογίζομαι γάρ. The reference to δόξα in *v.* 17 leads to the
consideration of all that is involved in that final and full manifestation of GOD.

οὐκ ἄξια κ.τ.λ. Cf. 2 Cor. iv. 17 f. ἄξια...πρός, no exact parallel
to this use:=are of no weight in comparison with:=οὐδενὸς ἄξια ; cf.
Plato, *Gorg.* p. 471ᴇ, qu. S. H. For the use of πρὸς=compared with,
judged by the standard of, cf. Gal. ii. 14; 2 Cor. v. 10; Eph. iii. 4;
Kuhring, *De praep. Gr.* p. 22.

μέλλουσαν ἀποκαλυφθῆναι. A periphrasis for fut. part. but emphasising the certainty of the event. ἀποκ. aor. refers to the final
revelation; cf. Gal. iii. 23, 1 Pet. v. 1.

εἰς ἡμᾶς. Cf. ἐπί, i. 18; ἐν Gal. i. 16: εἰς implies the shedding of the glory upon us from an external source: for the thought cf. 2 Cor. v. 2.

19. γάρ introduces the expression of the wide range of the future revelation.

ἀποκαραδοκία. Phil. i. 20 only, Lft. The subst. seems not to be found elsewhere = concentrated expectation (cf. ἀποβλέπειν).

τῆς κτίσεως. Of the physical creation, cf. Giff. The renovation of nature was part of the Jewish Messianic hope. It is essentially the hope of the restoration of the state of nature before the Fall, when the earth was cursed for man's transgression. Cf. S. H. p. 210, ref. Isa. lxv. 17—25, Enoch xlv. 4, Schürer E.T. II. 2, p. 172 f. The remarkable, and perhaps unique, feature here is the suggestion of an almost conscious participation of nature in the 'larger hope'; and the interpretation in this sense of its movements and strife and waste. If we are right in understanding the passage so, it is an anticipation of a very modern kind of sympathy. Cf. Edersheim, ii. p. 441; Stanton, J. and Chr. Mess., 310 f., 350 f.

τὴν ἀποκάλυψιν τ. υ. τ. θ. Cf. Lk. ii. 32, 35; 2 Thes. ii. 3 f. only, of persons other than divine. It is the climax of the φανέρωσις described in 2 Cor. iv. 11, iii. 18, when the veil shall be removed, all the disturbing influences of earthly conditions and judgments, and the true sons of GOD stand out in their true light. That manifestation will bring the 'new heavens and the new earth,' to which all the strife and movements of nature tend.

20. τῇ γὰρ ματαιότητι = the purposelessness, futility which the world of nature exhibits, until the conception of nature is itself brought under the larger conception of GOD's eternal providence.

ὑπετάγη. Prob. ref. Gen. iii. 17, 18.

διὰ τὸν ὑποτάξαντα = for the purposes of Him who so subjected it; cf. on v. 10, Heb. ii. 10. S. Paul here connects the actual condition of nature with the Fall, as he does the actual condition of human nature in c. v., no doubt in dependence on Gen. iii. 17.

ἐφ' ἐλπίδι with ὑπετάγη. The subjection to vanity is a commonplace: the novelty here lies in the vision of hope.

21. ὅτι καὶ αὐτὴ ἡ κτ. Not man only but the natural creation with him will be set free.

τῆς δ. τῆς φθ. = τῆς ματαιότητος. N. the echo, but in a different sense, in 2 Pet. ii. 19. φθορά, in St Paul chiefly or always physical, in 2 Pet. generally moral, occurs only in Ro., 1 Co., Gal., Col. and 2 Peter.

ἐλευθερία. Cf. Gal. iv. 23 f.

τῆς δόξης τ. τ. τ. θ.   δόξα almost=ἀποκάλυψις, but describes the character revealed rather than the process of revealing :=the true character manifested fully,)(φθορά 1 Cor. xv. 42.

τέκνων, 'children,' as one in character with GOD in Christ, cf. above 17.

22. οἴδαμεν. The appeal to common experience.

συνστ. καὶ συνωδ. συν. not with man, but throughout all its parts, members and organisms. The cpds only here; for ὠδῖν. cf Mt. xxiv. 8; the thought is of the pangs of birth=ἐφ' ἐλπίδι κ.τ.λ.

23. καὶ αὐτοί. We Christians, though we have the earnest of the Spirit and of freedom, ourselves still find our body in bondage, not yet fully emancipated.

τὴν ἀπαρχὴν τ. πν.   ἀπ. only here in this connexion; cf. ἀρραβών, Eph. i. 14 ; 2 Cor. v. 5 : and cf. 2 Cor. v. 1—5 for a fuller expression of this thought.

υἱοθεσίαν. Cf. 15 ; Eph. i. 5.   υἱὸς marking privilege rather than nature, υἱοθεσία=putting into that position of privilege ; to privilege character must be brought to correspond ; consequently the word suggests a process, and may be used either of the beginning of the process (v. 15) or of the end as here, or of the whole (Eph. *l. c.*) ; cf. Westcott on Eph. *l. c.*

τὴν ἀπολύτρωσιν. Cf. on iii. 24. This word too indicates a process, not a finished act ; cf. Eph. i. 7 ; Col. i. 14. Here and Eph. i. 14, iv. 30 it is used to name the object for which the Spirit is given. So 1 Cor. i. 30 Christ is our ἁγιασμὸς καὶ ἀπολύτρωσις. The simple verb is used of the beginning of the process, 1 Pet. i. 18 ; cf. Heb. ix. 12. The fundamental texts are Mt. ᾽xx. 28 ; ‖ Mk. x. 45. N. Eph. i. 10 connects man's redemption and the destiny of creation, as here.

τοῦ σώματος ἡ.   The body : because (1) the body had become the seat of sin and death (vii. 24, viii. 11) : (2) it is through the body that man is connected with the physical creation. The redemption of the physical organism of man's life has a far-reaching effect upon all related physical creation ; cf. 1 Cor. xv. 51—54 ; Phil. iii. 21.

24. γάρ. These clauses explain the στενάζομεν...ἀπεκδεχόμενοι.

τῇ γὰρ ἐλπίδι. "Hope gives a definite shape to the absolute confidence of faith. Faith reposes completely on the love of GOD. Hope vividly anticipates that GOD will fulfil His promise in a particular way" Westcott, *Heb.* x. 23 ; cf. Hort, 1 *Pet.* p. 86 ; cf. Gal. v. 5 ; Eph. i. 18, iv. 4 ; Col. i. 27 ; 1 Th. v. 8. For the connexion with ἐσώθημεν, 1 Pet. i. 3 (with Hort's note (p. 34), "The new order of things is represented as in a manner all one great, all-pervading hope ").

The article = this hope, namely of the redemption of the body ; cf. vii. 25. The dative can hardly mean 'by this hope' but 'in this hope' ; cf. S. H. Salvation, as ἀπολύτρωσις and υἱοθεσία, is a process, and it begins with faith, on man's part, and is carried on in an atmosphere or condition of hope, the hope of complete redemption.

ἐλπὶς δὲ. Hope implies a fulfilment still future, and that demands the expectancy of a steady endurance.

25. δι' ὑπομονῆς = in a condition of endurance. ὑ. is steady resistance to adverse influences; and this is the peculiar Christian temper under present conditions ; cf. Heb. xii. 1 ; 1 Thes. i. 3 ; 2 Thes. iii. 5 ; Rev. xiv. 12 ; for διά cf. ii. 27, xiv. 20.

26—end. This section enforces the above description of the Christian life, by the evidence of experience that GOD Himself helps man in this endurance of hope, the Holy Spirit v. 26, the Father v. 28, the Son v. 34.

26. ὡσαύτως δὲ καὶ κ.τ.λ. As hope is the link of fellowship between man and creation, so the attitude of hope wins the help of the Holy Spirit, it is the link of fellowship in action between GOD and man.

τὸ πνεῦμα. Picks up and expands the hint of v. 16. N. that the Spirit here is definitely represented as in a reciprocal relation to the Father which we can only describe as personal.

συναντιλαμβάνεται. Cf. Lk. x. 40 ; = puts His hand to the work in cooperation with us. The work as shown by v. 16 and the following sentences is prayer as the first expression of the character of sonship.

τῇ ἀσθενείᾳ ἡ. = with us in our weakness. Weakness associated with hope necessarily falls to prayer. In that action the Spirit helps. ἀσθ. = all in ourselves that makes it hard to endure.

γάρ. Introduces explanation of our weakness.

τὸ τί προσευξ. Cf. Blass, p. 158. The groaning (of v. 23) finds no adequate or formulated expression : we know we are in want but how to express our need in particular we know not ; it utters itself in a cry of appeal (v. 16) : and in that cry we are conscious that the Spirit joins in terms inexpressible by us, but intelligible to Him whose Spirit He is. The Father understands the Spirit framing the utterance of the children.

ὑπερεντ. only here ; cf. v. 35. στεναγμοῖς, cf. Acts vii. 34. ἀλαλήτοις, only here ; cf. 2 Cor. xii. 4.

27. ὁ δὲ ἐραυνῶν τὰς καρδίας. Cf. Rev. ii. 23 ; Ps. vii. 10 ; Jer. xvii. 10 ; 1 Cor. ii. 10. The point seems to be that GOD's knowledge of the hearts of men and their needs enables Him to understand the particular line (τὸ φρόνημα) of the Spirit's intercession which is uttered with and through man's spirit; cf. Acts xv. 8, i. 24; Lk. xvi. 15; Gal. iv. 6.

ὅτι, 'that.' κατὰ θεόν = after the standard and measure of the character of GOD, not with the imperfection of human utterance.

ὑπὲρ ἁγίων = on behalf of men who belong to GOD, (so ‖ κατὰ θεόν), and therefore in pursuance of His will for them.

28. The thought passes from man's striving in prayer with the help of the Spirit, to GOD's constant activity for man, to promote that good, which is the object, even when unexpressed or inexpressible, of the children's prayer.

οἴδαμεν, of an acknowledged fact of experience or conviction.

τοῖς ἀγαπῶσι τ. θ. The true temper of childhood, answering to and counting on the ἀγάπη of the Father; cf. 35, 39. The fundamental attitude on both sides now comes to the front. The dat. = for: see next note.

πάντα συνεργεῖ. συν. is intr. (Mk xvi. [20]; 1 Cor. xvi. 16; 2 Cor. vi. 1; Ja. ii. 22) = helps, so Herm. *Sim.* v. 6. 6; πάντα is the 'inner accusative' = helps in all ways, gives all needed help; cf. Blass, p. 90; cf. Polyb. xi. 9. 1, πολλὰ συνεργεῖν τὴν ἁρμογὴν τῶν ὅπλων εἰς τὴν χρείαν. S. H. qu. *Test. xii. Patr.* Issach. 3; Gad 4 where συν. = 'help' simply. Chrys. and Theodorus seem to make it tr., taking GOD for subject and referring πάντα to apparently adverse circumstances. Origen takes πάντα for subj. but makes it refer to GOD's action described in vv. 29 f., *Philocal.* (Robinson) p. 229.

[ὁ θεός.] Whether we read this or not, we should supply it as subj. to συν. The whole point of vv. 28—30 is that GOD gives active help, etc. To make πάντα subj. introduces a quite alien thought, unless with Origen it is strictly referred to vv. 29 f.

εἰς ἀγαθόν, tr. for their good.

τοῖς κατὰ πρόθεσιν κλητοῖς οὖσιν. πρόθεσις = purpose, of man (Acts xi. 23, xxvii. 13; 2 Tim. iii. 10), of GOD (ix. 11; Eph. i. 11, iii. 11; 2 Tim. i. 9), describes the whole purpose of GOD for man, which results in the call. It is shown in its elements or stages in vv. 29, 30. The call falls into the lines of the purpose and is conditioned by it alone. Cf. vb of man i. 13, of GOD Eph. i. 10 (*al. supra* iii. 25).

29. ὅτι because, explains πάντα συνεργεῖ, the whole long process of GOD's good will to man, a will which is act.

οὕς. The consideration is confined, here, to Christians = τοῖς ἀγ. τ. θ. as His children. The aorists throughout refer to the definite acts of GOD which have come within their experience.

προέγνω. ἔγνων in the Bible, when used with a personal object, implies not mere knowledge, but recognition of the object as in personal relation to the subject; the first act, if we may say so, of GOD's mind towards man, which then develops in acts of will. Jerem. i. 5; cf. Isa. xlix. 1, 3, 5; Ex. xxxiii. 12, 17. So here, xi. 2; 1 Pet. i. 2, 20 (see Hort)=recognition, previous designation to a position or function. Here=the recognition of them as children, a recognition formed in the eternal counsels of GOD; cf. Mt. vii. 23; 1 Cor. viii. 3; Gal. iv. 9; 1 Cor. xiii. 12.

προώρισεν. Cf. 1 Cor. ii. 7; Eph. i. 5, 11; in all these passages refers to that character which GOD meant men to have by being brought into union with Him through Christ. So here, of GOD's provision of a certain relation or character which should be, therefore, men's true character, and should be gained by conformity to the character of Christ. The thought is not of determining something which in consequence could not be otherwise, but of drawing the lines of a true destiny, which still required further conditions for fulfilment; cf. Phil. ii. 12, 13, and note on i. 4.

συμμόρφους κ.τ.λ. = to share in the character which is exhibited in His Son, as Incarnate. συμμ., cf. 2 Cor. iii. 18, Phil. iii. 10, where the character is described as in process of development; and so perhaps Gal. iv. 19. In Phil. iii. 21 the reference is to the consummation of the process. εἰκών, cf. 1 Cor. xv. 49, 2 Cor. *l.c.*, ct. *supra* i. 23. The reference is to the true human character seen in Jesus, the Incarnate Son : man is meant to make that character his own under his present conditions by gradual growth, for complete achievement in the end. τοῦ υἱοῦ because it follows upon the relation of children. Consequently the likeness is also a likeness of GOD ; cf. Col. iii. 10; Wisd. ii. 23, and there is an underlying reference to Gen. i. 26.

εἰς τὸ εἶναι α. That He, as firstborn, might have many brethren. GOD's purpose is to people His household with children, brothers of the Son.

πρωτότοκον. Cf. Lk. ii. 7; Col. i. 15, 18; Heb. i. 6; Rev. i. 5; for a kindred idea cf. Heb. ii. 10. On the word cf. Lft on Col. *l.c.* The question whether πρ. is used in reference to the eternal nature of the Son, or to His resurrection, does not arise here ; as the stress is on ἐν π. ἀδ., not on πρ. The word, however, is an important link with Col.

30. ἐκάλεσεν. Of the stage in which GOD's purpose is first made known to the individual, in the call to be a Christian heard and, in this case, obeyed. A favourite idea in S. Paul and S. Peter ; cf. i. 1, 7.

ἐδικαίωσεν. Justified sc. in answer to faith, as they are οἱ ἀγα-
πῶντες τ. θ.

ἐδόξασεν. This is generally taken to refer to the final glory of the
future state, cf. 19. But the aorist is a difficulty, and is not satis-
factorily explained. 2 Cor. iii. 18, iv. 11 show that even under present
conditions there is conferred upon Christians a 'glory' or manifestation in them of GOD, which is plain to those who have eyes to see.
It is the 'glory' of the regenerate life in Christ, the manifest working
in them of the Spirit, the earnest and promise of that future state.
This passage is full of the ideas of 2 Cor. iii. 4—iv. 12, and we
may therefore without hesitation interpret ἐδόξασεν by the help of
that passage; cf. Joh. xii. 23, xvii. 1: and n. 1 Pet. ii. 12 (for the
effect upon others) and esp. above iii. 23 n.; so = σύμμορφους κ.τ.λ.
29.

31—39. The confidence inspired by this evidence of the love of
Christ and GOD. The love which is the ground of the whole relation
of GOD to man is shown in its intensity (31), and its power as
revealed in Christ (34, 35 a): then the consequences are drawn
(35 b—39).

31. εἰ ὁ θεὸς κ.τ.λ., as is shown by the above enumeration.

32. ὅς γε κ.τ.λ. N. the piling up of emphasis—ἰδίου—πάντων—
τὰ πάντα. For ἰδίου cf. 3 τὸν ἑαυτοῦ υἱόν.

33. κατὰ ἐκλεκτῶν θ. Against men whom GOD has chosen: the
bare words give tremendous emphasis.

θεὸς ὁ δικαιῶν. In the face of GOD's acquittal, the condemnation
of the world is as nothing; cf. 1 Cor. iv. 9 f.; 2 Cor. ii. 16; cf.
Isa. l. 8, 9.

34. Χρ. 'Ι. The whole process of the Son's action in redemption,
from the Incarnation to the Ascended Life, is given in the succession
of forcible phrases: in them His love is shown.

35. θλίψις κ.τ.λ. External circumstances, however desperate in
seeming, cannot separate.

36. ἕνεκεν σοῦ κ.τ.λ. Ps. xliv. 22.

37. διὰ τοῦ ἀγ. ἡ. v. 35, n. aorist.

38. θάνατος κ.τ.λ. None of the spiritual powers or influences
which beset men's lives can separate; cf. Ps. cii. (ciii.) 11 f., cxxxviii.
(cxxxix.) 7 f. Behind all the powers, conditions, influences, is GOD in
His name of love.

39. τῆς ἀγάπης τ. θ. τ. ἐ. Χρ. 'Ι. τ. κ. ἡ. The full phrase sums
up the whole argument from i. 16.

E. ix. 1—xi. 36. THE REJECTION OF THE GOSPEL BY ISRAEL.

The theme of i. 16, 17 has been worked out; it has been shown that the Gospel is a power of GOD unto salvation for them that believe, a power needed by Gentile and Jew alike, guaranteed on condition of faith and in response to faith by the love of GOD, and adequate to man's needs as shown in history and in individual experience; and a brief description has been given of the actual state of the Christian in Christ and of the certainty and splendour of his hope, resting upon the love of GOD. Naturally at this point the question of the Jews arises: they were the typical instance of a people brought into close and peculiar relation to GOD, and they therefore afford a crucial case of GOD's dealings with such. How then did it come to pass that they rejected the Gospel? What is their present state? their future destiny? and how does this affect Christians? The answer is found in the conditions under which GOD selects men for the execution of His purposes. It is important to bear in mind that the selection throughout is regarded as having reference not to the final salvation of persons but to the execution of the purpose of GOD. Underlying the whole section is the special object of S. Paul to justify himself in preaching the Gospel to the Gentiles.

CHAPTER IX.

IX. Israel's rejection of the Gospel (a great grief and incessant pain to S. Paul and (4) a great problem in the economy of redemption), (6) is not due to a failure of GOD's word, for the condition of acceptance was not a carnal descent but a spiritual, and depended upon GOD's selection of men for special purposes. (14) This selection was righteous, because it was directed to the execution of His purpose of mercy and was the effect of mercy, by revealing to men His power and character, and (19) acted in accordance with qualities exhibited by men, in their response, as creatures, to the purpose of their creation, shown in the case of Israel, (24) as diagnosed by the prophets, (30) partly succeeding and partly failing to grasp the true nature of righteousness and the means of its attainment.

1. ἀλήθειαν, κ.τ.λ. Cf. 1 Tim. ii. 7; 2 Cor. xi. 31, vii. 14, xii. 6; Gal. i. 20: in all cases a strong assertion of his personal truthfulness, in a statement which would be challenged. Here his deep personal interest in Israel is asserted; his championship of the Gentiles had no doubt been interpreted as hostility to Jews.

ἐν Χριστῷ = as a Christian; cf. 2 Cor. ii. 17, xii. 19; Phm. 8. In this anarthrous and simple form the phrase is confined to S. Paul (all except 2 Thes. and Pastorals) and 1 Pet.; and seems simply to mark the Christian position.

συνμαρτυρούσης. ii. 15, viii. 16 only. In ii. 15 and here the συν is perhaps simply perfective; cf. Moulton, p. 113. Otherwise the conscious reflection is cited as a confirming witness to the uttered statement.

τῆς συνειδήσεώς μου. Cf. 2 Cor. i. 12, v. 11. = all that I know of myself; cf. ii. 15 n.

ἐν πνεύματι ἁγίῳ. Cf. 1 Cor. ii. 11, 12, xii. 3. Not merely 'in my spirit as consecrated,' but 'in the light of or under the control of the Holy Spirit.' ‖ ἐν Χριστῷ. 1 Cor. xii. 3 is decisive for this meaning.

2. ἀδιάλειπτος. 2 Tim. i. 3 only. Adv. Rom. i. 9 and 1 Thes. (3) only.

3. ηὐχόμην. Cf. Acts xxv. 22; Gal. iv. 20; Phm. 13. Here of an impracticable wish, 'I could have prayed if it had been possible'; Blass, p. 207. Contrast Acts xxvi. 29.

ἀνάθεμα, lit. a thing set up in a temple and so destroyed as far as use by man goes (LXX. Lev. xxvii. 28); then devoted to destruction (Deut. xiii. 15), cursed (LXX. Josh. vii. *al.*); cf. Nägeli, p. 49. Followed by ἀπό only here; cf. vii. 2, κατήργηται ἀπό; cf. 1 Cor. xii. 3, xvi. 22; Gal. i. 8, 9.

αὐτὸς ἐγώ. vii. 25, xv. 14; 2 Cor. x. 1, xii. 13. ?=instead of them.

ἀπὸ τοῦ χριστοῦ = so as to lose all that the Messiah means to a Jew and to a Christian. For ὁ χρ. cf. vii. 4, viii. 35, ix. 5. The reference when the article is present (except perhaps where it is due to an article with a governing word) seems always to be to the office of Messiah as exhibited and interpreted in Jesus.

ὑπὲρ—κατὰ σάρκα, to distinguish them from the spiritual family of Christ: the Church is now the true Israel. τ. σ. μ. κ. σ. explains τ. ἀ. μ.

4. οἵτινες. This form of the relative marks the characteristic which is the occasion of his feeling; cf. Moulton, p. 91 f.; Blass, 172; Hort, 1 *Pet.* ii. 1 f. 'Never absolutely convertible with ὅς,' M., 'seeing that they are.'

εἰσιν, they still are in spite of what has happened.

Ἰσραηλεῖται, the name which marks the religious privilege of the nation; cf. Joh. i. 48; below xi. 1; 2 Cor. xi. 22: and for Ἰσραήλ cf. below 6; 1 Cor. x. 18; Gal. vi. 16; Eph. ii. 12; closely connected with the expectation of the Messiah and His kingdom, Acts i. 6. The following enumeration gives the details which are all involved in this name, and emphasises the paradox of the rejection of the Gospel by a people so prepared.

ἡ υἱοθεσία. Not LXX. or class. but common in inscriptions; cf. Deissmann, *B. S.* II. p. 66. In N.T. Rom., Gal. (1), Eph. (1) only. This is the only place in which it refers to the sonship of Israel. Was it current among the Jews? cf. Exod. iv. 22; Hart, *Ecclus.* p. 302 f.

η δόξα. Cf. Lk. ii. 32; 2 Cor. iii. 7 f. The reference is to the Shechinah, the visible sign of the presence of GOD among His people.

αἱ διαθῆκαι. The plural marks the successive repetitions and ratifications of the covenant from Abraham to Moses; cf. Acts iii. 25; Lk. i. 72; for the plural Eph. ii. 12.

ἡ νομοθεσία, the legislation—the positive revelation of GOD's will which distinguished Israel from all other nations. Only here in N.T. and LXX. canon : 2 Macc. vi. 23 ; 4 Macc. v. 35.

ἡ λατρεία, the ordered services of the Temple ; cf. Heb. ix. 1, 6.

αἱ ἐπαγγελίαι, primarily of the promises made to Abraham ; cf. Gal. iii. 16, Heb. vii. 6, but including the whole prophetic revelation as touching the Messiah, cf. 2 Cor. i. 20; Acts xiii. 32: Hart, *Ecclus.* p. 306.

5. οἱ πατέρες. Cf. xi. 28, xv. 8 ; 1 Cor. x. 1 ; Heb. i. 1, viii. 9 (qu.); Lk. xi. 47 ; Joh. vi. 49 ; Acts xiii. 32. On the Jewish insistence on the merits of the fathers cf. S. H., p. 330. The term includes the whole ancestry of Israel, not merely the Patriarchs.

ἐξ ὧν, with τὸ κατὰ σάρκα. ὁ χρ. the Messiah. τὸ κ. σ.; as regards merely human origin, cf. i. 3; cf. 1 Clem. xxxii. 2 (F. C. Burkitt, *J. T. S.*, v. p. 455). On the constr. cf. Blass, p. 94, cft Heb. ii. 17; below xii. 18, xv. 17: "the accus. of reference has already become an adverbial accus."

ὁ ὢν ἐπὶ πάντων, κ.τ.λ. I adopt the stopping of W. H. mg. (σάρκα · ὁ ὢν κ.τ.λ.). This clause is an ascription of blessing to God, in His character as supreme ruler of all things, the author and director of all the dispensations of His Providence, tr. 'He who is over all, even God, is blessed for ever, Amen.' See Add. Note, p. 219.

6—13. The present condition of Israel has not been explicitly stated in *vv.* 1—5, but implied in S. Paul's wish that he might have been ἀνάθεμα ἀπὸ τοῦ χριστοῦ for them. They are ἀνάθεμα ἀπὸ τοῦ χριστοῦ in spite of all their privileges : yet not all; and the fact that some have accepted the Gospel shows that the Word of God, the basis of their call and privilege, has not utterly failed; indeed that Word itself drew distinctions even within the seed of Abraham, between the descent of nature and the descent of promise or spirit ; and again in the children of Isaac between the one chosen of God for His purposes and the one not chosen.

In this section, then, the first line of argument is stated : the condition of Israel depends solely on God's choice for the execution of His purpose.

6. οὐχ οἷον—ὅτι. A unique combination : cf. Field, *ad loc.* He decides that οὐχ οἷον is in vulgar use a strong negative=nequaquam, ne minimum : 'It is by no means the fact that....'

δὲ contrasts with the implicit thought of *vv.* 4, 5 : this wonderful dispensation has not ended in failure on God's part.

ἐκπέπτωκεν. Absolute use not common. Here=to fail of its purpose (cf. Polyb. IV. 82. 8); cf. Ecclus. xxxi. 7, slightly different.

ὁ λόγος τοῦ θεοῦ=the utterance of the purpose of God, as given in promises and covenants to Israel; cf. Joh. x. 35: a rare, perhaps unique (S. H.), use in N.T.; for the thought cf. iv. 14 =Gal. iii. 17.

οὐ γὰρ πάντες κ.τ.λ., blood relationship does not of itself admit to the spiritual position.

7. οὐδ᾽ ὅτι κ.τ.λ., nor does descent of flesh make children, in the sense of the promise, as witness Ishmael's case; cf. Joh. viii. 33 f.

σπέρμα, sc. κατὰ σάρκα; cf. xi. τέκνα, sc. ἐπαγγελίας or τοῦ θεοῦ. ἀλλ᾽ Ἐν Ἰσ. Gen. xxi. 12.

8. τοῦτ᾽ ἔστιν κ.τ.λ., the principle of selection is seen at work in the choice of lines and persons for the execution of God's purpose: the starting point is God's promise to Abraham, including both the birth of a son and the blessing of the Gentiles.

λογίζεται εἰς σπέρμα, are reckoned as seed, sc. of Abraham for the purposes of the promise: n. σπέρμα is applied here more narrowly than in 7, as the quotation in that verse suggests.

9. ἐπαγγελίας κ.τ.λ. This utterance, which was directly connected with the blessing (Gen. xxviii. 10), is a matter of promise.

10. οὐ μόνον δέ, κ.τ.λ. The same principle is seen in the selection of one of two sons, born at one birth of one father and mother, even before birth or any act on their part.

11. ἵνα ἡ κατ᾽ ἐκλογὴν κ.τ.λ. The purpose of God (the execution of His promise to bless the Gentiles) is carried out by a principle of selection, not as a matter of favour bestowed on merit but as a choice of fit instruments for attaining the end. πρόθεσις, cf. viii. 28, here primarily of the purpose indicated in the promise. ἐκλογή, cf. Heb. ix. 15 (below *v.* 21), selection: God selects nations and individuals not primarily for their own interest, but for work to be done for Him : the ἐκλογὴ becomes definite in a 'call,' κλῆσις; both are subservient to His purpose; men and nations are His σκεύη; cf. 1 Thes. i. 4; 2 Pet. i. 10: *infra* xi. 5; Hort, 1 *Pet.* i. 1.

οὐκ ἐξ ἔργων κ.τ.λ., with ἐρρέθη. The word which determined their position was not the result of works already done by them by way of reward, but the result of God's call to service.

12. ὁ μείζων κ.τ.λ., Gen. xxv. 23, where it is the nations represented by their founders rather than or at least as much as the founders themselves that are under consideration : throughout S. Paul is speaking of God's purpose as dealing with nations; cf. S. H. *ad loc.*

13. Mal. i. 2, where the words describe the several fates of

Israel and Edom, the disappearance of the latter and the desolation of their land being contrasted with the wideness of GOD's love for Israel. That is to say, history confirms the selection : Israel, with all its faults, served GOD's purpose ; Edom did not.

The object, then, of these references is to show the character and object of the call of GOD—it is a choice of instruments for a definite purpose ; and the call has not failed because of the failure of individuals, provided that there are still real instruments of His purpose doing His service (*v.* 21), and forming a remnant through which His work is carried on (27, xi. 5). That S. Paul was combating an actual position—of the irreversible validity of the call of Israel after the flesh—is shown by S. H. p. 249. But the question arises as to the justice of GOD in this discrimination ; and this question is handled in the next section.

καθάπερ γέγραπται. The words of the prophet are quoted to show that the actual course of history bore out the statement made to Rebecca. Jacob and his descendants had proved to be objects of GOD's love, Esau and his descendants, the Edomites, objects of GOD's hate. Malachi, as Genesis, refers to the nations.

ἐμίσησα. Only here in N.T., and here as a quotation, is the verb used to describe GOD's attitude to a man or men ; cf. Heb. i. 9 ; Rev. ii. 6. S. Paul uses the natural language of the Jew, in enforcing an argument based upon Jewish conceptions. It is essentially not Christian language. The truth underlying it is the necessary hatefulness of the character and conduct embodied in the history of Edom.

14—33. This choice of GOD is not unjust, because it flows from His Mercy, not from man's disposition or efforts. (17) Pharaoh himself was raised up to give an instance of GOD's power and to make wide proclamation of His Name : GOD's will works whether in mercy or in hardening. (19) If you ask what room is there for moral blame, seeing that GOD's will is irresistible? I reply, that man has no right to protest against GOD the conditions of his nature : any more than the vessel can quarrel with the maker for the uses to which it is destined. (22) It was GOD's will to make plain the conditions which should incur His wrath and to bring home to man's knowledge His power ; in doing so He bore long with those who served only to exhibit wrath and were formed by character only for destruction, His patience serving to reveal the great stores of revelation of Himself opened out to such as served to exhibit His mercy, formed and prepared for such revelation, men called now in our persons not only from Jews but also from Gentiles. (25) This action of GOD's will is witnessed by the prophets both as regards the call of Gentiles (27) and as regards the call of only a remnant of Israel, representing the true Israel. (30) What then is the conclusion? That the righteousness (which is the purpose of GOD for man) is found among Gentiles, who for so long made no effort to attain it, while Israel missed even the law of righteousness at which they aimed. (32) And the reason is, that they neglected the one condition of attainment, namely faith : stumbling on the very rock of which the prophet spoke.

S. Paul is here defending his position, that the true people of GOD, the true Israel, now consists of a remnant of Israel and an incoming of Gentiles, both accepted on the ground of faith, against the objection that this involves an incredible rejection of the main stock of Israel : he shows how such an event was definitely contemplated by the prophets (25—33), and justifies it by the consideration of GOD's use of man for the execution of His purpose. Man is made for such use; and according to his character he serves that use, either negatively by showing the awful consequences of GOD's wrath upon sin (cf. i. 17 f.), and an instance of His power, or positively by showing the operation of GOD's loving mercy and self-revelation. The responsibility of man is maintained because he is a living instrument, who has the choice of faith or rebellion. He has no right to quarrel with the necessity which imposes this choice or the consequences which follow it ; they are the conditions of his being a man at all. The clue to the meaning is to be found in the fact that the dominant thought is not that of man's personal destiny and final salvation or the contrary, but the thought of GOD's call to service, and the relation of man to GOD in the execution of that service. The call of man to take part in this work of GOD is a crowning instance of GOD's mercy to man. The work has to be done; but it may be done either with man's cooperation or against his will. The story of man is in the first case a revelation of GOD's mercy, in selecting men for certain uses, in the second a revelation of GOD's wrath, in visiting the failure to execute His purpose. The clue to the nature of man's responsibility is given in *v.* 32. See Add. Note, p. 222.

14. τί οὖν ἐροῦμεν; introduces a difficulty, as in vi. 1.

μὴ...; Can there be unrighteousness in GOD? is this choice of persons mere προσωπολημψία ? (ii. 11)? Cf. iii. 5, where the problem here worked out is just stated.

παρὰ τῷ θεῷ. Cf. Hort, *S. James* i. 17 = in GOD ; παρὰ being used instead of ἐν from an instinct of reverence; cf. Mk x. 27; Rom. ii. 11.

μὴ γένοιτο. Cf. iii. 4, vi. 1.

15. τῷ Μωυσεῖ γὰρ κ.τ.λ. = LXX. Exod. xxxiii. 19. In the original the force lies in the assertion of effective mercy. S. Paul applies it as asserting selective mercy (cf. 18). The mercy of GOD depends upon His Will. But how does this exclude the charge of unrighteousness, as γὰρ implies that it does? It can only do so, on the unexpressed assumption that GOD's Will is essentially and necessarily righteous; cf. iii. 6. But this is the very point raised by the objector: and we should have expected it to be expressed in the most explicit form. The context however shows that it is not the general mercy of GOD 'over all His works' which is here being considered, but His mercy in selecting human instruments for carrying out His work of redemption; ἔλεος is closely connected with χάρις (cf. Hort, 1 *Pet.* p. 30). Cf. xi. 30 f.

16. ἄρα οὖν. It follows therefore on a consideration of the whole circumstances—a combination very frequent in Rom. (8) and once each in Gal., Eph., 1 and 2 Thes. only.

οὐ τοῦ θέλοντος κ.τ.λ. Sc. ἡ ἐκλογή ἐστιν: the choice for the particular service depends not on man's will or effort, but on GOD's mercy.

τρέχειν. Metaph. only in S. Paul and Heb. xii. 1. Cf. περιπατεῖν.

17. λέγει γὰρ κ.τ.λ. Exod. ix. 16 (LXX. ἕνεκεν τούτου διετηρήθης ἵνα...ἰσχύν...): apparently an independent translation of the Hebrew. εἰς τοῦτο points forward to ὅπως: ἐξήγειρα, "used of GOD calling up the actors on the stage of history; cf. Hab. i. 6; Zech. xi. 16; Jer. xxvii. 41," S. H. So Lipsius, Zahn, *al.* Cf. ἀνέστησεν, Acts ix. 41. Giff. takes ἐξηγ. = 'I raised thee from thy sickness.' Pharaoh is cited as an unwilling instrument of GOD's mercy: in his case and person the purposes of GOD's mercy and the revelation of His character (ὄνομα) are secured, although the process involves for him a 'hardening': that is due to his attitude towards GOD's purpose.

18. σκληρύνει. Cf. Exod. vii. 3, 22 *al.*: the only place in N.T. where the hardening is directly attributed to GOD. Cf. Acts xix. 9; Heb. iii. 8 *al.* The 'hardening,' which is immediately the result of man's own attitude, is so by reason of the conditions imposed in creation on man's nature and consequently is an act of GOD; cf. i. 24, xi. 8.

19. ἐρεῖς μοι οὖν κ.τ.λ. You will say to me, In this case what room is still left for faultfinding? If men are thus appointed to be instruments of GOD's use whether for mercy or hardening, how can they be responsible? how can GOD find fault? The answer is, on the one hand, that the question cannot be properly raised by man as against GOD, because man has to accept the conditions of his creation, and on the other hand that the revelation of GOD's wrath is itself turned by the patience of GOD into a revelation of mercy. The answer does not seem to us sufficient, for it still leaves the fundamental point unsolved—why are some men to be the subjects of the revelation of wrath in order that the mercy may be revealed in others? If moral responsibility is to be maintained, the cause of this difference must be seen to lie in the man himself. But this is not brought out until we get to *v.* 31 where the cause of Israel's failure is named as want of faith. Can we use this particular instance to interpret the whole argument? If we are meant to, it is strange that it should be left so late, and unapplied to the general problem. The reason for this perhaps is that S. Paul's mind is really absorbed in the particular problem of Israel, and does not attempt to elucidate, perhaps did not feel the weight of, the general problem. See Add. Note, p. 222.

τῷ γὰρ βουλήματι κ.τ.λ. The question assumes that the hardening is the primary purpose of GOD. The use of the term **βούλημα** slightly exaggerates the statement ὃν θέλει κ.τ.λ.; βούλομαι involving "volition guided by choice and purpose; θέλει expressing the mere fact of volition" (Hort, *James,* p. 32): but the distinction cannot be used to help the situation here.

ἀνθέστηκεν has ever succeeded in resisting (cf. xiii. 21): if the hardening is GOD's will, how can a man help it?

20. ὦ ἄνθρωπε. Cf. ii. 1, 3; cf. James ii. 20 only (*v.* 1 Tim. vi. 11), thou that art mere man. For the idea cf. Wisdom xii. 12.

μενοῦνγε. Cf. x. 18; Phil. iii. 8 only; μενοῦν, Lk. xi. 28. Corrective, 'rather than put such a question consider...,' Blass, p. 270.

ἀνταποκρινόμενος. Lk. xiv. 6 only.

μὴ ἐρεῖ τὸ πλάσμα κ.τ.λ. Is. xxix. 16, xlv. 9; cf. lxiv. 8; Jer. xviii. 1—6; Ecclus. xxxiii. 13; 2 Tim. ii. 20, 21. The metaphor emphasises the absurdity of the creature who quarrels with the conditions of his creation: and it brings out also again the point that man and, in particular here, nations are made for use and must subserve that use. It must not be pressed to the denial of spontaneity in man, which would be contrary to all S. Paul's ethical teaching. Men are living or personal instruments.

21. εἰς τιμὴν for honourable use, εἰς ἀτιμίαν for dishonourable use; cf. 2 Tim. *l.c.*

22. εἰ δὲ.... No apodosis follows: the current is broken by the introduction of prophetic passages *v.* 25 f. What apodosis was intended? The thought passes from the abstract relation of Creator to created to GOD's actual government of men, as seen in His dealings with those who oppose and those who obey His Will: the principles of government are declared in the words ἤνεγκεν and προητοίμασεν, the attitude in π. μακροθυμία, the end in the revelation of GOD's power and character, whether by wrath or mercy. The apodosis required, then, is some such appeal as 'what fault can we find here?' It should be remembered that the revelation of wrath is just as necessary for the moral education of man as the revelation of mercy. They are in fact the two sides of the shield.

θέλων = in willing, or while willing: the clear exhibition of wrath is one side of GOD's revelation to man, and is given in the fact and consequences of sin; cf. i. 18 f. The wrath of GOD towards sin is as true an outcome of His loving purpose for man, as is His pleasure in righteousness. The participle describes not the reason (because) nor a contrast (although), but the general condition under which the action of the main verb takes place.

ἐνδείξασθαι τὴν ὀργὴν exactly ‖ i. 18 = to give an instance of...; cf. iii. 25; 2 Thes. i. 5; 1 Tim. i. 16.

γνωρίσαι τὸ δυνατὸν αὐ. γνωρίσαι = to bring to the knowledge of men. τὸ δυνατὸν, His power seen in combating sin no less than in effecting righteousness.

ἤνεγκεν σκεύη ὀργῆς. Jer. l. (xxvii.) 25; Is. xiii. 5 (Heb.), but in both these passages the meaning is 'brought out weapons by which to inflict His purpose of wrath.' Here = 'bore with...instruments of wrath'; cf. ii. 4, iii. 25, 26; 2 Pet. iii. 9, 15 (Mayor cft 1 Pet. iii. 20; Ps. lxxxvi. 15; Is. xxx. 18 al.). Cf. Exod. xxxiv. 6.

σκεύη ὀργῆς. Instruments whose only use now is for the wrath of GOD. The image of the preceding verse is continued but the form is changed (ὀργῆς not εἰς ὀργήν) = not 'destined for wrath' but fit only to exhibit or effect wrath (cf. S. H.). They have become so fit, by their own neglect of what they could know of GOD (cf. i. 18 f.). So

κατηρτισμένα εἰς ἀπώλειαν marks that their present state is the result of a course of preparation, and this must be found (again in accordance with i. 18 f.) in their own conduct. Cf. Lk. vi. 40; 1 Cor. i. 10; Eph. iv. 12 (-μός). ἀπώλειαν)(σωτηρίαν, cf. i. 32; Mt. vii. 13; Phil. iii. 19; 1 Tim. vi. 9.

23. ἵνα γνωρίσῃ. The object of the patience of GOD is to bring home to men's minds 'the wealth of His glory'; cf. xi. 32, 33. ἵνα depends on ἤνεγκεν. The patience effected this object, because the mercy was revealed in spite of the opposition of sinners, such as Pharaoh or unfaithful Israel; and was recognised as all the more abundant because of that opposition. The redemption of Israel from Egypt, and the saving of a remnant and call of the Gentiles, were all the more signal triumphs of GOD's purpose for the opposition that was overcome. Hence the emphatic τὸν πλ. τ. δ.

If καὶ is read before ἵνα (as S. H.), we may take the final clause either (1) as practically connected with ἐν πολλῇ μακροθυμίᾳ 'bore with much long-suffering and with the object of making known' (so S. H.); but the sequence is disjointed; or (2) as connected with ἐνδείξασθαι, wishing to give an instance of His wrath and to make known His grace; where we have the same combination of constructions as in 1 Cor. xiv. 5; and the sequence is good: but the intervention of the main clause makes this very difficult, though perhaps not impossible.

τὸν πλοῦτον τῆς δόξης. πλ. specially characteristic of Eph. and Col.: but cf. also ii. 4, xi. 33; Phil. iv. 19:=the inexhaustible abundance. δόξα here of the revelation of GOD's character in His dealings with man, in thought closely ‖ Eph. ii. 7: the great acts of redemption reveal GOD to man. Cf. Eph. i. 18.

ἐπί. Towards or over as in Eph. ii. 7: depends on the whole of the preceding phrase.

σκεύη ἐλέους ‖ σκεύη ὀργῆς, instruments fit for the use of His mercy; such as He can use for His merciful purposes.

ἃ προητοίμασεν. Which instruments He prepared beforehand for bringing about this revelation of Himself. For the word cf. Eph. ii. 10 only. The σκ. ἐλ. are prepared by GOD Himself; the σκ. ὀργῆς make themselves so, by rejecting His methods of preparation. The reference is to the training through history and life, not to 'election,' Giff.

εἰς δόξαν. δ. must have the same meaning as in the preceding clause=for revelation of His purpose and character. The thought of final glorification is not included here; cf. viii. 30.

24. οὓς καὶ ἐκάλεσεν. The attraction of οὓς (to ἡμᾶς) marks the turn of thought from regarding the persons as instruments to regarding the instruments as persons: the personal agency of men comes out.

ἡμᾶς. Even us, or in us—or perhaps—which He actually called us to be.

οὐ μόνον κ.τ.λ. Here the underlying thought of the whole passage becomes explicit: and its importance is marked by the anacoluthon: instead of finishing his sentence S. Paul goes on at once to illustrate the fact of this call from prophetic sayings. It may also be that he shrank from enforcing his argument that the unbelieving Jews were σκεύη ὀργῆς.

25—29. The four quotations are cited to show that the prophets contemplated that the choice of the chosen people would be maintained only in a remnant, and that there would be a choice of others also. There is warrant in Scripture for both sides of his proposition; not only for God's working κατ᾽ ἐκλογήν, but also for the assertion that the ἐκλογὴ in fact involved a call of Gentiles and at least contemplated a falling away of Israelites, or, as he here prefers to call them, Jews.

25. Hos. ii. 23. The original refers to the restoration of the ten tribes, who had fallen from their privileged state. S. Paul applies this to the inclusion in the privileged state of Gentiles who had not possessed it; on the principle that, if God could bring back the disowned, He could call in those who had not before been called. Cf. 1 Pet. ii. 10 (and Hort's note).

26. Hos. i. 10 describes the reunion of Israel into one nation under one head: again S. Paul extends the reference.

ἐν τῷ τόπῳ=Palestine in Hosea: here=the countries of the Gentiles.

θεοῦ ζῶντος. Cf. Acts xiv. 15; Westcott on Heb. iii. 12.

27. The next two quotations justify the claim that Israel's call survives in a remnant.

Is. x. 22. The context speaks of a remnant saved by trust in God. LXX. is followed but slightly altered; the first phrase is from Hos. i. 10, a clear proof that the quotations were from memory (or from a catena?).

τὸ ὑπόλιμμα. Sc. only the remnant.

28. λόγον γὰρ συντελῶν κ.τ.λ. Cf. Is. xxviii. 22=LXX. πράγματα: λόγον w. ποιήσει, 'shall effect a reckoning upon earth, completely and briefly.'

29. Is. i. 9=LXX.

30—33. What conclusion is to be drawn? The facts are plain: Gentiles have attained a state of righteousness, though they were not seeking it: Jews, who sought it, have not attained. And the reason too is plain; what faith gave the one, lack of faith lost for the other: and this again corresponds to a prophetic warning.

30. τί οὖν ἐροῦμεν; Cf. viii. 31.

ὅτι κ.τ.λ. introduces the answer to the question: but the answer is incomplete till the second subsidiary question 32 διὰ τί is answered.

διώκοντα...κατέλαβεν, pursuing...overtook; cf. Phil. iii. 12; Exod. xv. 9; Field, ad loc.

δικαιοσύνην δὲ κ.τ.λ. Corrective=a righteousness given by God in response to faith, not as a result of works nor as yet worked out in life; cf. i. 17.

31. Ἰσραὴλ. The name of privilege; cf. on v. 4.

νόμον δικαιοσύνης. A law embodying righteousness, almost=a legal righteousness; cf. ii. 23, Wisd. ii. 11.

ἔφθασεν did not reach; cf. 2 Cor. x. 14; Phil. iii. 16. Only in 1 Thes. iv. 15 does the idea of anticipation certainly occur.

32. διὰ τί; Sc. οὐκ ἔφθασεν.

ὅτι. Sc. ἐδίωκεν. ὡς ἐξ ἔργων = with the idea that they could attain by starting from works.

τῷ λίθῳ τοῦ π. Allusion to Is. viii. 14, LXX. λίθον πρόσκομμα. The sense in Isaiah is that the Lord of Hosts will be a sanctuary for Israel if they trust in Him: they will not then find Him as a stone to stumble against. The absence of faith makes Him so. ·

33. Is. xxviii. 16, LXX. with λιθ. π. κ. π. σ. substituted for λίθον πολυτελῆ κ.τ.λ. and other slighter variations; cf. x. 11; 1 Pet. ii. 6 (see Hort).

In the original, the stone is the Divine King or Kingdom of Israel (in contrast with alien alliances), the recognition of which is to steady the mind of the people: the trust in its divine mission will not be baffled by disappointment (cf. Hort, *l.c.*). The Apostolic interpretation sees this 'stone' in the Messiah, recognising as so often in Christ the fulfilment of what had been said of the true Israel. A good instance of the re-interpretation of O.T. in the light of Christian experience (cf. Mt. xxi. 42 parallels; Acts iv. 11 qu. Ps. cxviii. 22). S. H. refer to Justin M. (*Dial.* 36, p. 122 l. 34, p. 112 D, Otto) and suggest that λίθος was a name for the Messiah among the Jews from an early (? pre-Christian) date. The point of the quotation here is that the Jews instead of trusting in this stone (of foundation for the true Israel, cf. Eph. ii. 20) had taken offence at it as revealed in Christ (1 Cor. i. 23) and trusting instead in their own works had come to grief. The tendency of Judaism at this time, in St Paul's view, was to trust in their performances of law instead of drawing life from communion with the living GOD; the rejection of the Messiah was the culminating instance of this tendency. This reason, why Israel εἰς νόμον οὐκ ἔφθασεν, suggests that Christ is the fulfiller of law; so cf. x. 4; Mt. v. 17; James i. 25.

καταισχυνθήσεται. Shall not be shamed by being disappointed in the object of trust; cf. *v.* 5; 2 Cor. vii. 14, ix. 4, x. 8.

CHAPTER X.

This chapter expands the theme of the last section, and, by showing that Israel failed through ignorance, culpable because in defiance of express warnings, illustrates one strain in the theme of c. ix. that man is responsible for his failure to respond to GOD's purposes.

(1—4) Israel's rejection of the Messiah due to ignorance of the relation of Christ to law and righteousness (5—15) though the demand of the new righteousness was not hard to meet and they were informed of it by (16—21) preaching of the apostles and warnings of the prophets.

1—4. With all my eager longing and prayer for Israel's salvation, I cannot but see and say that they have failed, not for lack of zeal, but for failing to recognise the nature of true righteousness and substituting an imagined righteousness of their own : they refused obedience to GOD's righteousness and to Christ as putting an end to law, for all believers, as an instrument of righteousness. They had put law in the place of GOD and could not accept Christ in the place of law.

1. ἀδελφοί. The personal appeal emphasises the depth of his feeling.

ἡ μὲν εὐδοκία. μὲν suggests a contrast between S. Paul's desire and the facts as he is forced to see them.

εὐδοκία = purpose. Cf. 2 Thes. i. 11; Phil. i. 15, in which places the idea of purpose involved in goodwill is clear; so probably Phil. ii. 13. The proof of this purpose had been given by his habit of preaching first to Jews, and by his incessant efforts to keep together the Jewish and Gentile sections of the Church.

καρδία involves will (2 Cor. vii. 3, ix. 7) and intelligence (Eph. i. 18, iv. 18) as well as affection. ἐμῆς = my whole heart.

ἡ δέησις. The genuineness of the purpose shown not by acts only but by prayer.

εἰς σωτηρίαν = ἵνα σωθῶσιν. Sc. ἐστίν.

2. ζῆλον. In a good sense; cf. Joh. ii. 17; 2 Cor. vii. 7, 11, ix. 2, xi. 2 only.

οὐ κατ᾽ ἐπίγνωσιν = without clear or true discernment of the will or character of God. "γνῶσις is the wider word and expresses knowledge in the fullest sense: ἐπίγνωσις is knowledge directed towards a particular object, perceiving, discerning, recognising; but it is not knowledge in the abstract; that is γνῶσις," Robinson, *Eph.* p. 254 (see the whole discussion).

3. ἀγνοοῦντες. The Jews and Gentiles failed for the same reason; cf. i. 18 f.; Eph. iv. 18.

τὴν τοῦ θεοῦ δικαιοσύνην = the righteousness which God exhibits in His own character and requires from men, contrasted with that righteousness which they tried to gain by their own efforts and methods. This is a decisive instance of the true meaning of the phrase; cf. i. 17.

ὑπετάγησαν. Cf. 1 Cor. xv. 28; James iv. 7; 1 Pet. v. 5, for the middle sense of the passive form. The revelation of God's righteousness in Christ required a surrender of preconceived ideas and habits and a submission : this the Jews did not give.

4. τέλος γὰρ κ.τ.λ. γὰρ explains why this submission was required. τέλος νόμου = an end of law, as an instrument of righteousness. Law promoted righteousness by revealing God's will and awakening the moral consciousness. That dispensation was ended by Christ, in whose Person and character God's will was fully revealed, and who at the same time, in His communicated life, gave the power of fulfilment to all who trust in Him. He thus also fulfils law, both as a revelation of and as a means to righteousness. But the special point here is that He ends the dispensation of law.

νόμου. The particular reference is of course to Jewish law: but it is stated comprehensively in accordance with S. Paul's view of Gentile conditions.

εἰς δικαιοσύνην = as regards righteousness, or for the purposes of righteousness.

παντὶ τῷ π. Cf. i. 16—the new condition marks the universality of the effect.

5—15. The reasonableness of such a submission is shown, and the relation of Christ to law explained, by the contrast between righteousness when sought as result of law, and righteousness resulting from faith. For the former S. Paul quotes Moses as laying down authoritatively that such righteousness can be attained only by complete obedience to law ; and that has been shown to be so difficult as to be impossible (cc. iii., vii.). For the latter S. Paul, while using O. T. language, does not quote it as authoritative, but freely adapts it to his purpose, using it because it is familiar and on his general principle of the fundamental unity of thought in O.T. and the Gospel; cf. S. H. for a full discussion.

5. ὁ ποιήσας κ.τ.λ.=Levit. xviii. 5, LXX. (ἄ). The stress is on ὁ. π. he that has done it, and he alone. ἐν αὐτῇ, 'by it.'

6. ἡ δὲ ἐκ π. δ. A personification, a dramatisation of the appeal of the Gospel to man, to make plain the nature of the demand made by it, in contrast to the demand made by the Law. The demand of the Gospel is not for impossible effort, but for trust and confession. Note that S. Paul finds faith-righteousness already included in O.T. teaching; cf. iv. 13 f.; Giff. on v. 10.

μὴ εἴπῃς κ.τ.λ. The allusions are to Deut. xxx. 11 f. The questions, which are set aside, embody the hesitations of the man who supposes that the facts, on which this righteousness is based, are dependent upon human activity, whereas they are the accomplished acts of GOD in Christ; and what is demanded is trust in Him who has done these acts, and confession of His Lordship.

τοῦτ᾽ ἔστιν. Simply explanatory=that is to say; so in vv. 7, 8.

Χριστὸν καταγαγεῖν...ἐκ νεκρῶν ἀναγαγεῖν. The reference is to the Incarnation and Resurrection. These are the fundamental acts of GOD by which His righteousness is revealed, and made possible for man. The fact that they are GOD's acts determines the human condition of righteousness, namely, faith in GOD through the incarnate and risen Son, and consequent confession of Him; cf. Phil. ii. 1—11.

7. τὴν ἄβυσσον for πέραν τῆς θαλάσσης, Deut. *l.c.*=ᾅδης of Ps. cxxxviii. 8, LXX.; Swete on Rev. ix. 1.

8. τὸ ῥῆμα τῆς πίστεως=the word in which faith, as the principle of righteousness, expresses itself. The actual ῥῆμα is Κύριος Ἰησοῦς: it is the expression of a faith which believes with the whole heart that GOD raised Him from death. The resurrection is the proof of the Lordship. This faith and confession is the demand of the Gospel righteousness. For the subj. gen. with ῥῆμα cf. Ac. xxvi. 25. Other explanations are—the message which has faith for its subject, cf. Joh. vi. 68; Acts v. 20 (S. H., Giff.), the message which appeals to faith (Lid.), the Gospel message (Oltramare ap. S. H.).

9. ὅτι=because.

ὁμολογήσῃς. Cf. Mt. x. 32 (∥ Lk.); 1 Tim. vi. 12; Heb. xiii. 15; 1 Joh. ii. 23.

ὅτι Κ. Ἰ. Cf. 1 Cor. xii. 3; 2 Cor. iv. 5; Phil. ii. 11; Acts ii. 36, xix. 5; above iv. 24; 2 Cor. iv. 14; Eph. i. 15; Phm. 5.

The simplest form of the Christian creed : κύριος the LXX. rendering of Jahweh is predicate to Ἰησοῦς; freq. in Acts in connexion with baptism and the first confession of faith (cf. Acts xvi. 31); cf. Knowling, *Witness etc.*, p. 261 f. The simple combination is most frequent in 1 Thes., but occurs in most of S. Paul's Epp. and Heb. xiii. 20, Rev. xxii. 20, 21, and elsewhere; cf. Robinson on Eph. v. 26.

καὶ πιστεύσῃς ἐν τῇ κ. σ. The aor. marks the initial act; the addition of ἐν τῇ κ. σ. distinguishes this act, as the expression (ἐν=with) of the whole heart, from bare assent to a fact; cf. Acts viii. 37 v.l., 1 Thes. iv. 14.

10. πιστεύεται=faith is formed, there is a state of faith, the condition, on man's side, of the state of righteousness.

ὁμολογεῖται=confession is made, a state of confession, the necessary condition for σωτηρία. The present tense in both cases marks the state of man's mind, not the mere act.

δικαιοσύνην—σωτηρίαν. The parallelism shows that the words are practically synonymous.

11. πᾶς κ.τ.λ. The quotation is suggested by the word σωτηρία; the confession based on faith will not be disappointed; then πᾶς suggests the wide range of the principle and leads to *v.* 12. Note πᾶς is added by S. Paul; but the universality is at once involved when πιστεύειν, possible to all, is laid down as the sole qualification; cf. i. 16, 17.

12. διαστολή. Distinction, or distinguishing (cf. 1 Cor. xiv. 7), that is, in the matter of faith, which is a common human quality.

ὁ γὰρ αὐτὸς κύριος. The same Person is Lord of all; the argument here lies in the universal reach of the term κύριος, as used in the confession Κύριος Ἰησοῦς.

πλουτῶν κ.τ.λ. The positive side, as from the Lord, of οὐ καταισχυνθήσεται.

τοὺς ἐπικαλουμένους α. Cf. Acts ii. 21, ix. 14, 21, xxii. 16; 1 Cor. i. 2; 2 Tim. ii. 22; 1 Pet. i. 17; commonly in LXX. for invoking Jehovah as the God of Abraham, Israel, etc. The phrase is therefore a natural consequence of using the term Κύριος of Jesus, and has the same significance; cf. Knowling, *op. cit.* p. 263 f.

13. πᾶς γὰρ κ.τ.λ. Joel ii. 32 qu. Acts ii. 21. N. the direct application to Christ of the O. T. phrase for Jehovah, as object of worship.

14. πῶς οὖν κ.τ.λ. The string of rhetorical questions at once justifies S. Paul's preaching to the Gentiles and shows that the Gospel has been offered to the Jews; they have failed, but not for lack of opportunity; this thought is developed in 16 f.

16—21. The quotations show that the refusal of the Jews to respond to the Gospel and the consequent call of Gentiles was

anticipated by prophets, from Moses to Isaiah, and typified by the
experience of the prophets themselves.

16. ἀλλ' οὐ πάντες κ.τ.λ. An objection taken by an imagined
interlocutor : you say 'all'; but *all* did not respond to the appeal of
the Gospel.

Ἡσαίας γὰρ κ.τ.λ. Is. liii. 1.

γὰρ = that was to be expected; for it was also the experience of the
prophets.

17. ἄρα κ.τ.λ. Then, as now, it was Christ's word heard by the
prophet and reported, which was the outward condition of faith.
N. the underlying thought that Christ spoke through the prophets;
cf. 1 Pet. i. 11.

διὰ ῥ. Χρ. The word is that which the prophet utters, and it is
Christ's word in the prophet. Pope (*J. T. S.* IV., p. 273 f.) argues for
taking ῥ. Χρ. here of the word spoken to the heart of the hearer; but
the thought is alien from the context.

18. ἀλλὰ κ.τ.λ. Israel has heard; ἤκουσαν though οὐχ ὑπήκουσαν. μὴ can it be pleaded that....

εἰς πᾶσαν κ.τ.λ., Ps. xix. 4, quoted not for argument but for
illustration : the Gospel has gone forth as widely as the utterance of
God spoken of by the Psalmist.

19. μὴ Ἰσραὴλ οὐκ ἔγνω; Can it be pleaded that Israel did not
understand, i.e. Israel, with its privilege of special revelation, cannot
plead ignorance in face of the explicit character of the warnings;
cf. Joh. iii. 10.

πρῶτος. From Moses onwards the warnings are explicit, of disobedience in Israel and acceptance among others.

ἐγὼ κ.τ.λ. Deut. xxxii. 21.

20. Ἡσαίας κ.τ.λ. Is. lxvi. f.

CHAPTER XI.

XI. GOD has still not rejected Israel. (1) A remnant is saved now as in the time of Elijah, (8) the hardening of the rest has for its object the salvation of the Gentiles and ultimately of Israel itself. (15) The privilege of the Gentiles is the same as the privilege of Israel; (17) in their case also it may be forfeited, (25) and even for Israel it points beyond the time of hardening to their ultimate salvation. (29) For the gifts of GOD are irreversible; His purpose is comprehensive mercy; His wisdom, knowledge and judgments are deeper than man can fathom, because they underlie the very origin, process and end of all creation.

1—12. The failure of Israel does not even now constitute a rejection by GOD. As in former times of apostasy there is a faithful remnant in whom the faithfulness and graciousness of GOD is still seen. And in this remnant lies the hope of restoration.

1. λέγω οὖν κ.τ.λ. picks up the thought of ix. 6. The reference to Ps. cxiv. 14, 1 Sam. xii. 22, enforces a negative answer.

μὴ ἀπώσατο κ.τ.λ. The form of the question involves a negative answer.

καὶ γὰρ ἐγὼ κ.τ.λ. explains the vehemence of μὴ γένοιτο; in such a rejection he himself would be involved and his whole position, that the Gospel is the climax and fulfilment of the earlier dispensation in its true spirituality, undermined.

Ἰσραηλείτης κ.τ.λ. Cf. 2 Cor. xi. 22; Phil. iii. 5.

2. προέγνω. Cf. viii. 29 n.

ἢ οὐκ οἴδατε κ.τ.λ. The point is that in a notorious case of a great apostasy there was no rejection by GOD, but a preservation of a remnant. So it is now.

ἐν Ἠλείᾳ "in the section which deals with Elijah," S. H. q.v.

ἐντυγχάνει—κατά. Cf. Acts xxv. 24 περί, 1 Macc. xi. 25 κατὰ; lit. approaches, and petitions, GOD against....

3, 4. 1 Kings xix. 10, 18.

4. ὁ χρηματισμός, subst.: here only in N. T.; cf. vb Mt. ii. 12; Acts x. 22; Heb. xii. 25; LXX. 2 Mac. ii. 4, app. in the sense of an oracle = χρησμός : but here, in direct reference to ἐντυγχάνειν, = reply ; cf. Deissmann *B. S.* p. 118, "ἔντευξις is a technical term for a petition to a king, χρηματίζειν the t.t. for the reply"; cf. Milligan, *Grk Pap.* 5, 5, 21 ; Polyb. 28. 14, 10 = answers to ἐντεύξεις of ambassadors (Schw. *Lex.*).

τῇ Βάαλ, on the fem. (LXX. τῷ) cf. S. H. : "the feminine article with the masc. name was due to the desire to avoid the utterance of the forbidden name Baal (Hosea ii. 16, 17) and the substitution in reading of αἰσχύνη, just as the name Jehovah was written with the pointing of Adonai ; usage most common in Jeremiah, occurs also in 1 and 2 Kings, Chronicles, and other Prophets ; not in Pentateuch" (summarised).

5. λίμμα only here in N. T. ; cf. ix. 27 (ὑπολ. or καταλ. seems to be the usual word in LXX.).

κατ᾽ ἐκλογὴν χάριτος on a principle of selection made by God's free grace, cf. ix. 11. The genitive marks the ground of selection and forestalls at once any sense of superiority or merit. It is God's free generosity, not their own deserts, which preserves the remnant ; cf. Eph. ii. 9. The statement seems to rest on the words κατέλιπον ἐμαυτῷ.

6. εἰ δὲ χάριτι, sc. γέγονεν ἡ ἐκλογή.

οὐκέτι ἐξ ἔργων. The 'remnant' are not saved in consequence of their works.

ἐπεὶ, otherwise, cf. 22 ; 1 Cor. xv. 9 ; v. Field *ad h.l.* ἡ χάρις the grace we are speaking of ; οὐ. γ. χ., loses its character of grace, cf. iv. 4.

7. τί οὖν ; sums up the argument : Israel missed its aim ; but not all Israel ; the select remnant gained it ; the rest were blinded ; cf. ix. 31.

ἐπωρώθησαν were 'dulled' or 'blinded' ; they failed to perceive the true way of attaining their aim ; exactly ∥ x. 3 ἀγνοοῦντες, not ∥ σκληρύνει, ix. 18. Robinson, *Eph.* 264 f., points out that πώρωσις, πωροῦν are used in N. T. not of the hardness of the will or obstinacy (σκληροκαρδία) but of the dullness of the understanding, dullness of sight or feeling being applied to the heart as the seat of intelligence ; cf. Mk viii. 17 ; Joh. xii. 40 ; 2 Cor. iii. 14 ; Eph. iv. 18 ; where the context is decisive, as here, *vv.* 8, 10. The whole discussion should be read.

8. καθάπερ γέγρ. Is. xxix. 10, Deut. xxix. 4, a free conflation.

πνεῦμα κατανύξεως, καταν. Isa. *l.c.* Ps. ix. 3 only. ' Torpor ' seems to be the meaning of the noun, but is not easily paralleled by the uses of the verb (Isa. vi. 5, Dan. x. 15 are nearest) : perhaps produced by the influence of κατανυστάζω, cf. S. H. n., Field. In any case the idea is of the dulling of the spiritual sense as in ἐπωρώθησαν.

ὀφθ. κ.τ.λ.   Cf. Mk iv. 12 qu. Isa. vi. 9 f.

9. Ps. lxix. 22 f., xxxv. 8 (θήρα).   A terrible quotation : it implies that the Jews are to be reckoned among those enemies of GOD and persecutors of His suffering people on whom the Psalmist imprecates these curses, the sustenance of their lives is to become a snare and trap and retribution for them, their eyes are to be darkened and their strength broken.   The justification of this use of the passage is that to the Psalmist also the persecutors were his own people.   The punishment is inevitably found in the very privileges and faculties which they had misused.   So the situation described is typical of the present situation = now, as then, the wrath of GOD works side by side with His grace.

θήρα = a net ; cf. Ps. xxxv. 8 only.   ἀνταπόδομα, cf. Lk. xiv. 12 (only in N. T.).

11. λέγω οὖν.   The moral of the situation is drawn ; it does not end in the ruin of the Jews ; it has for its first result the offer of salvation to Gentiles, and that gives a hope of a still wider purpose ; cf. *v.* 25 f.   Their ruin may be disciplinary.

ἔπταισαν κ.τ.λ.   The context sharpens the meanings of the words : ἔπταισαν and πέσωσι thus contrasted = stumbled to their final ruin, though the two words are much more nearly synonymous in common use ; ἔπταισαν is also defined by the use of παράπτωμα, a slip aside, a trespass, as it is suggested by σκάνδαλον (9) (S. H.).   ἵνα ranges in its use from definite purpose to simple result (cf. Moulton, p. 206), so paraphrase : Is the ruin of Israel the only and final result of their fall?   Not at all ; the immediate result is the offer of salvation to the Gentiles ; this should rouse Israel to competition, and we can see that if Israel's defeat has enriched the world, their restoration and completion may still enormously increase that gain.   That is the end we may anticipate ; cf. 15.

παράπτωμα, a slip from the straight.   Pauline except Mk xi. 25 f. (∥ Mt. vi. 14 f.).   The dative = the occasion.

ἡ σωτηρία τ. ἔ. = the salvation which we preach *has come* to the Gentiles.

παραζηλῶσαι echoes x. 19.

12. ἥττημα = defeat : they have been defeated in their efforts after righteousness (so 1 Cor. vi. 7 of defeat in a case at law) ; cf. Field *ad loc.*   He points out that there is a lack of correspondence between ἥττημα and πλήρωμα as there is between παράπτωμα and πλοῦτος.   There is no justification for translating ἥττημα by ' loss.'

πόσῳ μᾶλλον.   Sc. πλοῦτος ἔσται.

πλήρωμα.   Cf. Robinson, *Eph.* p. 255 f.: he shows that substantives in -μα represent the result of the action of the verb, and may be either active or passive.   Here = the completing of Israel, i.e. the adding the rest to the remnant; cf. *vv.* 15, 26.

13—33. The relative positions of Jews and Gentiles, which have just been described in brief, are now elaborated, to show that they both stand or fall on the same principle, of GOD's grace and man's faith; bare privilege cannot save either.   The argument of i.—iii. is thus completed.   There it was shown that both failed in the same way; here that both must be saved in the same way.   (13) Now my word to the Gentiles: though I make much of my office as preacher to the Gentiles, in the hope of stimulating Israel to take up their place in the Gospel—an end of supreme value and (16) natural— (17) yet Gentiles must remember that they owe their present state to their being included in the true life of Israel, (19) and may, as did Israel, by lack of faith in the goodness of GOD, come under His severity.   (23) Israel, too, by recovery of faith may be reinstated. (25) The truth is that the love of GOD persists over all: Israel's partial blindness leads to the call of the Gentiles, that, when completed, to restoration of Israel; (30) all have been shown to need, that they may receive, GOD's mercy.   (33) So we get a glimpse of the unfathomable wisdom and knowledge of GOD, His impenetrable judgments and untracked ways, in His supreme government of all things and elements in the universal plan : His is the glory for ever.

13. ὑμῖν δὲ—τοῖς ἔθνεσιν.   A dramatic turn: not, of course, implying that those to whom he was writing were all Gentiles; cf. ii. 1, 17.

ἐφ᾽ ὅσον μὲν οὖν κ.τ.λ.   The particles must be separated.   οὖν = well then, introducing what he has to say to Gentiles.   μὲν finds its antithesis in δὲ, *v.* 17.   His stress upon the mission to the Gentiles does not prevent him seeing their real position.   There is still the note of apologia: from ix. 1 he has been defending his position as apostle of the Gentiles; and here he completes the defence.   Hence the emphatic ἐγώ.

ἐφ᾽ ὅσον, so far as I am...; the description does not exhaust the meaning of his office; it has a bearing upon Jews as well.

ἐθνῶν ἀπόστολος.   This seems to be the only instance in N.T. of the gen. after ἀπ. describing the persons to whom the apostle is sent.

τὴν διακονίαν.   Of the apostolic office; cf. 2 Cor. iv. 1, v. 18; 1 Tim. i. 12.

δοξάζω.   Cf. Jo. viii. 54; Heb. v. 5; Rev. xviii. 7 = magnify.   The

Apostle may magnify his office, for the purpose which he states ; but this must not lead his converts to exult over the excluded (κατακαυχῶ, v. 17).

14. παραζηλώσω. Another echo of x. 19.

15. ἀποβολὴ, Acts xxvii. 22 only. *vv.* 15, 16 are parenthetic, justifying the statement of purpose in 14 and repeating the idea of 12.

καταλλαγὴ κόσμου. Cf. v. 10, 11 ; Eph. ii. 12—16, and 2 Cor. v., 18, 19. καταλλ. verb and subst. only in Rom., 1 and 2 Cor. (ἀποκ., Eph., Col.).

ἡ πρόσλημψις. The reception of them (see Hart, *Ecclus.* p. 302 ; cf. 1 Sam. xii. 22).

ζωὴ ἐκ νεκρῶν = life after death : the sharpest contrast that human experience affords. In what reference ? It must include not merely the recovered Israel but the reconciled world. It seems therefore to point to the final consummation at the second coming, cf. viii. 18 f., and esp. Acts iii. 19 ff., where the repentance of Israel is the necessary preliminary of that coming ; cf. 1 Cor. xv. 28. So S. H., who point out the same reference in i. 26. It explains then the πόσῳ μᾶλλον of v. 12.

16. εἰ δὲ ἡ ἀπαρχὴ, κ.τ.λ. The metaphor is from Numbers xv. 20, 21. ἁγία in both clauses is used in its technical sense of consecrated to GOD's use, without immediate reference to the character of the thing or person consecrated : but the consecration shows the true destiny of the thing consecrated. The verse gives the ground for the hope of a πρόσλημψις of Israel. The consecration of the firstfruits, of the root, involves the consecration of the whole organism. It is not annulled by the lapse of some members. New members are brought in by the mercy of GOD ; but this does not exclude the possibility of the recall of those who fell away ; such is the resourcefulness of the mercies of GOD. Thus ἀπαρχὴ and ῥίζα = the patriarchs (cf. S. H. and Giff.) ; the φύραμα and the κλάδοι = the generality of Israel ; those that remain faithful are the true Israel, the remnant on which faithful Gentiles are grafted. So the true life of Israel persists in the Church in Christ. For this use of ἀπαρχή, cf. 1 Cor. xvi. 15, 2 Thes. ii. 13 (*v.l.*), James i. 18, Rev. xiv. 4. The thought is present in viii. 19.

17. εἰ δέ τινες κ.τ.λ. δέ introduces the antithesis to μὲν of 13 ; μὴ κατακαυχῶ τῶν κλάδων)(τὴν διακονίαν μου δοξάζω. The point of the simile is that the Gentiles owe their present inclusion in the stock of Israel, the chosen people, solely to that mercy of GOD which first made a chosen people : the condition of permanence for them is the same as it has been for Israel, namely, faith ; they have no reason then to boast over the discarded members of that stock, but rather to fear for themselves, lest they too should fail in the condition, and further to hope for those members, that the same creative act of God, which has brought them, the Gentiles, into union with this source of life, may also restore those who have cut themselves off from it. The argument is closely ‖ 1 Cor. x. 1—13.

The true Israel is the root or stock with the branches, individual members, whether new or old. The underlying thought is the unity of the life in and from Christ, constituting the unity of the new Church. We have the elements here of the thought of the 'one man in Christ' which is developed in Eph. ; cf. Hort, *R. and E.*, p. 179 ; cf. Joh. xv. 1 ff. ; Jer. xi. 16.

τινες τῶν κλάδων. Not all Israel were apostate ; the remnant remained as a stock with some branches.

σὺ...ἐγένου. The singular emphasises the obligation of the individual.

ἀγριέλαιος. See Ramsay, *Pauline Studies*, p. 223 f. He refers to Prof. Fischer 'Der Oelbaum' to show that two processes of grafting were used in the cultivation of the olive : (1) the ordinary process of grafting a noble olive shoot on a stock of the same kind, all original branches of the stock being cut away, and the grafted shoot forming the tree. This was done when the stock was still young. (2) An exceptional process was employed to invigorate an old olive tree which was failing : the failing branches only were cut away, and a shoot of wild olive was grafted. The effect was both to invigorate the old tree and its remaining branches and to ennoble the new graft. According to Prof. Fischer this process is in practice in Palestine at the present day. If we may suppose it to have been in use in S. Paul's time, it affords an admirable illustration for his subject. The fact seems to have been discovered first by Prof. Fischer and commentators from Origen downwards appear to have no knowledge of it.

ἐν αὐτοῖς. Among the branches which remained.

συνκοινωνός. Partner with the remaining branches in the root which supplies the richness of the olive. The root here too is the 'remnant' as in Christ ; cf. 18.

18. μὴ κατακαυχῶ. ' Do not triumph over' (as you are in danger of doing (cf. Moulton, p. 125)).

19. οὖν. The Gentile is represented as justifying his triumph by the fact that his inclusion was the purpose of their rejection.

20. τῇ ἀπιστίᾳ—τῇ πίστει, dative marking the cause or occasion. Cf. *v.* 30, iv. 20 ; 2 Cor. ii. 13 ; Blass, § 38. 2 (1898). For ἀπ. π., cf. Mk ix. 24.

μὴ ὑ. φ. Give up these high thoughts of yourself; school yourself to the humility of fear; cf. 1 Tim. vi. 17.

22. ἴδε οὖν. This being so observe how in God there is both goodness and severity, meeting in each case the position taken by man.

ἴδε only here w. accus. N. the absence of articles.

ἐπιμένῃς. With dat., vi. 1; Phil. i. 24; Col. i. 23; 1 Tim. iv. 16 only. He says τῇ χρ. not τῇ πίστει to emphasise this absence of all merit and the need of dependence on God's grace exclusively; the thought of πίστει is included in ἐπιμένῃς.

ἐπεὶ, otherwise; cf. xi. 6.

23. As the Gentiles came to share in the hope of Israel, so fallen Israel may share the hope of the redeemed Gentile. He now explicitly declares his hope for Israel, hinted in *v.* 12.

δυνατὸς γάρ κ.τ.λ. The same power which grafted the Gentile branches can graft again the broken branches of Israel, and indeed (24) the exercise of power is less, as they naturally belong to the stock.

24. ἐκ τῆς κατὰ φ. ἀγρ. From the wild olive to which you naturally belonged. So παρὰ φύσιν contrary to your natural origin, οἱ κατὰ φύσιν those who naturally belong to it.

25—32. The argument is summed up in a picture of the wide and patient purpose of God : the end is to bring both Jew and Gentile under His mercy : in the process both have sinned (cc. i. 18—iii.) and experienced His wrath, owing to the same cause in them. But the waywardness of man has no counterpart in God : His gifts and calling are not withdrawn or changed, and will triumph in the end.

25. οὐ θέλω ὑ. ἀγνοεῖν. Cf. i. 13; 1 Cor. x. 1, xii. 1 *al.*, always with ἀδελφοί; a solemn emphasis of a fundamental truth.

τὸ μυστήριον τοῦτο. This secret of God's providential government; cf. xvi. 25; 1 Cor. xv. 51. The word in S. Paul always has the sense of a secret of God's purpose now revealed. In its fullest sense, it is the purpose of redemption in Christ, especially as including all mankind : so of the Incarnation (1 Tim. iii. 16), of the crucifixion (1 Cor. ii. 1, 7), of the consummation (Eph. i. 9), of the inclusion of the Gentiles (Eph. iii. 3, 4; Col. i. 26, 27, *infra* xvi. 25); here of the final reunion of Jew and Gentile in one Church (cf. Eph. ii. 11 f.). S. H.

ἐν ἑαυτοῖς φρόνιμοι. φρ. has special reference to plans devised for effecting their salvation : they must take God's plan, not find one in their own imaginings; cf. xii. 16 1 Cor. iv. 10. There is nothing quite parallel in the use of the verb; but cf. σοφός 1 Cor. i. 19 f., and σοφίας v. 33.

ὅτι πώρωσις κ.τ.λ. The briefest possible summary of the whole argument.

ἄχρι οὗ κ.τ.λ. Cf. Lk. xxi. 24.

τὸ πλήρωμα. Cf. on v. 12.

εἰσέλθῃ. Of entering into the kingdom; cf. Mt. vii. 21, 13; Lk. xiii. 24, S. H.; so also σωθήσεται.

26. καὶ οὕτως, so and only so: πᾶς Ἰ. = τὸ πλήρωμα αὐτῶν v. 12. The idea is that Israel as a nation will have its part fully in the consummated kingdom of Christ (cf. 1 Cor. xv.) and in this final reconciliation S. Paul sees the fulfilment of the promises. What fate awaits those Israelites who fell away, he does not consider. Jewish eschatology seems to have provided for the inclusion of all Israel in the Messianic kingdom by means of a general resurrection. But this question of the ultimate salvation of individuals is as completely ignored at this point, as it has been throughout these chapters.

καθὼς γέγραπται κ.τ.λ., Is. lix. 20. ἐκ Σιὼν is substituted for ἕνεκεν Σ. LXX. and ' to S.' Hebr.; the last clause is from Is. xxviii. 9. The context in Is. concerns the sins of Israel, and the verses quoted give the promise of redemption. This hope, which contemporary Judaism applied to a restoration of Israel by the establishment of the Messianic kingdom in Jerusalem, S. Paul sees fulfilled in the final return of the Christ and the establishment of His spiritual kingdom. For *Sion* thus spiritualised cf. Gal. iv. 26; for the new covenant, 2 Cor. iii. 6 f. For the Jewish interpretation of these passages, cf. S. H. The context is quoted in c. iii.

28. κατὰ μὲν. The verse states in another form the fact laid down in 25 b. Hence the asyndeton. The Gospel preached by S. Paul, by its abolition of law and inclusion of Gentiles, involved, as a matter of fact, the throwing of the greater part of Israel into a state of hostility to GOD: that hostility was incurred for the sake of the Gentiles: but that does not involve a change in GOD's original purpose in selecting Israel; His love still holds towards them for the sake of the fathers in whom that purpose found its first expression and a true response; cf. above v. 1.

τὴν ἐκλογήν. The choice made long before—of Abraham and Israel; cf. xi. 5, ix. 11.

τοὺς πατέρας, ix. 5; Acts iii. 25, xiii. 17; 32; *infra*, xv. 8; 1 Cor. x. 1; Heb. i. 1, viii. 9 (qu.). There seems no strong reason for limiting the reference to the Patriarchs. The plural seems to include the whole ancestry of Israel, here regarded as the object of GOD's love shown in

His earlier dispensation. It is for the sake of them, on whom He had lavished so much, that their wayward descendants are still not allowed to travel beyond the range of His love.

29. ἀμεταμέλητα γὰρ κ.τ.λ.   ἀμεταμ., 2 Cor. vii. 10 only.

τὰ χαρίσματα, only here of GOD's gifts outside the Gospel dispensation ; its use for the privileges of the Jew (ix. 4—6) is a remarkable instance of S. Paul's sense of the unity of revelation : the use of the words marks the fact that the privileges of the Jew were the free gifts of GOD's love, and, as such, could not be forfeited by rejection, though their operation might be suspended. The love which gave is still there. So

ἡ κλῆσις. The call to service, and ultimately to the kingdom, still holds, if Israel will hear.

30. ὥσπερ γὰρ. Another ground for the hope in 25 b found in a parallel between the actual experiences of Gentiles and Jews.

ὑμεῖς. Cf. *v.* 13 ; the whole section is addressed to Gentiles.

ποτὲ ἠπειθήσατε. Cf. Eph. ii. 12, iv. 18 : the Gentile state was due to the refusal to obey the voice of GOD speaking to them ; i. 19 f.

νῦν δὲ, now that you have heard and received the Gospel.

ἠλεήθητε τῇ τ. ἀπ. You came under the mercy of GOD owing to their disobedience = 28 a. As a matter of fact the opposition of the Jews led to the preaching of the Gospel to Gentiles ; cf. Acts xii. 9 f., xiii. 46 *al.*

31. νῦν, again under the Gospel, ἠπείθησαν refused to obey GOD's voice speaking in the Gospel, τῷ ὑ. ἐ. owing to the mercy shown to the Gentiles : the wide range of the Gospel was in S. Paul's experience the principal cause of offence to the Jews. This construction gives a clear and fitting sense : others take τῷ ὑ. ἐ. with ἐλεηθῶσιν ; but this involves a very awkward order and does not give a quite clear sense.

ἵνα καὶ αὐ. νῦν ἐλ. In order that they in their turn under the Gospel may experience the mercies of God, in contrast, that is, with their present subjection to His wrath, not with their former covenant relation, as that also was a state of mercy.

32. συνέκλεισεν γὰρ κ.τ.λ. Cf. iii. 9, 19, 23 ; Gal. iii. 22.

τοὺς πάντας. Jew and Gentile alike, regarded as classes : in both classes there were numerous exceptions, but neither class as such was exempt from the doom of disobedience ; both need the mercy which is GOD's ultimate purpose. The point here, as throughout, is to set aside any claim for special consideration on the ground of privilege. Privilege is a sign of GOD's love but not a guarantee of man's response ; and in the failure of that response men fall under the judgment of GOD.

ἵνα—ἐλεήσῃ. "There is a Divine purpose in the sin of mankind, and in the disobedience of the Jew: the object of both alike is to give occasion for the exhibition of the Divine mercy," S. H. Man's disobedience is GOD'S opportunity.

33—36. In dealing with this awful problem the last and deepest thought is, how infinite is the wealth and wisdom and knowledge in GOD, how far we are from being able to explore all His judgments or to track out all His ways; He reveals, but to none is His mind open, from none is His counsel drawn, to none is He in debt: He is the source, the ruler, the end of all: man can offer him nothing but the glory which is His due: so let us offer.

These verses contain at once a profound confession of faith in the goodness and wisdom of GOD, in spite of all the problems which experience raises and does not solve, and a confession of humility and reserve as regards the reasoning which has been given. Something has been seen and said of the purpose and ways of GOD, but not all: enough to confirm faith and to awake worship and praise; but not to explain everything: glimpses of the end to encourage man in the time of probation; but not more than glimpses. The fundamental postulates of faith are the wisdom of GOD and His all-embracing and loving purpose; these are the only sure guide among all the problems of experience, and they are a sufficient guide.

33. ὦ, the only place where S. Paul uses the exclamation except with a vocative.

βάθος. Cf. viii. 39; 1 Cor. ii. 10; Eph. iii. 18: there is the suggestion of depth impenetrable to human thought.

πλούτου. If coordinate with σοφίας and γνώσεως, represents χάρις or ἀγαπή, and this might be justified by ii. 4, x. 12, xi. 12; cf. Phil. iv. 19; it is a favourite word in Eph.; cf. esp. i. 7, ii. 7, iii. 8. The argument of the preceding chapters has developed the thought both of the love and of the wisdom of GOD. Yet here the dominant thought seems to be rather of the ways in which GOD conceives and brings about, if we may so speak, His ends; and consequently it is better to take πλούτου as governing the other genitives.

καὶ σοφίας καὶ γνώσεως. Combined also Col. ii. 3. σοφία is attributed to GOD by S. Paul with special reference to the wisdom with which the divine dispensations are ordered for the execution of His purpose, especially in the culminating dispensation of the Gospel, the means taken for the redemption of man from sin. ‖ δι' αὐτοῦ, 36; cf. 1 Cor. i. 19 f., ii. 7; Eph. iii. 10; Col. ii. 3. This is in accordance with the current use of the word, which applied specially to the philosophy of conduct, rather than to metaphysical speculation.

καὶ γνώσεως. Knowledge of what men and things really are, the necessary basis of σοφία as thus used. This is probably the only place where the subst. is used of GOD's knowledge, cf. Acts i. 24, xv. 8, nor is the verb commonly so used; 1 Cor. iii. 20; 1 Joh. iii. 20 (1 Cor. viii. 3; Gal. iv. 9; 2 Tim. ii. 19, slightly different, cf. viii. 29 n.). The thought seems to be of that complete knowledge of the nature of man and the issues of action which the wisdom of His dispensation reveals; so ∥ εἰς αὐτόν, v. 36.

θεοῦ. The absence of the article emphasises the character of GOD as GOD.

ἀνεξεραύνητα. Cf. 1 Pet. i. 10 ἐξηραύνησαν; the simple verb not uncommon in N. T. (Jo. Pa. Pet. Rev.); an Ionic word preserved in Trag. and revived in the κοινή; cf. Milligan Pap. 139 : on the form ἐραυν- for ἐρευν- cf. Thackeray Gr. I. p. 78. This adj. in Prov. xxv. 3 Symm. =that cannot be completely probed by searching; cf. ἀνεκδιήγητος 2 Cor. ix. 15, v. Nägeli, p. 23.

τὰ κρίματα. Cf. ii. 2; Jo. ix. 39. His judgments have been the subject of these chapters.

ἀνεξιχνίαστοι. Eph. iii. 8, LXX. (Job); not found elsewhere (ἐξιχνεύω, Trag.), Nägeli, p. 62.

αἱ ὁδοί. Cf. Rev. xv. 3 (qu.); Heb. iii. 10 (qu.); Acts xiii. 10, xviii. 26; Jo. xiv. 6. Here of the ways along which GOD moves in His government of creation.

34.   Isa. xl. 13 f., qu. 1 Cor. ii. 16; cf. Wisd. ix. 13, 17.

35.   Job xli. 11 (Heb.).

36.   ὅτι refers not to the preceding verse only but to the whole explanation vv. 33—35.

ἐξ αὐτοῦ κ.τ.λ. In close relation to the context, ascribing to GOD as GOD the whole origin, direction, and end of all these elements in the ordering of creation, and in particular of human life and destiny which have been under discussion. The thought gives strength and hope to faith. The nearest parallel in thought is 2 Cor. v. 18, in language 1 Cor. xi. 12.

ἐξ αὐτοῦ. From Him as creator and giver. ∥ πλοῦτος v. 33.

δι' αὐτοῦ. Through Him as ruler and guide, cf. xvi. 26; ∥ σοφία, v. 33. The same rare use of διά as is found in 1 Thes. v. 14 (=under the guidance of Jesus), Hebr. iii. 16 (διὰ Μωυσέως); cf. Kuhring, Diss. de Praepos. (Bonn, 1906) who quotes from Papyri only. So Heb. ii. 10. In 1 Cor. viii. 6 the use is different; cf. Joh. i. 3; διά being used of the Son as agent of creation=Heb. i. 2. Blass (p. 132) qu. Aesch. Ag. 1486.

εἰς αὐτόν. 1 Cor. viii. 6. He is the end to which all this leads,
‖ γνῶσις v. 33 ; cf. 2 Cor. v. 18 θεὸς ἦν ἐν Χρ. κόσμον καταλλάσσων ἑαυτῷ.

αὐτῷ ἡ δόξα. Cf. xvi. 27 ; Ephes. iii. 21 ; Gal. i. 5 ; Phil. iv. 20 ;
1 Tim. i. 17 ; 2 Tim. iv. 18. In all cases evolved by the thought of
God's mercies, either general or special. ἡ δόξα, sc. ἐστίν ; cf. 1 Pet.
iv. 11 and Lft ad Gal. i. 5 := to Him belongs the glory seen in all His
works.

ἀμήν. The word at the end of prayers and praises marks the
assent of others to the utterance. In these passages it emphasises
the statement by the express assent given to it by the Apostle. Cf.
Dalman, p. 227, Swete on Rev. i. 5 (ref. to Chase on Lord's Prayer
p. 168 f.).

CHAPTER XII.

In this section S. Paul deals with the consequences of the principles he has worked out as they affect the character and the conduct of the Christian life. The main principles are two : (1) The Gospel offers to the Christian power to conform his life and conduct to the will of GOD (i. 16), the use of that power depending solely on faith or trust, as man's contribution to the result. (2) Service in the execution of GOD's purposes is the fundamental demand made upon man by his relation to GOD; this principle has been exhibited as the explanation of Israel's failure (ix.—xi.) ; and is now to be expounded in its positive bearing, as determining the main characteristics of the Christian life. In the course of this argument two main thoughts come into prominence. The power, as has been already shown (vi. 1 ff.), is the life of Christ in man, due to the living union given by the Spirit in baptism. And consequently the service is the service due from members of a spiritual society or body, conceived as potentially coextensive with humanity, the service due both to the Head and to the other members. The special instances of the operation of this power in service are determined by the conventions of the time and of the situation in which S. Paul found himself and those to whom he is writing. The section may be summarised as follows :

XII. 1—2. The general principle is stated.

3—5. The right attitude of mind ⎫ in view of the social relations and mutual obligations of Christians.

6—21. The right use of gifts ⎭

XIII. 1—10. The true relation to the civil power and the outside world.

11—14. The urgency of the times calls for the new character in man.

XIV.—XV. 13. The special care for scrupulous brethren and Christian duty towards them.

XII. 1—2. The consequence to be drawn from this exposition of the working of GOD's compassion towards man, in the call of Jews and Gentiles and in His dealing with them, is the duty to offer the whole nature and capacity of a man, in living and consecrated service for GOD's use, in the way He pleases, as the reasonable work of a man: and this duty requires a refusal to fashion oneself to meet the demands of what is merely temporary and transitory, and a determination to undergo a radical transformation and renewal of mind, so as to test the will of GOD, in all its goodness, acceptance, and perfection, as the determining factor in conduct and character.

1. οὖν. Cf. v. 1; Eph. iv. 1; Col. iii. 1. The exhortation presents the true state of a Christian as the consequence of all that has gone before.

ἀδελφοί. The appeal is to their realisation of their relation to each other and to the Father.

διὰ τῶν οἰ. τ. θ. Cf. xv. 30; 1 Cor. i. 10; and esp. 2 Cor. x. 1. The compassionate dealings (plur.) of GOD enforce the exhortation: || 'If GOD so loved us…,' 'If then ye were raised with Christ…'=This being GOD's attitude towards you, make the due response. διὰ, see v. 3.

οἰκτιρμῶν. Cf. 2 Cor. i. 3. In O.T. the compassions of GOD are the basis of the covenant with Israel; cf. Exod. xxxiv. 6; Is. lxiii. 15; Lk. vi. 36. The plural signifies the concrete instances of compassion in all the long history, cf. Ps. l. 1 (LXX.), 2 Sam. xxiv. 14. They have been the burden of the preceding chapters.

παραστῆσαι. Cf. vi. 13—19; 2 Tim. ii. 15, the only passages where it is the act of the man himself. Of others' action cf. Lk. ii. 22; 2 Cor. xi. 2; Col. i. 28: of GOD's action, 2 Cor. iv. 14; Eph. v. 27; Col. i. 22. The sacrificial suggestion seems to be always due to the context, not to the word itself.

τὰ σώματα ὑμῶν. Cf. σεαυτόν, 2 Tim. *l.c.*; τὰ μέλη, ἑαυτούς, vi. *l.c.* For the thought, cf. 1 Cor. vi. 20. The body is of course more than the flesh: it is the organic vehicle or instrument (ὅπλα, vi. 13) of the mind or spirit which it uses for its own activities under present conditions of human life. This instrument is to be presented to GOD now for His use, and that involves a change and new development of the mind, which was formerly directed to using the body without regard to GOD. The body is not to be neglected, but used in this new service. And the reference is to personal activities in the social life.

θυσίαν. Cf. Mk xii. 33; Eph. v. 2; Phil. ii. 17, iv. 18; Heb. xiii. 15, 16; 1 Pet. ii. 5 (with Hort's note). In 2 Cor. ii. 14 f. the word does not occur but the thought is closely similar. In all these passages the conception is that the living activities of the man, in the condition of his life on earth, are devoted to service of GOD by service of man, as a thankoffering. The type of sacrifice implied is not the expiatory but the thanksgiving. The motive is given by the mercies received (διὰ τῶν οἰ.); the method is the imitation of the earthly life of Christ (cf. below, vv. 3—21; Eph. l.c.). The 'sacrifice' is not negative merely, in self-denial and surrender, but positive, a willing dedication of self to service in the power of the new life. This is the force of the epithet. It is to be observed that this is the only sense in which S. Paul uses the word θυσία.

ζῶσαν. The offering takes effect not by destruction or repression of life, but by its full energy; cf. vi. 13.

ἁγίαν. Set apart and consecrated to GOD.

τῷ θ. εὐάρεστον. By this full energy of life so consecrated man pleases GOD: cf. ὀσμὴ εὐωδίας, 2 Cor. ii. 14. Cf. Hort, l.c., p. 113 b.

τὴν λογικὴν λατρείαν ὑ. In apposition to the whole clause παραστ. κ.τ.λ. This offering to GOD of the life in its daily activities is the service dictated by the reasonable consideration of man's nature and his relation to GOD.

λογική. 1 Pet. ii. 2 (only). In both passages (see Hort on 1 Pet. l.c.) the word has reference to the rational element in man, which, as the mark of his divine origin and the organ of control over the animal nature in its passions and appetites, is his distinctive characteristic. It has its origin in Stoic philosophy, but had spread into common use and may be supposed to have become part of popular psychology. Here as an epithet of λατρεία it indicates that the service described corresponds to the higher nature of man, in contrast to such action as would be a mere assimilation through the lower nature to the ways of a transitory world: so this thought comes out in the next verse where the idea of λογικὸς is taken up by τοῦ νοός. Perhaps 'rational' is the best translation, but it comes very near to 'spiritual'; cf. 1 Pet. ii. 5 (πνευματικὰς θυσίας) and Phil. iii. 3; Heb. viii. 5 f., ix. 14 (qu. Hort, p. 112); cf. also i. 9.

λατρείαν. See Westcott, Heb. p. 232 (ed. 1889). In LXX. and N.T. alike the verb and subst. are always used of service to GOD or gods (but see Deut. xxviii. 48), Judith iii. 8 of divine worship offered to Nebuchadnezzar: distinguished from λειτουργία by this limitation and from δουλεία by its voluntary character. It included the whole ritual service of Israel (cf. ix. 2; Heb. ix. 1, 6) but also all personal service offered to GOD, as Lord and Master. For its use here of service in life cf. i. 9; Phil. iii. 3; Heb. xii. 28.

2. καὶ μὴ κ.τ.λ. This service of GOD involves a change in attitude

of mind: it must no longer be set on meeting the demands of 'this world' by an adaptation which can only be superficial, but by a steady renewal of its true nature must work a radical transformation of character, till it accepts as its standard of action the Will of GOD, in all its goodness for man, its acceptance by GOD, and its perfection in execution. This sentence develops the consequence of 'presenting our bodies etc.,' says what that means for a man and explains what is involved, especially, in ζῶσαν and λογικήν; cf. closely Eph. iv. 22—24.

μὴ συνσχηματίζεσθε, 'cease to adapt yourselves to' (see Moulton, p. 122 f.), as you have done in the past; cf. Eph. *l.c.* 1 Pet. i. 14 adds this point explicitly.

συνσχημ. Of an outward adaptation which does not necessarily spring from or correspond to the inner nature. Here the whole point is that the true nature of man demands the repudiation of 'the world's' claims, and so far as the man tries to meet those claims, he is not acting upon or satisfying his true nature. On the word, see Lft, *Phil.*, pp. 125—131; Hort ad 1 Pet. i. 14. Cf. μετασχηματίζω of disguise, 1 Cor. iv. 6; 2 Cor. xi. 13—15. In Phil. iii. 21 the outward fashion is made to correspond to the true expression of the inner nature.

τῷ αἰῶνι τούτῳ. The phrase always implies contrast to ὁ αἰὼν ὁ μέλλων, even when the latter is not expressed. Rarely is it purely temporal (Mt. xii. 32); but generally the moral contrast is emphasised (Lk. xvi. 8, xx. 34), perhaps always so in S. Paul (? Eph. i. 21; Tit. ii. 12). The moral significance (as in the use of κόσμος, cf. Eph. ii. 2) depends upon the idea of the transitory and superficial character of 'this age' when treated as of independent value: its standards and claims all deal with what is superficial and transitory in man, that is, with his lower nature, ignoring the eternal in him.

μεταμορφοῦσθε. Execute such a change in the manner of your life as shall correspond to your true nature; cf. 2 Cor. iii. 18, where the same process is described but with more explicit statement of the divine influence at work and the new character gained. The word occurs also in Mk ix. 2 = Mt. xvii. 2 only. But cf. also viii. 29; Phil. iii. 10, 21.

τῇ ἀνακαινώσει τοῦ νοός. The renewal of the mind is the means by which the transformation is gradually effected. Cf. Eph. iv. 23, where ἀνανεοῦσθαι corresponds to μεταμορφοῦσθε here, and τῷ πν. τ. ν. ὑ. to τῇ ἀνακ. τ. ν. ὑ. here. 2 Cor. iv. 16 gives the closest parallel, cf. Col. iii. 10. This renewal is the work of the Holy Spirit (Tit. iii. 5) primarily, but of course requires man's energy of faith; so personal action (μεταμορφοῦσθε) is required.

τῇ ἀνακαινώσει: the article=which is open to you in Christ: the word has its full force=the making fresh and new again, as it once was: the mind has become old and worn; by the Holy Spirit it is made fresh again and vigorous with youth; cf. τὸν παλαιὸν...τὸν καινὸν ἄνθρωπον, Eph. iv. 22, 24; 2 Cor. *l.c.* Cf. also 2 Cor. v. 17; Rev. xxi. 4. The youthful joy and vigour of Christians was the constant wonder of observers. The word brings out vividly the contrast with the prevailing pessimism of contemporary thought. The effect of the Spirit is fresh vitality and a true direction of the mind.

τοῦ νοός. The mind is the faculty by which man apprehends and reflects upon GOD and divine truth. As it is moved by the spirit or by the flesh it develops or degenerates; cf. c. vii. 25 n. Cf. Eph. iv. 17; Col. ii. 18; 1 Tim. vi. 5; Tit. i. 15.

εἰς τὸ δοκ. κ.τ.λ. The aim of the whole effort (εἰς τὸ dep. on μεταμορφ.) is to test what is GOD's will for man both in general and in the particular details of life. The action of the mind is not conceived of as speculative, but as practically discovering by experiment more and more clearly the lines upon which the change of nature and conduct must work. The thought is expressed fully in 1 Cor. ii. 6—16, esp. cf. *vv.* 12 and 16. Contrast *supra* i. 28.

δοκιμάζειν=to test or find out by experiment.

τί τὸ θέλημα τοῦ θεοῦ=what the will of GOD is for your new life; cf. ii. 18; Eph. i. 9, v. 17; Col. i. 9; 1 Pet. iv. 2. The apprehension of the will is essential to the true conduct of the new life.

τὸ ἀγαθὸν κ.τ.λ. The will of GOD here as in *ll.cc.* means not the faculty which wills, but the object of that will, the thing willed (cf. Giff. *ad loc.*); consequently these epithets are applicable: the object of GOD's will, here, is the character of the new life in detail, and this is good, as regards man's needs, acceptable, as regards his relation to GOD, and perfect, as being the proper and full development of man's nature. It is noticeable that here only in N.T. are any epithets given to τὸ θέλημα τ. θ.

These two verses, then, summarise, in the most concise form, the practical duty which follows upon man's relation to GOD as described; they describe conditions of the Christian life as it depends upon the power for salvation to be appropriated by faith: and introduce the detailed applications now to be made.

3—8. The connexion seems to lie in the emphasis just laid upon mind as the instrument of the formation of the new character. This leads to the charge to keep that mind in the attitude and quality proper to one who derives from GOD faith, by which he can use the given power, and in its use is bound by his relation to Christ and the other members of the body. These considerations (3) exclude all self-importance, enforce self-restraint, and (4—8) dictate the object, service in the one body, and therefore the quality and temper of mind in details of service.

3. γάρ enforces the charge just given by a description of the right temper of mind for men in their circumstances.

διὰ τῆς χ., 'on the authority of'; cf. 1 ; 1 Thes. iv. 2, and perhaps 1 Tim. iv. 14 ; 2 Tim. ii. 2 : the accus. xv. 15 has a different suggestion.

τῆς χ. τῆς δοθ. μοι. Cf. i. 5, xv. 15 ; 1 Cor. iii. 10, xv. 10 ; Gal. ii. 9 ; Eph. iii. 2, 7. His commission to preach the free favour of GOD to all, and his own share in this grace, authorise him to insist to every one of them upon its conditions; cf. Robinson, *Eph.*, pp. 224 f. The aor. part. of course refers to his call.

παντὶ τῷ ὄντι ἐν ὑ. All Christians stand on the same level and under the same conditions, whatever their special gifts.

ὑπερφρονεῖν...φρονεῖν...σωφρονεῖν. φρονεῖν here describes the quality (as νοῦς the faculty), not the object or contents, of thought or mind; cf. xi. 21, xii. 16 ; 1 Tim. vi. 17, and perhaps Phil. ii. 5. In all other places it is used of the object or contents as in Mt. xvi. 23=Mk viii. 33; Acts xxviii. 22 : and freq. in S. Paul. ὑπερφρ. only here. φρονεῖν S. Paul only exc. *ll.cc.* σωφρονεῖν Pauline, exc. Mk v. 15 ‖ Lk., 1 Pet. iv. 7. It is impossible to represent the play on words in English with the same epigrammatic point. The clue to the full thought is given by 1 Cor. ii. 16 and Phil. ii. 5 f. The 'mind' of the Christian must reproduce, in his place and capacity, the 'mind' of Christ, of whom he is a member.

παρ' ὃ δεῖ φρονεῖν. Cf. the use of παρά with comparatives, Heb. i. 4, iii. 3, and also Heb. i. 9 *al., infra* xiv. 5. δεῖ, as the subject of GOD's mercies and gifts.

σωφρονεῖν = that sound habit of mind which holds to the realities of a man's position, and does not err either by excess or defect : used of sanity, Mk v. 15 ; 2 Cor. v. 13. εἰς τό = up to the point of. The elements of this σωφροσύνη are explicitly stated in Eph. iv. 2. Comparing viii. 1, we may say that this σωφροσύνη consists in recognising the law of the new life.

ἑκάστῳ picks up the παντὶ and emphasises the distinctness of each in the common life : prob. governed by ἐμέρισεν, and transposed for emphasis.

ἐμέρισεν. I.e. at his call, in baptism=1 Cor. vii. 17 only ; cf. 2 Cor. x. 13 ; Mk vi. 41 ; Heb. vii. 2 ; μερισμὸς, Heb. ii. 4 : the faith which is the condition of the reception of the Spirit in baptism is itself a gift of GOD.

μέτρον πίστεως. μέτρον does not=μέρος or μέρις, as most commentators take it; in N.T. it always has its proper significance of
'a measuring instrument.' Consequently the genitive must be a
genitive of definition, a measuring instrument consisting in faith.
The point is that faith was given to each as a measure by which
to test his thinking of himself, to see whether it is true and sound
thinking: faith is such a measure because it recognises the true
relation of the man to GOD and his true position in the society of
Christ; cf. xiv. 23 n. So far as a man's thinking of himself conforms to his faith, so far is it true and sound thinking (μέτρον is
suggested by σωφρονεῖν). He will then think of himself as deriving
all that he has from GOD, having nothing from himself, and therefore
bound to serve GOD in all things and to claim nothing for himself:
so his mind will be busy in that transformation which will be a
presenting of a living offering to GOD. This thinking in faith will
also show him his special call and aptitudes in the one body.

The usual interpretation makes μέτρον πίστεως=a specific measure
or portion of faith: but this, besides the strain on the word μέτρον,
involves serious difficulties, and practically forces commentators who
adopt it to take πίστεως as equal to χάριτος.

4. καθάπερ γάρ.... Cf. 1 Cor. xii. 12—27. The reason for this
exercise of sober thought in contrast to exaggerated thought of self,
is the position of the Christian as a member of a body in Christ. In
1 Cor. *l.c.* the comparison is developed in far greater detail and is
applied to elucidating the various functions which the several personal
members perform in the body. Here stress is rather laid on the
temper of mind in which the several gifts should be utilised, as
illustrating the detailed exhibition of σωφροσύνη. In Eph. iv. both
lines of thought are combined. The difference of aim in the several
passages accounts for certain differences of phraseology.

ἐν ἑνὶ σώματι κ.τ.λ. A favourite analogy with S. Paul. It brings
out (1) the dependence of all on the one life received from the union
with Christ (cf. vi. 1 f.), (2) the mutual dependence of each on each
and all for giving effect to that life in each, (3) the common share
of each and all in the work to which that life is directed. While the
idea of this diversely organic unity of life and aim in Christ underlies
all S. Paul's ethical teaching, it may be said to be the single subject
of Eph. where it is fully and positively developed. S. H. rightly
point out that the comparison of a social organism to the body was
very common in ancient writers.

τὰ δὲ μέλη πάντα κ.τ.λ. But the members have not all the same
business or mode of action.

5. οἱ πολλοὶ κ.τ.λ. We who are many, being in Christ, are one
body; cf. viii. 1—10. The connexion of the individual with Christ,
made in baptism, is a connexion of life, given by the presence of His
life in him. Lut this life is one and the same for all who are baptised
into Him; therefore the connexion of the individual is not only with
Christ but with all who are instinct with the same life. The in-
dividuality however is not thereby submerged, but socialised, so to
speak: it is developed by being brought into these new and living
relations and has its part in the organic whole. The emphasis here
is not on the connexion with Christ, which is assumed, but on the
consequent connexion with others. So in 1 Cor. x. 17, xii. 13; Eph.
ii. 16, iv. 4. In 1 Cor. xii. 27, Eph. i. 23, iv. 12 *al.*, the stress is on
the relation to Christ.

τὸ δὲ καθ' εἷς. Cf. Mk xiv. 19, [Joh.] viii. 9. "*κατὰ* is used as
an adverb distributively. M. Gr. *καθείς* or *καθένας*=each," Moulton,
p. 105. **τὸ...**=as regards our several individualities; cf. ix. 5, xii. 18;
Blass, p. 94. The accus. of reference has become an adverbial accus.

ἀλλήλων μέλη. Cf. Eph. iv. 25, where also the stress is on the
mutual obligations in the society; otherwise *μέλη Χριστοῦ* (1 Cor. vi.
15, xii. 27; Eph. v. 30). Thus again the special direction of the
σωφροσύνη is indicated.

6. ἔχοντες δὲ κ.τ.λ. *δὲ* brings out, in contrast with the unity just
emphasised, the difference of function indicated in 4 b. But, as we
have different gifts, we must use them in relation to others, in service.
Some place a comma after *μέλη*; but the balance of the sentences
and the connexion of thought are against this.

χαρίσματα—χάρις. *χάρις* is the one gift of life in Christ, given to
all; *χάρισμα* is the special character which this gift assumes as
differentiated in each. "*χάρις* is the vital force of the *σῶμα τ.
χρ.* which flows from Christ through all its living members; *χάρισμα*
a special determination of this force to enable a particular *μέλος* to
do its part towards the whole *σῶμα*," Lid.; cf. 1 Pet. iv. 10; 1 Cor.
xii. 4, 7 (where *τὸ πνεῦμα* takes the place of *χάρις*).

τὴν δοθεῖσαν ἡμῖν. Cf. 3 (*δοθείσης—ἐμέρισεν*) of baptism.

εἴτε προφητείαν κ.τ.λ. A very characteristic series of elliptical
clauses. What is the ellipse? The first member of each clause
clearly describes a *χάρισμα*, the second member its manner of use;
the context demands that all these uses should be instances of
σωφροσύνη, the sober thought of self as meant for service; the ellipse
must, then, be supplied in each case to bring out this point.

προφητείαν. The decisive passage in S. Paul is 1 Cor. xiv. 1—33;
the Rev. claims to be a book *προφητείας* (i. 3, xxii. 7 f.); here=a

χάρισμα, the gift or power of prophecy as 1 Cor. xii. 10, xiii. 2 ; as a particular act, 1 Cor. xiv. 22 ; 1 Thes. v. 20 ; 1 Ti. i. 18, iv. 14. It may include foretelling, but its normal exercise has οἰκοδομὴ in view (1 Cor. xiv. 3, 5, 26), i.e. exposition of divine truth in such a way as to bring out the condition of the human heart (1 Cor. xiv. 25) and to encourage and console. It seems to differ from διδάσκειν as involving the consciousness of acting under direct inspiration, rather than of drawing upon personal experience and reflexion. It is clear from 1 Cor. xiv. 32 that S. Paul had to heighten and spiritualise the current thoughts about 'prophecy' and 'prophets.'

κατὰ τὴν ὀ. τ. π. Sc. we must use this gift—προφητεύωμεν.

κατὰ τὴν ἀναλογίαν = in due or full proportion to or correspondence with.

τῆς πίστεως. The faith which animates and enlightens the prophet. The aim of προφητεία is οἰκοδομή ; its inspiration therefore must be the faith of the προφήτης ; and that faith must be allowed free play, so that he delivers all that he believes, "without exaggeration, display, or self-seeking," Giff. Lid. follows the Latin as against the Greek fathers in taking τῆς πίστεως = the Christian Faith (objective), and κατὰ τὴν ἀναλ. = " according to the majestic proportion, etc."; but this is exactly a case where the instinctive interpretation of the Greek fathers is decisive. Moreover, the context requires here a reference, not to an external standard, but to the temper and spirit in which the action is performed.

7. εἴτε διακονίαν κ.τ.λ. Sc. ὦμεν ; cf. 1 Tim. iv. 15, ἐν τούτοις ἴσθι ; so with the next two clauses, thoroughness and devotion are insisted upon.

διακονίαν. The widest word for service, including the functions of apostles, prophets, etc., but here probably of personal service in the community ; cf. Phoebe xvi. 1. ἐν τῇ διακ., the special way of serving given to each.

ὁ διδάσκων. The change of form probably merely the result of instinctive literary feeling. The teacher is distinguished from the prophet (Acts xiii. 1 ; 1 Cor. xii. 28 ; Eph. iv. 11) perhaps as expounding, elucidating and systematically imparting truth rather than discovering and declaring it. It is of course a distinction of functions not of persons. See above, v. 6.

ἐν τῇ διδασκαλίᾳ. Cf. 1 Tim. iv. 13, 16. The act or practice of teaching, not the thing taught (so generally in the Pastoral Epp.).

8. ὁ παρακαλῶν. S. Paul is not thinking only of gifts qualifying for office, but of all gifts which help the society and its members. So here of the gift of stimulus or encouragement, especially in the application of truth to conduct; cf. 1 Tim. vi. 2; Tit. i. 9, ii. 15.

ὁ μεταδιδοὺς κ.τ.λ. Here and in the two following clauses we have to supply an imperative from the participle.

ἁπλότητι, liberality; cf. 2 Cor. viii. 2, ix. 11, 13; Ja. i. 5; where see Hort : S. Paul's use seems to be definitely=liberality.

ὁ προϊστάμενος, very general, for any one in a position of control or guidance; cf. 1 Thes. v. 12; 1 Tim. iii. 4 f., v. 17 (*al.* Tit. iii. 8, 14).

ὁ ἐλεῶν, only here and Jude 22 (outside the Gospels) of human mercy. ἐν ἱλ. cf. Ecclus. xxxii.(xxxv.) 11, Prov. xxii. 8 S. H.; perhaps there is a special reference to works of compassion, with almsgiving or healing. Cf. ἐλεημοσύνη, Mt. vi. 2 f.

9. The classification of the following clauses is not systematic : some refer to duties to Christians, some to non-Christians, some to both; and the different references are intermixed (cf. τῇ θλίψει, v. 12; εὐλογεῖτε κ.τ.λ. 14). Throughout recognised characteristics or conditions of the Christian life are named, and the temper of mind enjoined in which they should be exercised or treated. These commands, then, elements of Christian law, are not rules of action but principles of conduct. The Christian law is not embodied in external precepts, but in the example of Christ, adopted by faith. The contrast with the Jewish law is exactly the same as in the Sermon on the Mount. The particulars can all be signally paralleled from the Gospel account of Jesus.

9. ἡ ἀγάπη ἀνυπόκριτος. As in 1 Cor. xiii. S. Paul passes from the question of χαρίσματα to a καθ᾽ ὑπερβολὴν ὁδός, the way of love, so here in passing to an enumeration of instances of Christian character in general, as distinct from special gifts, he begins with ἀγάπη. It is to be observed that all these characteristics are the result of the 'power for salvation' which the Gospel brings; and they illustrate the metamorphosis which character undergoes to become Christian.

ἀνυπόκριτος, 'without dissimulation' A. V., 'without hypocrisy' R. V.; better perhaps 'unfeigned.' ὑπόκριτος = playing a part, unreality being implied; cf. 2 Cor. vi. 6; 1 Tim. i. 5 (πίστις); 1 Pet. i. 22. Christian love must be real.

ἀποστυγοῦντες κ.τ.λ. This clause insists on the necessity of an uncompromising moral standard, easily ignored by any merely class morality or forgotten by a sentimental benevolence. The moral sternness of the Gospel is here strongly represented; cf. 1 Thes. v. 22 (but there the reference is more limited). S. H. connect this clause with the preceding, and take τὸ πονηρὸν and τὸ ἀγαθὸν to mean the evil and good in others; but this is farfetched, and blunts the point of both injunctions. The participles express avoidance and adherence in the strongest possible way.

τὸ πονηρόν. The only certain instance of the substantival neuter of this adj. in N. T.; exc. Lk. vi. 45 ‖ Mt., wh. compare.

κολλώμενοι, gen. in N. T. with dat. of person, but cf. Acts viii. 29; freq. in Patr. Apost., qu. *Did.* 5, 2.

10—21. Note the remarkable coordination of participles, adjectives, infinitives (15), and imperatives. All should be translated by the imperative; cf. Moulton, pp. 180 f., 222; cf. 1 Pet. ii. 18, iii. 1, 7, 8 f., iv. 8 f.; cf. Col. iii. 16, 17; 2 Cor. ix. 11, 13; Eph. iv. 2, 3; Hebr. xiii. 1—5. The participles are all durative in action, implying habits. So the imperatives, except δότε, v. 19, which implies a single act once for all. The negatives with participles and imperatives follow the general rule of μὴ with the present imperative and imply the giving up of former habits; cf. Moulton, p. 122 f. All are instances of the σωφροσύνη which is the result of the μεταμόρφωσις.

10. τῇ φιλαδελφίᾳ. Cf. 1 Thes. iv. 9; 1 Pet. i. 22 (in LXX. only in 4 Macc.). A recognised duty, therefore liable to formalities; this must be provided against by an eager feeling of affection as to real members of a family.

φιλόστοργοι. Always of family affection; so 2 Macc. ix. 21 *al.* Polyb. *al.*

τῇ τιμῇ. Cf. xiii. 7; Joh. iv. 44; 1 Tim. vi. 1; Heb. iii. 3; 1 Pet. iii. 7, of respect paid by man to man.

ἀλλήλους προηγούμενοι. We have to choose between (1) an unparalleled construction=giving each other a lead; this requires the genitive: (2) an unparalleled sense 'each considering another superior to himself.' Even if we take (1) the proper meaning would be 'taking the lead of each other,' which is the opposite of the evident sense. (2) assumes that the compound follows the sense of ἡγεῖσθαι=to hold, consider, τινὰ τοιοῦτον, the only sense in·which the simple verb is used in N. T. except in the participle. This is supported by Phil. ii. 3 and Theodoret's παραχωρείτω δὲ ἕκαστος τῶν πρωτείων τῷ πέλας. Chrys. wavers: (1) τὸ σπουδάζειν τῇ τιμῇ νικᾶν τὸν πλησίον; (2) λέγει οὐ τιμᾶτε ἀλλὰ προηγεῖσθε; and although no parallel to this sense of the compound can be found, it is possible and suits the context.

11. τῇ σπουδῇ, in the zealous diligence which Christian practice requires.

ὀκνηροί, of hesitation from whatever cause, so sluggish, idle; cf. Mt. xxv. 26.

τῷ πνεύματι prob.=with or by the Holy Spirit—the source in the man of all the activities which are being urged. ζέοντες, cf. Acts xviii. 25 ; ζεστός, Rev. iii. 15, 16. The whole phrase)(ὀκνηροί.

τῷ κυρίῳ δουλεύοντες. The fervour inspired by the Spirit is to be used in the service of the Lord ; cf. Acts xx. 19 ; 1 Pet. ii. 16. The two clauses remind them of the power and the allegiance which are the background of the whole exhortation. The alternative reading τῷ καιρῷ is attractive, both because it brings this clause more into line with the neighbouring clauses and as parallel to Gal. vi. 10 ; Eph. v. 16 ; Col. iv. 5. But the parallels are not quite convincing—there the man is urged to make himself master of opportunity, here to be its slave, a very different and even dubious exhortation. And if we take τῷ πνεύματι as above we get an excellent sense and parallel.

δουλεύοντες. Of the relation of Christians in general ; cf. vi. 18, xiv. 18 ; 1 Thes. i. 9 ; otherwise generally of apostles or ministers till Rev.

12. τῇ ἐλπίδι χαίροντες. Cf. xv. 13 ; dat. = because of your hope ; their hope is motive of joy ; and hope naturally springs from the thought of the Spirit and the Lord ; cf. Rev. xxii. 17.

τῇ θλίψει. In your tribulation—a recognised condition of the Christian profession ; cf. 1 Thes. i. 6, iii. 3 f. *al.* S. H. call attention to the regular appearance of this note of persecution from the beginning of S. Paul's Epp.

ὑπομένοντες. Absol. as 2 Tim. ii. 12 ; Heb. xii. 7 ; 1 Pet. ii. 20. It takes the accus. of the object.

τῇ προσευχῇ προσκαρτεροῦντες. Cf. Acts i. 14, ii. 42, vi. 4 ; Col. iv. 2 ; your practice of prayer ; in this and the two following clauses the subst. is governed by the verb.

13. ταῖς χρείαις. Cf. Acts xxviii. 10 ; Phil. ii. 25, iv. 16, 19 ; Tit. iii. 14 = the needs. On μνείαις see crit. note, p. xlv.

κοινωνοῦντες. κοιν. = to be partners or act as partners ; the dat. of the thing marks the matter in which the partnership is exercised : cf. xv. 27 ; 1 Tim. v. 22 ; 1 Pet. iv. 13 ; 2 Joh. 11 ; dat. of person = the persons with whom the partnership is formed, cf. Phil. iv. 15 ; Gal. vi. 6 ; the gen. of the thing, the matter which the partners share ; cf. Heb. ii. 14. So here = acting as their partners in the matter of their needs : goes further than μεταδιδούς, *v.* 8, as implying personal service ; cf. 1 Tim. vi. 18.

τὴν φιλοξενίαν διώκοντες. Cf. ix. 30, 31, xiv. 19 ; 1 Cor. xiv. 1 ; 1 Thes. v. 15, *al.* This use confined to Pauline writings (incl. Heb., 1 Pet.) ; not the mere exercise, but the active search for opportunity is implied. Hospitality, a recognised duty, is to be carefully cultivated ; cf. 1 Pet. iv. 9 ; 1 Tim. iii. 2 ; Tit. i. 8.

14. εὐλογεῖτε κ.τ.λ.   Cf. Lk. vi. 28 (Mt. v. 44); 1 Cor. iv. 12; 1 Pet. iii. 9.   This clause inserted here shows that the order is not systematic.

15. χαίρειν κ.τ.λ., for infin.=imper. cf. Phil. iii. 16, "familiar in Greek, esp. with laws and maxims," Moulton, *l.c.*; here used in preference to the participle perh. on grounds of euphony.

16. τὸ αὐτό..., maintain that mutual agreement with each other which is the basis of peace; cf. xv. 5; 2 Cor. xiii. 11; Phil. ii. 2, iv. 2.

μὴ τὰ ὑψ. A potent source of danger to peace.   τὰ ὑψ. φρ.= ὑπερφρονεῖν, *v.* 3, xi. 21; 1 Tim. vi. 17; cf. ὑπερήφανος, Jas. iv. 6; 1 Pet. v. 5; here it refers to the estimate of self in comparison with other men; in all other passages of an overweening estimate of self in relation to God.

τοῖς ταπεινοῖς, always masc. in N.T. and O.T., exc. Ps. cxxxvii. 6 (where Heb. suggests *persons*), in contrast with ὕψος, Lk. i. 52; Jas. i. 9.   The antithesis to τὰ ὑψηλὰ has led some commentators to take it as neut. here.   But, against this, is not only biblical use, but the context; masc. gives a better expansion of τὸ αὐτὸ κ.τ.λ., and better suits the verb συναπαγ.

συναπαγόμενοι.   No real ‖ to this use is given: Gal. ii. 13; 2 Pet. iii. 17 pass.   Chrys. gives συμπεριφέρου, συμπεριέρχου; cf. Field, *ad loc.* =put yourselves on a level with, accommodate yourselves to. S. H. (though preferring the neuter) qu. Tyn. Cov. Genev., 'make yourselves equal to them of the lower sort.' Rhem., 'consenting to the humble.'

μὴ γίνεσθε φρ. παρ᾽ ἑ.   Prov. iii. 7; with parallel clause ἐπὶ σῇ σοφίᾳ μὴ ἐπαίρου=avoid self-conceit; cf. xi. 25.

17. μηδενὶ κακὸν κ.τ.λ.   1 Thes. v. 15 f.; 1 Pet. iii. 9 f.

προνοούμενοι καλὰ κ.τ.λ.   Prov. iii. 4, LXX.; 2 Cor. viii. 21; the sense is well given by Chrys.: πρόνοιαν ποιεῖσθε τοῦ καλοὶ φαίνεσθαι ἐν τῷ μηδενὶ διδόναι ψόγου πρόφασιν, he compares 1 Cor. x. 32.   Lid. cft 1 Thes. iv. 12; 1 Pet. ii. 12.   There is a common standard of honour which Christians must by no means ignore; cf. 2 Cor. iv. 2.

18. εἰ δυνατόν, τὸ ἐξ ὑμῶν κ.τ.λ.   If it is possible, at least as far as depends on yourselves.   The accumulation of conditions emphasises the difficulty of the precepts; cf. Field.

19. ἀγαπητοί.   N. the appeal to the treatment which they have received from God, as enforcing this most difficult act of self-denial.

δότε τόπον.   The aor. marks the instantaneous and final character of the act.   τόπον, 'room' or 'opportunity'; cf. Eph. iv. 26; Heb. viii. 7, xii. 17; Acts xxv. 16.

τῇ ὀργῇ.   The wrath of God; as v. 9; 1 Thes. ii. 16; cf. 1 Pet. iv. 19.

γέγραπται γάρ κ.τ.λ.   Deut. xxxii. 35 Heb. ;   see Giff. on form of quotation.

20. ἐὰν πεινᾷ κ.τ.λ.   Prov. xxv. 21 ; for ψώμιζε cf. 1 Cor. xiii. 3.

ἄνθρακας πυρὸς κ.τ.λ.   The context in Prov. and here forbids us to take this as a symbol of mere punishment or vengeance.   The 'coals of fire' are pains, but healing pains, of remorse and repentance. Lid. qu. Jerome and Aug. in support of this interpretation; cf. 1 Pet. ii. 15, iii. 16.

21. μὴ νικῶ κ.τ.λ. sums up 17—20.   Comm. qu. Sen. *de benef.*, VII. 31, vincit malos pertinax bonitas.   Wetst. gives a long catena of ∥.

CHAPTER XIII.

1—7. Relation to civil authorities.

There is no introduction or formula of connexion. This is still part of the new σωφροσύνη. It is to be observed that the reasons for civil obedience are fully and clearly given, even with repetitions, as though the matter required explicit treatment. Yet the occasion for the introduction of the subject is not explained or hinted at. It is possible that S. Paul may have had reason to fear, or may have feared that others would expect, that the Christian societies might inherit some of the turbulence of the Jewish, esp. there may have been a danger that Christians at Rome would be infected. Or again, the Christian theory of the civil order may have been raised by the emphasis laid upon the kingdom. And the necessity of clear views may have grown upon S. Paul's mind with his gradual approach to the centre of the Empire, and his realisation of the importance for the propagation of the Gospel. The establishment of Christian societies in so many places and the development of their internal organisation would also bring this question into prominence, as it did that of legal proceedings (1 Cor. vi.). At the same time, it is to be noticed that the treatment of the question, though definite, is quite general; there is no sign either in the argument or in the tone of the passage of any special urgency: and we may conclude that it is due simply to the desire for completeness in indicating the outlines of Christian duty and the character and temper in which it should be fulfilled.

Note further some significant omissions. (1) The question of duty as between rival claimants to civil authority is not touched. (2) Nor is the question of duty to a corrupt and unjust authority: it is assumed throughout that the authority is just and has for its aim the good. (3) Nor is the question of conflict between the civil and spiritual authorities.

S. H. have an excellent excursus on the question, pp. 369 ff. Cf. also E. von Dobschütz, *Die Urchristlichen Gemeinden*, p. 95 (Leipzig, 1902). Cf. 1 Pet. ii. 13—17; 1 Tim. ii. 1 f.; Mt. xxii. 15 f. ‖ Lk.

1. **πᾶσα ψυχή.** Cf. ii. 9 (Rev. xvi. 3, of fish) ; Acts ii. 43, iii. 23. L. & S. give ‖ from Greek class. poetry. Epictet. fr. 33 ψυχαί = slaves.

ἐξουσίαις, of persons holding civil authority Lk. xii. 11 ; Tit. iii. 1 only ; cf. 1 Cor. xv. 24 ; Eph. i. 21 *al.* ; Col. i. 16 *al.* ; 1 Pet. iii. 22.

ὑπερεχούσαις. Simply of superiority in any degree ; cf. 1 Pet. ii. 13.

οὐ γάρ ἐστιν ἐξ. κ.τ.λ. S. Paul lays down the principle that the fact of authority being established involves the divine ordinance of it. The two clauses state the same principle, in a negative and a positive form. The repetition emphasises the point.

2. **ἑαυτοῖς.** Emphatic : will bring judgment upon themselves.

κρίμα λήμψονται. Of the civil judgment involved by their acts ; cf. Lk. xxiii. 40, xxiv. 20.

3. **γάρ.** The justice of the government is assumed : so 4 a.

τῷ ἀγαθῷ ἔργῳ. Hort favours P. Young's conj., ἀγαθοεργῷ ; cf. 1 Tim. vi. 18, ἀγαθοεργεῖν ; tempting but hardly necessary.

τὸ ἀγαθὸν ποίει. Cf. 1 Pet. ii. 15.

4. **ἔκδικος εἰς ὀργὴν.** Cf. 1 Thes. iv. 6 : for the execution of wrath ; the wrath of offended authority.

5. **ἀνάγκη.** "The necessity is twofold, external on account of 'the wrath' which the magistrate executes, internal on account of conscience towards GOD." Giff.

διὰ τὴν συνείδησιν. Cf. Acts xxiii. 1, xxiv. 16, 'because of your own conscience' : because, as your paying tribute shows, you recognise them as authorities duly constituted, and therefore ministers of GOD. Hence it is a matter of conscience towards GOD ; cf. 1 Pet. ii. 19. See Add. Note, p. 209.

6. **φόρους.** Lk. xx. 22, xxiii. 2 only, direct taxes on persons, houses or land. **τέλος** of customs, taxes on trades.

λειτουργοί, of public service or office ; here as administering public functions committed to them by GOD : the connexion of the word with public service of religion is secondary.

εἰς αὐτὸ τοῦτο, to this very end, i.e. of securing social order and obedience, τὸ ὑποτάσσεσθαι.

προσκαρτεροῦντες, absol.: cf. Acts ii. 46.

7. **ἀπόδοτε,** pay as their due, οὐδὲ γὰρ χαρίζῃ τοῦτο ποιῶν · ὀφειλὴ γάρ ἐστι τὸ πρᾶγμα, Chrys.

8—10. The question of duty to the civil power leads to a summary of the principle which underlies all duty towards man, found in the duty of love, τὴν μητέρα τῶν ἀγαθῶν Chrys. : still the exposition of the properly Christian character.

8. **μηδενὶ μηδὲν.** The repetition of the negative gives a strong

emphasis to the injunction.   ὀφείλετε in pres. = remain under debt to no man in any matter, except in love.

εἰ μὴ τὸ ἀλλήλους ἀγαπᾶν.   ἀλλήλους must be given as wide a reference as μηδενὶ; love is a permanent debt (pres. infin.) that can never be fully discharged; cf. Aug. *Ep.* cxcii. 1 (qu. Lid.) "semper autem debeo caritatem quae sola etiam reddita detinet redditorem." This sums up all the teaching of xii. 3—xiii. 7.

ὁ γὰρ ἀγαπῶν κ.τ.λ.   This is the only way of fulfilling law, and this does fulfil it.

τὸν ἕτερον.   Apparently used by S. Paul to give the widest possible extension to the principle : anyone with whom a man is brought into relation : it avoids vagueness (not πάντας ἀνθρώπους or τοὺς ἄλλους) by its individual note and bars all casuistry as to 'the neighbour'; cf. Lk. x. 29.   It is grammatically possible to take τὸν ἕτερον with νόμον (cf. Hort on James ii. 8 *ad fin.*) ; but the phrase would be strained, and the context (ἀλλήλους—τὸν πλησίον) is against it.

νόμον πεπλήρωκεν.   Cf. Mt. v. 17: *supra* viii. 4; Gal. v. 14 and subst. *v.* 10.   νόμος is quite general, though as the next verse shows the Decalogue is the crucial instance.   πεπλ. perfect, has by that continuing act fulfilled and does fulfil, not abolished or done away.

9. τὸ γὰρ κ.τ.λ., n. sing. = the injunction regarded as one, contained in the several ἐντολαί following.

οὐ μοιχεύσεις κ.τ.λ.   The order differs from the Hebr. text in Ex. xx. 13; Deut. v. 17: follows the B text of Deut. LXX., as also Lk. xviii. 20; James ii. 11; Philo *de decal.*, Clem. Alex. *Strom.* vi. 16 S. H. N. the ninth commandment is omitted (but inserted in some MSS.).

ἐν τῷ λόγῳ τούτῳ = in this saying of Scripture.

ἀνακεφαλαιοῦται, is summed up and included.   Eph. i. 10 only.

ἀγαπήσ. τ. π. σ. ὡς σ.   Levit. xix. 18, where the context seems to limit it to Israelites : here the context has already given the widest interpretation.

10. κακὸν οὐκ ἐργάζεται.   The negative expression corresponds to the negative form of the precepts in *v.* 9.   Love cannot do any of these evils to the neighbour ; therefore it fulfils law.   Its positive effect in going beyond any possible extension of positive precepts is implied in *v.* 8.

ἡ ἀγάπη = the love which Christians owe to all.   It is to be noted, again, that in laying down the moral requirements of Christian conduct, S. Paul avoids rules and insists on the quality which in its proper operation belongs to the Christian as such and produces conduct conformable to the character of the life which is in him.

11—14. The exhortations to the detailed development of the

Christian character are enforced by the reminder that the times are
critical, and demand effort ; that the full 'day' of Christ's coming is
near : and the contrast between the life of the natural man and of
the regenerate is drawn in a few bold lines. The whole is summed
up in the description of the Christian aim, as a repeated effort to
'put on the Lord Jesus Christ,' and a complete abandonment of the
satisfaction of the lusts of the flesh; a return to the thought of xii.
1, 2.

11. καὶ τοῦτο, cf. 1 Cor. vi. 6, 8 ; Eph. ii. 8 ; cf. καὶ ταῦτα,
Heb. xi. 12; resumes with emphasis the whole exhortation.

εἰδότες. Cf. Lk. xii. 56 ; Mk xiii. 33=realising the character of
the present period and its demands upon you.

τὸν καιρόν. Cf. 1 Cor. vii. 29 ; Eph. v. 16; 1 Pet. iv. 17; Rev. i. 3,
xxii. 10; Lk. xxi. 8; almost technical for the period before the Second
Coming, S. H.

ὅτι explains the characteristics which they ought to realise.

ὑμᾶς ἐξ ὕπνου ἐγερθῆναι. ὕπνος metaph. only here ; cf. Eph. v.
7—14. Here the contrast is not with the heathen state, but of the
awakened and alert spirit with the sleeping and inert : a warning
against acquiescence in the present. Giff. cft Mt. xxv. 1 f.; perh. cf.
1 Cor. xi. 30.

ἡ σωτηρία. Cf. v. 9 ; 1 Pet. i. 5 ; 1 Thes. v. 8, 9. It is not
always clear whether the word is used of the present state in which
the Christian is by faith : or the final state which is the object of his
hope and is brought about by the Second Coming. Here the context
decides for the latter.

ἐπιστεύσαμεν. We became believers—a good instance of the 'ingressive' aorist; cf. Moulton p. 129 f.; cf. [Mk] xvi. 16 ; Acts ii. 44,
xix. 2 ; 1 Cor. iii. 5, xv. 2 ; Gal. ii. 16 ; Eph. i. 13 ; Heb. iv. 3.

12. ἡ νὺξ κ.τ.λ. 1 Thes. v. 2—7 ; Rev. xxi. 25, xxii. 5. προεκ.
' is far spent' (advanced) : A. and R.V., aor. marks the point reached.
The night is almost gone, the signs of the coming day are already in
the sky.

ἀποθώμεθα οὖν κ.τ.λ. Here the contrast with the heathen life
seems to come out. N. the aor., it is to be a single act done once for
all. τὰ ἔργα τ. σ. the deeds which are characteristic of the darkness.
τὰ ὅπλα τ. φ., the weapons needed for the work to be done in the
light ; cf. 1 Thes. v. 6—8, where both thoughts are more fully
expressed. Eph. v. 10 f. describes the warfare of the light. Taking
v. 14 into account, we see that there is a reference here, as in 1 Thes.
and Eph., to the Messianic warfare in which the Christian, as ἐν
Χριστῷ, has to take his part.

13. ὡς ἐν ἡμέρᾳ κ.τ.λ. The conduct (περιπ.) must befit the day and its occupations.

14. ἐνδύσασθε. Metaph. only in S. Paul (exc. Lk. xxiv. 49) ; cf. Gal. iii. 27 ; Eph. iv. 24 ; Col. iii. 10, with 11 *ad fin.* The closest parallel in thought, though not in language, is Eph. *l.c.*, as the reference is not primarily to baptism (as in Gal. *l.c.*, Col. *l.c.*) but is the repeated effort to realise the Christian character, that is the character of the Christ as living in the Christian. The metaphor is found in O.T. Job xxix. 14 ; Ps. cxxxii. 9 ; cf. Lk. *l.c.* Col. iii. 12 after 10, 11, shows the meaning of the metaphor, and gives us a clear hint that in describing the details of Christian character S. Paul is consciously reproducing the elements of the character of our Lord, as we learn them from the gospels. In estimating the amount of acquaintance with the Gospel story which S. Paul had, this fact must be given full weight. The aorist here has the 'constative' force (Moulton, p. 130), i.e. describes as one effort the constantly repeated efforts of growth in the Christian character.

τὸν κύριον 'I. Χρ. The full name is remarkable, contrast Gal. *l.c.* If it is the correct reading, it emphasises (1) the indwelling of the Christ, (2) the model given by the life of Jesus on earth, (3) the motive of obedience and allegiance to the Lord.

τῆς σαρκὸς κ.τ.λ. Cease to provide for the flesh with a view to desires : the negative with the present imperative has its idiomatic force (Moulton, p. 122 f.).

πρόνοιαν μὴ ποιεῖσθε = μὴ προνοεῖσθε ; cf. reff. ap. Field, *ad loc.* ; cf. Mt. vi. 25 ; Lk. xii. 22 f. ; Phil. iv. 6.

εἰς ἐπιθυμίας, quite general, of all desires of the flesh : the needs and desires of the flesh must no longer be the controlling motives in the life of the new man. = τὰ ἐπὶ τῆς γῆς, Col. iii. 2 ; Eph. iv. 22 is more limited : so Gal. v. 16 ; 1 Pet. ii. 11.

CHAPTER XIV.

XIV. (1) Scruples must not be allowed to separate brethren : (3)
they do not separate from GOD : (4) we have no right to judge those
who, in their particular choices of action, all own allegiance to the
one Lord : (10) judgment is reserved for God.

(13) The true Christian way is to avoid all offence to brethren in
matters indifferent, and, positively, to concentrate our aim upon the
weightier matters.

XV. (1) The fundamental Christian principle is mutual service
and help, after the model of the Christ, and in that endurance and
encouragement which GOD gives to promote harmony in His service.

(7) This mutual service and reception is the proper consequence
in the Christian life, of Christ's service and reception of Jew and
Gentile unto GOD's glory, the foundation of the hope, joy and peace
of all Christian men.

1. τὸν δὲ ἀσθενοῦντα κ.τ.λ. S. Paul passes to a special case
(δὲ) of the duty of love and the consequence of the corporate character
of the Christian life : we may perhaps regard it as a special case of
the injunction, xii. 16.

ἀσθ. τῇ πίστει, iv. 19; cf. 1 Thes. iii. 10, v. 14 ; 1 Cor. viii. 7 f.
Cf. iv. 20; 1 Cor. xvi. 13. τῇ πίστει = his faith—the weakness lies
in the fact that his faith in GOD through Christ does not carry him
to the detailed conclusions as to the true use and place of all material
things and acts in the spiritual life : it is not a wrong faith, but
a faith which in certain directions is ineffective. The cause of this
ineffectiveness is assigned in 1 Cor. viii. 7, as the associations which
certain acts have with the sins of the former heathen life. These
prevent him from realising the full Christian ἐξουσία (ib.).

προσλαμβάνεσθε. Phm._17 ; Acts xviii. 26 ; here xi. 15, xv. 7 ;
make it a rule to take him into your company and intimacy, whoever
he may be.

μὴ κ.τ.λ. = but not; the negative qualification is expressed separately, to give its full scope to the positive injunction.

εἰς διακρίσεις διαλ. For settling doubts, or deciding difficulties; cf. 1 Cor. xii. 10 ; Heb. v. 14. This is the only meaning of διάκρισις in N. T. and suits the context well : διαλογισμοί = thoughts involving doubts and scruples ; cf. Mt. xvi. 7, 8 ; Lk. v. 22. They are not to aim at deciding the questions which the weak brother raises in his mind, in the spirit of judging. It is a fine piece of charity to take a man, opinions and all.

2. ὃς μὲν κ.τ.λ. The absence of connecting particle shows that this is an illustration of the principle.

ὃς μὲν—ὁ δὲ ά. Cf. Blass, p. 145. πιστεύει, has faith to, so far as to—no ‖ to this use; Acts xv. 11 the only other case of inf. after π. is different. Giff. qu. Dem. *Onet.*, p. 866, προέσθαι δὲ τὴν προῖκ᾽ οὐκ ἐπίστευσεν.

λάχανα ἐσθίει, i.e. refuses to eat meat. This is the only clear evidence that an ascetic vegetarianism existed among the Christians of this time. It is very remarkable that S. Paul should choose this form of asceticism as his illustration ; and the reason must be sought in special conditions at Rome. The practice may have been due mainly to the imitation of contemporary asceticism (cf. von Dobschütz, *op. cit.*, p. 93 f., Lietzmann, Romans, p. 65). But it is conceivable that these influences may have been at least reinforced by the difficulty in which Christians found themselves of avoiding εἰδωλόθυτα (cf. 1 Cor. viii.). For tender consciences a solution was ready, in the avoiding of animal food altogether ; cf. the wide statement 1 Cor. viii. 13. The whole argument shows that it is not a case of sects imposing rules on others, but of private scruples and practice. See Introd. p. xxx.

3. ὁ ἐσθίων, sc. κρέα. The injunction is put in form as if the preceding statement had been negative, κρέα οὐκ ἐ.

μὴ ἐξ. —κρ. The idiomatic use = give up despising—judging; cf. *v.* 13. ἐξουθενείτω. The contempt which ignores :)(προσλαμβάνεσθαι ; cf. Lk. xviii. 9 ; Acts iv. 11 ; 1 Cor. i. 28, vi. 4.

κρινέτω. The judgment which makes sins out of what are not sins. Both tempers are subversive of ἀγάπη.

ὁ θεὸς γὰρ κ.τ.λ. This implies the principle of the whole argument against the validity of the law for Christians : but in such a way as to assume that there is now no controversy on the matter. His admission to the body of Christ carried no such conditions. The aor. must refer to that admission in baptism.

4 σὺ τίς εἶ κ.τ.λ. : the tables are turned : in judging him as a

sinner thou art committing a sin of presumption, in judging one who
is not accountable to thee.   For the dramatic form, cf. 1 Cor. iv. 7 f.

ἀλλότριον οἰκ.   Cf. Lk. xvi. 13.   οἰκ. only here used of the relation
of the Christian to the Lord, but cf. δοῦλος, and οἰκονόμοι of apostles,
οἰκία of the Christian family.   ἀλλ. belonging to and therefore accountable to another master.

στήκει.   Cf. 1 Cor. xi. 13 : a present, formed from the perf. ἕστηκα
(which is used for the present) probably to allow of emphasis on the
durative action (as κράζω by the side of κέκραγα (= pres.)); cf. Moulton,
p. 147, 248.   Blass, p. 40 f., cft γρηγορεῖν, mainly found in imper.;
cf. 1 Cor. xvi. 13 ; Mk iii. 31.

5.   ὃς μὲν γὰρ κ.τ.λ.   A second instance is given—scruples as to
the observance of days.   Here it is almost inevitable to think of
Jewish influence (cf. Col. ii. 16): and all the more remarkable is the
detached way in which the case is treated : as long as such observance
is not made occasion for judging others, it is open to individual choice.

κρίνει—παρ'.   No exact parallel : =judges or esteems one day as
superior to another for certain purposes : and perh. distinguishes one
day from another.   Cf. on xii. 3.

πληροφορείσθω, be assured.   Cf. iv. 21; Col. iv. 12 : *al.* 2 Tim. iv.
7; Lk. i. 1.

6.   ὁ φρονῶν τὴν ἡμ.   Cf. viii. 5 ; Phil. iii. 19 ; Col. iii. 2 ; Mk
viii. 33 (‖ Mt.).

κυρίῳ φρονεῖ.   Dat. to denote the person whose interest is affected,
Blass p. 111.   *Anarthrous κύριος* is used (1) after O.T. as a name for
God, *passim.*   (2) of Christ, very rarely without the addition of 'I. or
Χρ. or both : and then only with a preposition (2 Cor. xi. 17 ; Eph.
vi. 8=Col. iii. 20 (?); 1 Thes. v. 17) or in gen. after anarthrous subst.
(1 Cor. vii. 25 ; 1 Thes. iv. 15 ; 2 Tim. ii. 24).   There is no clear
parallel to the use in this passage if we take κ. as=the Lord Christ.

So tr. to a master: he has a master to whom he is responsible and
in view of whom he forms his opinion ; the master is Christ.   See next
verse.

7.   οὐδεὶς γὰρ ἡμῶν κ.τ.λ.   None of us Christians.   As Christians
we all recognise our subordination, in living and in dying, to the one
Lord.   It must be assumed then that the particular rules a man
makes for himself are made with that reference, and must be treated
with respect by others accordingly.

ἑαυτῷ, for his own ends, with regard to himself (not by himself) ;
as contrasted with the Lord's ends : the assertion of course involves
the supposition that the Christian is living up to his calling.

ἀποθνήσκει.   The service of the Lord is not exhausted by the life of the servant; it is regarded and furthered in his death also.   The decision of time and manner of death, just as the regulation of the details of life, therefore lies with the Lord not with the servant; cf. Phil. i. 21 f.; cf. Lid.

8. τῷ κυρίῳ, for the Lord; dat. as above, 6.

τοῦ κυρίου ἐσμέν. The whole argument rests on the position of Christians as δοῦλοι τοῦ κυρίου.

9. εἰς τοῦτο γὰρ κ.τ.λ. To establish this relationship was the object of Christ's death and resurrection. Note that in dealing with these secondary matters S. Paul bases his argument on this external relation, not on the deeper vital relation ἐν Χριστῷ; cf. S. H.; cf. 1 Cor. vi. 20.

ἔζησεν. Came to life—ingressive aorist: clearly of the entrance into the Resurrection life, in which He became κύριος. S. H. Lid.

ἵνα καὶ ν. κ. ζ. Cf. Lk. xx. 38: the absence of the article emphasises the state of the persons.

κυριεύσῃ=to establish his lordship over—(ingressive aor.). Is there a reference here to the Descent into Hell? Lid. cft Phil. ii. 10; Eph. iv. 9. The order ν. κ. ζ. is remarkable, and suggests such a ref.   1 Pet. iii. 18 f., iv. 6 f. may be partly dependent on this passage; cf. x. 7.   Swete, *Ap. Creed,* pp. 56 f.

10. σὺ δὲ τί κ.τ.λ. The dramatic emphasis is again applied as in v. 4; but here the appeal is based on the equality of brethren.

πάντες γὰρ κ.τ.λ. The common responsibility to one Lord is now put in its most forcible form, of ultimate responsibility to GOD as judge; cf. 1 Pet. iv. 5.

τῷ βήματι τ. θ. 2 Cor. v. 10 (τοῦ χριστοῦ) of the judgment seat; cf. Acts xxv. 10 *al.*

11. γέγραπται γάρ. Isa. xlv. 23, xlix. 18 (conflat.).

ἐξομολογήσεται. Cf. xv. 9; Mt. xi. 25; cf. Phil. ii. 11.

12. ἄρα οὖν. The final conclusion on this line of argument: each man will account to GOD, and to Him alone.

λόγον δώσει. Elsewhere ἀποδίδοναι Mt. xii. 36 *al.*

13—23. While Christian freedom is to be maintained, it must not be so maintained as to violate charity. S. Paul has developed in the strongest terms the Christian right, and consequently the wrong of judging. Now he develops the higher considerations, which should influence the strong, in suspending their rights for the greater matters of righteousness, peace and joy, for love's sake. The principle is enforced by repetition; cf. 14 *a* and 20 *b,* 15 *b* and 20 *a*; in each case some fresh aspect enforces the principle. The argument is the same as in 1 Cor. viii. 9—13.

13. μηκέτι οὖν κ.τ.λ. concludes the preceding argument.

κρίνατε=make it your judgment—different from κρίνωμεν; cf. Acts xv. 19.

τιθέναι κ.τ.λ. To *lay* a stumblingblock or trap for your brother; cf. Mt. xviii. 6, 7; 1 Cor. viii. 9=προσκοπή 2 Cor. vi. 3; *supra* ix. 33; 1 Pet. ii. 8.

σκάνδαλον. Orig. a trap=σκανδαληθρόν (LXX. tr. for noose, snare), then any cause of offence. It seems generally to include the idea of 'causing to sin' as well as that of 'offending,' so Mt. *l.c.* and xvi. 23; 1 Joh. ii. 10.

14. οἶδα καὶ πέπεισμαι κ.τ.λ. A very strong assertion of the complete abolition of legal definitions of clean and unclean, not however by way of controversy, but as fully admitting the principle maintained by the 'strong.'

ἐν κυρίῳ 'I. Cf. 1 Thes. iv. 1, 2 where διὰ τοῦ κ. 'I. repeats ἐν κ. 'I. of *v.* 1: the force of ἐν here seems to be 'on the authority of,' and it is a direct appeal to the teaching of Jesus recognised as authoritative (κυρίῳ); cf. for kindred cases of ἐν 1 Cor. vi. 2, xiv. 11; Mt. xii. 24; Acts xvii. 31; cf. Blass, p. 130 f. The reference would then be to such teaching as is contained in Mk vii. Gif. on the other hand takes ἐν κ. 'I.=ἐν Χριστῷ, "the conviction is that of a mind dwelling in communion with Christ, and therefore enlightened by His Spirit." So Lid. S. H. But this interpretation seems to strain the language (=ὡς ὢν ἐν...) and to neglect the peculiar force of the combination ἐν κ. 'Ιησ. The name 'Ιησοῦς (without Χριστός) seems in S. Paul always to suggest some act, teaching or characteristic of Jesus in His life on earth. Cf. Zahn *ad loc.* (p. 578 f.); Weiss (p. 561).

εἰ μή='still,' πλήν; cf. Blass, p. 216.

κοινόν. The technical term for 'unclean,' i.e. in itself and making the person who does or takes the thing unclean; cf. Heb. x. 29; Rev. xxi. 17; Mk vii. 2; Acts x. 14, 28, xi. 8. So the verb *ll. cc.*; Acts xxi. 28; Heb. ix. 13.

15. γάρ. *v.* 14 is a parenthetic admission and qualification, γάρ refers back to *v.* 13. The whole passage is curiously elliptic and interjectional.

διὰ βρῶμα. Owing to meat—that meat which you in your strength and freedom take, but he regards with scruples.

κατὰ ἀγάπην περ. Cf. viii. 4; 1 Cor. iii. 3: love no longer rules your conduct, as of course it ought to do.

μὴ...ἀπόλλυε. Cf. 1 Cor. viii. 11: the pres. act. of this verb occurs only here and Joh. xii. 25. Moulton, p. 114, includes this verb among those in which the prep. has the effect of 'perfectivising' the action of the verb. Here it must be the 'linear perfective,' i.e. describe the process which inevitably leads to the end. 'Do not bring to ruin as there is danger of your doing.' The point seems to be (as in 1 Cor. *l.c.*) that the example which encourages the weak brother to do what he feels to be wrong is destructive to him.

ὑπὲρ οὗ Χρ. ἀπ. The strongest appeal to the Christian. You ruin him to save whom from ruin Christ died, 1 Cor. *l.c.*; cf. Mt. xviii. 6, 7.

16. μὴ οὖν. As this ruin is the result of such action, do not give occasion for such a charge being brought against what is for you and in itself good.

βλασφημείσθω. The result of such an action would be that an evil character could be imputed to what is in itself good; cf. ii. 24, iii. 8; 1 Cor. x. 30 ; 1 Tim. vi. 1.

τὸ ἀγαθόν=your freedom, a good gained by your faith=ἡ ἐξουσία 1 Cor. viii. 9; ἡ γνῶσις *ib.* 11.

17. οὐ γάρ κ.τ.λ. No question of fundamental principle is raised; you may suspend your freedom in such matters: for the fundamental matters are etc.

οὐ γάρ ἐστιν ἡ. β. τ. θ. Cf. Mt. vi. 31—33, *ib.* v. 3 f. This is one of the clearest particular cases of the influence of the teaching recorded in the Gospels upon S. Paul's thought and language; cf. S. H. p. 381. Knowling, *The witness of the Epistles*, p. 312; id. *The Testimony of S. Paul to Christ*, p. 316 f.

ἡ βασιλεία τοῦ θεοῦ. Here and 1 Cor. iv. 20 only does S. Paul speak of 'GOD's sovereignty' as a present condition: in other places he speaks of it as a future condition, participation in which is dependent upon character formed in the present life; cf. 1 Cor. vi. 9, 10, xv. 50; Gal. v. 21; Col. iv. 11 (?); 1 Th. ii. 12, 2 Th. i. 5. In Col. i. 13 the present condition is regarded as the sovereignty of His Son or Christ. The two conceptions are combined in Eph. v. 5 and 1 Cor. xv. 24; cf. Lk. xxii. 29 f.; Joh. xviii. 36. (Robinson, *Eph.* p. 117.) On the meaning of the phrase='government or sovereignty of GOD,' cf. Dalman, *The Words of Jesus*, E. T., p. 91 f. Dalman, *op. cit.* p. 135, points out " that the phrase (in Jewish literature) never means the locus of the divine sovereignty but the power itself in its present and future manifestations in the teaching of Jesus. The idea is closely connected with the 'life of the future age,' and includes comprehensively the blessings of salvation." The use here regards the effect of GOD's government as already operative in those that are His and producing in them that condition of life which is a fit preparation for the future life when the 'sovereignty' will be fully revealed. For the connexion of ἡ βασ. τ. θ. with δικαιοσύνη in S. Paul cf. Sanday, *J. T. S.*, I., p. 481.

βρῶσις καὶ πόσις, 'eating and drinking'; cf. Lk. xxii. 30. The Gospel gives a metaphorical description of the common life of joy and love in the future life. S. Paul here declares that the character of that life does not depend on these external matters but on the moral and spiritual state.

δικαιοσύνη κ.τ.λ. Cf. Pss. 96—99, descriptions of the revealed and established sovereignty of Jehovah and the conditions it brings in; cf. Dalman, *op. cit.*, p. 136; cf. also Lk. xvii. 21: and Mt. v. 3—12.

δικαιοσύνη. Here 'righteousness,' as describing the condition of those who do GOD's will—cf. the negative 1 Cor. vi. 9, 10; Gal. v. 21.

εἰρήνη. Peace with GOD and between man and man; cf. 1 Thes. v. 23 (after 12—22), 2 Thes. iii. 16 (after 6—15).

χαρά. The natural outcome of righteousness and peace; cf. xv. 13; Gal. v. 22.

ἐν πνεύματι ἁγίῳ. In the Holy Spirit—inspired by and dependent on Him; cf. Gal. *l.c.*, 1 Thes. i. 6.

18. ὁ γὰρ ἐν τούτῳ κ.τ.λ. Cf. xv. 3, the service of the Christ involves the adoption of His principle of 'not pleasing Himself.'

ἐν τούτῳ=in this matter, of conduct as regards things in themselves indifferent.

δουλεύων τῷ χρ. This is the true service of the Christ (the Messiah) in contrast with pretended services; cf. Hort, *Eccl.*, p. 111; cf. below xv. 3, 4.

δόκιμος τοῖς ἀν. Contrasted with μὴ βλασφημ. ὑ. τὸ ἀγαθόν: men will not be able to find fault.

19. ἄρα οὖν, 'so then after all': brings to the front some of the implications of the preceding verses, for further enforcement of the appeal.

τὰ τῆς εἰρήνης. The aims which the peace established by Christ dictates.

τῆς οἰκοδομῆς τῆς εἰς ἀλλ. οἰκ.=the building up of the individual character so that each can take his place in the one building. This is a duty which each Christian owes to each; cf. 1 Cor. xiv. 3; 2 Cor. xii. 19, xiii. 10.

20. κατάλυε τὸ ἔργον τοῦ θεοῦ. The οἰκ., the duty of Christian to Christian, is GOD's own work; cf. 1 Cor. iii. 9; Acts xx. 32. καταλ. is suggested by the metaphor of building; cf. Mk xv. 29; Gal. ii. 18; 2 Cor. xiii. 10.

πάντα μὲν καθαρά. The admission of *v.* 14 is repeated, to bring out more explicitly the harm which may be done by insisting on rights; 1 Cor. x. 23, viii. 9.

ἀλλὰ κακὸν, sc. your use of this principle, τὸ τῇ ἐξουσίᾳ χρῆσθαι. The assumption, as throughout, is that the weak brother may be led to act against his conscience by the example of the strong.

διὰ προσκόμματος. Under conditions which will make him fall. διὰ *w. gen.* expresses the conditions of an action; cf. ii. 27, viii. 25; 2 Cor. ii. 4; Blass, p. 132 f.

21. καλὸν κ.τ.λ. Cf. 1 Cor. viii. 13.

μηδὲ ἐν ᾧ, sc. πράττειν τι.

22. σὺ π. κ.τ.λ. π. ἔχεις = πιστεύει v. 2. It is not necessary to exhibit your faith in this matter to men: to be taken with the preceding.

μακάριος κ.τ.λ. gives the final contrast between the really strong and the weak : the one with a clear conscience is to be envied (cf. Ja. i. 25) : the doubter must not claim the freedom he does not feel.

ἐν ᾧ δοκιμάζει. ἐν ἐκείνῳ ὃ δοκ. in the matter which he passes as right and sound; cf. 1 Cor. xvi. 3; 2 Cor. viii. 22; 1 Thes. ii. 4 (pass.).

23. ὁ δὲ διακρινόμενος κ.τ.λ. Cf. James i. 6, 'he that hesitates or doubts,' who wavers in his judgment ; cf. iv. 20 ; Acts x. 20.

κατακέκριται is at once condemned by the act, not by the doubt.

οὐκ ἐκ πίστεως, 'because the action does not spring from faith.' It is not the result in him, as it is in the other, of faith: and action which cannot justify itself thus proceeds from some other motive, which necessarily makes it sinful. Faith here as throughout is the man's faith in GOD through Christ. This faith settles for the man the principles and details of conduct. Only that conduct is right for him which springs properly from this faith. When a man's faith either gives no answer to a question as to conduct or condemns a particular line, the conduct is sinful. Thus we are given here a practical rule for individual action: not a general principle of the value of works done outside the range of Christian profession and knowledge. It has been constantly used for the latter purpose. Cf. S. H. "faith is used somewhat in the way we should speak of a good conscience." It is important to observe the negative character of the phrase. It does not follow that everything which a man believes he may do is right ; cf. Lid.

CHAPTER XV.

1—6. The negative principle just laid down—of self-suppression in the interests of the weak—does not exhaust the Christian's duty: there is a positive obligation to share his burdens and to consult his wishes, for his good. This is to do as the Christ did.

1. ὀφείλομεν δέ. But beyond this we have a positive duty to fulfil; cf. for this reference of duty to the example of Christ 1 Joh. ii. 6, iii. 16, iv. 11; Gal. vi. 2; Eph. v. 2.

ἡμεῖς οἱ δυνατοί. S. Paul includes himself, but he does not here dwell on his own example as he does to his own converts; cf. 1 Cor. ix. 1—23. οἱ δυνατοί = who are able; cf. 2 Cor. xiii. 9.

τὰ ἀσθενήματα, only here. The several acts and instances of ἀσθένεια.

βαστάζειν. Cf. Gal. vi. 2, not merely = 'to put up with,' but to help in bearing the load; cf. xii. 13. The strong would adopt the practices of the weak, when in their company, and so help them to bear the burden of these self-imposed regulations; cf. 2 Cor. xi. 29; 1 Cor. ix. 22. This gives full meaning to the following negative clause.

2. ἕκαστος ἡ. κ.τ.λ. puts the positive duty in corresponding form: with two qualifications securing that these concessions should not be mere sentimental benevolence, but aim at the good, in conduct, and keep in view what would strengthen the individual character; cf. on xiv. 19.

3. καὶ γὰρ ὁ χριστός. Who is at once the standard and the inspiration of the Christian's conduct. ὁ χρ. The Christ as we know Him in the life of Jesus.

ἀλλὰ καθὼς γέγρ. Ps. lxix. 9: for constr. cf. ix. 7. The Christ submitted Himself to the reproaches heaped upon GOD, rather than please Himself. The quotation illustrates Christ's principle in the extremest case: and the argument from it is *a fortiori*, Christians should act upon the principle in lesser difficulties. S. H. take it that S. Paul is using the quotation in a different sense from the original—taking σε=another man: but this seems unnecessary. The Psalm is frequently quoted in relation to Christ (Joh. ii. 17; Mt. xxvii. 27—30, 34; Joh. xix. 29; and also xi. 9; Acts i. 20, Lid.).

4. ὅσα γὰρ κ.τ.λ. γὰρ in a manner apologises for a not very obvious quotation, and S. Paul takes the opportunity of insisting on the value of O.T. for Christians.

προεγράφη. Cf. i. 2; Eph. i. 12 τοὺς προηλπικότας; Gal. iii. 8.

εἰς τὴν κ.τ.λ. 'With a view to'—this was their purpose; cf. 2 Tim. iii. 16.

ἡμετέραν. 'Of us Christians.' **διδασκαλίαν,** teaching, instruction. So perhaps always in N.T. (not=doctrine).

διὰ τῆς ὑ. κ. διὰ τ. π. τ. γρ. 'By the endurance and by the encouragement of the scriptures.' The repetition of διὰ seems to separate the two phrases and limit τῶν γρ. to the second (not so, Gif., Lid.): then=by means of the steadfast endurance proper to the Christian and with the help of the encouragement afforded by the scriptures. If, on the other hand, we connect both subst. with τῶν γραφῶν it is difficult to find a clear meaning for the first: Lid. "the patience of which the O.T. gives such bright examples"; Gif. "the patience is that which the scriptures give"; both seem strained. The two subst. have a special reference here to the 'burdens to be borne.'

τὴν ἐλπίδα. The Christian attitude of hope. ἔχωμεν=maintain—the proper durative sense; cf. v. 1. Moulton, p. 110. This statement of the use of the O.T. scriptures must be compared with 2 Tim. iii. 16: they imply (1) that the O.T. has a permanent value for the Christian, (2) that that value is two-fold, (a) for instruction, discipline and encouragement of the Christian, (b) as witnessing to Christ in whom is the Christian hope. The statements do not go beyond this, S. H.; cf. Lid.

5. ὁ δὲ θεὸς κ.τ.λ. The thought passes rapidly from the scriptures to the one Author of the truth they contain, of the power of endurance, and of encouragement; and from the particular instance of unity to the general principle, and from the special end of service of the brethren to the all-inclusive end of the glory of GOD.

ὁ θεὸς τῆς ὑπ. καὶ τῆς π. This gen. after θεὸς is confined to S. Paul (exc. Heb. xiii. 20; 1 Pet. v. 10) and to prayers: the gen. describes a gift of GOD in each case, εἰρήνη (xv. 33; 2 Cor. xiii. 11; Phil. iv. 9; 1 Thes. iv. 23; Heb. xiii. 20); ἐλπίς (xv. 13); παράκλησις (2 Cor. i. 3); ἀγάπη (2 Cor. xiii. 11); χάρις (1 Pet. v. 10). In each case the gift mentioned has special ref. to context. So here=that GOD who enables us to endure and encourages us by the scriptures. O.T. ‖s are not frequent and chiefly in Psalms, in prayers τῆς σωτηρίας most common; cf. Ps. xvii. 46; xxx. (xxxi.) 5; xli. (xlii.) 8; lxi. (lxii.) 7.

τὸ αὐτὸ φρονεῖν. The unity of mind and interest, easily impaired if difference of opinion is allowed to affect personal relations, is the best preventive of such dissension : the words carry us back to xii. 16 and indicate the presence beneath the surface of the argument of the fundamental theme, the union of Jew and Gentile in Christ : this becomes explicit in *vv.* 7 ff.

ἐν ἀλλήλοις. Cf. εἰς ἀλλήλους xii. 16 = mutually.

κατὰ Χρ. Ἰησ. After the manner and rule of Christ Jesus—as exemplified in His life on earth and His mission (Christ) of reconciliation ; cf. 2 Cor. v. 18—vi. 3 f. This combination and order are confined to S. Paul (throughout) and Acts (? Mt. i. 18).

6. ὁμοθυμαδὸν. Acts (10) and here only : with one heart and mouth,—the expression of τὸ αὐτὸ φρονεῖν.

δοξάζητε τ. θ. "A phrase much used in both O.T. and N.T. for all forms of human recognition of GOD's true character and work, rendered by word or by act," Hort, 1 *Pet.* ii. 12. The special subject of recognition is here indicated by the full description.

τὸν θεὸν κ. π. τ. κ. ἡ. Ἰ. Χρ. Cf. Phil. ii. 11 with context from *v.* 2. This full description is a compendium of the Gospel, especially as the Gospel of reconciliation ; and comes suitably here as the climax of the detailed exhortations to unity, echoing the appeal of xii. 1 to 'the compassions of GOD.' The whole economy of creation and redemption comes from GOD, revealed as the GOD and Father of our Lord Jesus Christ, and as in Him 'reconciling the world to Himself.' The full phrase occurs only in benedictions (Eph. i. 3 ; 2 Cor. i. 3 ; 1 Pet. i. 3 ; cf. Col. i. 3) or other places of special solemnity (here and 2 Cor. xi. 31 nearly). Both θεὸν and πατέρα are to be taken with τ. κ.; cf. Hort on 1 Pet. i. 3 (p. 29).

7—13. This is the final stage of the appeal for unity in the new life : and therefore goes to the bottom of the question, the unity of Jew and Gentile. It is not mere toleration that is needed, but full reception, based on the mind and work of Christ.

7. διὸ κ.τ.λ. This verse resumes and restates *vv.* 5, 6. προσλ. ἀ. ‖ τὸ αὐτὸ φρονεῖν ; καθὼς κ.τ.λ. ‖ κατὰ Χρ. Ἰησ.; εἰς δόξαν ‖ ἵνα κ.τ.λ.

διὸ. On all the grounds stated in xiv. 1—xv. 6.

προσλ. ἀλλ. As in xiv. 1 but wider—each other, in spite of all the differences which tend to separate man from man; cf. xi. 15 ; Phm. 12, 17 ; Acts xviii. 26, xxviii. 2. Does this connexion involve the conclusion that "the relations of Jew and Gentile were directly or indirectly involved in the relations of strong and weak"? see S. H. qu. Hort.

καθὼς καὶ κ.τ.λ. resumes the whole argument of i.—xi. incl.

Those chapters show how the Christ brought all men to Himself, with all their differences and all their sins.

ἡμᾶς. Us Christians, including already representatively Jews and Gentiles.

εἰς δόξαν τοῦ θεοῦ. With a view to glorifying GOD; cf. xi. 33—36.

8. λέγω γὰρ explains and justifies the statement ὁ Χρ. προσελ. ἡμᾶς, by showing that the call of Jew and Gentile alike was a true instance of service rendered by Christ to GOD in bearing the burdens of the weak.

διάκονον γ. περιτομῆς. A very remarkable phrase, n. (1) the órder throws emphasis on διάκονον, the natural order being γεγενῆσθαι διάκονον περιτομῆς (Blass, p. 287—8). (2) then by διάκονον so placed is emphasised that aspect of the work of Christ which specially affords an example of service to others, and so it clinches the appeal to the strong to bear the burdens of the weak. The fundamental use of διάκονος for menial service to a master makes the word especially appropriate to this purpose. (Cf. Hort, *Chr. Eccles.*, p. 202 f.; cf. Lk. xii. 37; Mt. xx. 28, ‖ Mk and n. Joh. xiii. 13—16.) (3) περιτομῆς will in this case define the burden which the διάκονος took up, and stand for the whole order of preparatory law which is summed up in the fundamental requisite of circumcision: an exact parallel to this conception is given in Gal. iv. 4; cf. 1 Cor. ix. 20. The gen. is objective, ‖ 2 Cor. iii. 6 καινῆς διαθήκης; Eph. iii. 7 εὐαγγελίου. He has so taken up the burden of circumcision and used it in the interests of GOD's truth as to etc. (4) γεγενῆσθαι, a strong perfect (γεγονέναι might have been ambiguous, as it is sometimes aoristic; cf. Moulton, p. 146) implying the whole process of Christ's διακονία as completed by Him and realised in the experience of S. Paul and the Church in its final purpose and result, the common call of Jew and Gentile alike, so 'has proved to be...' (the form here only in N.T., part. Joh. ii. 9 only. For LXX. cf. Thackeray § 24: for papyri Mayser, p. 391).

ὑπὲρ ἀληθείας θεοῦ names the object of the διακονία, but, instead of the personal object (τῷ θεῷ), the character of GOD which this service vindicates, and so explains εἰς δόξαν τοῦ θεοῦ=in the interests of GOD's truth, i.e. truthfulness; cf. iii. 4, 7; cf. Ps. xxx. (xxxi.) 6; Briggs, Ps. xv. 2 (*Internat. Com.* I. p. 115) = 'faithfulness, reliableness'; Kirkpatrick, Ps. lxxxv. 10. The faithfulness is vindicated by the fulfilment of the promises made under the covenant in all their comprehensive inclusion of Jew and Gentile together.

εἰς τὸ κ.τ.λ. With both βεβαιῶσαι and δοξάσαι (cf. Blass, p. 236): the aor. marks the result of the διακ. γ. as done once for all:=so that He established the promises and the Gentiles glorified God. Both Jew and Gentile received the full benefit of the service—the one in the fulfilment of the promises, their special treasure (ix. 4; Eph. ii. 12) and the other in the call of God's mercy.

βεβαιῶσαι. Here simply 'confirmed,' 'established' by fulfilling; cf. iv. 16; Heb. ii. 2. Perh. in all other places in N.T. the meaning 'warrant' or 'guarantee' is to be preferred.

τὰς ἐπ. τῶν πατέρων. Cf. Acts xiii. 32, xxvi. 6. No other instance of this gen. w. ἐπαγγ.: obj. gen. 'made to...' It might be 'possessive'; for the whole thought cf. 2 Cor. i. 20.

τῶν πατέρων, ix. 5 n.

9. τὸ δὲ ἔθνη...δοξάσαι. The two infinitives under one article mark the fact that the twofold result is really one: the confirmation of the promises comes by the call of the Gentiles. The δὲ marks the contrast between τὰ ἔθνη and τῶν πατέρων; the one result brought a double benefit, to Jews and to the Gentiles:='while for their part.'

ὑπὲρ ἐλέους. Cf. xi. 30, 31: =on account of mercy received; nearly =περί, v. Blass, p. 135. The order puts emphasis on ὑπὲρ ἐλέους; the absence of the article emphasises the character of the new state.

καθὼς γέγραπται. The four quotations all illustrate the union of Jew and Gentile in 'the promises': the first three as uniting in rendering praise to God for His mercies, the last as sharing in the promise of the Davidic king.

διὰ τοῦτο κ.τ.λ. Ps. xviii. (xvii.) 49 (Κύριε after ἔθνεσιν) the triumph of David over his enemies and the establishment of his throne is the effect of Jehovah's faithfulness to His servant, and must be celebrated not only in Israel but among the heathen. These then have some share in the knowledge of Jehovah and His faithfulness.

10. εὐφράνθητε κ.τ.λ. Deut. xxxii. 43, from the Song of Moses, in close connexion with the execution of vengeance on God's enemies, and the consequent rejoicing of heaven, sons of God and all the angels of God. In this triumph, then, the Gentiles are to share.

11. αἰνεῖτε κ.τ.λ. Ps. cxvii. (cxvi.) 1 (om. καὶ bef. ἐπαιν. LXX.). The Gentiles are called upon to praise God for His lovingkindness and faithfulness to Israel (so here ἀλήθεια and ἔλεος).

12. ἔσται ἡ ῥίζα. Isa. xi. 10 LXX. The climax of the most definite Messianic passage in Isa. i.—xl.; the Messiah, the Davidic king, will include the Gentiles in His dominion by their voluntary 'resort' to Him (for ἐλπιοῦσιν—'seek' R.V., 'resort' Cheyne).

13. ὁ δὲ θεὸς τῆς ἐλπίδος. The God who gives us this hope; cf. on v. 5. τῆς ἐλπίδος suggested by ἐλπιοῦσιν v. 12 must refer definitely to the hope of the gathering of all to Christ, Jew and Gentile (cf. xi.

13—16, 25 ff.) as already there has been a representative gathering (v. 7).

πληρῶσαι κ.τ.λ. Joy and peace are the proper consequences of such a hope, as fulfilling what love makes desirable, and putting men at peace with each other in view of the event.

ἐν τῷ πιστεύειν = in the active exercise of faith in GOD, that He will accomplish this promise.

εἰς τὸ περ. The result of this faith, invigorated by the temper of joy and peace, is to increase the activity of this hope in them : their hope in this accomplishment will be more real and vigorous.

ἐν δυνάμει πν. ἁγ. The original power of all exercise of Christian grace—in power from the Holy Spirit; cf. 19, Lk. iv. 14 only; cf. Eph. iii. 16; 2 Thes. i. 11; cf. Hort on 1 Pet. i. 5.

πνεύματος ἁγίου. The Holy Spirit : for abs. of article cf. 1 Pet. i. 5 ἐν δυνάμει |θεοῦ; 1 Cor. ii. 5, 2 Cor. vi. 7; so 2 Cor. xiii. 4 (ἐκ); 2 Tim. i. 8 (κατὰ) and without preposition; 1 Cor. i. 18, 24: in fact the combination is always anarthrous.

G. CONCLUSION.

xv. **14—33.** Explanation of the occasion of writing.

14—33. The letter passes to personal matters (a) 14—21 a delicate apology and justification of the letter itself: it is not sent with a view to supplementing deficiencies of the Roman Christians, but partly, at least, to remind them of the great truths of the Gospel, and justified by the writer's commission and experience, all under Christ, and of Christ's work among the Gentiles through him, (b) 22—29 it is the outcome of the affection which has always made him eager to visit them, and now that his work in Achaia and the east is finished, he proposes to visit them on the way to Spain, first fulfilling a commission of love and gratitude from his Gentile churches to Jerusalem, where he hopes that his visit will be accompanied by a consummate blessing of Christ. (c) 30—33. Meantime he almost passionately begs for their prayers that he himself may be rescued from the attacks of the unbelievers in Jerusalem, and that the service he is engaged upon may be thoroughly acceptable to the Church there, that he may come to them in the joy of accomplished purpose and be refreshed with them for further effort. He concludes with the prayer that the GOD of that peace, which he is hazarding all to promote, may be with all at Rome, overcoming their differences too.

The object of this section is clearly to forestall misconceptions and to establish a thorough understanding and mutual sympathy between writer and readers. The dominant interest of S. Paul at the time is shown to be the cementing of the union of Jew and Gentile within the Church, the crucial example and the earnest of the establishment of the full peace of God between man and man in all their differences. This brings in the note of deep and almost passionate feeling: and corresponds with the tone and interest of the whole Epistle. The object of the proposed journey to Rome, for which this letter is a preparation, is shown to be twofold: (*a*) to make personal acquaintance with the Roman Church and to advance the Gospel among them, (*b*) to secure a base of operations for renewed missionary activity, in Spain.

14. πέπεισμαι δὲ κ.τ.λ. He deprecates the interpretation of the letter as involving any distrust or depreciation of them.

ἀδελφοί μου. A specially intimate and affectionate appeal.

καὶ αὐτὸς ἐγώ. I, without waiting for others to tell me, of my own knowledge and confidence. Is there an underlying reference here to a letter from Aquila and Priscilla which has given him full information about the Christians in Rome? See on xvi. 3.

ὅτι καὶ αὐτοί. You, of your own initiative, without requiring help from me.

ἀγαθωσύνης. In LXX. the meaning of kindliness, benevolence, occurs in Neh. ix. 25, 35, xiii. 31 (of God) and perhaps Judges viii. 35, ix. 16. The same meaning suits best in Gal. v. 22; Eph. v. 9 (see Robinson); 2 Thes. i. 11 ("denotes a human quality always in S. Paul =moral excellence, but implies specifically an active beneficence" Findlay). Only in S. Paul, *ll. cc.* in N.T., not found in cl. Greek. Ep. Barn. ii. 9 of God. So here 'goodness towards others' picks up the thought of c. xiv.

π. τ. γνώσεως. This again is suggested by the subject of xiv; cf. 1 Cor. viii. 1 ff.; but of course has a wider reference.

νουθετεῖν. Acts xx. 31 and Epp. P. only; 1 Cor. iv. 14 ὡς τέκνα)(ἐντρέπων; Col. i. 28 ‖ διδάσκοντες, so iii. 16; 1 Thes. v. 12, 14 a work of οἱ προϊστάμενοι; 2 Thes. iii. 15 ν. ὡς ἀδελφόν; 'admonish,' 'warn'; 'rebuke' is too strong. c. xii. is a good instance of νουθεσία; cf. νουθεσία 1 Cor. x. 11; Eph. vi. 4; Ti. iii. 10.

15. τολμηροτέρως=in somewhat bold terms: the comparative gives an apologetic note, which is observable throughout the passage: he will not seem, in any way, to be forcing himself upon them either in teaching or in person.

ἔγραψα. The epistolary aorist; cf. Eph. vi. 22 (ἔπεμψα); 1 Cor. v. 11, ix. 15; Gal. vi. 11; Phm. 19, 21.

ἀπὸ μέρους can hardly mean 'in parts of the Epistle': rather with ὡς 'partly by way of reminding you.' He could not honestly feel that the Epistle did nothing but remind them of what they knew. ἀπὸ μέρους qualifies an overstrong statement xi. 25, xv. 24; 2 Cor. i. 14, ii. 5 (only).

ἐπαναμ., here only. Herm. *Vis.* 4. 1. 7 (only, in Pat. Ap.), Plat. Dem. (L. & S.). ἐπ. over again, with the hint that it may be superfluous.

διὰ κ.τ.λ. The impulse was due to the grace—constituting an obligation.

τὴν χάριν τὴν δοθ. μοι. Cf. xii. 3; cf. 1 Cor. iii. 10, xv. 10; Gal. ii. 9; Eph. iii. 2, 7, 8; Phil. i. 7; Col. i. 6. In all these passages χάρις has direct reference to S. Paul's commission as an apostle to the Gentiles; and here and elsewhere to the definite act by which he was commissioned, in his call. 'Grace was given to him for his ministry to the Gentiles—to the Gentiles through his ministry.' See Robinson, *Eph.* pp. 225 f.

16. λειτουργὸν Χρ. Ἰησ. Cf. xiii. 6 n.; cf. Phil. ii. 25 (ὑμῶν—λειτουργὸν τῆς χρείας μου=εἰς ἐμέ); Christ Himself is a λειτουργός, Heb. viii. 2; cf. S. Paul 2 Cor. ix. 12; the Philippians Phil. ii. 17, 30; cf. here xv. 27; 2 Cor. ix. 12; angels Heb. i. 7: in a more special sense Lk. i. 23; Acts xiii. 2; Heb. ix. 21, x. 11. The classical meaning of a public service performed to the community still colours the word. S. Paul adds here the name of the authority, who orders the performance, and the persons to whose benefit it is directed. As compared with διάκονος the public and representative character is emphasised. The Ecclesiastical usage for services of public worship is to be interpreted by rather than to interpret the wider use. Here the context gives it the specially religious sense.

εἰς τὰ ἔθνη with λ.; cf. πρός με Phil. ii. 30.

ἱερουργοῦντα. Only here in N.T. 4 Macc. **vii.** 8 (Sixtine edtn; Sw. δημιουργοῦντες) with τὸν νόμον, but the doubt as to text makes this passage useless. Subst. 4 Macc. iii. 20=sacrifice. The verb is rare and late. It is used (1) abs.=to act as priest in sacrifice: (2) with accus. when the object is the victim sacrificed; and in the pass. of victims. It is very difficult to apply this sense here; τὸ εὐ. τ. θ. can hardly be the matter offered as a victim; the next clause shows that the matter of the offering is the Gentiles or the consecrated lives which they bring: and this agrees with the other uses of sacrificial terms by S. Paul (θυσία xii. 1 n.; cf. Hort, 1 Pet. ii. 5, λειτουργία Phil. ii. 17). As however ἱερουργεῖν prop.=to be a ἱερουργός, the transitive use must be secondary: and we may perhaps take it here as abs. and τὸ εὐαγ. as an accus. of reference=exercising a priesthood in reference to the Gospel of GoD. So Lid., S. H. *al.* i. then specialises the meaning of λειτουργόν, and τὸ εὐαγ. describes the rule or standard of this priesthood, in contrast with the priesthood of the law; cf. Heb. vii. 28. So Rutherford tr. "discharging priestly duties of the Gospel of God." The accus. with the verb would then correspond to the gen. with the subst. μυστηρίων ἱερουργός qu. from Galen. See Field, *ad loc.*

ἵνα depends ὑα the whole preceding clause λ. Χρ. ʼΙ. ἰ....

ἡ προσφορά τῶν ἐθνῶν, for the gen. cf. Heb. x. 10 only. In προσφορὰ and προσφέρειν the dominant notion is of 'approach to God,' the offering symbolising the approach of the offerer to God's presence; cf. Westcott, Heb. x. 10; Hort, 1 Pet. ii. 5, p. 111 a. The gen. is probably therefore objective. The Gentiles are the offering which S. Paul as Gospel-priest brings to God; this is the matter of the ministry which he exercises under Christ Jesus.

εὐπρόσδεκτος; cf. 1 Pet. ii. 5 = δεκτός, Phil. iv. 18; εἰς ὀσμὴν εὐωδίας, Eph. v. 2 (cf. 2 Cor. ii. 14 f.); τῷ θεῷ εὐάρεστον, xii. 1.

ἡγιασμένη ἐν πν. ἁγ. gives the ground of acceptability; cf. πνευματικός, 1 Pet. ii. 5.

17. ἔχω οὖν. οὖν refers to the preceding statement of his mission—being in this relation to Christ Jesus and engaged on this work for Him, I am bold beyond what I should be if I were acting on my own account; shows how this statement justifies τολμ. ἔγραψα.

ἔχω καύχησιν = καυχῶμαι, emphasising the durative action.

ἐν Χρ. ʼΙ. In my union with and service of Christ Jesus.

τὰ πρὸς τὸν θεόν. As regards my relation to God: accus. of ref. Blass, p. 94; cf. Heb. ii. 17.

18. οὐ γὰρ κ.τ.λ. The comparison with 2 Cor. x. 8 f. seems to show that a double qualification of καύχησις is compressed into this rather clumsy declaration (1) I will only boast of my own works (not ἐν ἀλλοτρίοις κόποις), (2) I will not dare to boast of these works as my own, but only as Christ's achievements through me: the thought of (1) crops up again in *v.* 20, of (2) in 19.

εἰς ὑπακοὴν ἐθνῶν. Cf. xvi. 19; to effect obedience (to Christ, of faith) on the part of Gentiles.

λόγῳ καὶ ἔργῳ. In speech and action: i.e. both in the preaching of the Gospel and in exemplifying it in life: more specific than 2 Cor. x. 11; cf. Lk. xxiv. 9; Ac. vii. 22; Col. iii. 17; 2 Thes. ii. 17; 1 Joh. iii. 18.

19. ἐν δ. σημείων καὶ τεράτων. Cf. 2 Cor. xii. 12. There is no doubt that S. Paul himself claimed to work miracles; cf. Heb. ii. 4; Acts pass.

ἐν δυνάμει πν. ἁγ. Cf. 13, the climax of the manifestation of the power of the Gospel.

ὥστε after κατειργάσατο.

ἀπὸ Ἱερ.—Ἰλλυρικοῦ. This geographical measure of his work in the Gospel is in conception exactly ‖ 2 Cor. x. 14—16 (there too, as he is addressing the Corinthians, Corinth itself is the limit): n. that in S. Paul's view Jerusalem is the beginning for himself as for the other Apostles (cf. Hort, *R. E.* pp. 39 ff.).

κύκλῳ. With μέχρι τ. Ἰ., marking the course of his missionary journey : as S. H. with the Greek commentators whose verdict on such a question of language is weighty. *Al.* take it with Ἱερ. but (1) S. Paul did not preach as a missionary in Judea, (2) κύκλῳ could hardly include Syria, (3) it would need the article.

Ἰλλυρικοῦ clearly marks the furthest point as towards Rome which his preaching had reached at the time he was writing this letter (in Corinth). The name was given to the western districts of the province of Macedonia (Mommsen, *Provv.* I., p. 299 f.). It would mark his nearest approach to Rome: as at Thessalonica he had been on the direct road to Dyrrhachium, the most direct route from the East to Rome. It is most probable that μέχρι is exclusive; (1) it is not easy to find a place in the Acts for any preaching in the interior of the province of Macedonia, scarcely in Acts xx. 2 ; (2) there were then no important towns till the sea coast was reached, the inhabitants being " a confused mass of non-Greek peoples." It was not S. Paul's practice to preach in such country districts : (3) in marking limits μέχρι would be more naturally exclusive ; cf. Mommsen, *ib.*, 256 n. ; but see Ramsay, *Gal.* p. 276.

πεπληρ. τὸ εὐ. τ. χρ. 'The Gospel of the Christ' has special reference to the call of the Gentiles and missionary work among them; cf. 1 Cor. ix. 12; 2 Cor. ii. 12, ix. 13, x. 14; Gal. i. 7; Phil. i. 27. πεπληρ. he has completed the preaching throughout all this area—by establishing the Gospel in all the principal centres. The statement must be taken in connexion with S. Paul's own conception of his mission and of the methods by which it could be carried out: cf. again 2 Cor. x. 13 f.; cf. Ramsay, *Pauline Studies*, p. 77 f. For constr. cf. Col. i. 25 ; Acts xiv. 26.

20. οὕτως δὲ κ.τ.λ. qualifying πεπληρωκέναι :=but always with the eager desire.

φιλοτιμούμενον. This word is a good illustration of meaning determined by use, rather than by derivation. The primary (derivative) sense is 'to be ambitious': in the 'general usage of the best Greek writers'='to make one's best efforts.' So 2 Cor. v. 9 a heightening of θαρροῦμεν καὶ εὐδοκοῦμεν ; 1 Thes. iv. 11 (only, in N.T.); cf. Polyb. I. 83 (qu. Field) ἐφιλοτιμεῖτο ‖ μεγάλην ἐποιεῖτο σπουδήν.

οὐχ ὅπου ὠνομάσθη Χρ. Cf. Eph. i. 21; cf. Jerem. xxxii. 15 (xxv. 29) = was named as an object of allegiance and worship; cf. 1 Cor. i. 2; Isa. lxvi. 19.

ἵνα μὴ ἐπ᾽ ἀλλ. θ. οἰκ. Cf. 2 Cor. x. 15 and for θεμ. 1 Cor. iii. 10; ἀλλ. = laid by another.

21. καθὼς γέγρ. Isa. lii. 15.

22—29. διὸ καὶ κ.τ.λ. This work has detained him; but its completion leaves him free to fulfil his long cherished purpose, as soon as a special mission, in the interests of his work, has been fulfilled at Jerusalem. His visit to Rome has for its object a journey to Spain, for which he wishes to enlist their sympathy and support. The complication of motives and purposes here as so often leads to incomplete and involved sentences. The hesitancy of expression is partly due to his delicacy; he will not seem either to have neglected the Church in Rome, or to force himself upon them. So he explains his delay and in the same breath his reason for coming, as an appeal for their help in his work.

διὸ καὶ = this was just the reason why I was so constantly being hindered from etc.

ἐνεκοπτόμην. Cf. 1 Thes. ii. 18; 1 Cor. ix. 12 (subst.); (Polyb. 24. 1. 12 lect. dub.); cf. Witkowski, *Ep. Priv.* 24 ἡμῖν ἐνκόπτεις καλά 'you are hindering us finely.' No class. instance is quoted for this meaning. N. imperfect, 'I was constantly being hindered.'

τὰ πολλά. Adverb. accus. (= πολλάκις) akin to the accus. of the inner object; cf. Blass, p. 94.

τοῦ ἐλθεῖν. Cf. Blass, p. 235: more commonly the pleonastic negative is inserted after verbs of hindering.

23. τόπον ἔχων = having opportunity or opening; cf. xii. 19; Eph. iv. 27; Heb. viii. 7, xii. 17; Acts xxv. 16.

κλίμασι. 2 Cor. xi. 10; Gal. i. 21, 'districts'; cf. Ramsay, *Gal.*, p. 278 ff. = 'a comparatively small geographical district'; cf. Polyb. x. 1. 3.

ἐπιπόθειαν. Here only; cf. 2 Cor. vii. 7, 11; vb i. 11, *al.*; adj. Phil. iv. 1; 'eager longing.'

ἐπ. ἔχων—ἀπὸ ἱ. ἐ. Cf. Moulton, p. 119; 2 Cor. xii. 19; Joh. xv. 27. The linear present in this combination is best expressed by our perfect, 'having had for several years past'; Burton § 17 cft Acts xv. 21 *al.*; but cf. Blass, p. 189.

24. ὡς ἂν πορεύωμαι. In 1 Cor. xi. 34; Phil. ii. 23 ὡς ἂν w. aor. subj. = 'as soon as I shall have': here = 'when I am on my way to,' 'on my journey to Spain' Rutherford. In LXX. ὡς ἂν w. aor. subj., = when, is frequent: only once in this sense with pres. subj. (Prov. vi. 22); cf.

Moulton, p. 167 (where he notes the use of the futuristic present in the subj. mood) and Blass, p. 272. This use appears to be Hellenistic. In cl. Gr. ὡς ἄν is final ; and this use would make good sense here : but it seems to have died out ; cf. however Witkowski, *Ep. Priv. Gr.* 1. 3.

ἐλπίζω γὰρ. A parenthesis occasioned by the mention of Spain— the ultimate object of his journey west.

θεάσασθαι. To visit, only here in N.T.; cf. 2 Chr. xxii. 6 LXX. only. My visit to you is to be 'in passing.'

ὑφ' ὑ. προπεμφθῆναι. Cf. 1 Cor. xvi. 6 ; 2 Cor. i. 16 ; Tit. iii. 13 ; 3 Joh. 6 ; Acts (3) it implies assistance and speeding for the journey, and so here enlists the interests of the Romans for his work in Spain, and claims their support.

ὑμῶν—ἐμπλησθῶ. Cf. *Od.* xi. 452 υἷος ἐμπλησθῆναι...ὀφθαλμοῖς.

ἀπὸ μέρους. 'In some degree.' R.

25. νυνὶ δὲ. The sentence is broken off, to allow of explanation of still further delay ; this journey was much in his mind, both for the interest of it, and the danger ; cf. Hort *R. and E.*, p. 43.

διακονῶν τοῖς ἁγίοις. Cf. 2 Cor. viii. 4, 9, 20, ix. 1 f. This service for the saints occupied a great part in S. Paul's mind at this time : it symbolised in a most expressive form the union of Jew and Gentile in the one Church : we may indeed say that the same thought so eagerly cherished and indefatigably pursued appears in the mission to Jerusalem and in the Epistle to the Romans. The synchronism cannot have been accidental. Introd. p. xiv.; Hort, *R. and E.*, p. 40 ff.; Rendall, *Expositor*, Series IV., vol. 8, p. 321 f.

26. ηὐδόκησαν of men ; cf. 2 Cor. v. 8, xii. 10 ; 1 Thes. ii. 8, iii. 1; 2 Thes. ii. 12 ; subst. Lk. ii. 14 (v.l.) ; Rom. x. 1 ; Phil. i. 15 only.

Μακ. καὶ 'Αχ. The provinces are named to include all the Churches in them ; cf. 2 Cor. ix. 2 f. The Churches of Galatia are also named in this connexion 1 Cor. xvi. 1 ; cf. the list of companions Acts xx. 4.

κοινωνίαν τινὰ ποιήσ. 'To make a contribution' Rutherford. Contribution is rather too cold a word. κοιν.=act of partnership or fellowship ; cf. 2 Cor. ix. 13 where εἰς πάντας brings out the fuller meaning : so here τινα=a kind of partnership to help the poor etc. The act united the Gentile Churches in fellowship with each other and with the Church in Jerusalem whose poor they were helping ; cf. also 2 Cor. viii. 4.

27. γὰρ corroborates—yes indeed ; Blass, p. 274 f.

τοῖς πν.—τοῖς σαρκ. Cf. 1 Cor. ix. 11.

λειτουργῆσαι. Cf. Phl. ii. 30 (-ία) 25 (-ος) of service from man to man.

28.　τοῦτο=this business—of his mission in this cause.

ἐπιτελέσας.　'When I have put a finish to'; cf. Phil. i. 6 : the word is used in the same connexion in 2 Cor. viii. 6, 11.

σφραγισάμενος αὐ. τὸν καρπὸν τούτον.　Deissmann, *B. S.* II. 65, 66, quotes from Papyri instances of sealing bags of corn etc. to prevent their being tampered with and so to secure them for the assignee : and following Theod. Mops. and Lipsius tr. 'bring it safely into their possession.'　This will be an instance, then, of the commercial metaphors not infrequent in S. Paul (cf. βεβαιοῦν, χειρόγραφον, ἀρραβών).　The present of money, symbolising brotherly fellowship, is the fruit received by the Jerusalem Church as the result of the spiritual labours of S. Paul, working on their behalf among the Gentiles.　The seal was primarily a mark of ownership and authenticity and then secondarily of security and correctness (cf. Mt. xxvii. 66) as here.　So Rutherford "when I have securely conveyed to them this return."　So Chrys., Theodt (Cramer's *Catena* iv. p. 512).

αὐτοῖς=οἱ ἅγιοι (*v.* 25) in Jerusalem.

ἀπελεύσομαι for Attic ἄπειμι; εἶμι had fallen out of use in popular language, Blass, p. 52 ; cf. Thackeray, p. 257, 267.

εἰς Σπανίαν.　Cf. S. H.　Whether S. Paul visited Spain or not is doubtful.　That he should have intended to is completely in accordance with his general plan of mission work ; cf. Introd. p. xii ; cf. Ramsay, *Paul the Tr.*, p. 255.

29.　ἐν πληρώματι εὐλογίας Χριστοῦ = bringing with me Christ's blessing in its full completeness.　He feels no doubt (οἶδα) that, if he succeeds in reaching Rome, that is, in getting safe through his mission to Jerusalem, he will have been successful too in the great aim of that mission, that is, in producing a signal manifestation of the union of Jew and Gentile and securing a full acknowledgement of it.　This he regards as a complete execution of Christ's blessing—i.e. GOD's blessing offered in Christ to all mankind (cf. Gal. iii. 9, 14 ; Eph. i. 3) and, if he comes to them at all, it will be with this supreme achievement.　See also Acts xx. 24 ; *infra v.* 31 and Hort *R. and E.*, p. 42.

ἐν πλ.　This use of ἐν is to be compared with ἐν ῥάβδῳ ἢ ἐν ἀγάπῃ (1 Cor. iv. 21), ἐν μαχαίρᾳ Papp.=using or wearing, or furnished with ; "haec exempla ad vestitum pertinent, significantia qua veste quis indutus, deinde quibus rebus ornatus et instructus sit," Kuhring *Prepos. Graec.* ; cf. Deissmann, *B. S.*, p. 115.

30.　παρακαλῶ δὲ κ.τ.λ.　This urgent appeal reveals, as by a lightning flash, the tension of mind in which S. Paul was living at the time : the supreme importance of this mission was only rivalled by its extreme dangers. The hostility of the Judaizers and still more of the unbelieving Jews naturally culminated at the moment when the success of his work was on the point of being secured; cf. Acts xx. 3. It is no wonder that to himself at one time success at another the dangers were more obvious (cf. Acts xx. 22—25, xxi. 4, 13). Here, as he above appealed to their support for his projected work in Spain, he appeals for their prayers in this great crisis.

διὰ τοῦ—διὰ τῆς κ.τ.λ. See xii. 3 n. 'on the authority of.'

τῆς ἀγάπης τοῦ πνεύματος. A unique phrase: not ‖ Gal. v. 22; Col. i. 8. The idea = viii. 26 f. The parallelism of the clauses points to the meaning—the love which the Holy Spirit has for us and works in us—not the latter only.

συναγωνίσασθαι. Only here; cf. for the simple verb Col. i. 29, iv. 12, of strenuous effort. N. aor., the case brooks no delay.

ἐν ταῖς προσευχαῖς marks the way in which they can help in this supreme struggle.

31. ἵνα κ.τ.λ. The two elements in the situation are already marked: (1) rescue of S. Paul from the enemy who thought by one blow to shatter the work, (2) acceptance of the offering and its meaning by the Church in Jerusalem.

τῶν ἀπειθούντων. Cf. Acts xiv. 2 *supra*, x. 21, xi. 30; 1 Pet. ii. 8.

32. συναναπαύσωμαι. Only here in N.T., sc. after the ἀγών. As they shared the struggle, so they should share the relief and rest.

33. ὁ θεὸς τῆς εἰρήνης. The God who has given and will secure the peace, which Christ has won, and which is now at stake; cf. *v.* 5 n. The prayer naturally concludes the impassioned appeal of the last few verses; cf. Hort, *R. and E.,* p. 52.

CHAPTER XVI.

1. συνίστημι δὲ κ.τ.λ. This verse is in close connexion with the preceding section : he has explained his desire to visit them, the reasons for delay ; instead of coming, he is writing and commends to them the bearer of the letter.

συνίστημι. Cf. 2 Cor. iii. 1 ; cf. Milligan, *Greek Papyri*, 14. 5, and for instances of letters of introduction *ib.* 8, and for the word *ib.* 3. 2, 5 = 'I introduce, commend' hereby. The common formula makes it clear that Phoebe was the bearer of this letter.

Φοίβην. Mentioned only here. Wetstein qu. Suet. *Aug.* for the name.

τὴν ἀδελφὴν ἡμῶν. Cf. Phm. 2. S. Paul seems to give this title (with ἡμῶν and μου) to fellow workers to whom he was under obligation for personal service; of Titus 2 Cor. ii. 13 ; anon. viii. 22 ; Epaphroditus, Phil. ii. 25 ; Timothy, 1 Thes. iii. 2 ; and the phrase may here anticipate the πρ. καὶ ἐμοῦ αὐτοῦ of *v.* 2.

οὖσαν [καὶ] διάκονον τῆς ἐκκλ. As ἡ ἀδ. ἡ. marks a relation to S. Paul, this phrase marks her relation to the Church : and the form of the phrase suggests that διάκονον implies an official position. If so, it is the only mention of this office in N.T. (unless we take 1 Thes. iii. 11 in this sense). The next mention is Plin. *Ep.* x. 96. 8 duabis ancillis quae ministrae dicebantur : then later still in the Apostol. Constitutions. The existence of such an office cannot be thought improbable even at this early stage, in view of the social condition of women ; cf. S. H. Against this is the very general use of διάκονος

N 2

and διακονία (cf. 1 Cor. xvi. 15) in this group of Epistles, and the unlikelihood that the word would be used in the official sense in this
passage alone; n. also the similar combination in 1 Thes. iii. 2; cf.
Ency. Bibl. 'Deacon' and Hort *Eccles.* p. 207 f. On the whole there
seems to be insufficient reason for taking it officially. So in the
ordinary sense 'being also one that ministers to...,' an additional
ground of commendation.

τῆς ἐκκλ. τῆς ἐν Κ. The address of 2 Cor. i. 1 and xv. 26 above
suggest that there were other Churches in Achaia besides Corinth.
This was one of them.

Κενχρεαῖς. The seaport of Corinth on its eastern shore; cf. Acts
xviii. 18, xx. 3. See Introd. p. xi.

2. προσδέξησθε. Lk. xv. 2; Phil. ii. 29.

ἀξίως τῶν ἁγίων. In a manner worthy of the saints—as saints
should.

παραστῆτε, help; cf. 2 Tim. iv. 17.

ἐν ᾧ ἂν κ.τ.λ. This suggests that Phoebe was going to Rome on
her own business, and that S. Paul used the opportunity of sending
his letter.

προστάτις. Only here in N.T.; cf. προῖστασθαι, xii. 8; 1 Thes. v.
12; 1 Tim. v. 17; cf. Witkowski, *Ep. Priv.* 48. 9, *ib.* 9. 4, 'protectress.'
A word used technically to mean the representative or patron; but
here to describe the way in which Phoebe 'looked after' any who
wanted her help.

3—16. Greetings; see Lightfoot, *Phil.* pp. 171 ff. S. H. *ad loc.*

3. Πρίσκαν καὶ Ἀκύλαν; cf. Acts xviii. 2, 18, 26; 1 Cor. xvi. 19;
2 Tim. iv. 19. We first hear of this pair at Corinth, where they were
found by S. Paul on his first visit and that connexion was formed
which lasted for the rest of his life. They had then lately come from
Rome, and presently went with S. Paul to Ephesus, where they
remained while he went on his way to Jerusalem. At Ephesus they
were when Apollos arrived, and probably were influential in the small
Church there, as they put Apollos in the way of full Christian
teaching. They were there still, or again, when S. Paul wrote 1 Cor.,
certainly nine months, perhaps more than a year, before this Epistle.
Now they are at Rome, and again some years later (2 Tim.) in the province of Asia. A difficulty has been raised about this frequent change
of home: and it has been directed against the originality of this passage
in this place. But, apart from the migratory habits of Jews engaged in
business, it is clear from Acts, 1 Cor. xvi. 19 and this passage that A.
and P. had given themselves to the work of propagating the Gospel:
and it is not unreasonable to conjecture that just as they were left

behind at Ephesus (Acts xviii. 18) to begin the work there and to prepare for S. Paul's return, so they may now have been sent by him to Rome to prepare the way for his intended visit; and returned to Asia at a later date, perhaps when he himself was released from Rome. This conjecture is supported by the fact that S. Paul's intention to go to Rome was already formed at least before he left Ephesus (Acts xix. 21). It would explain his knowledge of the Christians who were at Rome at this time, both of those who seem to have centred round these two and of the other groups mentioned. For if they went to Rome to prepare for S. Paul's visit, they would naturally communicate with him as soon as they had got into full touch with the Church there. The list of salutations gains much in naturalness and point, if we can suppose it to have been based on information sent by A. and P. And we may see in such a letter from Rome the direct occasion of S. Paul's letter and even in some degree the influence which determined its character. (Zahn, *Einl.* p. 275, also makes this suggestion.) See Introd. p. xii f.

τοὺς συνεργούς μου. Cf. 2 Cor. viii. 23; Phil. ii. 25, iv. 3; Col. iv. 11; Phm. 24; 1 Thes. iii. 2 (v. l.): in all cases of sharing in the apostolic labours. Jews as they were, they were devoted workers in the Gospel with S. Paul, and shared his mission to the Gentiles: see below on π. αἱ ἐκκ. τ. ἐ.

4. οἵτινες. 'For they,' 'seeing that they,' a ground for this prominent greeting.

ὑπὲρ τῆς ψ. κ.τ.λ. We have no further information about this. It may have been either at Corinth or at Ephesus.

ὑπέθηκαν. In this sense only here in N.T. = 'they pledged' risked, cf. Plat. *Protag.* 313 A (L. and S.); for the form cf. Thackeray, 23 § 10.

εὐχαριστῶ. The only place in the N.T. where the verb or subst. is used with a human object (cf. and ct Acts xxiv. 3).

π. αἱ ἐκκλ. τῶν ἐθνῶν. A unique combination and very significant. It emphasises their share in carrying the Gospel to the Gentiles, and shows the purpose of this elaborate reference to them. πᾶσαι. We know of P. and A. at Rome, Corinth and Ephesus only. But Corinth and Ephesus mean Achaia and Asia: and their influence, direct and indirect, may well have gone further. The occasion for gratitude should not be limited to this special service rendered to S. Paul.

5. καὶ τὴν κατ' οἶκον κ.τ.λ. Cf. 1 Cor. xvi. 19. It is natural to suppose that as P. and A. had formed a centre at Ephesus they would also form one at Rome. This phrase suggests that S. Paul had heard from them since their arrival at Rome: and this to some extent supports the suggestion that they had gone there to prepare the way

for him. Some communication from them may have been the direct
occasion for this letter. Zahn suggests that all the names that follow
to *v*. 13 are to be included in this group of Christians, *vv*. 14, 15
naming two other groups. This seems probable.

For the 'Church in the house' cf. Col. iv. 15; Phm. 2; Acts xii.
12; cf. S. H., Lft ad Col. *l.c.* "no clear example of a separate building
set apart for Christian worship before the third century, though
apartments in private houses might be specially devoted to this
purpose"; cf. Hort, *Eccles.* 117.

Ἐπαίνετον. "Not an uncommon name in inscriptions from Asia
Minor" S. H. Zahn suggests that he was an early convert of P. and
A. at Ephesus and possibly worked under them in their trade, and
so accompanied them to Rome.

τὸν ἀγ. μου. This phrase (and below 8, 9) marks of course personal
intimacy (contrast *v*. 12).

ἀπαρχὴ τῆς 'Α. εἰς Χρ. means that he was the first or at least
among the first converts at Ephesus, therefore of P. and A.; cf.
1 Cor. xvi. 15.

6. Μαρίαν. As this name may be either Roman or Jewish, it
tells us nothing. The *v.l.* Μαριάμ would be decisive.

ἥτις...εἰς ὑμᾶς. It may be questioned whether the reading ὑμᾶς is
not too difficult to come under the *praestat ardua* rule. The names
before and after at least to *v*. 9 inclusive are all of personal friends
and some of fellow-labourers of S. Paul. It is unlikely that one who
was known to him only by report would be included at this point.
Moreover the selection of one person at Rome as having laboured
much for them is remarkable. If ἡμᾶς be read, the ἥτις clause here
is exactly ‖ οἵτινες κ.τ.λ. in 7 and brings the name into line with the
others. But see Introd. p. xxv.

7. Ἀνδρόνικον. A Greek name, used, as so often, by a Jew.
Zahn, p. 607 n. 56, remarks that Jewish names are rare in the Jewish
inscriptions of Italy. This name occurs among members of the
imperial household, S. H.

Ἰουνίαν. Probably for Junias = Junianus a man's name, though not
a common one.

τοὺς συγγενεῖς μου, i.e. Jews. So 11, 21; cf. ix. 3.

συναιχμαλώτους. Cf. Col. iv. 10; Phm. 23. We have no ground
for identifying the occasion.

οἵτινές εἰσιν κ.τ.λ. (1) ἐπίσημοι = marked men, notable : here of
course in a good sense; ct Mt. xxvii. 16. Class. both in good and bad
sense; cf. 3 Macc. vi. 1 (not elsewhere in LXX. of persons). (2) ἐν
τοῖς ἀποστόλοις (*a*) among the apostles sc. of Christ, themselves being

reckoned as apostles: so Ltt *Gal.* p. 96 n. 1, S. H. *ad loc.* This is
the obvious meaning. In that case, according to S. Paul's use, they
must belong to the class which he describes in Gal. i. 17 as τοὺς πρὸ
ἐμοῦ ἀποστόλους. He uses the term to include members of the
primitive community who had received their commission from the
Lord Himself, a class not limited to the Twelve (e.g. Barnabas,
perhaps Silas), S. Paul himself being its latest member (1 Cor.
xv. 8). (*b*) Others take it=men of note in the judgment of the
Apostles (Gif., Zahn). There is no advantage in this rendering,
unless it is assumed, wrongly, that A. and J. cannot have been
apostles. We may conclude then that A. and J. were among
the earliest preachers of the Gospel, and that they had shared
S. Paul's labours, as well as his imprisonment. They are now at
Rome, and may have been among those who first brought the Gospel
to Rome. See Introd. p. xxv, Add. Note, p. 225.

οἵ—γέγοναν ἐν Χρ. We should probably supply ἀπόστολοι; = 'Who
were made and have been apostles in Christ.' The form ἐν Χρ. is
occasioned by the turn of phrase: if he had repeated ἀποστ. he would
have written ἀποστ. Χριστοῦ. This is quoted as a clear use of γέγονα
as aoristic; cf. Joseph. *c. Apion.* 4. 21 ὀλίγῳ πρότερον τῆς Πεισιστράτου
τυρραννίδος ἀνθρώπου γεγονότος qu. Moulton, *Prol.* p. 146, who quotes
two instances from papyri, though he doubts the use in N.T.; cf. Dr
Weymouth *ap.* S. H. But we have to note that πρὸ ἐμοῦ gives a
mark of time='even longer than I': and the use is ‖ to the case of
perf. with πάλαι (see Moulton, p. 141). Cf. Joh. vi. 25; Mt. xix. 8,
xxiv. 21; 1 Cor. xiii. 11; Gal. iii. 17; 1 Tim. v. 9. There is no clear
case of the strictly aoristic meaning of this form in N.T. For the
form -αν cf. Thackeray, pp. 209, 212; Mayser, p. 323; Moulton, p. 52:
cf. Col. ii. 1; Acts xvi. 36, and γέγοναν, Rev. xxi. 6 only: it is a case
of the gradual intrusion of the weak aorist form into the perfect and
strong aorist.

8. Ἀμπλιᾶτον. S. H. refer to inscriptions showing that this
common slave name occurs among the imperial household: but in
particular, to a chamber in the cemetery of Domitilla, one of the
earliest of Christian catacombs, containing the name AMPLIATI, in bold
letters of the end of the first or beginning of the second century. The
single personal name suggests a slave: the honour of an elaborately
painted tomb suggests that he was very prominent in the earliest
Roman Church: the connexion with Domitilla seems to show that it
is the name of a slave or freedman through whom Christianity had
penetrated into a second great Roman household. See the whole
note.

9. Οὐρβανόν· " A common slave name, found among the members of the (imperial) household," S. H.   The name of course tells us nothing as to nationality. He may have been a Jew or a Greek.

τὸν συνεργὸν ἡμῶν· Prob., as S. H., a general description of working in the same cause as S. Paul and his companions, not necessarily of personal fellowship; cf. Phm. 1 only: elsewhere always μου (v. 3, 21; Phil. ii. 25, iv. 3; 2 Cor. viii. 23 (ἐμὸς); Phm. 24).

Στάχυν· " Rare but found in the imperial household," S. H.; cf. Witkowski, Ep. Priv., p. 73.

10. Ἀπελλῆν. A name borne by Jews; cf. Hor. Sat. I. v. 100, see Lft.

τὸν δόκιμον ἐν Χρ. marks some special difficulty faithfully overcome; cf. 1 Cor. xi. 19 ; 2 Cor. x. 18 ; 2 Tim. ii. 15 ; Ja. i. 12.

τοὺς ἐκ τῶν Ἀριστοβούλου prob. = Aristobulus, brother of Herod Agrippa I., who lived a long time in Rome and was a friend of the Emperor Claudius. οἱ ἐκ τ. = some of his slaves, probably now connected with the imperial household, though treated as a separate group; A. being either dead or resident in Palestine. Zahn, ad loc. Lft, S. H.

11. Ἡρῳδίωνα. Coming between the two groups of slaves, prob. belonged to the former : the name suggests a connexion with the Herod family.

τοὺς ἐκ τῶν Ναρκίσσου. N. is reasonably identified with the freedman of that name, powerful under Claudius and put to death by Agrippina shortly after Nero's accession. S. H., Lft.

12. Τρύφαιναν καὶ Τρυφῶσαν, perh. sisters, and belonging to the last-named group. The names are found in household inscriptions : Tryphaena in one case with Tryphonilla, in another with Τρυφω[ν or σα]. Zahn, Einl. pp. 297—8.

Περσίδα κ.τ.λ. A slave name (not in the household inscriptions) : the special emphasis (τὴν ἀγ....πολλά) indicates some special knowledge on S. Paul's part, possibly personal, though μου is omitted.

13. Ῥοῦφον κ.τ.λ. The unique epithet (unless cf. 2 Joh. 1, 13) suggests that there was some marked peculiarity attending his conversion, and the reference to his mother points to personal connection with S. Paul; perh. = Rufus of Mk xv. 21 (Swete's note).

14. Ἀσύνκριτον. The two groups of five persons now following make it probable that we have here two more centres of Christian life in Rome, known to S. Paul by report, but not otherwise ; there are no distinguishing epithets. The names are all slave names, many of them found among the imperial household.

Πατρόβαν, abbrev. for Patrobius.

ʽΕρμᾶν, abbrev. for Hermagoras or other variations on Hermes.

15. Φιλόλογον. The name may suggest the occupation, in the secretariat or the record department; cf. Lft, *op. cit.* p. 177 n. 1.

Ἰουλίαν. Very common, and esp. in the imperial household.

Νηρέα. Cf. S. H. on the association of this name with the early history of the Roman Church.

Ὀλυμπᾶν = Olympiodorus.

16. ἐν φιλ. ἁγίῳ. Cf. 1 Cor. xvi. 20; 2 Cor. xiii. 12; 1 Thes. v. 26; 1 Pet. v. 14 (ἀγάπης): earliest reference to the 'kiss of peace' in the Christian service is in Just. Mart. *Apol.* i. 65. S. H.

αἱ ἐκκλησίαι πᾶσαι τοῦ χριστοῦ. The phrase is unique in N.T.: S. Paul speaks of αἱ ἐκκ. τῶν ἁγίων (1 Cor. xiv. 33), τῆς Γαλατίας *al.* (Gal. i. 2 *al.*), τῶν ἐθνῶν (v. 4), τοῦ θεοῦ (1 Cor. xi. 16; 2 Thes. i. 4): for the inclusion of Χριστός in the phrase we have only Gal. i. 22; 1 Thes. ii. 14 : for the relation of Χριστός to (αἱ ἐκκ.) ἡ ἐκκλ. cf. Eph. v. 23 f.

(1) ὁ χριστός in this Ep. emphasises the relation of Christ as Messiah to Gentiles as well as Jews (Hort, *Eccles.* p. 111, cft vii. 4, ix. 3, 5, xv. 3 and 7). Hort, *l.c.*, concludes that the phrase refers to the Churches of Judea: but the limitation to a single group seems quite inconsistent with the emphatic πᾶσαι; and he himself gave up this view, *R. and E.* p. 53. *v.* 4 shows such a limitation; so Gal. i. 22; 1 Thes. ii. 14. The force of the phrase seems rather to lie in its formal assertion of the equality and unity of all the Churches, as equally and together belonging to the Christ, in whom, as truly conceived, the ancient barriers are thrown down and mankind is one in GOD's mercy; cf. xi. 25 ff. It is a definite step to the ἡ ἐκκλησία of Eph.

(2) In what sense can S. Paul convey this greeting? "Doubtless S. Paul had information which enabled him to convey this greeting," Hort, *R. and E.*, p. 53. We may however go further. There were in his company at Corinth representatives, probably all formally appointed (cf. 2 Cor. viii. 19, 23), of many if not of all (cf. Acts xx. 4) of the Churches of his own foundation. He may have regarded himself or there may have been others in his company who could be regarded, as representing the Church in Jerusalem; cf. Igna. *Trall.* 12 ἀσπάζομαι ὑμᾶς ἀπὸ Σμύρνης, ἅμα ταῖς συμπαρούσαις μοι ἐκκλησίαις τοῦ θεοῦ; cf. id. *Magn.* 15. The inclusion of the Jewish churches is parallel to the emphasis on his Jewish friends in the above greetings.

(3) For πᾶσαι in emphatic position cf. 1 Cor. vii. 17 and ct 1 Cor. xiv. 33; 2 Cor. viii. 18, xi. 28.

17—20. A brief but pointed warning against teachers, who under fair seeming introduce divisions and offences. The fundamental

strain in the Epistle, the assertion that in the Gospel all men are
united to each other and to GOD in Christ, has been enforced by the
long list of greetings, giving detailed and practical point to teaching
and exhortation. It is natural that before ending S. Paul should
give a clear and strong warning against those elements in the Christian
society which tended to establish divisions and to create or continue
practices which were the cause of offence. Phil. iii. 18 f. is a close
parallel, in the general character of the warning following upon the
exposition of the teaching which the persons indicated endanger, and
in the immediately added contrast with the true state of Christians.

17. ἀδελφοί. Cf. xii. 1, xv. 14, 30; Phil. iii. 17. **σκοπεῖν.** 'Keep
an eye upon'; cf. Gal. vi. 1; Phil. ii. 4, iii. 17 (for imitation).

τοὺς τὰς δ. κ.τ.λ. These persons are described in quite general
terms : the warning is based on S. Paul's own experience in Asia
Minor and Greece, rather than on any particular information from
Rome, and may be due to the event described in Acts xx. 3. See
Introd. p. xi.

τὰς διχοστασίας. '*The* divisions' of which he had had such bitter
experience and which no Church could be ignorant of; cf. Phil. i.
15 f.; Gal. v. 20; cf. Phil. iii. 18 f. The great instance was the
attempt to maintain division between Jew and Gentile in the Church:
subsidiary to this but probably at this time more practically operative
was the attempt to set up authorities in rivalry to S. Paul. In both
cases the effect would be to establish two rival Churches in every
locality, and to render nugatory the union in Christ.

τὰ σκάνδαλα. Such teachings and precepts as put difficulties in
the way of the practical exercise of Christian love, reinstating those
barriers of convention and exclusiveness which had been done away
in Christ; cf. xiv. 13.

παρὰ τὴν διδ. with τὰς δ. καὶ τὰ σκ.; for ἐμάθετε cf. Eph. iv. 20;
Phil. iv. 9 (in a similar connexion). The 'teaching' is all the
instruction which led them to become Christians and informed them
in what true Christianity consists (ἐμάθετε).

18. οἱ γὰρ κ.τ.λ. The warning is against men who claimed to be
true servants of Christ and were not; cf. 2 Cor. xi. 13 : therefore
Judaising Christians, not necessarily themselves originally Jews.

τῇ ἑαυτῶν κοιλίᾳ. Cf. Joh. vii. 38; Phil. iii. 19 (metaph. only in
N.T.)=selfish desires and objects in the widest sense. He does not
say ἑαυτοῖς because they are not even serving their own true interests.

διὰ τῆς χρ. The 'fair speech' employed by them or characteristic
of them; cf. Gal. iii. 1, iv. 17. S. H. qu. Jul. Capitol. *Pertinax* 13,
χρ. eum appellantes qui bene loqueretur et male faceret.

εὐλογίας seems to get a bad meaning here by its connexion with χρ. S. H. qu. Aesop *Fab.* 229, p. 150 ed. Av. In N.T. elsewhere always of 'blessing.' Plat. *Rep.* 400 D of fine speech, in a good sense.

τῶν ἀκάκων=simple, guileless, and therefore unsuspicious; combined with εὐήθης Diod. Sic. *ap.* Wetstein;)(πανοῦργος Dio Cass., *ib.*; cf. Prov. i. 4; Heb. vii. 26. S. Paul is careful not to suggest that they have as yet any hold upon the Church.

19. γάρ justifies his appeal to them and what they had learnt.

ἡ—ὑπακοή. Their response to the teaching—obedience; cf. 2 Cor. x. 5 ; above vi. 17; 2 Thes. i. 8.

ἀφίκετο (only here in N.T.); cf. 1 Thes. i. 8, *supra* i. 8. This would not be a natural form of expression, if S. Paul was writing to a Church with which he was personally acquainted.

ἐφ' ὑμῖν. The warning is not due to his distrust of their present state, but to apprehension of what the future may bring.

σοφοὺς—ἀκεραίους. Cf. Mt. x. 16; Phil. ii. 15 only; cf. Lft. In Polyb. the word=uninfluenced from without (cf. Schweighäuser's Index). So here=admitting no influence for evil.

20. ὁ δὲ θεὸς τῆς εἰρήνης. The GOD who gives us our peace which these men are breaking up; cf. xv. 33 and xv. 5 n.

τὸν Σατανᾶν. Cf. 2 Cor. ii. 5—11, xi. 14. One special work of 'the Satan' is to set men at variance; cf. 1 Thes. ii. 18 and cf. Gen. iii. 15?.

ἡ χάρις κ.τ.λ. There is no parallel to the position of these words before more greetings. For the whole question see Add. Note, p. 233.

21—23. Greetings from companions.

21. Τιμ. ὁ συνεργός μου. Cf. on 3. The last we have heard of Timothy is in 2 Cor. i. 1. He probably accompanied S. Paul to Corinth ; unless we detect him in 2 Cor. viii. 18.

Λούκιος. Perh. = Acts xiii. 1, not=Luke (Lucanus, Λουκᾶς).

Ἰάσων. Cf. Acts xvii. 5—7, 9, the host of S. Paul at Thessalonica: he had probably accompanied or preceded S. Paul ; cf. 2 Cor. viii. 23.

Σωσίπατρος. Cf. Σώπατρος, Acts xx. 4, of Beroea. Was he in charge of the contribution from Beroea ?

οἱ συγγενεῖς μου. Cf. *v.* 7 n.

22. Τέρτιος ὁ γράψας κ.τ.λ. On S. Paul's use of an amanuensis cf. 1 Cor. xvi. 21; Gal. vi. 11; Col. iv. 18; 2 Thes. iii. 17. S. H.

23. Γάϊος ὁ ξ. μου. Perh.=1 Cor. i. 14: for ὅ. τ. ἐ. cf. *v.* 4 ; prob. refers to hospitality exercised by Gaius in Corinth to all Christian travellers—not to his house being the place of assembly for Corinthian Christians. It is not probable that they had only one such place.

Ἔραστος. Cf. 2 Tim. iv. 20.

οἰκονόμος. "In civitatibus Graecis saepe commemoratur" Herwerden; cf. Dittenberg for Ephesus, Magnesia, Cos; and for Egypt, Pap. Berl. *al.*; ' the treasurer.'

Κούαρτος ὁ ἀδελφός. S. Paul seems to use this title of men who were closely associated with him in his work. Cf. 1 Cor. i. 1, xvi. 12; 2 Cor. i. 1, viii. 22; Eph. vi. 21; Phil. ii. 25 *al.*

25—27. It appears from *v.* 22 that the whole letter was written by Tertius from dictation up to this point. We may conclude that S. Paul wrote these last verses in his own hand, by way of signature; cf. Gal. vi. 11; 2 Thes. iii. 17.

The doxology forms a conclusion, unique in S. Paul's Epistles, the only parallels in Epp. are 2 Peter iii. 18 *b*; Jude 24, 25. For other doxologies in S. Paul, concluding and summarising a section, cf. Eph. iii. 20, 21; 1 Tim. i. 17; cf. also 2 Tim. iv. 18; Heb. xiii. 21; *supra* xi. 33—36. This doxology sums up, tersely but completely, the main conception of the Epistle, and reproduces its most significant language. In particular, it is so closely related to i. 1—17 that it takes the place of a categorical statement that the description there given of S. Paul's mission has been justified by the detailed arguments of the Epistle. The comparison is drawn out below.

25. τῷ δὲ δυναμένῳ—Χριστοῦ. Cf. i. 16 τὸ εὐαγγέλιον, δύναμις γὰρ θεοῦ ἐστὶν εἰς σωτηρίαν.

στηρίξαι. Cf. i. 11—12, of God; 2 Thes. ii. 17, iii. 3; 1 Pet. v. 10 (a near ‖). ὑμᾶς. The need for strengthening is indicated in i. 11, xvi. 17—20. "The pronouns face each other with an emphasis which in such a context is hard to explain till we remember the presaging instinct with which S. Paul saw in the meeting of himself and the Roman Christians the pledge and turning point of victory"; Hort ap. Lft, *Biblical Essays*, p. 325; cf. i. 10 f., xv. 29—32.

κατὰ τὸ εὐαγγ. Adverbial to δυναμένῳ: κατὰ=as my Gospel declares; cf. ii. 16, xi. 28 in both cases with the same special reference as here to the inclusion of Gentiles, St Paul's distinctive Gospel.

καὶ τὸ κήρυγμα 'Ι. Χρ. explains τὸ εὐαγγέλιον, cf. i. 2, 3 εὐαγγέλιον θεοῦ—περὶ τοῦ υἱοῦ αὐτοῦ followed by the two clauses which severally correspond to the names 'Ιησοῦς and Χριστός, and are re-capitulated in *v.* 4 by the full name and title; for κήρυγμα cf. ii. 16, x. 8—15, xv. 15 f.; 1 Cor. i. 21, ii. 4; 1 Tim. iii. 16; 'Ι. Χρ. objective genitive.

κατὰ ἀποκάλυψιν κ.τ.λ. This should probably be taken as ‖ κατὰ τὸ εὐαγγ., describing in its character what that phrase states specifically. Cf. i. 16 f., xi. 25 f.; 1 Cor. ii. 6, 7, 10.

κατὰ ἀποκάλυψιν verbally = Gal. ii. 2; Eph. iii. 3; but the reference is different; nearer in thought is Gal. iii. 23; closest Eph. iii. 5—9; Col. i. 26; cf. ἀποκαλ. i. 17.

μυστηρίου. 'Of a secret'; cf. xi. 25; 1 Cor. ii. 1, 7—10, iv. 1; then Eph. i. 9, iii. 3—9, vi. 19 (‖ Col.); 1 Tim. iii. 16. The secret is the whole purpose of God for man's redemption, formed in and ultimately revealed in the Christ, as born of David's seed and marked by the resurrection as Son of God. In the argument of this Epistle, the special lesson of that secret, as revealed in Christ, is the union of all mankind in Him with God, as connected with justification by faith. The word has the same bearing in Eph., Col.: but there the special lesson is the development of this conception of union to illustrate the nature and work of the Church as such. In Romans this development is not directly treated but the foundation thought is here fully worked out.

χρόνοις αἰωνίοις. Cf. πρὸ χρόνων αἰωνίων 2 Tim. i. 9; Tit. i. 2, the only occurrences of the combination; cf. ἀπ᾽ αἰῶνος, Lk. i. 70; Acts iii. 21, xv. 18; Joh. ix. 32. It seems to be a vague expression for an indefinitely long time. πρὸ τῶν αἰώνων 1 Cor. ii. 7, Eph. iii. 9, 11 is more definite, but probably not very different in meaning. For the dative of extension of time cf. Lk. viii. 29 and epistolary formulae ἐρ-ρῶσθαί σε εὔχομαι πολλοῖς χρόνοις, Moulton, Prol. 75.

σεσιγημένον = ἀποκεκρυμμένον of 1 Cor. ii. 7, Eph. iii. 9 (= Col. i. 26). The silence of that long time past is contrasted with the utterance of the present; but it was not complete, as the next clause shows; cf. 1 Pet. i. 12, supra i. 2; Tit. i. 2. Tr. by pluperfect—'which had been kept in silence.'

26. φανερωθέντος. Cf. iii. 21 where exactly the same relation between the manifestation and the witness of prophets is expressed. The secret was manifested in the Person and history of Christ; He is the secret of God; cf. 1 Cor. i. 24.

νῦν = 'in our day' as contrasted with the χρ. αἰ.; cf. 1 Pet. i. 12 (Hort, p. 59), supra v. 11, xi. 30, 31.

διά τε κ.τ.λ. The τε connects γνωρ. closely with φαν., both in contrast with σεσιγ. 'But has in our day been manifested (in Christ) and made known.' The aorists should be translated by perfects. Then this clause tersely describes the apostolic preaching (1) in its support in the prophets, (2) in its commission from God, (3) in its direct aim, (4) in its range in the world.

διὰ γραφῶν προφ. For διὰ cf. 2 Tim. ii. 2 = on the authority of; cf. xii. 1, 3 n., an extension of the use of διὰ for the means or instrument: cf. a slight further extension = under the guidance of 1 Thes. iv. 14; Heb. iii. 16.

γρ. προφ. Cf. i. 2, iii. 21. The fact is seen throughout the Epp. and Acts; e.g. cc. ix.—xi., xv. 4, 9 ff.; cf. 1 Pet. i. 12; 2 Cor. i. 20; Lk. i. 70. The particular phrase is unique, and includes all the O.T. as all in its degree prophetic, cf. 2 Pet. i. 20. The absence of the article emphasises the character of all, rather than any specific writing.

κατ᾽ ἐπιταγὴν τ. αἰ. θ. corresponds to κλητὸς ἀποστ. ἀφωρισμένος (i. 1) and δι᾽ οὗ ἐλάβομεν χάριν καὶ ἀποστολήν (i. 5) but describes the authority of all apostolic work=διὰ ἀποστόλων; cf. 1 Tim. i. 1; Tit. i. 3.

τοῦ αἰ. θεοῦ. Only here in N.T. In LXX. Gen. xxi. 33; Isa. xxvi. 4, xl. 28; 2 Macc. i. 25; 3 Macc. vi. 12, viii. 16; for the idea cf. xi. 33—36; 1 Cor. ii. 7, x. 11; and Eph. iii. 9, 11; Col. i. 26; 1 Tim. i. 17; 2 Tim. i. 9; Tit. i. 2.

εἰς ὑπακοὴν πίστεως=i. 5 only; cf. xv. 18, xvi. 19, 1 Pet. i. 2; =to secure an obedience rendered by faith; ὑπ. in this sense only in the earlier epistles vi. 17, x. 16; 2 Thes. i. 8; 2 Cor. vii. 15.

εἰς πάντα τὰ ἔθνη. Cf. i. 5, xv. 11, xvi. 4; Gal. iii. 8; 2 Tim. iv. 17 and Rev. (saepe) for the whole phrase; cf. παντὶ τῷ πιστ. ᾽Ι. καὶ᾽Ε. i. 16.

γνωρισθέντος. Cf. ix. 22, 23; 1 Cor. xv. 1; Eph. vi. 19.

27. μόνῳ. Cf. iii. 30 where the 'singleness' of GOD is the basis of the universality of the Gospel, as here. See note ad loc. For μόνος cf. Joh. v. 44, xvii. 3; 1 Tim. i. 17, vi. 15 (in a similar connexion); Jude 25.

σοφῷ. Cf. xi. 33: specially of the wisdom which orders in detail the age-long and world-wide purpose. Cf. 1 Cor. i. 21—30; ii. 7; Eph. iii. 10; Col. ii. 3.

θεῷ. To GOD as GOD, sole and supreme Creator and Dispenser of all His wondrous dealings with men.

διὰ ᾽Ι. Χρ. As through Him GOD has manifested Himself to men, so through Him returns the due acknowledgment from man to GOD; cf. i. 8, vii. 25.

ἡ δόξα κ.τ.λ. Cf. xi. 36.

NOTE ON TEXT.

1. xvi. 20. *The Benediction.*

The case is stated by S. H. thus :

"אABC Orig.-lat. have a benediction at *v.* 21 only.

DEFG have one at *v.* 24 only.

L Vulg. *clem.* Chrys. and the mass of later authorities have it in both places.

P has it at *v.* 21 and after *v.* 27.

The correct text therefore has it at *v.* 21, and there only; it was afterwards moved to a place after 24 [presumably as in any case the more natural place] which was in some MSS very probably the end of the Epistle [e.g. FG], and in later MSS, by a natural conflation, appears in both."

Zahn holds that both benedictions are original, the slightly different form of the second (+ Χριστοῦ and πάντων) justifying the repetition.

2. xvi. 27. ᾧ om. B. 33. 72, Pesh., Orig.-lat., ins. rel. exc. αὐτῷ P. 31, 54.

The strongest argument for retaining ᾧ is the difficulty of the reading, and the consequent unlikelihood of its invention. But this principle must not be pressed to the adoption of an all but impossible reading. With ᾧ we can only explain on the assumption of a very awkward anacoluthon. Zahn and Weiss defend this by referring to the strong emotion, with which this passage is written. But even so this is not a natural anacoluthon; there is no parenthesis or interruption of thought; the sentence is regularly and strongly constructed up to Χριστοῦ, and throughout it is obvious that it is to end with ἡ δόξα; after the participial clauses, the dative has come, picking up τῷ δυναμένῳ and resuming the whole thought (μόνῳ σοφῷ); then διὰ Ἰησ. Χρ. again makes us expect ἡ δόξα, and cannot be connected with anything that has gone before: no amount of emotion could justify the insertion of ᾧ here, between the words that are crying for ἡ δόξα, and ἡ δόξα itself. It is a sheer though early blunder due to the frequent occurrence of the combination ᾧ ἡ δόξα. There is a closely similar case in *Mart. Polycarp.* xx. 2 (qu. by Weiss but with the wrong reading), τῷ δὲ δυναμένῳ πάντας ὑμᾶς εἰσαγαγεῖν ἐν τῇ αὐτοῦ χάριτι καὶ δωρεᾷ εἰς τὴν αἰώνιον αὐτοῦ βασιλείαν διὰ τοῦ παιδὸς αὐτοῦ τοῦ μονογενοῦς Ἰησοῦ Χριστοῦ δόξα, τιμή, κράτος, μεγαλοσύνη εἰς τοὺς αἰῶνας. Here ᾧ ἡ are inserted by two MSS before δόξα (Lightfoot, *Ap. Fathers* II. § ii. p. 983). Further, Jude 24, 25, clearly modelled on this passage, supports the omission of ᾧ; and even in Jude ℵ* am. and apparently aeth. insert ᾧ before δόξα.

ADDITIONAL NOTES.

A. συνείδησις, c. ii. 15.

The word is found only in the Pauline writings (Rom., 1 and 2 Cor., 1 and 2 Tim., Tit., 1 Pet., Heb.) except [Joh. viii. 9], and Acts xxiii. 1, xxiv. 16 (speeches of S. Paul). The verb (σύνοιδα) only in 1 Cor. iv. 4. In the LXX. it occurs only in Wisdom xvii. 11 (R.V. conscience), Eccles. x. 20 (R.V. heart), and perhaps Sir. xlii. 18 (R.V. knowledge). The verb, Job xxvii. 6; Lev. v. 1; 1 Macc. iv. 21; 2 Macc. iv. 41. The two passages which make clear the use of the word are Job *l.c.*, οὐ σύνοιδα ἐμαυτῷ ἄτοπα πράξας, and Wisdom *l.c.*, πονηρία...ἀεὶ προσείληφεν τὰ χαλεπὰ συνεχομένη τῇ συνειδήσει. In both these passages it is the state of mind which is conscious of certain actions in their moral aspects.

The customary meaning of the substantive follows the use of the verb. σύνοιδά τινί τι = to be privy to the action of another; σύνοιδα ἐμαυτῷ τι or τι πράξας = to be privy to an action or thought of my own; but, as a man in general cannot help being privy to his own thoughts and actions, the phrase is used with the special meaning of the recognition or feeling of the character, and especially the moral character, of one's own thoughts or actions. So we get first the simple meaning, the feeling or knowledge that we have done or thought certain things imputed to us, and, secondly, the more definite meaning, the feeling or knowledge that such thoughts or actions are right or wrong. This feeling can be appealed to as a witness to character, either by the man himself appealing to his self-consciousness in support of a statement, or by others appealing to the man's own consciousness of himself. So Wisdom xvii. 11, R. V. "Wickedness, condemned by a witness within, is a coward thing, and being pressed hard by conscience (τῇ συνειδήσει) always forecasts the worst lot," the consciousness of being wrong makes a coward of the man. Here the conscience or consciousness is an incorruptible witness before whose evidence the man trembles. Cf. Polyb. xviii. 26. 13, οὐδεὶς οὕτως μάρτυς ἐστὶ φοβερὸς οὔτε κατήγορος δεινὸς ὡς ἡ σύνεσις ἡ ἐγκατοικοῦσα ταῖς ἑκάστων ψυχαῖς, where the last phrase = ἡ συνείδησις. It is rather as a witness than as a judge that ἡ συνείδησις is regarded in ordinary Greek use : and it is only as a witness that it is appealed to in N. T.

In Romans the word occurs three times, ii. 15, ix. 1, xiii. 5. In ii. 15 and ix. 1 it is used of a man's knowledge of himself, his motives and thoughts, called as a witness to his true character. In ii. 15 the Gentiles' self-consciousness, knowledge of their own minds, witnesses to their possession, in a sense, of law, and so confirms the evidence of their acts. In ix. 1 S. Paul's knowledge of himself, as controlled by the Holy Spirit, witnesses to the pain and distress he feels for Israel, and confirms the witness of the assertion which he makes as in Christ. In xiii. 5 there is no idea of witness, but the consciousness of their own motives and feelings as shown in the fact that they willingly pay tribute, is appealed to as an argument for obedience.

Closely parallel to Rom. ix. 1 is 2 Cor. i. 12, where the consciousness of motive is alleged as a witness to the truth of his confident assertion.

With xiii. 5 may be grouped the passages in which an epithet is attached (Acts xxiii. 1, ἀγαθή, xxiv. 16, ἀπρόσκοπος; 1 Tim. i. 5, 19, 1 Pet. iii. 16, 21, ἀγαθή; 1 Tim. iii. 9, 2 Tim. i. 3, καθαρά. Cf. Heb. ix. 14, καθαριεῖ τὴν συνείδησιν; Heb. xiii. 18, καλή; Heb. x. 22, πονηρά). In all these passages it is clear that the word indicates the self-consciousness which includes good or bad contents, as matter of feeling and experience, as simply a matter of self-knowledge, without any direct thought of judgment. So 1 Pet. ii. 19, διὰ συνείδησιν θεοῦ, a remarkable phrase, seems to mean, owing to a feeling of or about GOD, bringing Him as it were into the field of conscious motive. This feeling or consciousness can be dulled by evil courses (1 Tim. iv. 2; Tit. i. 15). External ordinances leave it untouched (Heb. ix. 9), but it can be cleansed (Heb. ix. 14, x. 21, 22).

In 2 Cor. iv. 2, v. 11 the Apostle appeals, for the recognition of his claim, to the conscious experience (συνείδησις) which others have acquired of his character and life, their inner knowledge of him; in this use we have the substantival form of the verbal phrase σύνοιδά τινί τι. And it is possible that we have the same use in 1 Cor. x. 28, 29, where the συνείδησις may = the weak brother's knowledge of and feeling about the acts of the strong.

In 1 Cor. viii. 7—12 we have the remarkable epithet ἀσθενής, where if we translate συνείδησις as 'conscience,' we have the paradox of calling a sensitive conscience weak. We can hardly get a nearer translation here than 'feelings.' The man 'feels' that to eat εἰδωλό-θυτα is wrong. This 'feeling' cannot be justified by reason; it is due to association (τῇ συνηθείᾳ ἕως ἄρτι τοῦ εἰδώλου), and he cannot shake it off : it is called 'weak,' because in it the man is not really master of himself. The argument of the passage is directed to gaining from the strong a tender consideration for those who are in this weak state of feeling. It is a pity that the true character of many 'conscientious objections' of the present day is obscured by their association with our modern term 'conscience,' when they should be really described as συνείδησις ἀσθενής.

On the whole, then, we may say that in the N. T., as in common Greek use, συνείδησις describes rather a state of consciousness, than a faculty or act of judgment : some uses of the word 'conscience' correspond to this meaning of συνείδησις ; but in more cases than not the meaning will be adequately given by such renderings as 'consciousness,' 'self-knowledge,' or even simply 'heart.'

B. ON v. 13.

The usual interpretation takes ἄχρι νόμου = till the Mosaic law was given, and understands S. Paul to deny that sin could be imputed in the full sense to those who were ignorant of that law : consequently πάντες ἥμαρτον is regarded as = all men sinned in Adam. It cannot be denied that this interpretation is highly strained ; but the extreme complexity of the passage might be taken to excuse that, if two further objections did not arise : (1) By supplying ἐν τῷ ᾿Αδὰμ with π. ἥ. we assume the omission by the writer of words essential to the understanding of the passage ; (2) by taking ἄχρι νόμου = until the Mosaic law was given, and making the consequent assumption that sin was not imputed to Gentiles till they were aware of the Mosaic law (for the interpretation must extend so far), we make S. Paul say here that sin could not be imputed to the Gentiles, including Adam and the Patriarchs up to Abraham, because they had no law. But this is in direct contradiction with one main argument of the preceding chapters, and of course with the whole teaching as to the sinful state of Gentiles. I should further urge that for this meaning here the article would be indispensable before νόμου, as there is a specific reference to the Mosaic law as and when given. The interpretation given in the notes involves the difficulty (which I do not minimise) of translating ἄχρι νόμου = so far as there was law. ἄχρι is used frequently of time and place (Acts xx. 4, *al.*) : the gen. expresses generally the point of time or space reached ; but sometimes expresses also the interval before that point is reached; cf. ἄχρι καιροῦ, for a season (Lk. iv. 13; Acts xiii. 11); ἄχρι ταύτης τῆς ἡμέρας w. perfect (Acts xxiii. 1), ἄχρι τούτου τοῦ λόγου w. imperfect (Acts xxii. 22). The extension of meaning to=just in the degree that law, so far as there was law and no further, seems justifiable. If this meaning can be taken, then ἀλλὰ ἐβασίλευσεν κ.τ.λ. goes closely with ἁμ. οὐκ ἐλλογᾶται, as an indication that the punishment of sin being in evidence sin itself must have been there. καὶ ἐπὶ κ.τ.λ. brings out the fact that the sin was not on all fours with that of Adam, so making explicit the restriction hinted in ἄχρι νόμου, the unlikeness consisting in the fact that Adam sinned against a positive revealed command, men in general sinned against the internal law of a conscience, enlightened, if only partially. This interpretation is in strict agreement with the view put forward in the early chapters, and does not make S. Paul say anything but what he says explicitly.

C. νόμος.

νόμος and ὁ νόμος.

Gifford, Introd. pp. 41—48; S. H. p. 58; Lft, *Gal.* ii. 19, iv. 5; Hort, *R. and E.* pp. 24, 25.

Two questions have to be answered: (1) what was St Paul's conception of law? (2) what distinction is made by the presence or absence of the article?

(1) It is obvious that S. Paul's conception of law was derived primarily from his experience of the law of Moses, with the accretions of Pharisaic tradition (cf. iii. 17—20). Law was for him the expression of the Will of God in application to the conduct of man, as revealed to Moses and embodied in the written law and its authorised interpretations. The experience of his own religious growth, probably even before he became a Christian, threw into strong emphasis two characteristics of this revelation. First, that it put before man an exalted ideal of duty; the law was holy, righteous and good. Secondly, that neither in the law itself, nor in his own nature, could he discover any power which enabled him to fulfil the law. The law, in fact, was essentially an external standard, embodying declarations, apprehensible by man, of what was right; but not an internal power providing or imparting the ability to do what was right. To a nature which was capable of appreciating this standard, but did not find in itself the power nor even an unmixed desire to attain it, the result was that law produced a sense of sin, and a despair of righteousness,

an almost hopeless lack of correspondence between the conduct of man and the Will of God. To this experience the revelation of Christ came as a moral and spiritual revolution. The fundamental meaning, from the point of view of conduct or ethics, of that revelation was, that in Christ is offered to man not merely a new standard of knowledge or conduct, but a new power of action. The spiritual life, seen in Jesus, as man, crucified and ascended, is offered directly to man as a reinforcement of his own higher intelligence and will through the living union of man with the ascended Christ. It is a revelation of spirit, communicated to spirit, enabling man to live as a spiritual being. Its primary condition, on the part of man, is trust, the realisation, in act as well as in consciousness, of personal and vital dependence upon God through Christ. It is therefore, in the fullest sense, a complete deliverance from the sense of sin and despair of righteousness, which the bare knowledge of the law had produced : it supplies the power of which the law terribly emphasised the want.

Such were the conclusions of personal experience. But, further, from his Jewish training (cf. Giff. p. 436), S. Paul had already conceived of the Gentile state as also under law. They too had received an expression of the divine will, in manifold application to the conduct of life; a universality of law to which the universality of the new revelation corresponded. And this wide conception of the range of law led to the emphasising of the general aspect of law, in distinction from its special embodiment for Jews in the Mosaic code. And, in both cases, the same essential characteristic comes out. Law is for the Gentile too an external standard, not carrying with it the inner spiritual power of framing conduct according to its demands. The description then of the natural state of man under law is common to Jew and Gentile. The penetrating analysis of the experience of the Jew is typical of all men, as possessed of moral consciousness.

Two further points require to be stated. First this revelation in law was not properly twofold. In both cases law is the expression of God's will : the Mosaic law is only a more complete, clear and lofty expression : the law given, in conscience, to the Gentiles is on the same lines, but less complete. Consequently, in a certain sense, the Mosaic law was regarded as binding upon all men. This explains some of S. Paul's language, and also the insistence of the Judaisers on enforcing the law.

In the second place, it is not to be supposed that S. Paul denies to the pre-Christian world all power of doing God's will. It is clear (from ii. 14 *al.*) that he recognised a righteousness among Gentiles, and of course among Jews. The point of his argument is, that this righteousness was due, not to law, but to faith, in real though elementary activity. This is elaborately argued in the case of Abraham and his case is shown to be typical both for Jews and Gentiles (iv. 12, 16 f.; cf. Mt. viii. 11; Jo. viii. 39). The argumentation of c. vii. is, in a certain degree, abstract (cf. Introd. p. xli); it isolates, for the moment, the one influence upon man provided by law, in order to bring out the exact measure and character of that influence; it does not deny the other influences by which GOD has, in all ages and places, kept not only the knowledge of His will alive but also the actual fulfilment of it.

(2) Bearing these considerations in mind, we can answer the second question briefly. The distinction between νόμος and ὁ νόμος depends on the ordinary rules of the article. Generally νόμος, without the article, means law as such, without consideration of any particular form in which it may be known or embodied. It refers to the character of law, not to its particular mode or occasion. On the other hand ὁ νόμος means the particular law, which either ordinary experience, or the context in which it occurs, would bring to the mind of the hearer or reader. It follows, that νόμος without the article may refer to the Mosaic law, but, when it does, will refer to it in its character of law, rather than in its derivation from Moses (e.g. iv. 13). On the other hand, ὁ νόμος, while naturally and generally in S. Paul's use referring to the Mosaic law, may refer to some other law which is for the moment under consideration (e.g. vii. 3). Within these general rules, the interpretation in any particular passage must be determined by the context.

On the very peculiar uses in iii. 27, vii. 21, viii. 2, see notes.

D. ἁμαρτία.

Cf. Davidson, *O. T. Theology*, pp. 203 f. ; Westcott, *Epp. Joh.* pp. 37 ff. Kennett, *Interpreter*, July, 1910.

This word is used as the most general name for sin in itself and in all its forms. The original suggestion of 'missing' an aim or a way, contained both in the Hebrew (Davidson *l.c.*) and the Greek may be detected in such a phrase as iii. 23. But the word has got its full meaning from use. It includes ἀσέβεια, ἀδικία, ἀνομία, παράπτωμα, κακὸν ποιεῖν, πράσσειν, ἐργάζεσθαι. It is antithetic in its full range to δικαιοσύνη, as applied to men.

Two uses of the word must be distinguished. (1) It describes a state or condition in which men are, although it does not properly

belong to human nature as meant by GOD. (2) It describes particular acts and habits in which men choose what is wrong rather than
what is right.

(1) This use is found only in S. John (Ev., 1 Ep.) and S. Paul (Rom.,
1 and 2 Cor., Gal., 2 Thes. (v.l.) only). In S. Paul the use occurs twice
in Gal. (ii. 17, iii. 21), twice in 1 Cor. (xv. 56), once in 2 Cor. (v. 21),
and 2 Thes. (ii. 3 v.l.). On the other hand it occurs more than forty
times in Rom. (in cc. iii., v., vi., vii., viii.), in S. John Ev. six times,
in 1 Joh. five times (i. 8, iii. 4, 5, 8, 9).

(2) This use is found in Evv. Syn., Joh. (4), Acts, S. Paul (in
above Epp. (7), in Eph., Col., 1 Thes., Past. (6)), Heb., James, 1 and
2 Pet., Rev.

This second use is reinforced by the occurrences of ἁμαρτάνω, as well
as by ἁμάρτημα and other substantives which are more or less synonymous. The verb naturally is used of sinful acts and habits only ; and
always of the direct action of the man himself. In v. 12 indeed it
has been thought by some that a qualification such as ἐν ᾿Αδάμ must
be introduced, but this is quite unwarrantable. See note.

The explanation of this distribution is that S. Paul in this section
of the Romans and S. John (both Ev. and 1 Ep.) treat of sin in itself,
as in some sense distinguished from particular sinful acts and habits:
and they alone do so.

We will consider (1) in a little more detail, in relation to these
chapters of Rom. According to it, sin is regarded as a principle or
power, in itself external to and alien from man, but intruded into the
world by an act of man (v. 12) and gaining authority and establishing
a hold over man's nature (v. 21, vi. 12, 14, 17), owing to the character
of that nature, as composed of σάρξ and νοῦς or πνεῦμα (vii. 15 f.).

It is important to distinguish between the two stages of treatment.
First, the fact of the presence and power of sin, its true relation to
human nature, and the means of escape, are treated as matters of
general experience, historically whether (cc. i.—iii. summed up in
v. 12—21) of mankind in general or of the personal experience of
Christians (vi.). Secondly, in c. vii. 7—viii. 11 the examination of the
case is pursued by way of analysis of a single experience, in order
to bring out, psychologically, the real nature of this experience of
sin.

In the former passages the universality, power and effect of sin are
elaborated. In the latter what we may call the rationale of sin is
explained, as it occurs in man. In neither case is there any treatment of the existence or meaning of evil in itself. We are dealing at
no point with the metaphysical problem, but throughout with the

moral problem. This is made clear in a very remarkable manner, when we observe that S. Paul seems constantly to be on the verge of personifying sin, but never does so (cf. S. H. p. 145 f.). Considering that he undoubtedly believed in a power and powers of evil, this is most noteworthy. He would seem to abstain from any such reference because he wishes to concentrate the whole attention on man's responsibility and to exclude all secondary considerations whether of a metaphysical or other character. (Contrast 1 Joh. iii. 8—11; Ev. Joh. viii. 41, 44 f.) This is in accordance with the main object of these chapters, to bring out the universality and urgency of man's need which GOD meets by the power and the universality of the Gospel. Cf. Hort on James i. 14 (p. 24).

This emphasis on the responsibility of man for sin is most remarkable in v. 12, the beginning of the most obscure passage in the whole treatment. There we are told, one man was the cause of sin coming into the world, and death through sin; but the spread of death to all is made to depend on the fact that each and all at one time or another sinned (πάντες ἥμαρτον). It is not the sharing in but the repetition of the original act which brings all under the same doom of death. The statement is all the more significant, because it would be fully in accordance with the most prominent strain of O. T. thought to represent men as being under doom of death owing to the one sin, not because they were themselves guilty but because in them their first forefather was still being punished (Davidson, *op. cit.* p. 220). This idea is repudiated in the text almost in set terms; and the individualistic morality of the later prophets is explicitly adopted. The universality of sin, an assumption made in full accordance with O.T., is not regarded as being merely an universal liability to sin, but as an universal commission of sins. (So i. 18, iii. 23.) So in v. 14 actual sin is not denied in regard to any men, but only exact correspondence in character of the actual sins of some with the transgression of Adam. And so too in c. vii. the psychological analysis of man's nature, which is undertaken to show how he sins, shows sin to be in each the neglect to do what he knows to be right (cf. i. 18 *b*).

What then is the connexion between Adam and other men which is indicated in v. 12—21? And what is the line of analogy between that relation and the relation of men to Christ? Probably the true answer to these questions is that S. Paul does not give an answer in the sense in which we ask the questions. He is not in fact presenting a theory but appealing to acknowledged facts. Adam's act was the beginning of sin: owing to that act Adam died; and all died, because all sinned (12—15). The only hint of the nexus here is in the phrase

(v. 19) τοῦ ἑνὸς ἀνθρώπου. This suggests that there is a connexion with Adam in natural humanity, as there is a connexion with Christ in regenerate humanity. But the latter connexion does not attain a moral value without an act of each man, and we must conclude that neither does the former connexion assume a moral value without an act of each man. In accordance with this conclusion, v. 20 reminds us (cf. 14, vii. 9) that the single act of Adam's fall would not have been repeated, had not law, in whatever form, come within men's experience. All we can conclude is that there is a connexion of nature: and that in each man this nature, when in face of the knowledge of good and evil, fails as Adam failed. This failure is a matter of fact and observation, not explained by any theory. If we ask, what would have happened, in S. Paul's view, if Adam had not sinned, we can only answer that S. Paul does not ask or answer the speculative question. He gives no theory: he merely elicits the facts as they appeared to him.

When we pass to the psychological treatment of c. vii. 7—viii. 11 (cf. vii. 5), we find ourselves in presence of a distinction which has not been made explicitly in the preceding chapters, the distinction between σάρξ and πνεῦμα. And it is important to observe that σάρξ is used throughout the passage, not in its simple sense of human nature, as through its physical element transitory and perishable, but in the sense in which it admits of moral predications. S. Paul describes himself as σάρκινος, of a fleshly nature; and this is immediately supplemented by πεπραμένος ὑπὸ τὴν ἁμαρτίαν. Flesh is a source in him of action, and, being under the dominion of sin, prompts to wrong action. It does not cover his whole being, though it dominates it. There is behind all an ego (17) which resists its promptings, in sympathy with the good which the νοῦς apprehends, though it is not strong enough to carry it out. It is this ego which, in spite of the domination of the σάρξ, still preserves the knowledge of and the will to good. It is in fact the πνεῦμα which, when reinforced by the power of the life which is of and in Christ, asserts its supremacy, defeats sin in its stronghold, and makes the man free from the policy and power of the 'fleshly' element (viii. 1—11).

On this we observe in the first place that this analysis is undertaken in order to bring out the real function and character of law. Man's constitution properly understood shows how law, being itself spiritual, holy, righteous and good, may yet be an occasion of sin. And the reason is shown to lie in the actual behaviour of man in the face of the knowledge of law, not in the nature of law itself. But the transference of the sinful character from law to man necessitates further consideration of the nature of man. It might be supposed that man was essentially sinful. This is shown not to be the case. Sin is due not to man's nature in itself and therefore necessary, but to the play of the elements of that nature among themselves, to the domination of the transitory and perishable nature (σάρξ) over that element by which man is essentially man and inwardly related to GOD (πνεῦμα), or, to put it the other way, to the failure of that in man, which should rule, to establish its rule. The analysis represents that domination as complete, as far as action goes; but not complete so far as to extinguish the higher element. And this state is unnatural, in the truest sense: for it is the result of a passing under the power of sin (14). Why and how this comes about, S. Paul does not indicate; he describes it wholly by metaphors (ἀπέκτεινεν, πεπραμένος, ἐνοικοῦσι, ἀντιστρατευόμενον); he again gives no theory; he describes the fact, which he experiences, of the double forces at work in a man's consciousness. There is the knowledge of good, there is the wrong act, there is the sense of sin and helplessness: there is again the reinforcement of the spirit by the Christ and the change of balance. Sin is man's own act and yet not his true act: yet as his act it becomes a power dominating him by the use of what is truly part of himself. The whole process is within his own experience (vii. 5, 9, 14 f.). The sin which dwells in him is his own sin. In regard to 'flesh,' the flesh is not in itself sinful (*v.* 9) but neither is it in itself good; it is neutral till the man begins to use it, with the knowledge given by law: but just because it is neutral, it is not easily malleable to the uses of the spirit; the man lets it engross his activity, in contradiction to such uses, and becomes not only 'flesh' but 'fleshly'; the uses of the flesh supplant the uses of the spirit; and this disproportion or false relation, false to man's true nature, is the state of sin. Consequently, sin is still originally and essentially due to man's own act; it does not characterise flesh till an act of the kind has been committed: and when man's spirit is so far renewed and reinforced that its habitual actions are changed and reversed, the flesh itself becomes, even with its present limitations, no longer the field of sin but an instrument of the spirit; cf. vi. 12, viii. 11.

In regard to this passage as a whole, the question is asked whether S. Paul is here giving his own experience or dramatising in his own person what he conceives to be the general experience of men. There can be but one answer. The personal element is too definite, too sustained, and even too passionate, to allow the hypothesis of mere imagination. But even so there are two observations to be made. First the analysis of a personal experience is so far akin to the poetic dramatisation of common human experience, that both, if they are true and deep enough, carry us down to the fundamental facts and elements of human nature, which are common. The experience here analysed is typical just because it is so intensely and veraciously personal. Secondly, we are not to assume that in this analysis S. Paul is giving us the whole even of his pre-Christian experience. It is not his object to exhaust the account of himself, but to show his particular experience of the relation of law and sin. It is wrong to conclude that he could recognise in his pre-conversion life nothing but sin. As in Gentiles (ii. 15) and in Abraham and his true descendants (iv. 16 f.), so in himself he would recognise the presence, in its degree, both of the working of God's Spirit and of the response of faith, the *testimonium animae naturaliter Christianae*. What he gives us here is not an exhaustive account, but a description of the dominant character of his religious life before his conversion, and, undoubtedly, a very real and awful experience.

What conception, then, does S. Paul mean to convey by 'sin' as a power or influence? It seems to follow, from the above examination, that it is the conception of sin as a habit, formed by a succession of acts and seeming to acquire, and indeed acquiring for our experience, a control and mastery over a man, such as might be exercised by an external power. It comes to be felt as a power which holds man under bondage. And it is this feeling which S. Paul expresses by the metaphors, βασιλεύειν, δουλεία etc. But he does not go on to account for it, beyond the testimony of experience. He assumes its universality, as a matter of common acknowledgment. He describes its character in such a way as to connect it with the action of the human will. He shows its operation, in the springing up of a wrong relation between the two main elements in human nature. And the deductions he draws are the necessity for man in the first place of forgiveness and justification and in the second place of the re-creation of, or communication of a new life to, his spirit, and through his spirit to his whole nature. Beyond these limits he does not go.

E.   θάνατος IN CC. V., VI., VII.

The use of this word and its cognates, in these chapters, is a striking instance of S. Paul's method. He passes without hesitation from one meaning to another. In c. v. 12—21 the sense seems always to be that of natural death. In c. vi. it is used of the death of Christ upon the cross, of the death to sin in baptism, of

natural death or perhaps spiritual (16, 23); in c. vii. 1—3 of natural
death; 4, 6 of death to the former state of sin under law; 9 ff. of
spiritual death in sin. There is no attempt to harmonise these
various meanings; the context alone decides between them in each
case. And in some cases, as the notes have shown, it is by no means
easy to decide. The natural and the spiritual are too closely inter-
woven, not only in S. Paul's thought but in common religious
experience. It is interesting to notice that the metaphorical or
spiritual use of the term is rare in S. Paul's other epistles (2 Cor. ii.
16, iii. 7 (?), 2 Cor. v. 15; Gal. ii. 19; Col. ii. 20, iii. 3; 1 Tim. v. 6;
cf. νεκρός, Eph. ii. 5; Col. ii. 13; Col. iii. 5 only), and paralleled only in
S. John (1 Jo. iii. 14, v. 16, 17; Ev. v. 24, viii. 51 only) and perhaps
James i. 15.

F. ix. 5.

ὁ ὢν ἐπὶ πάντων θεὸς εὐλογητὸς εἰς τοὺς αἰῶνας ἀμήν.

The insertion of the participle throws emphasis on ὁ...ἐπὶ πάντων and
shows that it must be taken as subject and θεὸς as in apposition. Otherwise we should expect ὁ ἐπὶ πάντων θεός. ἐπὶ πάντων implies not mere
superiority (which seems never to be indicated by ἐπὶ with gen.) but
authority and government, = He who is supreme governor of all things,
a periphrasis for κύριος. πάντων is probably neuter and refers to the
whole process, in sum and in detail, of the ordered government and dispensations of the ages. The only other occurrence of ἐπὶ πάντων in
N.T. is in Eph. iv. 6. The question, therefore, whether the phrase can
be applied to ὁ χριστός depends not on any strict parallel, but on the
analogy of the use of κύριος: for this cf. x. 9 with 12; 1 Cor. xii. 3;
Phil. ii. 10, 11; and esp. 1 Cor. viii. 6; Eph. iv. 5; and generally the
application of κύριος, with its O.T. associations, to Christ; see Hort,
1 *Pet.* p. 30 f. It still remains open to question whether S. Paul
would name, as an attribute of the Christ, the management of the
dispensations; Heb. i. 3 (φέρων κ.τ.λ.) is only partly paralleled
by Col. i. 17; and S. Paul himself seems to reserve this function of
providential government to GOD as creator. The term κύριος seems
to be applied to Christ rather as sovereign over the present dispensation, than as the director of all the dispensations, the Son being
the agent of the operations of the Father: cf. xvi. 25, 26. It was probably some such consideration as this that led Hort to say (Appendix,
ad loc.) that the separation of this clause from ὁ χρ. τ. κ. σ. "alone
seems adequate to account for the whole of the language employed."
Neither S. H. nor Giff. elucidate this point. The question is not

whether the term θεὸς as predicate or the verbal εὐλογητὸς would be used of Christ by S. Paul (there is strong evidence for an affirmative answer); but whether he would assign to Him this function of deity. It is to be observed that it is generally agreed that the form of the phrase ὁ ὢν ἐπὶ πάντων throws the stress exactly on this function. These considerations point to a separation of this clause from the preceding; cf. 1 Clem. xxxii. 2.

Two questions remain: (1) is the insertion of the clause, if separated from the preceding, natural in the context? (2) does the run of the whole sentence allow of such separation?

As regards (1) the immediate context deals with GOD'S dispensation to and through Israel suggested by the strange paradox that the dispensation of the Gospel, expounded in the preceding chapters and in full climax in ch. viii., finds Israel alien. That the Gospel should have been prepared for in Israel, and that in spite of Israel's opposition the Gospel should now be in full course in its comprehensive universality, are both the results of GOD'S government or management of the dispensations: it is not unnatural that when the climax of the description of Israel's past has been reached, while the climax of ch. viii. is still in mind, S. Paul should turn to bless Him who directs and orders all, GOD worthy to be blessed for ever. The emphatic position and phrasing of ὁ ὢν ἐπὶ πάντων suits the turn of thought exactly. Nor is this assumption out of place here, in view of the great sorrow spoken of in v. 2 (as Giff.): that sorrow does not even for a moment suspend S. Paul's trust in the just and merciful government of GOD.

(2) It is no doubt true that the change of subject is abrupt: but it is of the very nature of an interjectional ascription to be abrupt: and the formal abruptness is compensated by the naturalness of the interjection.

Two further points require to be noticed. (1) It is argued that in ascriptions of blessing εὐλογητὸς always comes first in the sentence. But no order of words is so fixed that it cannot be changed for emphasis' sake: and the emphasis on ὁ ὢν ἐπὶ πάντων is amply sufficient to account for the order here; cf. Ps. lxvii. (lxviii.) 2 LXX. (2) It is argued that τὸ κατὰ σάρκα requires the statement of the other side of the nature of the Christ. But this argument ignores the reason for the mention of the Christ here at all, namely, to complete the enumeration of the privileges of Israel.

On the whole I conclude that the most natural interpretation is to place the stronger stop after σάρκα and to translate 'He that governs all, even GOD, be blessed for ever. Amen.'

It is perhaps necessary to observe that this comment is not in-fluenced by the consideration that S. Paul was not likely to apply the term θεὸς predicatively to Christ. The possibility of his doing so ought not to be denied in view of 2 Thes. i. 12, Phil. ii. 6, 2 Cor. xiii. 13, and other passages in which the Father and the Son are co-ordinated.

Prof. Burkitt (*J. T. S.* v. p. 451 ff.) argues that the ἀμὴν marks the clause as an ascription of blessing to GOD, not a description of nature. The ascription is here made, as an appeal for GOD's witness to the truth and sincerity of his statement in 1—4; cf. Rom. i. 25; 2 Cor. xi. 31. He takes ὁ ὤν (cf. Exod. iii. 14, 15; Rev. i. 4) as representing the 'Name of the Holy One,' the mere utterance of which with the necessarily accompanying benediction is an appeal to the final court of truth. So he connects "Rom. ix. 1, 5*b*, οὐ ψεύδομαι...ὁ ὤν, ἐπὶ πάντων θεός, εὐλογητὸς εἰς τοὺς αἰῶνας, ἀμήν: I lie not. The Eternal (Blessed is His Name!) I call Him to witness." While this argument seems to me conclusive as to the main con-nexion and intention of the clause, and the reference in ὁ ὤν to Exodus seems very probable, I still feel that the context and the Greek order point to connecting ἐπὶ πάντων with ὁ ὤν, nor does this seem inconsistent with such a reference. If ἐπὶ πάντων had been meant as epithet to θεὸς, I should have expected the avoidance of ambiguity by a change of order—θεὸς ἐπὶ πάντων.

A conjectural emendation of the text (ὧν ὁ for ὁ ὤν) has occurred to commentators from time to time. Jonas Schlicting in his commentary on the Romans (1656) mentions it, as likely to suggest itself, and points out the suitability of the climax, but rejects it as giving an unscriptural phrase. John Taylor (of Norwich, 1754) makes the same suggestion and justifies it as giving a proper climax. Wetstein refers to these and others, without comment. Bentley (*Crit. Sacr.* ed. Ellis, p. 30) mentions it, apparently with favour. John Weiss (*op. cit.* p. 238) adopts it, referring to Wrede, *Lic. Disp.*, a work which I have not seen. Hart, *J. T. S.* xi. p. 36 *n.*, suggests the same emendation.

Mr Hart supports the emendation, in a letter to me, as follows: " St Paul is writing here if anywhere as a Jew, and the relation of Israel to the GOD of Jacob forms the proper climax: Christian scribes altered the text because in their view that privilege was forfeited and had lapsed to the Church. I think this passage from Philo clinches the matter—*de praemiis* § 123 (M. ii. p. 428) (Lev. xxvi. 12) τούτου καλεῖ-ται θεὸς ἰδίως ὁ τῶν συμπάντων θεός, καὶ λαὸς ἐξαίρετος πάλιν οὗτος οὐ τῶν κατὰ μέρος ἀρχόντων ἀλλὰ τοῦ ἑνὸς καὶ πρὸς ἀλήθειαν ἄρχοντος, ἁγίου ἅγιος.—So St Paul says 'to whom belongs the supreme GOD, blessed be He for ever and ever, Amen.' But his reporters did not sympathise and desiderated an antithesis to κατὰ σάρκα, having identified the (abstract) Messiah with our Lord."

It will be seen that here again the justification of the conjecture depends on the propriety of the climax. The quotation from Philo does not, I think, carry us far. He is there emphasising the establishment of a personal relation between the GOD of all men and the individual saint, and he calls this single person a λαὸς ἐξαιρετός. Such language could of course be used by any Jew or Christian. We have a parallel in Heb. xi. 16: οὐκ ἐπαισχύνεται ὁ θεὸς θεὸς ἐπικαλεῖσθαι αὐτῶν, ἡτοίμασεν γὰρ αὐτοῖς πόλιν. But the point need not be laboured. Against this suggestion the following points may be urged:—(1) It ignores the effect of the ἀμήν in making the whole clause an ascription: see above. (2) The question is raised whether the idea embodied in the term 'The GOD of Israel' is naturally to be expected as the climax of the enumeration here made. It may be premised that that term is never used by S. Paul in his Epistles, or indeed in the N. T. except in Mt. xv. 31, Lk. xvi. 18, Acts xiii. 17. It does not occur, either explicitly or implicitly, in the other enumerations of the privileges of Israel (Rom. ii. 17, iii. 3, 2 Cor. xi. 22). Further, in this Epistle the whole argument has been based on the universal relation of GOD to man; and the very phrase ἐξ ὧν ὁ χριστὸς τὸ κατὰ σάρκα seems to exclude the divine relation of the Christ, and a fortiori the relation of man to GOD, from the list of the special privileges of Israel. Finally, the phrase ἐπὶ πάντων (see above), as referring directly to the governing and dispensing operations of GOD gives, almost necessarily, a wider range of reference than to the relations to Israel alone.

G. CAPP. IX.—XI.

The difficulty of the passage for us lies in the fact that we habitually think primarily of the destiny of the individual as such and the determination of his final position in relation to GOD: and we bring into this passage the problems of predestination and free-will as they affect the individual man. S. Paul's thought here is different. He is thinking, first, of the purpose of GOD and the work to be done in the execution of that purpose. He then sees in the selection of certain men and nations for this work, the determination, that is to say, of their position in regard to the work, a signal instance of GOD's graciousness and mercy. It is a high privilege to be called to assist in carrying out GOD's purpose.

Finally, he holds that, with this call and determination by GOD, there still remains to man the choice of acceptance of the call. If he accepts willingly, he becomes an instrument of mercy, that is an instrument in the execution of GOD's purpose for mankind. If he rejects the call and sets himself against the purpose, he still cannot escape from the position of an instrument; but, by his own act, he puts himself into that relation to GOD, which involves the exhibition of GOD's wrath on sin; he becomes an instrument of wrath, serving GOD's purpose still, but in spite of himself and to his own destruction.

Within the lines of this conception, we can see the rationale of S. Paul's treatment of individual cases. In the case of Esau and Jacob, the selection assigned to Jacob the leading part in the execution of the purpose, to Esau the part of a servant. In the history of Esau and his descendants, it is clear this part of a servant was rejected; Edom set itself in antagonism to Israel, fell under the wrath of GOD and received the doom implied in the word ἐμίσησα. In the case of Pharaoh, the selection assigned to him the rôle of giving a signal exhibition of GOD's power and proclamation of His Name. The way in which Pharaoh played that rôle was again the way of opposition: he set himself against the purpose of GOD: a 'hardening' of his own character and purpose was the result; where he might have been an instrument of mercy, he became an instrument of wrath; and while GOD's purpose of mercy in Israel was still fulfilled, Pharaoh was doomed. In the case of Israel, we see an ambiguous result. The selection, again, assigned to Israel the place in the execution of the purpose, which involved the storing up and ultimately the communication of GOD's purpose of mercy to all mankind. As the history of Israel develops, some are seen to accept this duty, others to reject it. There follows in part, a blinding of perception (πώρωσις ἀπὸ μέρους), an ignorance (ἄγνοια) of the end itself for which they are selected. The end itself cannot now be carried out by their means; and they are rejected. But this very rejection of part of Israel is a further revelation of GOD's true purpose in Israel; and the continued acceptance of the faithful remnant is a triumphant vindication of the patience of GOD and the permanence of His purpose. Only in the case of the faithless portion of Israel, does S. Paul's thought pass on to the ultimate issue for those who reject their proper work in the execution of the purpose. Here he derives from the fact of the original selection a far-reaching hope. He seems to suggest that the ultimate realisation of the purpose of GOD for all mankind, through the faithful stock, may itself produce such an effect upon the blinded Israel, that they too will see the truth and again come under the mercy of GOD (xi. 11, 12, 17—23, 28—32). In most remarkable language he speaks of the gifts and the calling of GOD being irreversible, and the love of GOD, manifested in the original selection and exhibited towards 'the fathers,' as still marking His real relation even to these children who have rejected its appeal.

We observe, then, in these chapters, as in the earlier, that S. Paul is dealing with what he regards as the facts of history and experience, and drawing his conclusions from them. He is not expounding a solution or even a statement of the metaphysical problems of pre-destination and freewill. He conceives of human experience as witnessing to a comprehensive and far-reaching purpose of GOD in His self-revelation to man. The destinies of men he sees as determined, on the one hand, by GOD's call to men and to families and nations to take part in the execution of that purpose, and, on the other, by the attitude which men, as individuals or families or nations, take up towards that call. The call assigns in each case a definite part and duty, not the same for all, but differentiated, that each may have his part. And in accordance with the way in which each undertakes the part assigned to him, comes success or failure for him. The grounds on which the several parts are assigned are hidden in the mystery of creation. The ultimate issue for individuals is hidden. What is known is that behind the vast purpose remains eternally the love of GOD, and in its execution is manifested inexhaustible wisdom and knowledge. If we feel, at first, a sense of disappointment, when we realise that we can get little light from these chapters on those metaphysical problems, a little reflection will show that the religious significance of the position here expounded is of enormously greater importance than any such solution could be. The conception of the whole process of the ages as being based upon the love of GOD, and directed in whole and in detail by His infinite wisdom and know-ledge; the conception of man as called to cooperate with GOD in the execution of this mighty plan; the assertion of man's undiluted re-sponsibility for playing his part in the place assigned to him, in free response to the call of GOD; here are ideas which touch life at every point, and have the power to inspire faith and to invigorate character in the highest degree.

On this question of election there is a very interesting discussion by Hort, in the *Life and Letters*, ii. p. 333.

H. APOSTLES.

1. This word, in the sense of a commissioned representative, is not found in Greek later than Herodotus (i. 21, v. 38). In classical Greek it means 'a fleet' or 'expedition.' It has not yet been found in Hellenistic Greek; but it would not be surprising if it should occur at that stage in the same sense as in the old Ionic language (cf. Nägeli, pp. 22—23).

2. In the Synoptic Gospels, the word is used by all three with reference to the Galilean mission of the disciples (Mt. x. 2; Mk iii. 14, vi. 30; Lk. vi. 13, ix. 10). It is possible that, as von Dobschütz argues, all these cases may be traced to S. Luke. But the use of the verb ἀποστέλλω in the same connexion (Mt. x. 5, 16, 40; Mk iii. 14, vi. 7) in Mt. and Mk makes it probable that the substantive also is original in these passages. Otherwise it is found in S. Luke only (xi. 49, xvii. 5, xxii. 14, xxiv. 10). But the verb, again, is used by the Lord both of His own mission, and of the mission of prophets, and of disciples, both in plain sayings and in parables. The quotation in Lk. iv. 18 may be the origin of the whole usage.

3. S. John uses the substantive only once (xiii. 16) to describe, though indirectly, the relation of the disciples to the Lord. He also uses the verb both of the Lord's own mission and of His mission of the disciples.

While these facts do not prove conclusively that the word was used of the Twelve by the Lord Himself, they show that the adoption of the title by the Twelve from the first would have been natural, if not inevitable.

4. The use in the Acts is consistent: (1) it is commonly used of the Twelve (Eleven) in the early chapters (i.—xi., xv.) only. They are otherwise described, as the Eleven (ii. 14) or the Twelve (vi. 2) only. It is to be noted that in this section the properly missionary work of the Twelve is the main subject: in c. xv. the conditions of missionary work are under discussion. The dominant use therefore of this term is natural: and its strict limitation to the Twelve shows that it already has an official sense. It is hardly possible, however, to say whether the word belongs to an early document used by S. Luke, or whether it is chosen by him as the best description in the circumstances of the character which the Twelve bear. There is nothing so far to show that he included any others than the Twelve in the title. (2) Twice and only twice he uses the word of Barnabas and Paul, on

their first mission (xiv. 4, 14). It is to be noticed that he does not use the word in describing the origin of the mission (ἀφορίσατε… ἀπέλυσαν, xiii. 2, 3) but in xiii. 4 he uses the remarkable phrase ἐκπεμφθέντες ὑπὸ τοῦ ἁγίου πνεύματος (xiii. 2, cf. xiv. 26). The commission and the work were not given by the Church but by the Holy Spirit, and under 'the grace of GOD.' We cannot say, therefore, that the term ἀπόστολος is here used of them as commissioned by the Church of Antioch. As with the Twelve, so with these two the commission is from above.

It is remarkable that the word does not appear again after c. xv. As regards the Twelve the explanation is obvious: they are not mentioned again[1]. But it is very remarkable that the term is never again used of S. Paul[2]. If we bear in mind how frequently S. Paul uses it of himself, the fact of its absence from this whole section of S. Luke would seem to militate against the suggestion that S. Luke is dependent on S. Paul for his use of the word; and to favour the supposition that in the earlier chapters he found it in his sources.

5. S. Paul's letters give us the earliest direct documentary evidence for the current meaning of the word: it is therefore important to consider in detail his use.

i. He uses the word of himself in the addresses of all his epistles, except 1 and 2 Thessalonians, Romans, Philippians and Philemon. In all cases the source of the apostleship is described, either by the simple genitive Ἰησοῦ Χρ. or Χρ. Ἰης., or in Galatians by an expanded prepositional clause having the same effect. The absence of the title in 1 and 2 Thessalonians is probably due to the greeting being a joint one from 'Paul, Silvanus and Timotheus': that he claimed the office is clear from 1 Thes. ii. 6. In Romans and Philippians, for different though cognate reasons, he suppresses the title : in Romans it is part of his delicate waiving of authority ; in Philippians it is one of the many marks of intimacy and affection. But in the introduction to the Romans he describes his own position in terms of the apostolate (i. 5, ἐλάβομεν χάριν καὶ ἀποστολήν) with the same indication of its relation to the Lord (δι' οὗ) as in Galatians.

The use of the word of himself is rare in other parts of the Epistles. Once in 1 Corinthians (ix. 1, 2) he insists on his position as apostle and the consequent rights. In the same epistle (xv. 7) he recalls its original basis. In 2 Corinthians we may say that the whole of cc. x.—xiii. are an assertion and defence of his apostolic

---

[1] Cf. Harnack, *Lukas etc.*, p. 200, n. 1.

[2] The verb occurs in this sense only in xxii. 2, xxvi. 17, S. Paul's speeches.

character, though he does not apply the word directly to himself except in xii. 12. In 1 Thes. ii. 6 and 1 Cor. iv. 9 he includes himself in the number of Χριστοῦ ἀπόστολοι or simply οἱ ἀπόστολοι. In 1 Tim. ii. 7, 2 Tim. i. 11 he refers to his appointment (ἐτέθην) as apostle. Finally, in Romans xi. 13 he speaks of himself as ἐθνῶν ἀπόστολος—the only place where he uses the word with an objective genitive: though in Gal. ii. 8 we have ἀποστολή with the same genitive.

There can be no doubt as to the meaning of the title to S. Paul. It involves a definite and direct appointment received from the Lord, to preach the Gospel, in particular to the Gentiles, to carry the due authority as representative of the Lord (cf. 2 Cor. v. 20), and to do the acts belonging to such an office. It is an independent and pleni-potentiary office, in the assertion of which often the whole cause of the Gospel proves to be involved. At the same time there is no trace that either the office or the name or the contents are new. Where there is explanation, it is of the nature of an appeal to acknowledged facts rather than of exposition of any new idea or interpretation. When his position is disputed, it is his right to the office which is challenged, not his presentation of it. Consequently we conclude that the idea of the office, in the full sense as conceived by S. Paul, was already present and the word current in the Church when he first used it.

ii. The question, however, arises, was it also current in a looser and wider sense? And as far as S. Paul's evidence goes this leads to an examination of those passages in which he either includes others with himself in the designation, or applies it to others apart from himself.

There are three classes of passages to be examined. First those in which there is a reference to all or some of the 'original apostles' whether exclusively or not; secondly, those in which the name is given to definite persons other than the original apostles; thirdly, those which speak of 'apostles' generally.

(a) To take first the references to the 'original' apostles.

Gal. i. 17, 19. The exact references in this passage are not clear. S. Paul first says that he did not go up immediately after his conversion to Jerusalem, πρὸς τοὺς πρὸ ἐμοῦ ἀποστόλους. The phrase implies his own inclusion at that time in the class of Apostles: it must, presumably, refer to the Eleven or Twelve; but whether it includes others besides them is an open question. Anyhow, it implies that they were all apostles in the full sense in which he claimed to be one. Secondly, he seems to include both Cephas and James the brother of the Lord in the class of apostles (*vv.* 18, 19): here we find an additional member of the class beside the Twelve, unless 'James the brother of the Lord' is, as is supposed by some, to be identified with James the Less. In the following chapter he speaks of James, Cephas and John as στύλοι δοκοῦντες.... And his language shows that they as well as Barnabas were included with him, on an equality, though with different spheres of work.

Here, then, we have the apostolate including, besides the Twelve, James (if not one of the Twelve), Barnabas and Paul. There is no question as to what an apostle is, only as to who are apostles.

1 Cor. ix. 5, μὴ οὐκ ἔχομεν ἐξουσίαν...ὡς καὶ οἱ λοιποὶ ἀπόστολοι καὶ οἱ ἀδελφοὶ τοῦ κυρίου καὶ Κηφᾶς; ἢ μόνος ἐγὼ καὶ Βαρνάβας οὐκ ἔχομεν ἐξουσίαν—

Here clearly Paul and Barnabas are assumed to be ἀπόστολοι. The clause ὡς καὶ...Κηφᾶς is strangely worded. But as Κηφᾶς is clearly one of οἱ λοιποὶ ἀπόστολοι, it would appear that οἱ ἀδελφοὶ τοῦ κ. must also be included in the class : i.e. other brethren of the Lord besides James.

1 Cor. xv. 7, εἶτα τοῖς ἀποστόλοις πᾶσιν.

This follows the mention of Cephas, the Twelve, the Five Hundred Brethren, James. It is possible that as 'the Twelve' in this enumeration include Cephas, so 'all the apostles' include the Twelve and James only. But it is more natural to understand the phrase, with its emphatic πᾶσιν, as including others. And in that case there were others, apostles in the same sense as the Twelve and James. There is no question here of a looser meaning of the word, but only of a wider range in its application.

2 Cor. xi. 5, xii. 11, οἱ ὑπερλίαν ἀπόστολοι.

In spite of the strong statement of certain critics, there is much to be said for referring this phrase to the same persons as are described in Galatians as οἱ πρὸ ἐμοῦ ἀπόστολοι. The exact range implied is not clear. If, however, it is to be taken to refer to those who are described in xi. 13 as μετασχηματιζόμενοι ὡς ἀπόστολοι Χριστοῦ, then the phrase is ironic, and describes the claim of those persons, not an admitted status. That claim may well have included a commission from the Lord, whether truly or falsely asserted; and indeed the words ἀπόστολοι Χρ. seem to imply that these persons did in any case make such a claim. In this event, as S. Paul does not exclude the possibility of others than the Twelve, James, Barnabas and himself having such a commission, we should have here definite evidence that there were others who rightly claimed the direct commission which is distinctive of the apostle in the strict sense of the word.

To return to 1 Cor. xv. 8, ἔσχατον δὲ πάντων κτλ. would seem to imply that to none later than S. Paul was such a direct communication addressed as could form the basis of the apostolic status. He was the last of the Apostles.

Consequently, if the name covers the wider range that has been suggested, it still excludes all whose conversion must be dated later than S. Paul's.

(b) We pass to the cases in which the word is used of others than those specifically named.

2 Cor. xi. 13, μετασχηματιζόμενοι ὡς ἀπόστολοι Χριστοῦ.

This passage has been a!ready dealt with. It supports both the strict meaning and the wide range of the word.

2 Cor. viii. 23, εἴτε ἀδελφοὶ ἡμῶν ἀπόστολοι ἐκκλησιῶν.

The context clearly decides that this phrase means 'representative agents of churches.' They are therefore called δόξα Χριστοῦ a manifestation of the power and the love of Christ, working in these churches to produce the exhibition of Christian brotherliness, in the contribution raised for the poor saints at Jerusalem. The whole passage deals with this contribution, and, in particular, with the precautions taken by S. Paul to have the whole matter put above suspicion. Representatives of all the contributing churches were associated with him in the company that conveyed the gift (see note on Rom. xvi. 16). Thus here we have a clear case of the use of the word not with a wider meaning, but in a different meaning, clearly defined by the genitive and by the context.

Phil. ii. 25, Ἐπαφρόδιτον τὸν ἀδελφὸν καὶ συνεργὸν καὶ συστρατιώτην μου ὑμῶν δὲ ἀπόστολον καὶ λειτουργὸν τῆς χρείας μου.

Here again the context defines the meaning. Epaphroditus has been sent to represent the affection and support given by the Philippians to S. Paul in his labours. He has brought the assurance of their eager and unfailing affection, of their keenness for the propagation of the Gospel, and a contribution in money for this purpose. He is the agent whom the Church has sent to minister to S. Paul's need. The sense of the word is exactly the same as in 2 Cor. viii. 23.

(c) In four passages—1 Cor. xii. 28; Eph. ii. 20, iii. 5, iv. 11—the word is used absolutely, twice to describe the first order of members of the Church, each with their distinctive function and work (1 Cor. xii. 28; Eph. iv. 11); once to describe the foundation on which the Church is built (Eph. ii. 20); once to describe the primary recipients of the Gospel revelation (Eph. iii. 5). There can be no question but that in these passages the word is used in its strict sense: but the range covered by it is left undefined.

We conclude, then, as to S. Paul's use of the word:

(i) In all but two passages, he uses it of commissioned preachers of the Gospel. Wherever he defines the source of the commission, it is referred to the direct intervention of the Lord. It is reasonable to infer that the same direct intervention is implied in those passages where there is no precise definition.

(ii) In two passages only is it used in another sense, and there the special sense is clearly defined.

(iii) There is no evidence that he used the word in such a general sense of 'missionaries' as would dispense with this condition.

(iv) He includes under the name, the Twelve, the Brethren of the Lord, himself, Barnabas, perhaps Silas and probably others unnamed (1 Cor. xv. 7); he must be taken to imply that all these men were original Apostles, in the sense that they received their commission from the Lord Himself.

(*d*) We now come to Rom. xvi. 7.

The obvious meaning of this passage is that Andronicus and Junias were themselves apostles. According to S. Paul's usage, this must mean that they were apostles in the strict sense, that is, that they had received their commission from the Lord Himself and probably (see above, on 1 Cor. xv. 8) before S. Paul. They were among the οἱ πρὸ ἐμοῦ ἀπόστολοι of Gal. i. 17. And this points to supplying ἀπόστολοι to γέγοναν—who became apostles in Christ even before me.

6. In other passages of the N.T. (*a*) we find the title ἀπ. Ἰ. Χρ. in 1 and 2 Pet. i. 1.

(*b*) In 2 Pet. iii. 2, Jude 17 we have a general reference to οἱ ἀπόστολοι (τ. κ. ἡ. Jude) as the original authorities for teaching.

(*c*) Rev. xviii. 20, the apostles are the first class in the Church, followed by οἱ προφῆται.

(*d*) Rev. xxi. 14, δώδεκα ὀνόματα τῶν δώδεκα ἀποστόλων τοῦ ἀρνίου are written on the twelve foundation-stones of the city.

(*e*) Rev. ii. 2, there are those who assert themselves to be apostles and are not as in 2 Cor. xi. 13.

The only passage which contributes new light is Rev. xxi. 14, where there is an apparent identification of 'the Twelve' and the 'Apostles.' It would appear that the number twelve has become symbolic: and we can hardly argue from this passage as to who were included in the class.

(*f*) Heb. iii. 1 gives us a unique description of our Lord as ἀπόστολος. This must be connected with those passages in Synn. Evv. and Joh., in which the verb is used by our Lord of His own mission.

7. In the Patres Apostolici the word is used exclusively of the original apostles as deriving their authority directly from the Lord. None are mentioned by name as apostles except S. Peter and S. Paul. Papias, who names several of the Twelve, does not use the word apostle.

The only exception to the rule is to be found in the *Didache*, where 'apostles' seem to be itinerant missionaries. The use is unique; unless Hermas, *Sim.* 9; 15, 4; 16, 5, are to be taken as implying a wider range. But *ib.* 17, 1 seems to limit the term ἀπόστολος to the Twelve; the others would be included under διδάσκαλοι. We must either suppose that the author of this portion of the *Didache* used what had become a current term for wandering evangelists: or that the application of the term to such is his own invention (see Dean Robinson, *J. T. S.*, April 1912, pp. 350—351). In either case it cannot be taken as evidence for the use or meaning of the term in the Apostolic times.

8. It has been suggested that the term is derived from contemporary Jewish practice. It is supposed that it was customary to send from Jerusalem persons representing the authorities to the various settlements of Jews of the Dispersion. The definite evidence for this is found in Justin *Dial.* 17 and 108, where he speaks of 'chosen men' being sent from Jerusalem to denounce the new Christian heresy. Saul's mission to Damascus is regarded as an instance of this procedure. The supposition is in itself, on general grounds, probable; but there is no evidence that the name 'apostles' was given to such persons: and it is obvious that the character of their office and business was widely different from that of the Christian Apostles.

Further, it has been suggested that a parallel may be found in the use of the name *apostoli*, for agents sent by the central authority to collect the annual tribute of the Jews of the Dispersion. But such agents do not seem to have been sent out till after the destruction of Jerusalem. Before that time, the process by which these contributions were remitted to Jerusalem is clearly described both by Philo (*de mon.*, Mang. II. 224: *leg. ad Caium*, Mang. II. 568, 592) and Josephus (*Antt.* xiv. 7, 2; xvi. 6 ff.). The contributions were stored up in a safe place in the locality and remitted to Jerusalem by the hands of members of the particular community, carefully selected. These people were called ἱερόπομποι (Philo) and the contributions ἱερὰ χρήματα. There is no hint of any agents from Jerusalem being concerned in the matter: and the persons actually engaged were not called 'apostles.' The real parallel to this arrangement is the measures taken by S. Paul for providing for the safe and trustworthy remission to Jerusalem of the contributions of the Gentile

Churches. It was not till after the destruction of Jerusalem, when we may suppose that it became necessary to provide further means for the consolidation of the relations with the central community, that we hear of 'apostles' sent from the centre for this and other purposes.

To sum up:

1. There is practically no evidence for the use of this term in the sense required in classical Greek later than Herodotus (Nägeli, *ad vb*).

2. It is used in LXX., 3 Kings xiv. 6 (A), of Ahijah the prophet; and of messengers, Isa. xviii. 2 (Q).

3. In Joh. xiii. 16 it is used as correlative to τὸν πέμψαντα: it does not occur elsewhere in S. John: but the verb is used both of the Lord's own mission and of His mission of the disciples.

4. In the Synoptic Gospels it is used in connexion with the Galilean Mission (by all three); otherwise only by S. Luke (thrice); in all cases with reference to the Twelve.

The verb is used in sayings attributed to the Lord, of Himself, of the O.T. prophets, and of the Twelve, in reference to the Galilean mission.

5. In Hebrews it is used of the Lord Himself.

6. It is used of the Twelve and of Barnabas and Paul in Acts; of the Twelve (? exclusively) in Rev. and (including S. Paul) in the Patres Apostolici.

7. In S. Paul it is used of himself (as 1 and 2 Pet.): of those who were apostles before him including the Twelve and others : of apostles as original and first order in the Church (so 2 Pet., Jude, Rev.), in no case with precise definition of range: and in two cases of agents commissioned by churches.

8. There is no distinct evidence that it was in use among the Jews in the Apostolic age.

9. The *Didache* is the only evidence in the first 150 years for its use among Christians in the more general sense of εὐαγγελιστής.

10. It is a probable conclusion that the word was derived from the Lord Himself; either that He called the Twelve apostles: or that His use of the verb to describe His own mission and theirs, led His followers who received the special commission to describe themselves as His ἀπόστολοι.

On this subject see Lightfoot, *Galatians*, pp. 92 ff. ; Von Dobschütz, *Probleme*, pp. 104 f. ; Batiffol, *Primitive Catholicism* (E.T. 1911), pp. 36 ff.; Hort, *The Christian Ecclesia*, pp. 22 f. ; Chapman, *John the Presbyter*.

I. Capp. XV., XVI.

A.

There is considerable difficulty as to the original place of the doxology (xvi. 25—27). The facts are as follows:

  I. The doxology is placed
     1. at the end of the Epistle (after xvi. 23 (24))
         i. by the MSS preferred by Origen (Ruf.),
         ii. by ℵBCDE minusc. 3, 4, def, Vulg., Pesh., Boh., Aeth., Orig. (Ruf.), Ambrosiaster, Pelagius, Aug., Sed., 16, 18, 137, 176.
     2. After xiv. 23
         i. Some MSS ap. Origen.
         ii. L, most minusc., Syr. Harcl., Goth., Theodoret, Joh. Damasc. : Antiochian recension and commentators.
     3. In both places AP 5, 17, Arm. codd.
     4. Omitted altogether
         i. Marcion ap. Origen. Codd. ap. Hieron. (in Eph. iii. 5) = Origen (Hort, Lft *Essays* p. 333).
         ii. FGg.

  II. There is some, very obscure, evidence that cc. xv. xvi.—23 (24) were omitted in some systems of Church lections. This depends on the list of capitula in Codices Amiatinus and Fuldensis, both of which seem to omit cc. xv. xvi. while including the doxology immediately after xiv. 23. The only other evidence for this omission is Marcion, ap. Origen (as generally interpreted, see below). G has a blank space after xiv. 23; but the attempt to show that in its ancestry occurred a manuscript which omitted cc. xv. xvi. seems to have failed.

  III. A variation of text, which has to be considered at the same time as the above, occurs in GF. In i. 7, 15 ἐν Ῥώμῃ is omitted by Gg (F defective), 47 mg. (note on i. 7). Some support has been sought for this omission in Origen and Ambrosiaster (Lightfoot), but without sufficient grounds. Zahn (Exc. I.) considers the reading to be original.

Origen's testimony is contained in the following passage from Rufinus' translation x. 43, Vol. VII., p. 453 ed. Lomm.

Caput hoc Marcion, a quo Scripturae Evangelicae atque Apostolicae interpolatae sunt, de hac epistola penitus abstulit; et non solum hoc, sed et ab eo loco, ubi scriptum est : " omne autem quod non est ex fide peccatum est :" usque ad finem cuncta dissecuit. In aliis vero exemplaribus, id est, in his quae non sunt a Marcione temerata, hoc ipsum caput diverse positum invenimus. In nonnullis etenim codicibus post eum locum, quem supra diximus, hoc est: "omne autem peccatum est": statim cohaerens habetur "ei autem qui potens est vos confirmare." Alii vero codices in fine id, ut nunc est positum, continent. Sed iam veniamus ad capituli hujus explanationem.

These statements, always with reserve as to the accuracy of Rufinus, have usually been taken to show that Origen had before him

    1.   Marcion's Apostolicon, omitting the whole of cc. xv. xvi.

    2.   Some Codices independent of Marcion, which included these chapters but put the doxology after xiv. 23.

    3.   Other Codices, which he accepted, which put it at the end, in its present place. But Hort, reading 'non solum *hic* sed et *in* eo loco,' interprets this statement as to Marcion to mean that he omitted the doxology in both places, and to have no reference to the rest of cc. xv. xvi. Zahn takes 'dissecuit' to mean 'mutilated or tore to shreds' (in contrast with 'penitus abstulit') and regards the statement as attributing to Marcion the omission of the doxology and the mutilation of xv. xvi. by corrections and omissions.

Hort's suggestion has not been adopted by other critics. Zahn's translation seems hardly adequate to the phrase "usque ad finem cuncta."

This testimony of Origen is probably to be supplemented from Jerome on Eph. iii. 5 (Vallarsi, vol. vii., p. 591 *b*) that the doxology is found "in plerisque codicibus." Hort (Lft, *B. E.*, p. 332) gives reasons for thinking that Jerome is here drawing upon Origen's commentary and therefore that we have again indirect evidence from Origen of the omission of the doxology being due to Marcion.

We have, then, evidence that in Origen's time there were three forms of the text.

    (*a*)   Marcion's text = i.—xiv. 23 (or i.—xiv. 23 + xv. xvi. 23 (24) altered).

    (*b*)   Nonnulli codices = i.—xiv. 23, xvi. 25, 27, xv. xvi. 1—23.

    (*c*)   Codices used by Origen = i.—xvi. 27 (= W. H.).

There is no existing textual support for (*a*). But

    (*a*)   Marcion's text + xv. xvi. 1—23 is the text of GFg.

    (*b*)   is supported by the MSS given above I 2. ii.

    (*c*)   is supported by the MSS given above I 1. ii.

There is therefore very strong MSS authority for preferring (*c*). But the question arises how the various changes came about.

Marcion's text is generally explained as due to the principles on which he revised the Gospels and Epistles. There is some difference of opinion as to whether he had any textual authority behind him.

Of the other variations three principal accounts have been given:

1. Lightfoot (*Bibl. Essays*, p. 287, 1893) holds that S. Paul himself made two recensions of his Epistle; (i) the original letter= i.—xvi. 23 sent from Corinth to Rome, (ii) a second edition altered to form a circular letter to a number of Churches unnamed, either late in or after the Roman imprisonment=i.—xiv. 23+the doxology, written for a conclusion, and omitting ἐν Ῥώμῃ in i. 7, 15. This letter was in circulation, and afterwards was completed by the addition of xv.—xvi. 23 (24). Against this theory it is argued (1) that no sign of the existence of this letter remains, though such might have been expected in the case of a circular letter addressed to various localities, unless the obscure testimony of the Capitulations can be alleged: (2) that it is inconceivable that S. Paul himself could have made a division after xiv. 23, the argument being continuous to xv. 13 (S. H.): (3) that the argument which Lightfoot himself bases on the uniqueness of the doxology in its present place as a conclusion holds with much greater effect against its position in the circular letter as conceived by him. These objections though of various weight are conclusive.

2. Hort holds that the W. H. text represents the original letter: that for purposes of reading in church cc. xv. xvi. were omitted, and the doxology placed at the end of xiv. 23: that the position of the doxology in church lections caused certain scribes to place it here, and either to duplicate or to omit at xvi. 23.

3. Zahn argues that the original position of the doxology was at xiv. 23. He bases this position on internal grounds: (1) the absence of a doxology at the end in all other epistles of S. Paul, (2) the anacoluthic character (leg. ᾧ) of the doxology implies a strength of emotion which is unlikely after the list of salutations, (3) its close connexion with the argument of xiv. 1—xv. 13, (4) the confusion of text (in connexion with the benediction) at xvi. 20, 23 can only be explained by the intrusion of the doxology, (5) its transference from after xvi. 24 to xiv. 23 cannot be accounted for. Some of these arguments are unsubstantial: (3) would be strong if the doxology occurred after xv. 13: but the interruption of the argument, if it is placed at xiv. 23, is strongly against this theory as it is against Lightfoot's.

4. S. H. differ from the above by giving an influential position to Marcion's text. They hold that (i) the original text was

that of W. H., (ii) Marcion cut off the last two chapters including the doxology partly on doctrinal grounds partly as unimportant for edifi-cation, (iii) Marcion's text, i.—xiv. 23 om. also ἐν Ῥώμῃ, i. 7, 15, had a considerable circulation and influence, (iv) for Church use it was supplemented by addition of the doxology i.—xiv. 23 + xvi. 25—27 (so arriving at Lightfoot's second recension), (v) this form of the Epistle was then supplemented by scribes by the addition of xv. xvi. 1—23, and in some cases by the addition of xv. xvi. 1—27, with a duplicate doxology. This explanation gets over the difficulty of the break at xiv. 23 by attributing it to Marcion's doctrinal objection to parts of xv. (e.g. xv. 8). It rests mainly upon the assertion of the influence of Marcion's Apostolicon.

On the whole it seems to give the simplest explanation of a very complicated problem.

5. Lake (*Expositor*, Dec. 1910) offers another explanation. He establishes the existence of a short recension i.—xiv. 23 + xvi. 25—27 and argues that this recension omitted ἐν Ῥώμῃ in c. i. The evidence for this recension is carried back (1) to the European type of the Old Latin Version (to which the capitulations of Cod. Amiat. are assigned), (2) to the African type of the same version, as evidenced by the fact that Cyprian fails to quote from cc. xv. xvi., and Tertullian *adv. Marc.* also omits all references to those chapters, although Marcion must either have omitted or mutilated them (see Origen, qu. above) : and (3) is supported by the evidence of MSS which have xvi. 25—27 after xiv. 23, on the ground that the doxology must naturally come at the end of the Epistle. He argues that the two recensions were both current till Cyprian's time ; and that the doxology was placed after xvi. 23, when the two were combined (Alexandrian MSS in Origen's time, Ambrosiaster and Jerome). It follows that no MS is preserved which has either recension in its original form.

His theory of the recension is that the short recension preceded the long, both being due to S. Paul himself. The short recension was written as a circular letter, a companion to Galatians (as Ephesians to Colossians), and this circular letter and Galatians were written considerably earlier than 1 Cor. In his winter sojourn at Corinth, S. Paul wishing to send to Rome a statement of his Gospel sent this circular letter with the addition of xv. xvi. 1—23, and the insertion of ἐν Ῥώμῃ in c. 1, to give it special application to the Christians at Rome.

This hypothesis is clearly very attractive. The textual criticism on which it is founded is comprehensive and strong. The absence of direct documentary evidence for the short recension may be partly accounted for by the lack of Old Latin evidence for the Epistle. But the difficulty besetting any theory which ends the Epistle, in one of its forms, at xiv. 23, is peculiarly strongly felt in this theory. The argument is brought to an abrupt conclusion, and it is really unfinished. Yet in a circular letter, accompanying Galatians, most of all should we expect the argument to be finished off and summed up. The abruptness of the conclusion is only emphasised by the doxology, or the grace and the doxology, supposed to follow immediately on 23. In fact in any theory of the textual variations, it ought to be regarded as fundamental that the separation between xiv. 23 and xv. 1—13 must have been due to violent interference with the original text—either of definite mutilation on doctrinal grounds, or of a mechanical arrangement for purposes of Church use.

The references for this discussion are Lightfoot, *Biblical Essays* (1893), Zahn, *Einl.* § 22, S. H. *Romans* lxxxv f., Westcott and Hort, Appendix *ad loc.*, Kirsopp Lake, *Expositor*, Dec. 1910.

B.

Two other questions have been raised as to these chapters, on internal grounds.

1. The doxology is said to belong, in style and thought, to a later period of S. Paul's writings than that of the Epistle to the Romans. Lightfoot accepted this view and supported it by a close comparison with the Epistle to the Ephesians (*Biblical Essays*, 317 f.) and the Pastoral Epistles: and met it by attributing the doxology to a recension made by S. Paul himself at a later period (see above). Hort met this argument by pointing out (1) the close correspondence of the doxology with the main thoughts and object of the Epistle, (2) the correspondence of the language and thought with particular expressions and conceptions found in Romans, 1 Corinthians (esp. c. ii.), Gal. and 1 and 2 Thes. (*l.c.* p. 327 f.). I have followed S. H. in adopting Hort's position here (see notes). The fact seems to be that the doxology sums up in terse and comprehensive form the positive view, which S. Paul had reached, of the relation of Jew and Gentile in Christ to each other and to God, as seen in relation to the whole purpose of God for man in creation and redemption. The Epistle to the Romans, as a whole, is a positive exposition of this theme, and so concludes the great period of strife through which S. Paul and the Gentile Churches had been passing. In the later Epistles, especially Ephesians and Colossians, this position is assumed as settled and made the basis for further teaching both positive and polemical on the nature and place

of the Christian Society. It is not, therefore, unnatural that the language in which here S. Paul sums up the position should be represented, both in earlier Epistles where the main thought crops out, and still more in the later, where it is the foundation of additional superstructure. The doxology is, in this very important sense, a link between the two groups of Epistles.

2. Some commentators have found a difficulty in the list of salutations in xvi. 3—16; and have argued that this must be a fragment of a letter addressed to the Church at Ephesus. There is no external evidence for separating these verses from the rest of cc. xv. xvi. As to the internal evidence it has been sufficiently shown by Lightfoot (*Philippians*, pp. 171—178, Caesar's Household) and S. H. (notes *ad loc.*), that both as regards individual names and groups, and in view of the combination of Roman, Greek and Jewish names, a strong case can be made out for Rome, and to some extent against Ephesus. These authorities I have followed, both in this matter and in regard to the presence of Aquila and Priscilla at Rome (see notes).

It may be further pointed out that in none of his Epistles addressed to Churches of his own founding does S. Paul send salutations to any individuals by name. Only in one case (1 Cor. xvi. 19) does he send to such a Church a salutation by name from individuals in his own company: and there the salutation is from *the group* centring round Aquila and Priscilla. In Col., written to a Church he had not visited, he sends salutations from six of his companions by name, and names two members of the Colossian Church, one for greeting, one for warning. The unexpected fact comes out that in writing to Churches which he knew intimately S. Paul's practice was to suppress all names. So far as this argument goes, then, it is against c. xvi. being addressed to Ephesus, and in favour of its being addressed to Rome. Nor is the reason far to seek; where he knew intimately large numbers, selection would be difficult if not invidious. On the other hand, where he knew few, he would lay stress on this acquaintance, as qualifying his want of familiarity with the Church as a whole.

INDICES

A. INDEX OF SUBJECTS.

B. GREEK.

This Index contains only the principal words which are commented upon in the notes.